# ROSARIO + VAMPIRE
## Season II

AKIHISA IKEDA

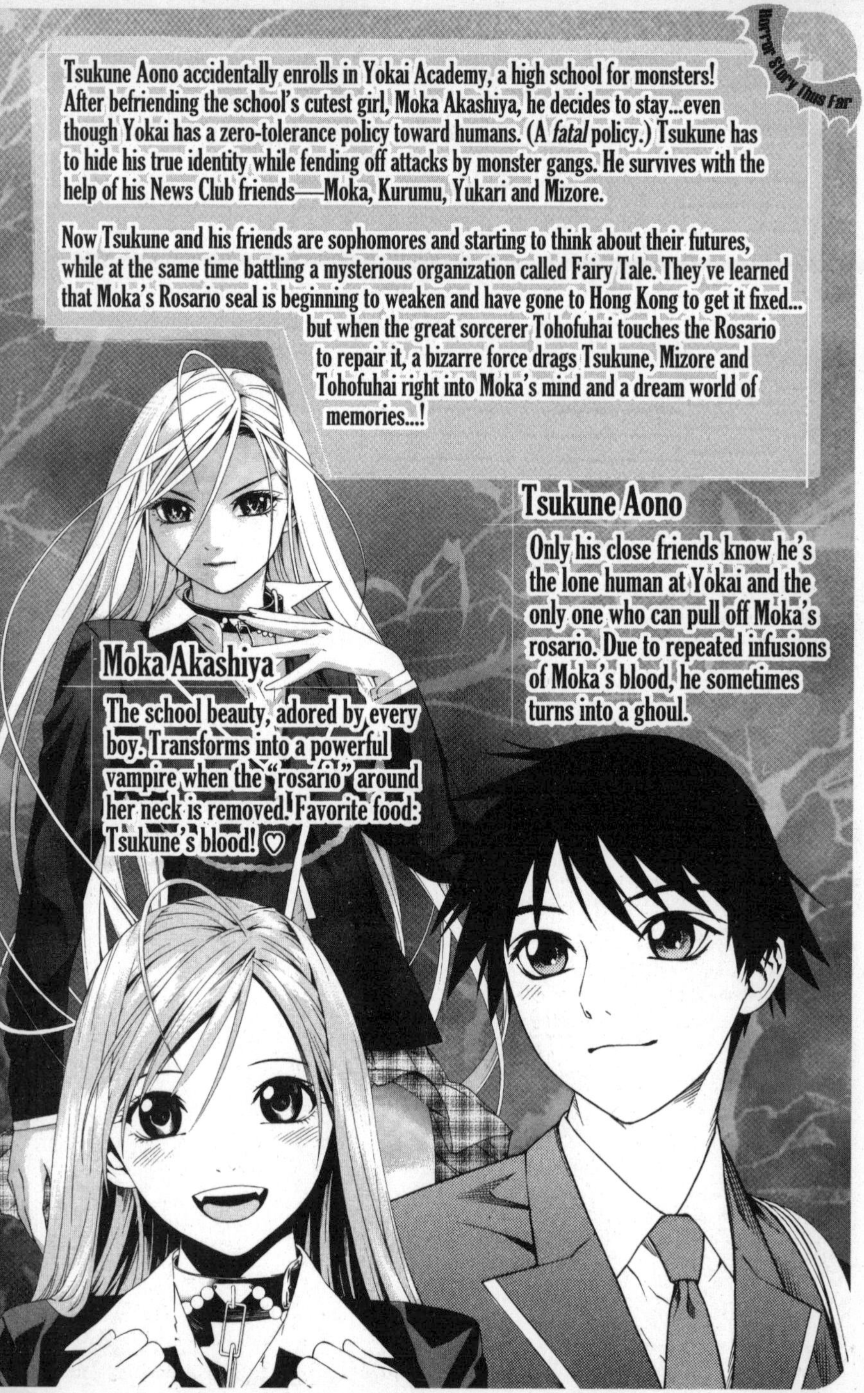
Horror Story Thus Far
Tsukune Aono accidentally enrolls in Yokai Academy, a high school for monsters! After befriending the school's cutest girl, Moka Akashiya, he decides to stay...even though Yokai has a zero-tolerance policy toward humans. (A *fatal* policy.) Tsukune has to hide his true identity while fending off attacks by monster gangs. He survives with the help of his News Club friends—Moka, Kurumu, Yukari and Mizore.
Now Tsukune and his friends are sophomores and starting to think about their futures, while at the same time battling a mysterious organization called Fairy Tale. They've learned that Moka's Rosario seal is beginning to weaken and have gone to Hong Kong to get it fixed... but when the great sorcerer Tohofuhai touches the Rosario to repair it, a bizarre force drags Tsukune, Mizore and Tohofuhai right into Moka's mind and a dream world of memories...!
Tsukune Aono
Only his close friends know he's the lone human at Yokai and the only one who can pull off Moka's rosario. Due to repeated infusions of Moka's blood, he sometimes turns into a ghoul.
Moka Akashiya
The school beauty, adored by every boy. Transforms into a powerful vampire when the "rosario" around her neck is removed. Favorite food: Tsukune's blood! ♡

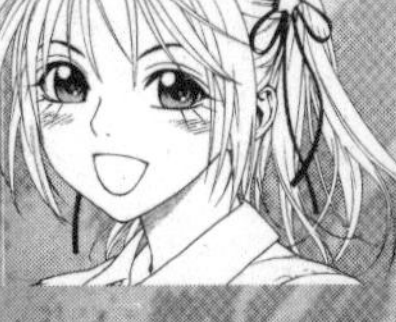

## Kurumu Kurono

A succubus. Also adored by all the boys—for two obvious reasons. Fights with Moka over Tsukune.

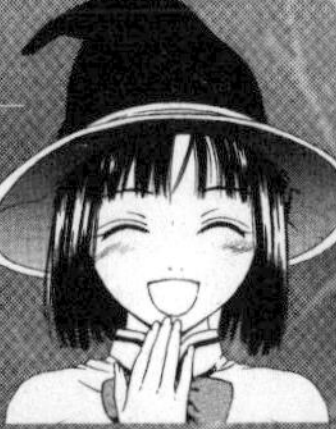

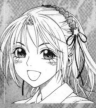

## Yukari Sendo

A mischievous witch. Much younger than the others but a real genius, she skipped several grades to get into the Academy. A sharp tongue for such a cute little thing.

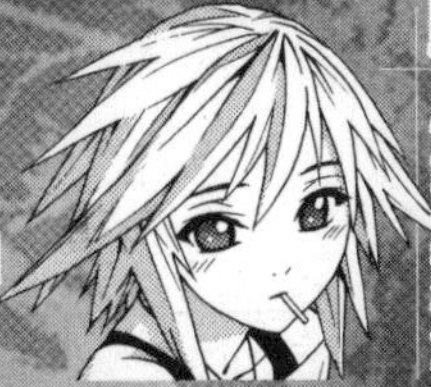

## Mizore Shirayuki

A snow fairy who manipulates ice. She fell in love with Tsukune after reading his newspaper articles.

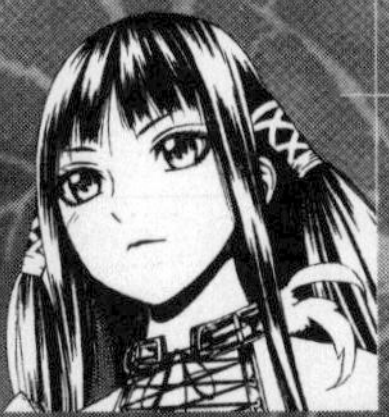

## Ruby Tojo

A witch who only learned to trust humans after meeting Tsukune. Now employed as Yokai's headmaster's assistant. A bit of a masochist.

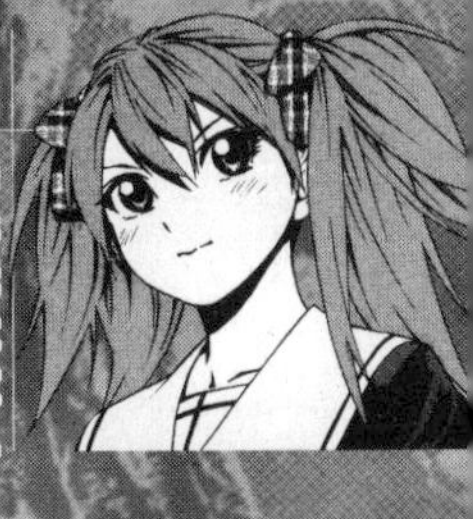

## Koko Shuzen

Moka's stubborn little sister. Koko worships Moka's inner vampiric self but hates her sweet exterior. Koko's pet bat transforms into a weapon.

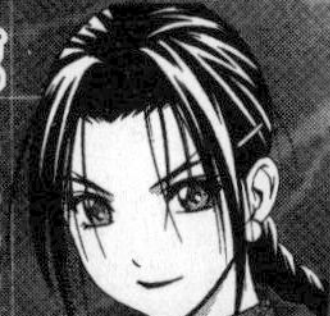

## Fangfang Huang

Freshman at Yokai Academy, the only son of a Chinese Mafia family that controls China's most dangerous monsters. Also a "Yasha," a Chinese demon who excels at transformation and sorcery. In awe of Tsukune.

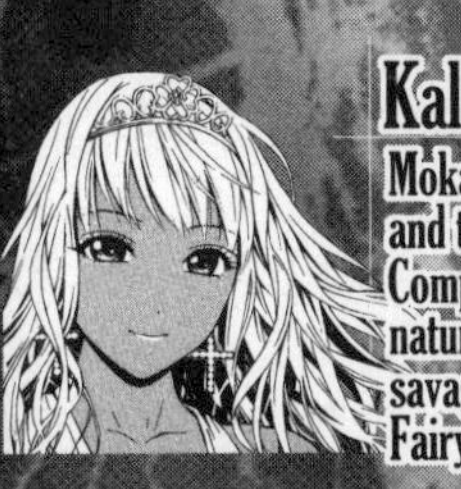

## Kalua Shuzen

Moka's elder sister and the middle daughter. Compassionate by nature, but works as a savage assassin for Fairy Tale.

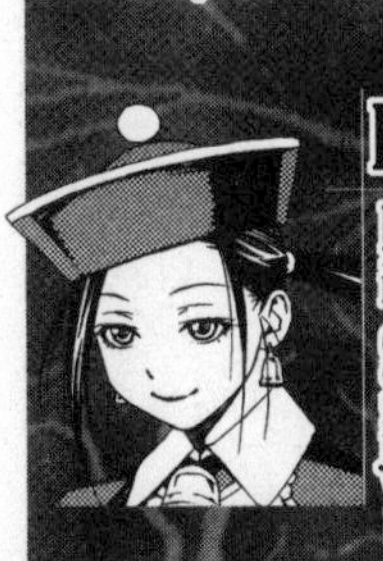

## Lingling Huang

Fangfang's elder sister, who is also late. Because she's dead. Reanimated as a Jiang Shi, a hopping zombie. A junior transfer student at Yokai.

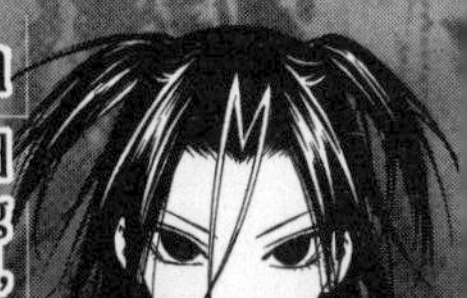

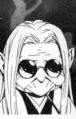

## Aqua Shuzen

Moka's elder sister and the eldest daughter. Having lost her mother as a child, she was raised by relatives in China. A master of Chinese martial arts.

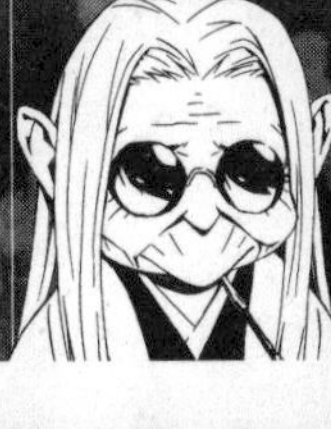

## Tohofuhai

Founder of the Huang Family, one of the three Dark Lords, and said to be the greatest sorcerer in the world—but now just a hardcore otaku?!

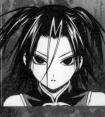

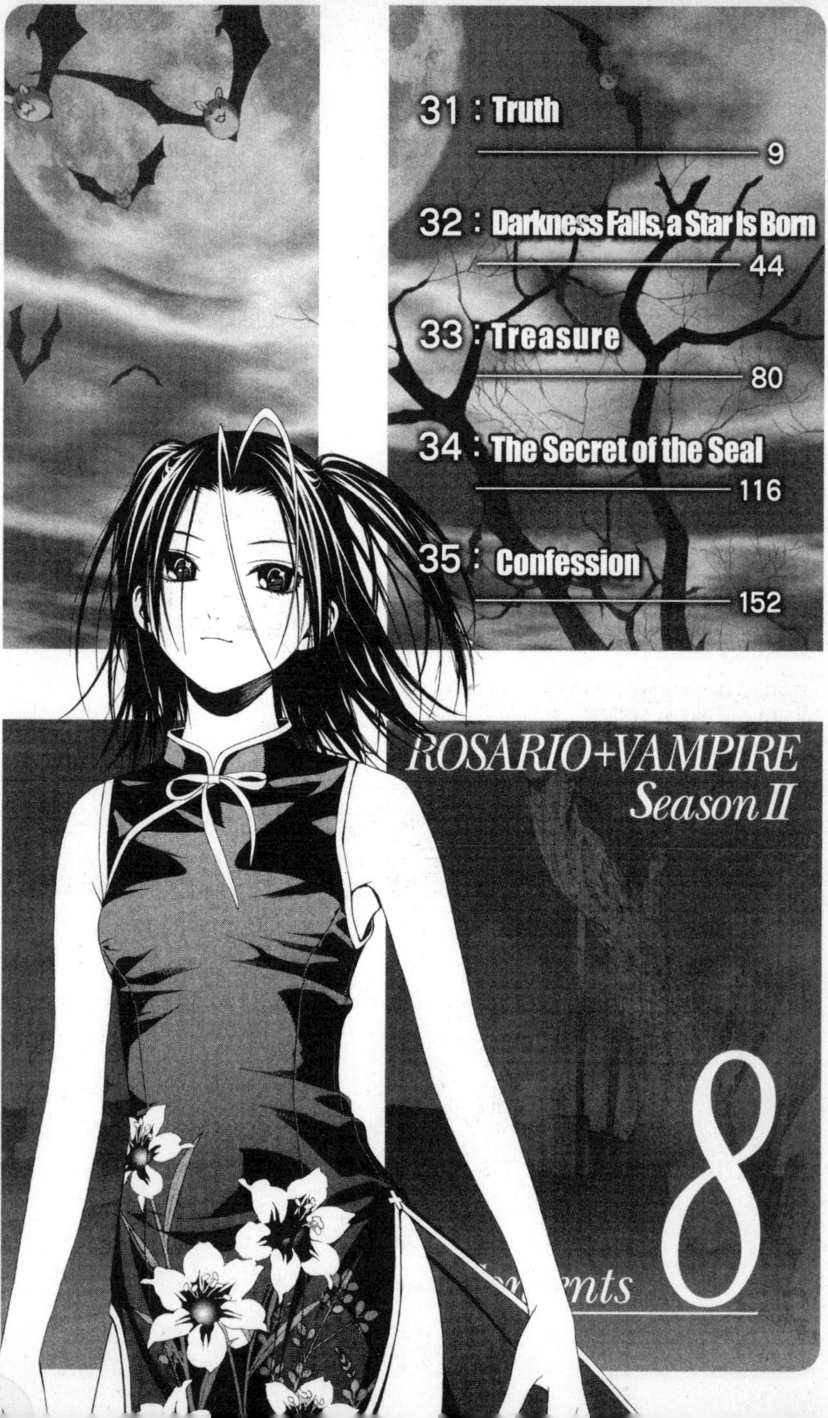

ROSARIO+VAMPIRE
Season II

# Contents 8

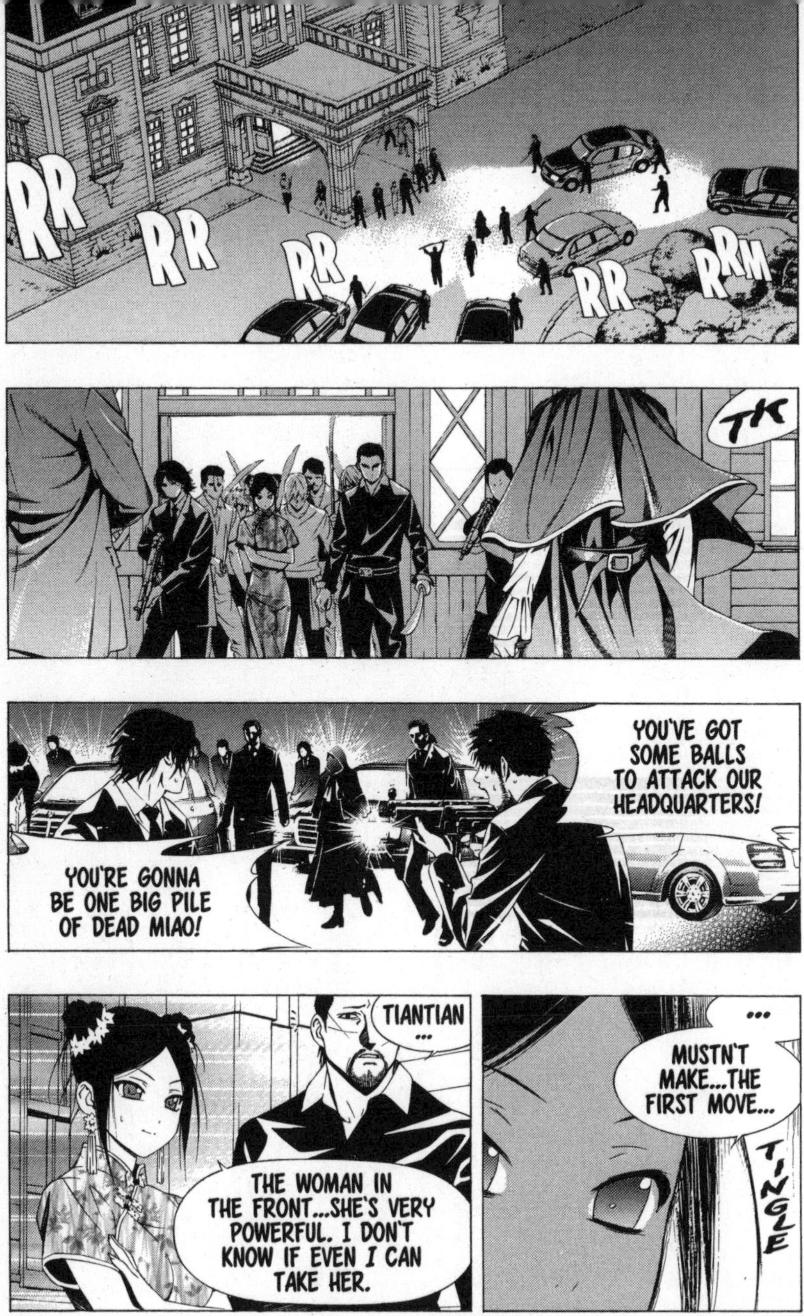
RRM
RR
RR
RR
RR
TK
YOU'VE GOT SOME BALLS TO ATTACK OUR HEADQUARTERS!
YOU'RE GONNA BE ONE BIG PILE OF DEAD MIAO!
...
MUSTN'T MAKE...THE FIRST MOVE...
TINGLE
TIANTIAN ...
THE WOMAN IN THE FRONT...SHE'S VERY POWERFUL. I DON'T KNOW IF EVEN *I* CAN TAKE HER.



# 31: Truth

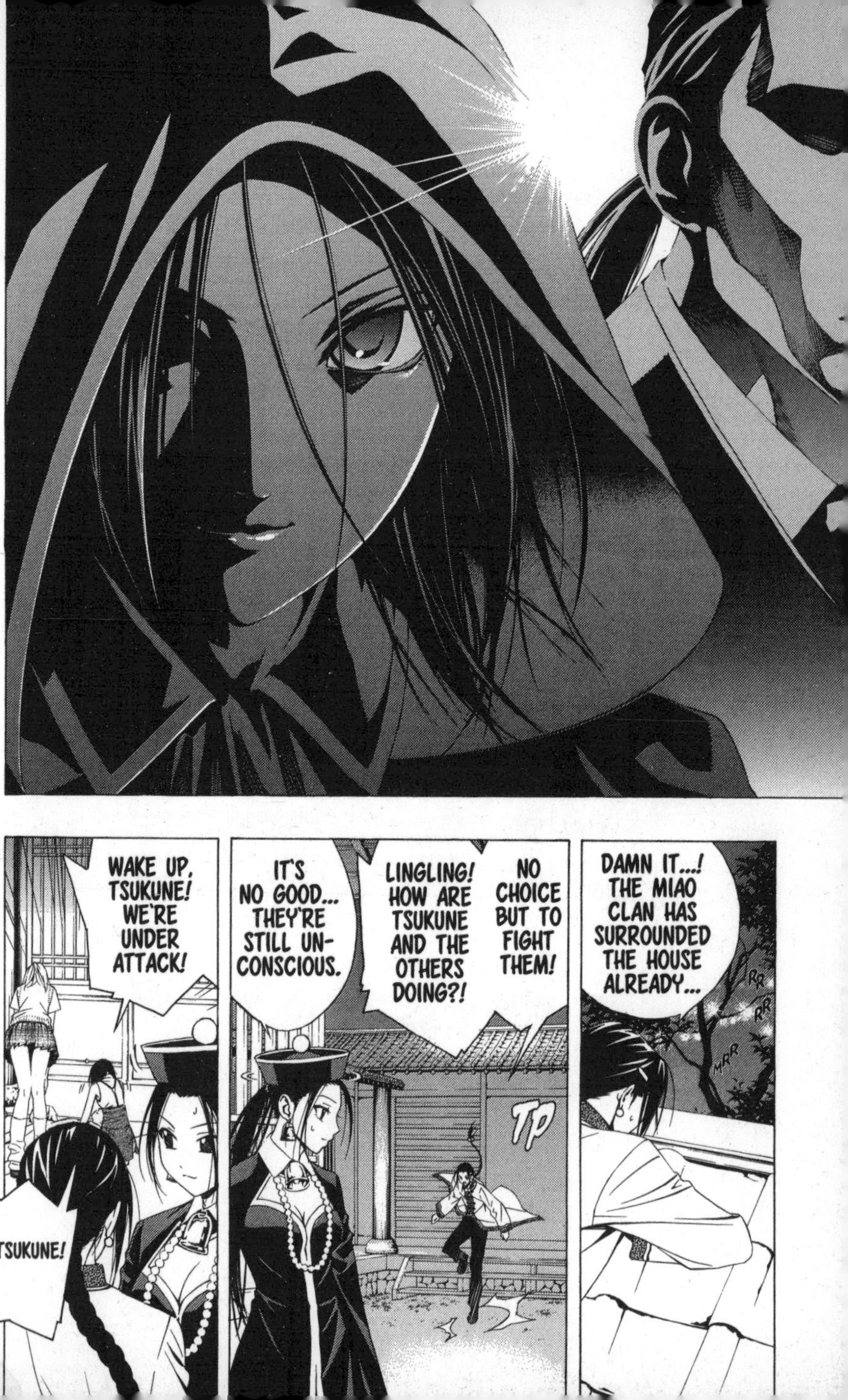
DAMN IT...! THE MIAO CLAN HAS SURROUNDED THE HOUSE ALREADY...
RR
RR
MRR
NO CHOICE BUT TO FIGHT THEM!
LINGLING! HOW ARE TSUKUNE AND THE OTHERS DOING?!
IT'S NO GOOD... THEY'RE STILL UN-CONSCIOUS.
TP
WAKE UP, TSUKUNE! WE'RE UNDER ATTACK!
TSUKUNE!

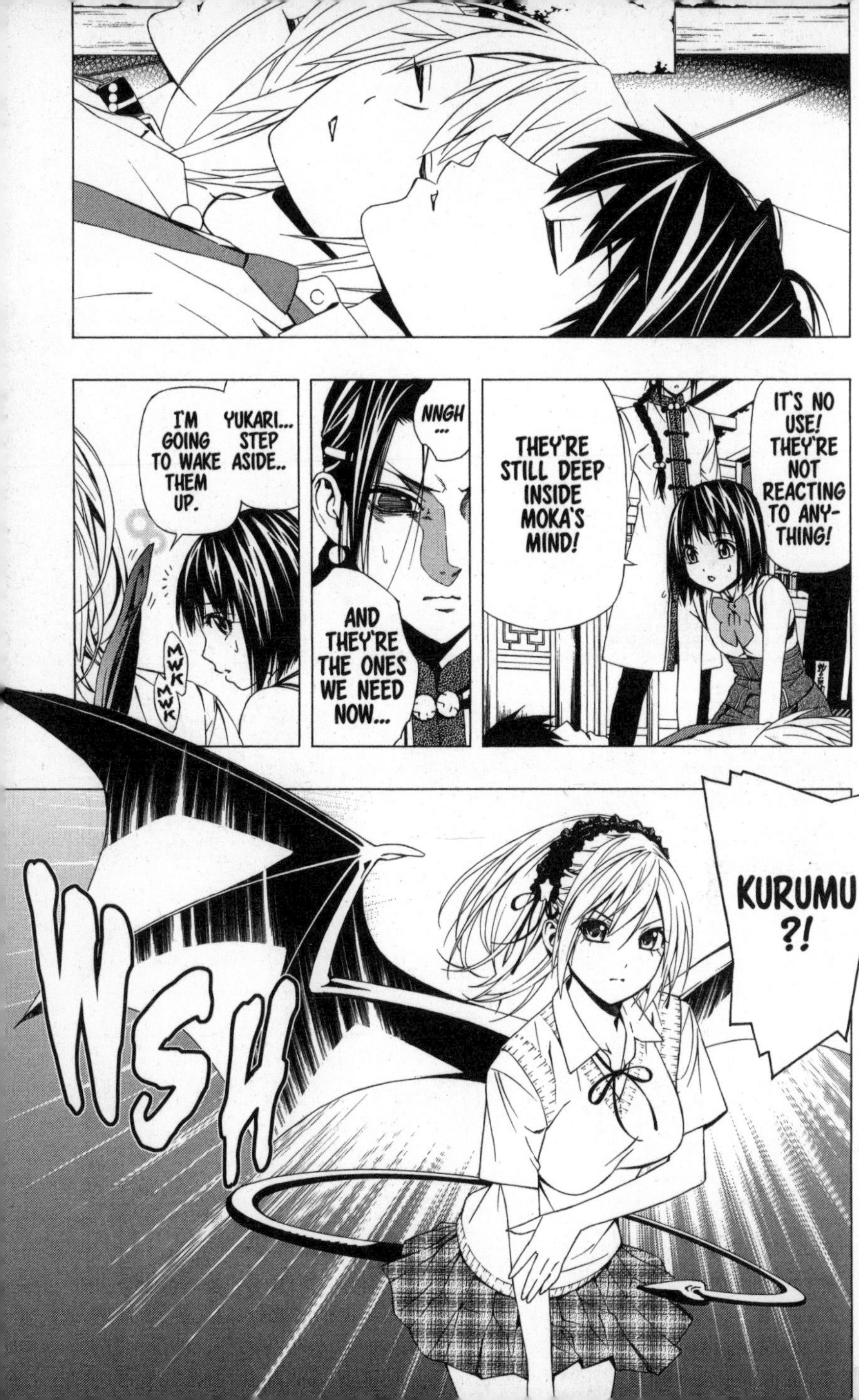
IT'S NO USE! THEY'RE NOT REACTING TO ANY-THING!
THEY'RE STILL DEEP INSIDE MOKA'S MIND!
NNGH...
AND THEY'RE THE ONES WE NEED NOW...
YUKARI... STEP ASIDE..
I'M GOING TO WAKE THEM UP.
MWK MWK
KURUMU?!
WSH

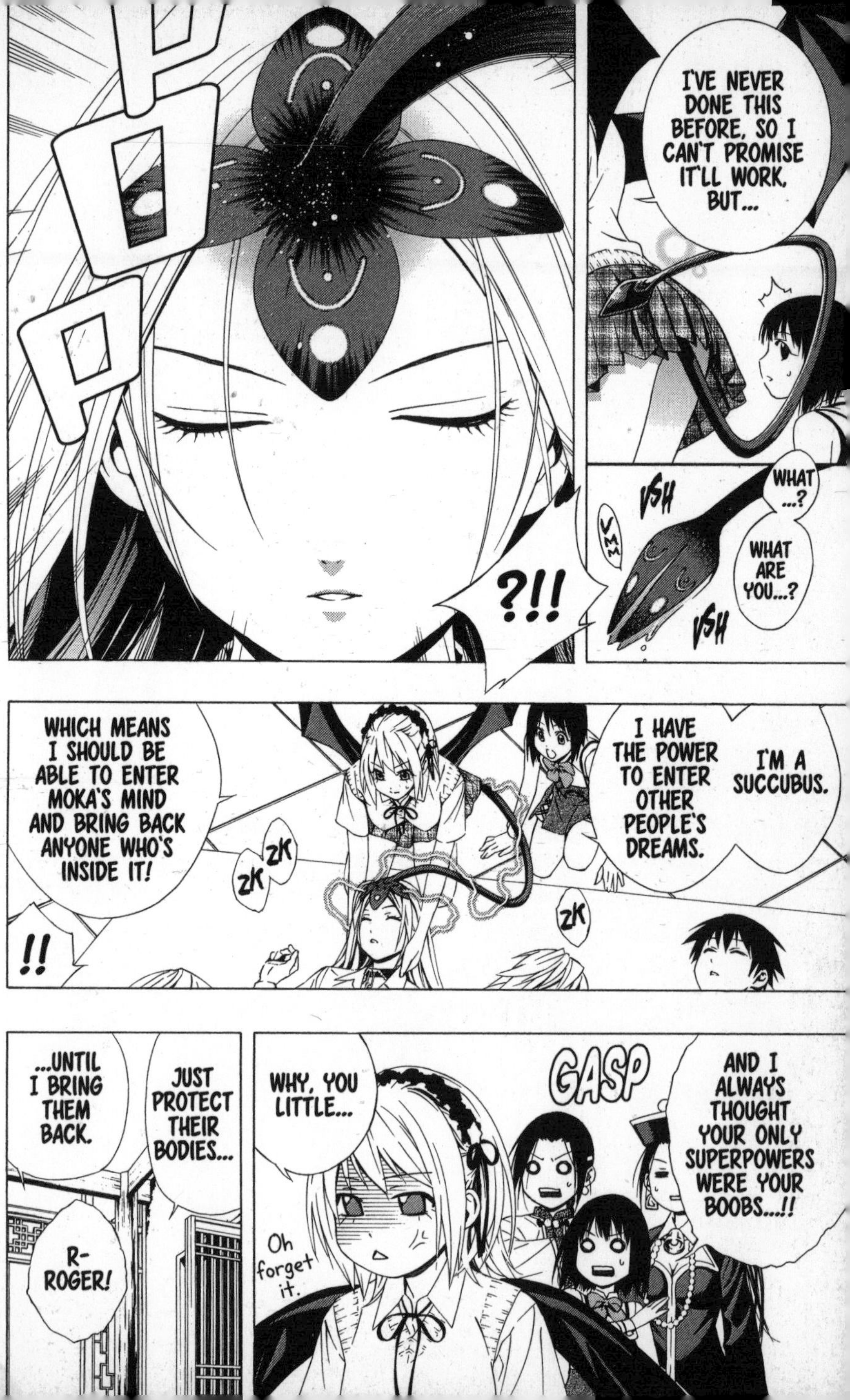
I'VE NEVER DONE THIS BEFORE, SO I CAN'T PROMISE IT'LL WORK, BUT...
VSH
UMM
WHAT ...?
WHAT ARE YOU...?
VSH
POP
?!!
I'M A SUCCUBUS.
I HAVE THE POWER TO ENTER OTHER PEOPLE'S DREAMS.
WHICH MEANS I SHOULD BE ABLE TO ENTER MOKA'S MIND AND BRING BACK ANYONE WHO'S INSIDE IT!
ZK
ZK
ZK
!!
AND I ALWAYS THOUGHT YOUR ONLY SUPERPOWERS WERE YOUR BOOBS...!!
GASP
WHY, YOU LITTLE...
Oh forget it.
JUST PROTECT THEIR BODIES...
...UNTIL I BRING THEM BACK.
R-ROGER!

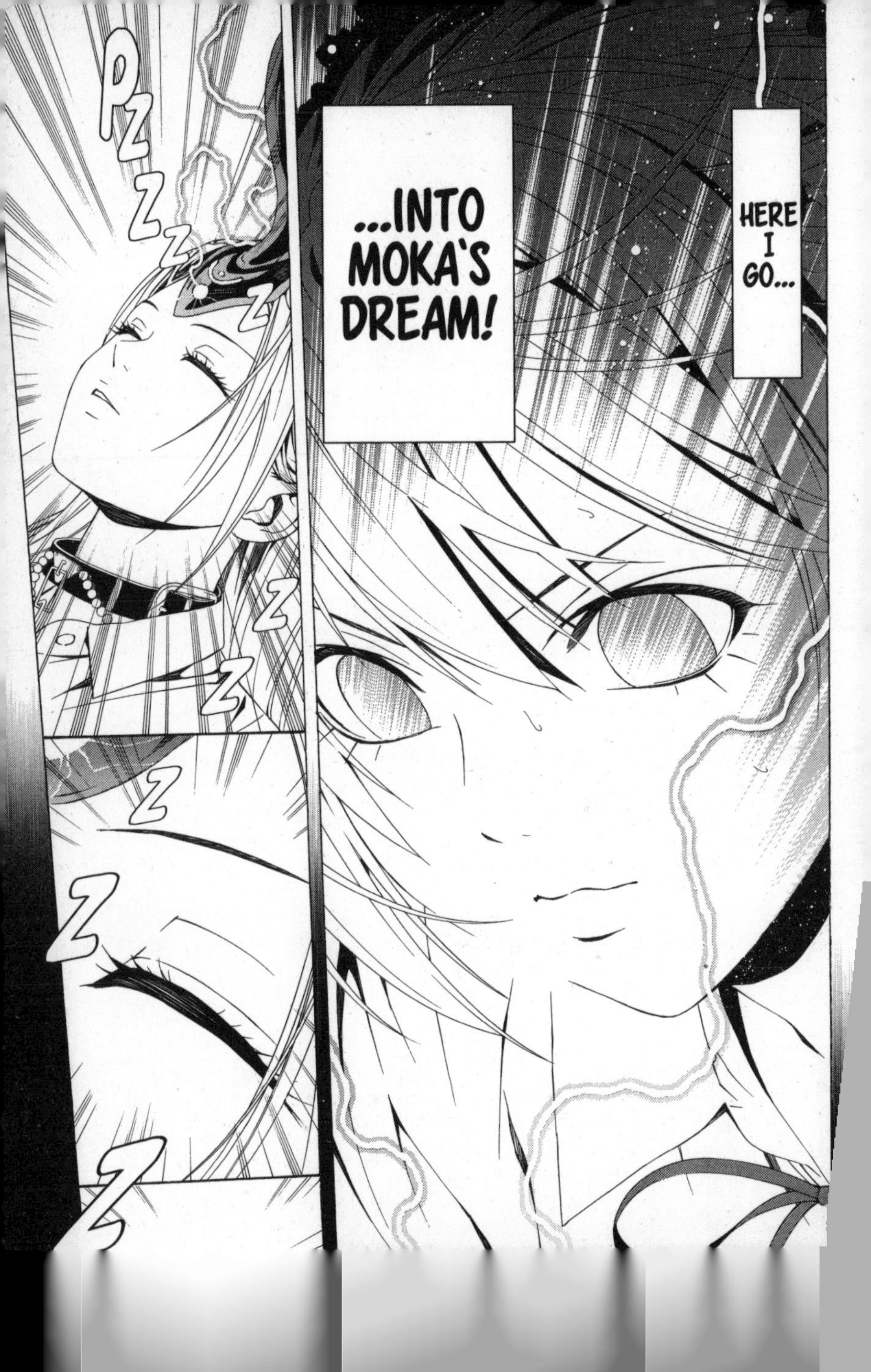
HERE I GO...
...INTO MOKA'S DREAM!
PZZZZZZ
ZZZ

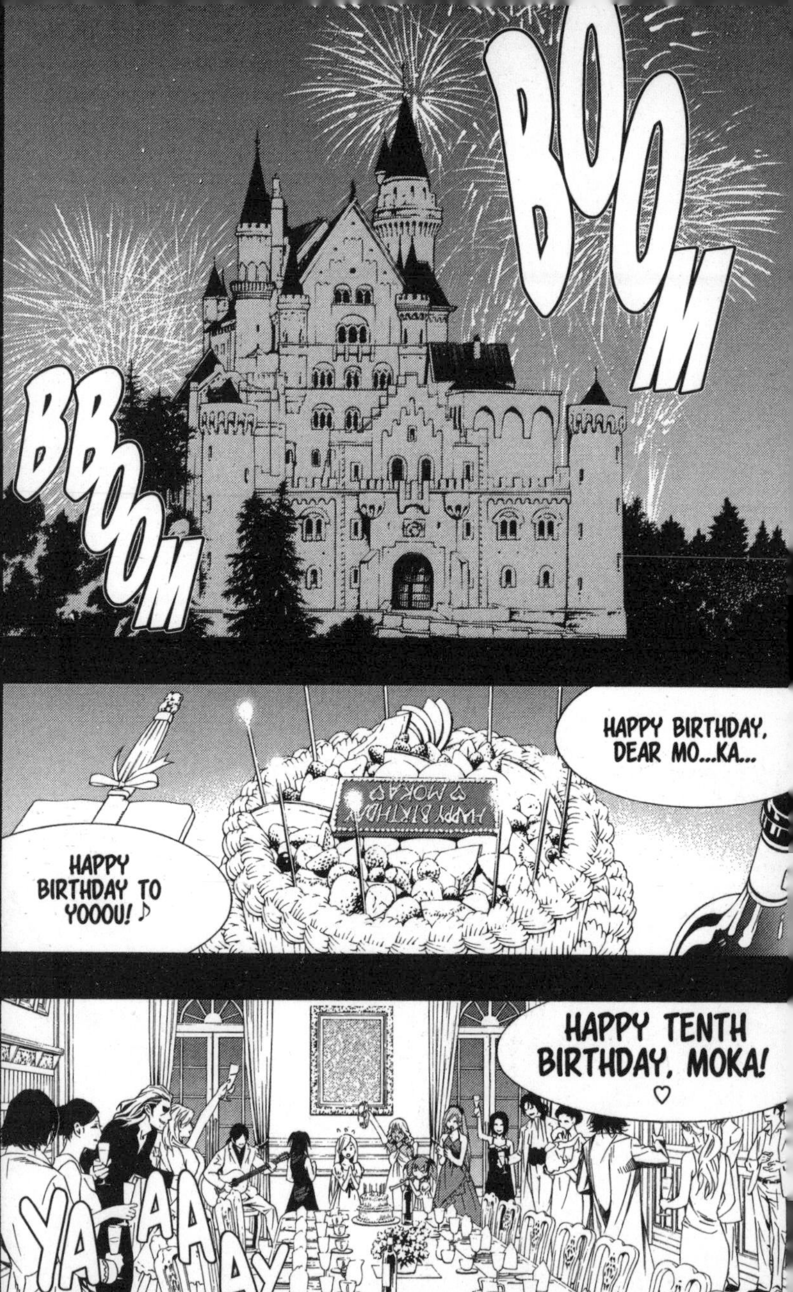
BOOOM
BBOOOM
HAPPY BIRTHDAY, DEAR MO...KA...
HAPPY BIRTHDAY ♡MOKA♡
HAPPY BIRTHDAY TO YOOOU! ♪
HAPPY TENTH BIRTHDAY, MOKA! ♡
YAAAAY

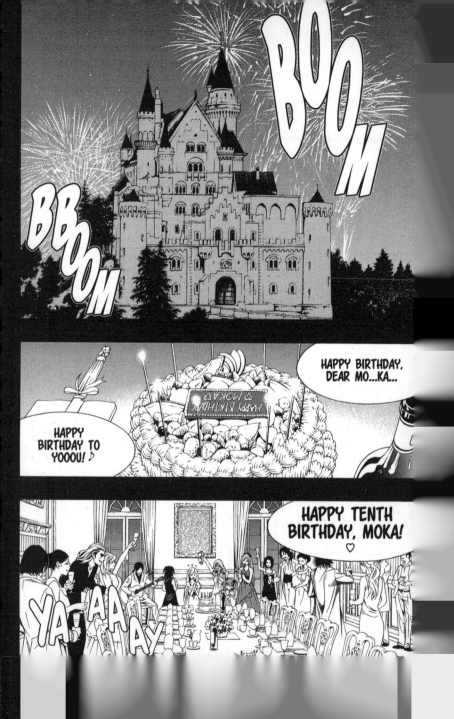

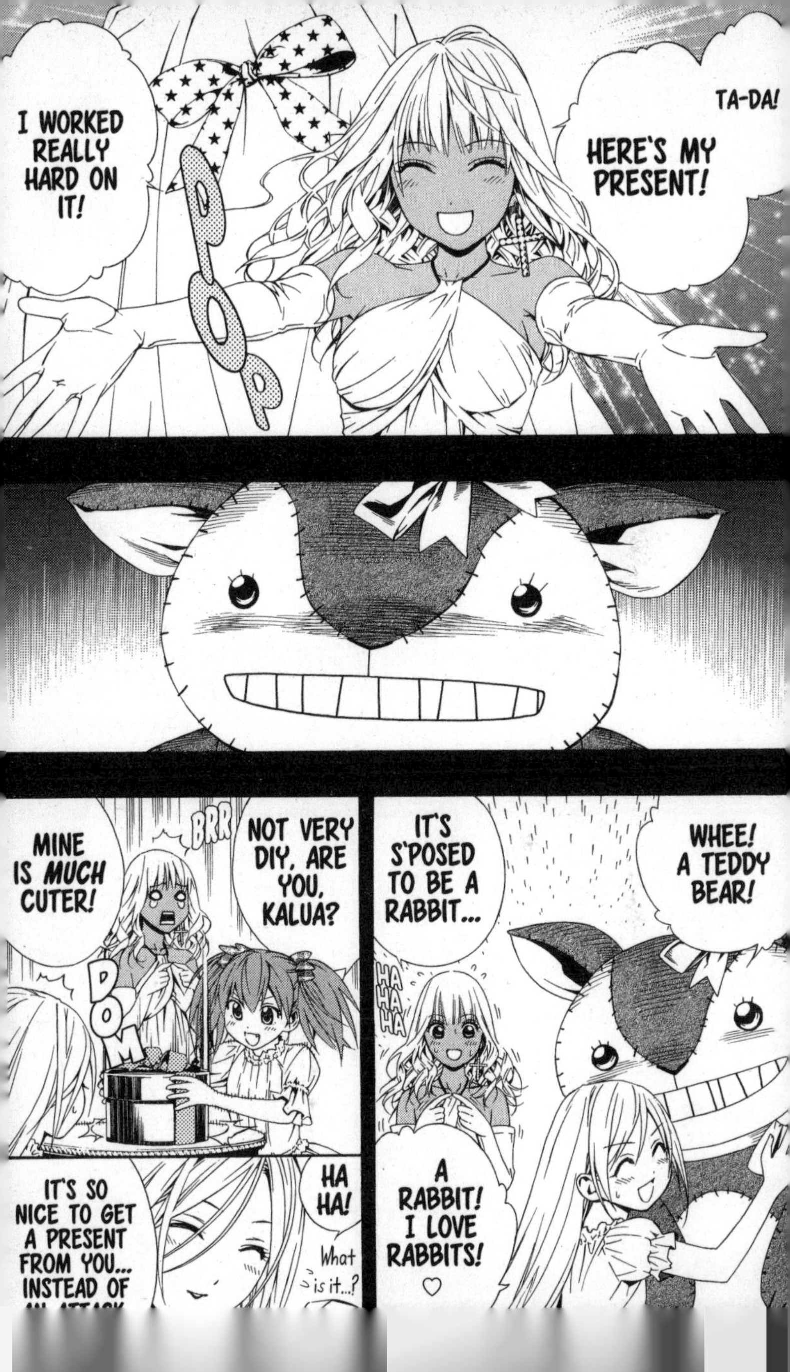
TA-DA!
HERE'S MY PRESENT!
I WORKED REALLY HARD ON IT!
POP
WHEE! A TEDDY BEAR!
IT'S S'POSED TO BE A RABBIT...
HA HA HA
A RABBIT! I LOVE RABBITS! ♡
NOT VERY DIY, ARE YOU, KALUA?
BRR
MINE IS *MUCH* CUTER!
DOM
HA HA!
What is it...?
IT'S SO NICE TO GET A PRESENT FROM YOU... INSTEAD OF

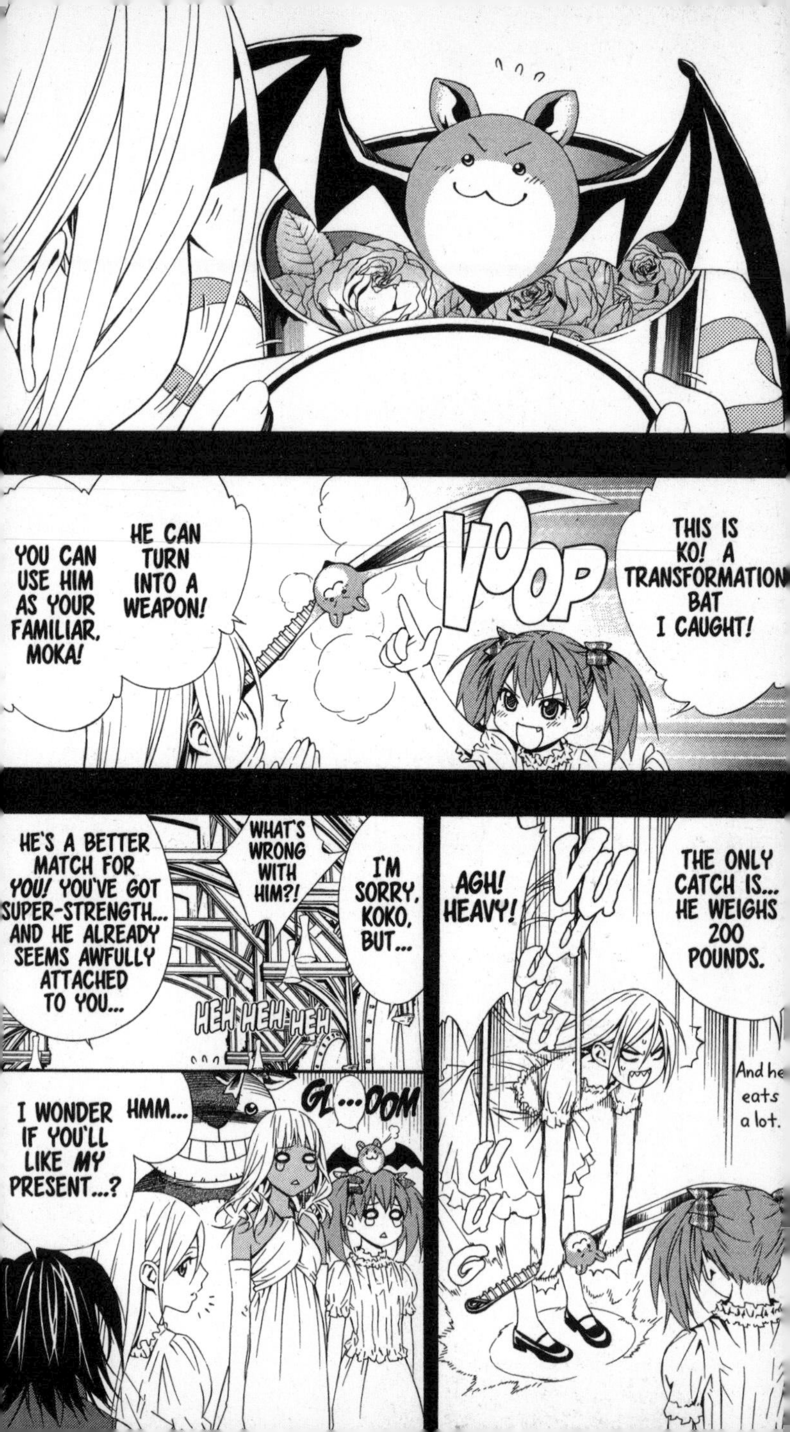
THIS IS KO! A TRANSFORMATION BAT I CAUGHT!
VOOOP
HE CAN TURN INTO A WEAPON!
YOU CAN USE HIM AS YOUR FAMILIAR, MOKA!
THE ONLY CATCH IS... HE WEIGHS 200 POUNDS.
AGH! HEAVY!
And he eats a lot.
I'M SORRY, KOKO, BUT...
WHAT'S WRONG WITH HIM?!
HE'S A BETTER MATCH FOR *YOU!* YOU'VE GOT SUPER-STRENGTH... AND HE ALREADY SEEMS AWFULLY ATTACHED TO YOU...
HEH HEH HEH
GL...OOM
HMM...
I WONDER IF YOU'LL LIKE *MY* PRESENT...?

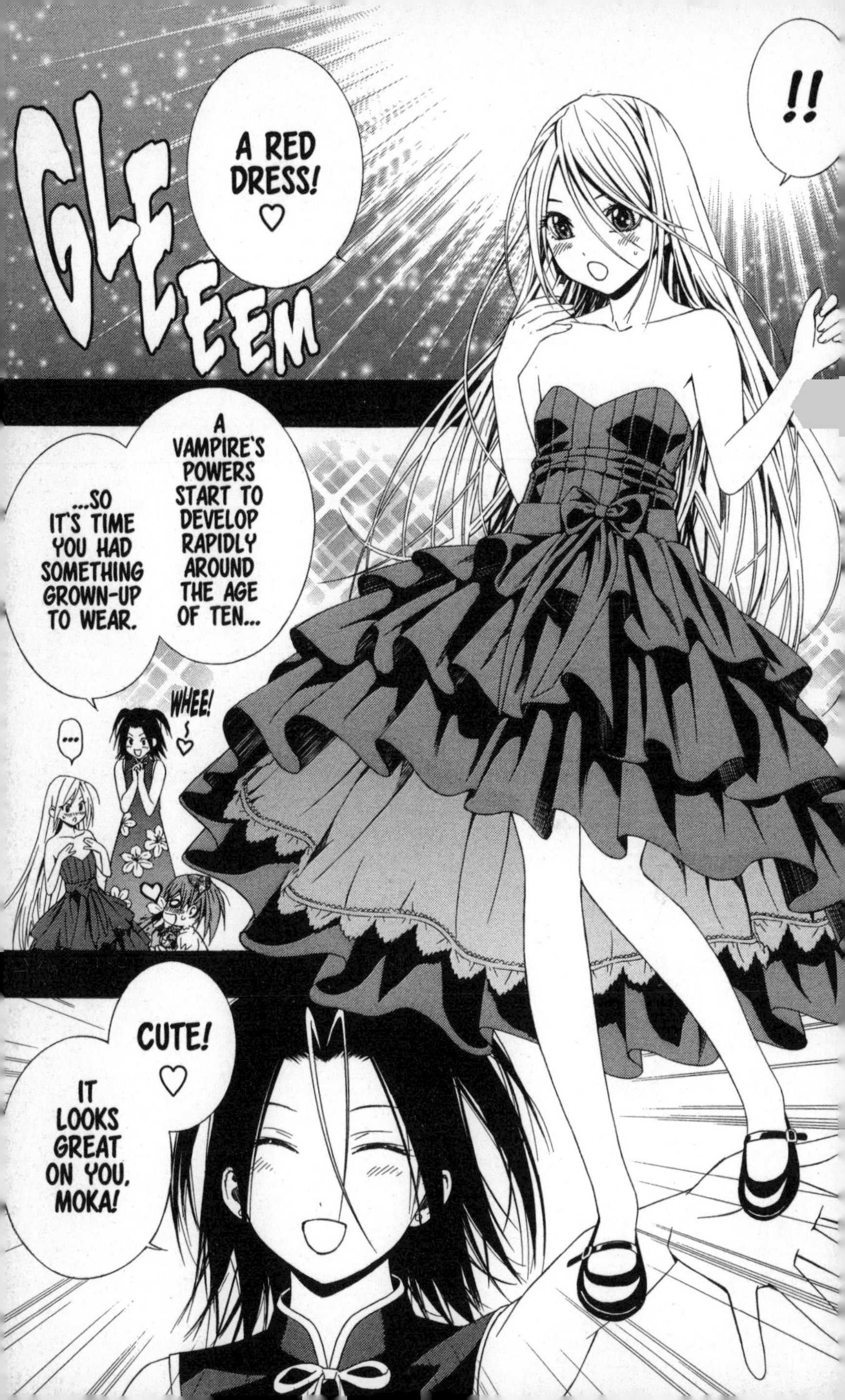
!!
A RED DRESS! ♡
GLEEEM
A VAMPIRE'S POWERS START TO DEVELOP RAPIDLY AROUND THE AGE OF TEN...
...SO IT'S TIME YOU HAD SOMETHING GROWN-UP TO WEAR.
WHEE! ♡
...
CUTE! ♡
IT LOOKS GREAT ON YOU, MOKA!

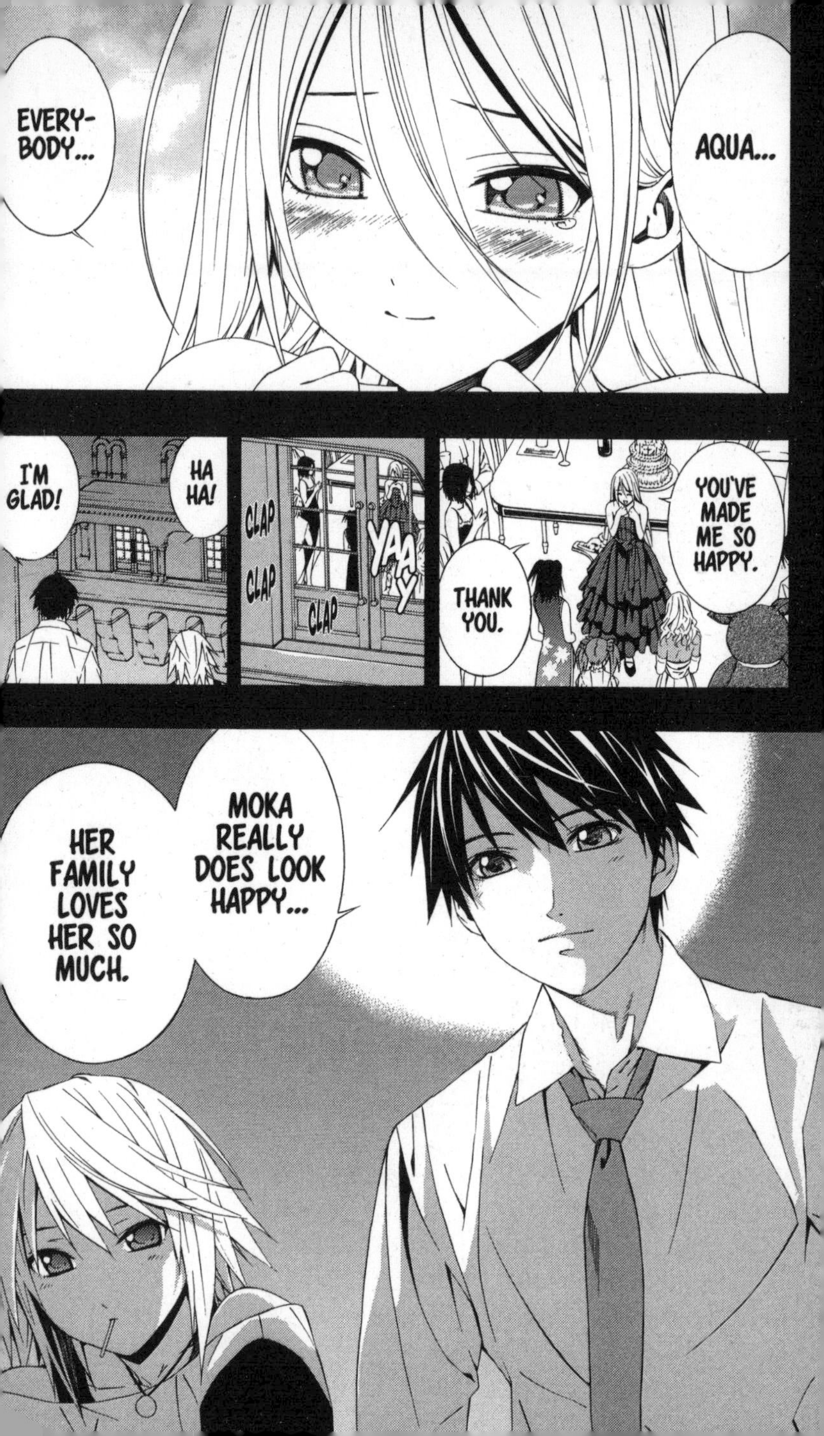
AQUA...
EVERY-BODY...
YOU'VE MADE ME SO HAPPY.
THANK YOU.
CLAP
CLAP
CLAP
YAAAY
HA HA!
I'M GLAD!
MOKA REALLY DOES LOOK HAPPY...
HER FAMILY LOVES HER SO MUCH.

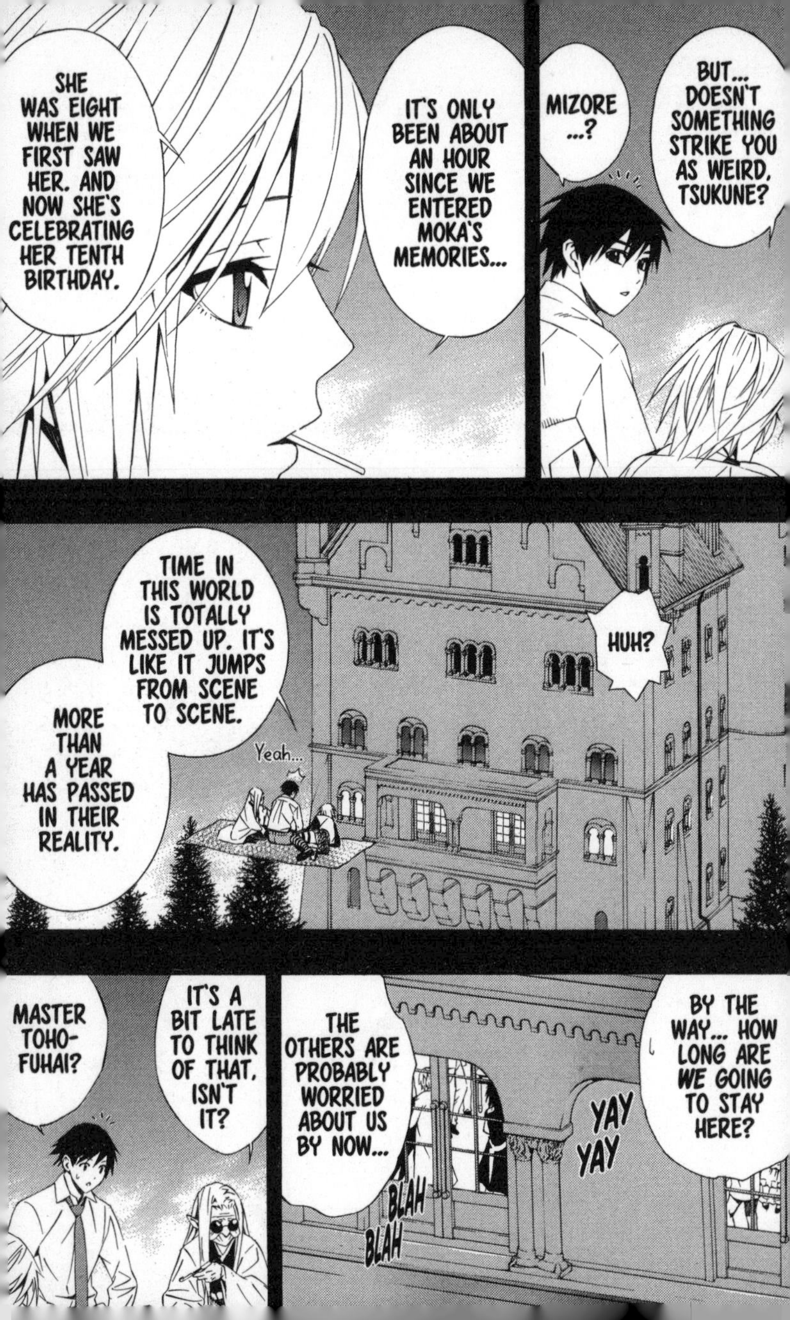
BUT... DOESN'T SOMETHING STRIKE YOU AS WEIRD, TSUKUNE?
MIZORE ...?
IT'S ONLY BEEN ABOUT AN HOUR SINCE WE ENTERED MOKA'S MEMORIES...
SHE WAS EIGHT WHEN WE FIRST SAW HER. AND NOW SHE'S CELEBRATING HER TENTH BIRTHDAY.
HUH?
TIME IN THIS WORLD IS TOTALLY MESSED UP. IT'S LIKE IT JUMPS FROM SCENE TO SCENE.
MORE THAN A YEAR HAS PASSED IN THEIR REALITY.
Yeah...
BY THE WAY... HOW LONG ARE WE GOING TO STAY HERE?
YAY YAY
THE OTHERS ARE PROBABLY WORRIED ABOUT US BY NOW...
BLAH BLAH
IT'S A BIT LATE TO THINK OF THAT, ISN'T IT?
MASTER TOHO-FUHAI?

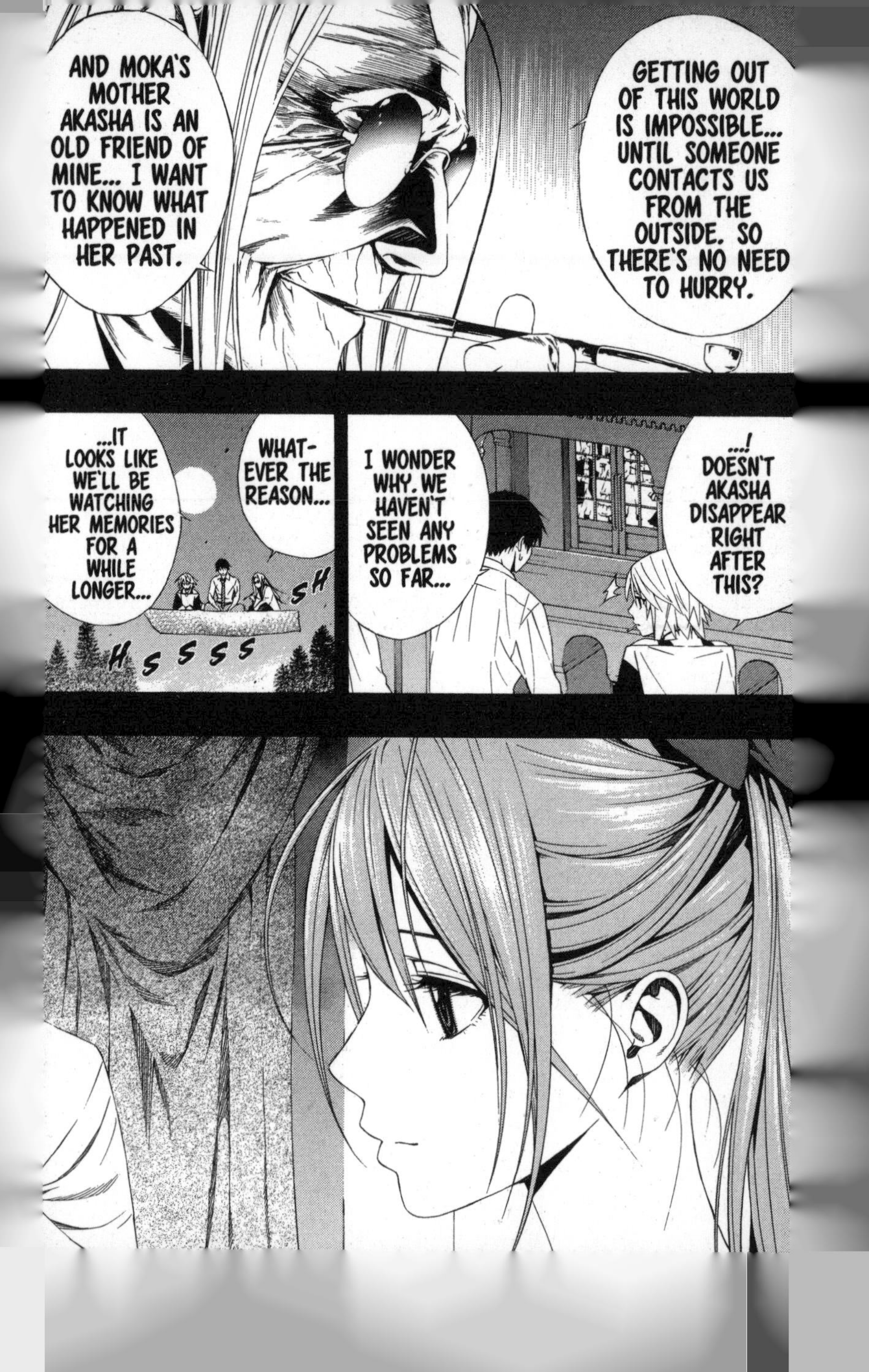
GETTING OUT OF THIS WORLD IS IMPOSSIBLE... UNTIL SOMEONE CONTACTS US FROM THE OUTSIDE. SO THERE'S NO NEED TO HURRY.
AND MOKA'S MOTHER AKASHA IS AN OLD FRIEND OF MINE... I WANT TO KNOW WHAT HAPPENED IN HER PAST.
...! DOESN'T AKASHA DISAPPEAR RIGHT AFTER THIS?
I WONDER WHY. WE HAVEN'T SEEN ANY PROBLEMS SO FAR...
WHAT-EVER THE REASON...
...IT LOOKS LIKE WE'LL BE WATCHING HER MEMORIES FOR A WHILE LONGER...
SHHSSSS

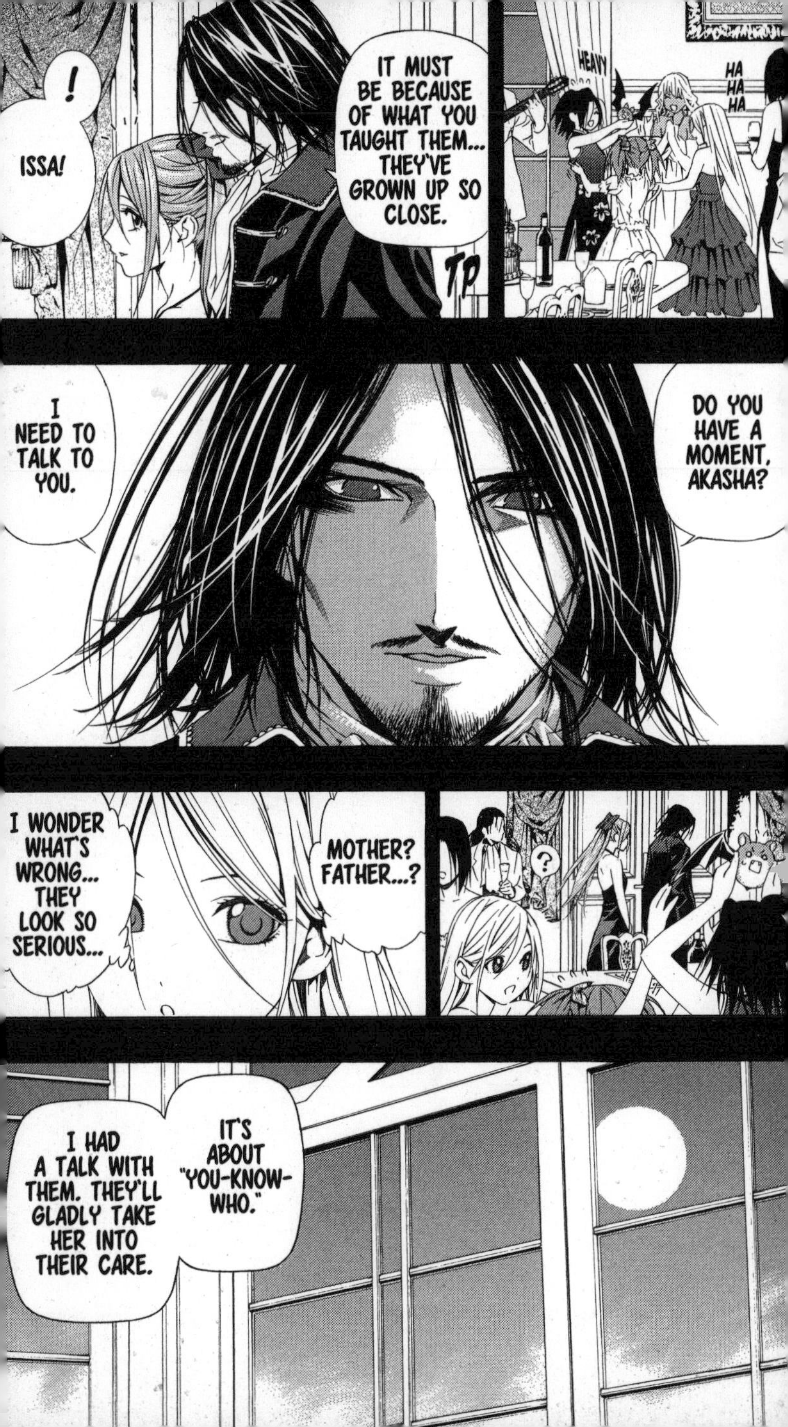
HEAVY
HA HA HA
IT MUST BE BECAUSE OF WHAT YOU TAUGHT THEM... THEY'VE GROWN UP SO CLOSE.
!
ISSA!
TP
DO YOU HAVE A MOMENT, AKASHA?
I NEED TO TALK TO YOU.
?
MOTHER? FATHER...?
I WONDER WHAT'S WRONG... THEY LOOK SO SERIOUS...
IT'S ABOUT "YOU-KNOW-WHO."
I HAD A TALK WITH THEM. THEY'LL GLADLY TAKE HER INTO THEIR CARE.

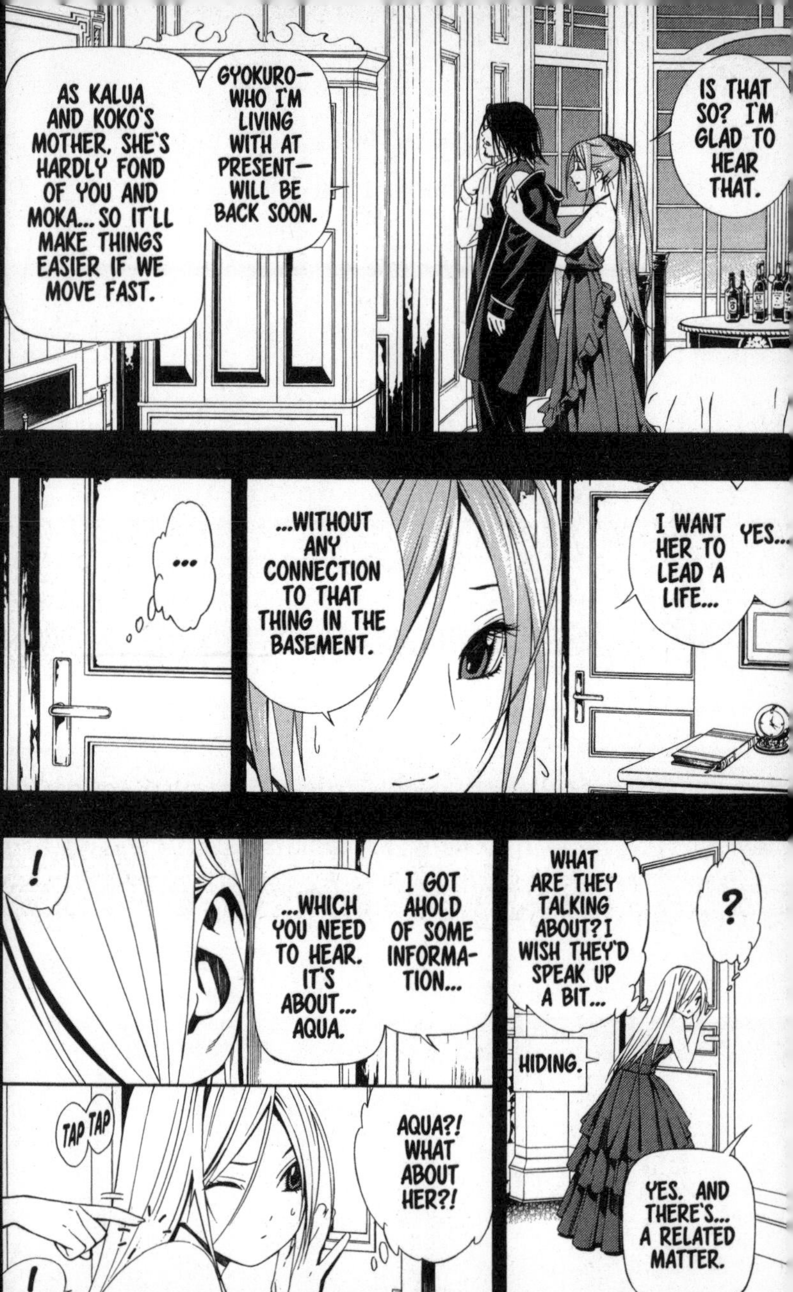
IS THAT SO? I'M GLAD TO HEAR THAT.
GYOKURO—WHO I'M LIVING WITH AT PRESENT—WILL BE BACK SOON.
AS KALUA AND KOKO'S MOTHER, SHE'S HARDLY FOND OF YOU AND MOKA... SO IT'LL MAKE THINGS EASIER IF WE MOVE FAST.
YES...
I WANT HER TO LEAD A LIFE...
...WITHOUT ANY CONNECTION TO THAT THING IN THE BASEMENT.
...
?
WHAT ARE THEY TALKING ABOUT?I WISH THEY'D SPEAK UP A BIT...
HIDING.
YES. AND THERE'S... A RELATED MATTER.
I GOT AHOLD OF SOME INFORMATION...
...WHICH YOU NEED TO HEAR. IT'S ABOUT... AQUA.
!
AQUA?! WHAT ABOUT HER?!
TAP TAP
!

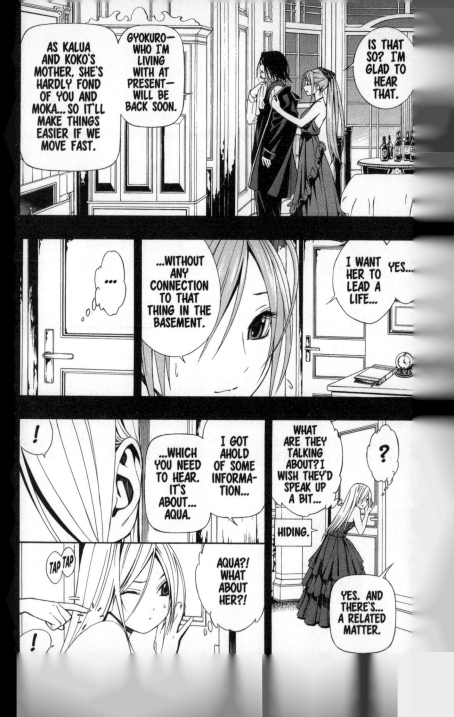

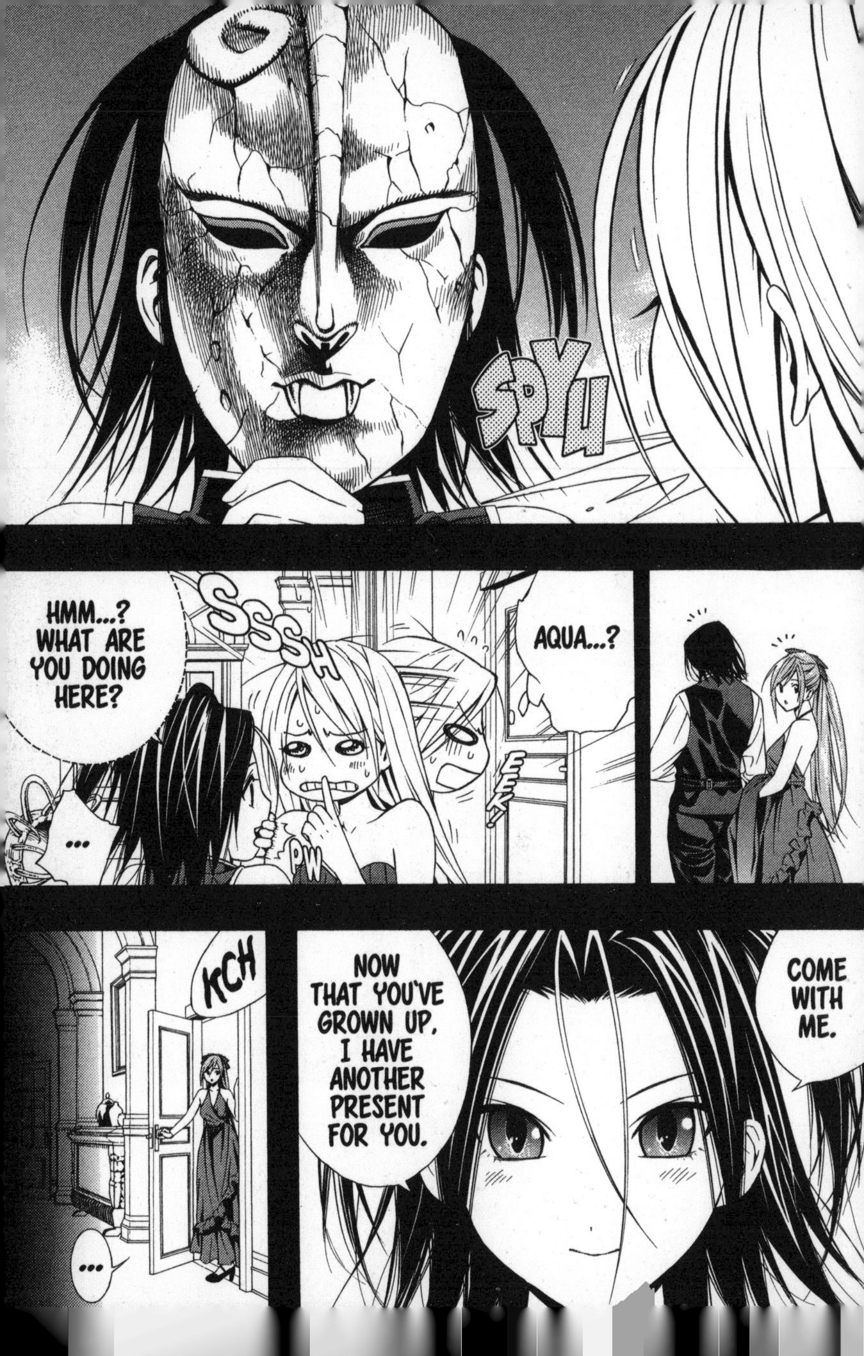
SPYU
AQUA...?
EEK!
SSSSH
HMM...? WHAT ARE YOU DOING HERE?
PW
...
COME WITH ME.
NOW THAT YOU'VE GROWN UP, I HAVE ANOTHER PRESENT FOR YOU.
KCH
...

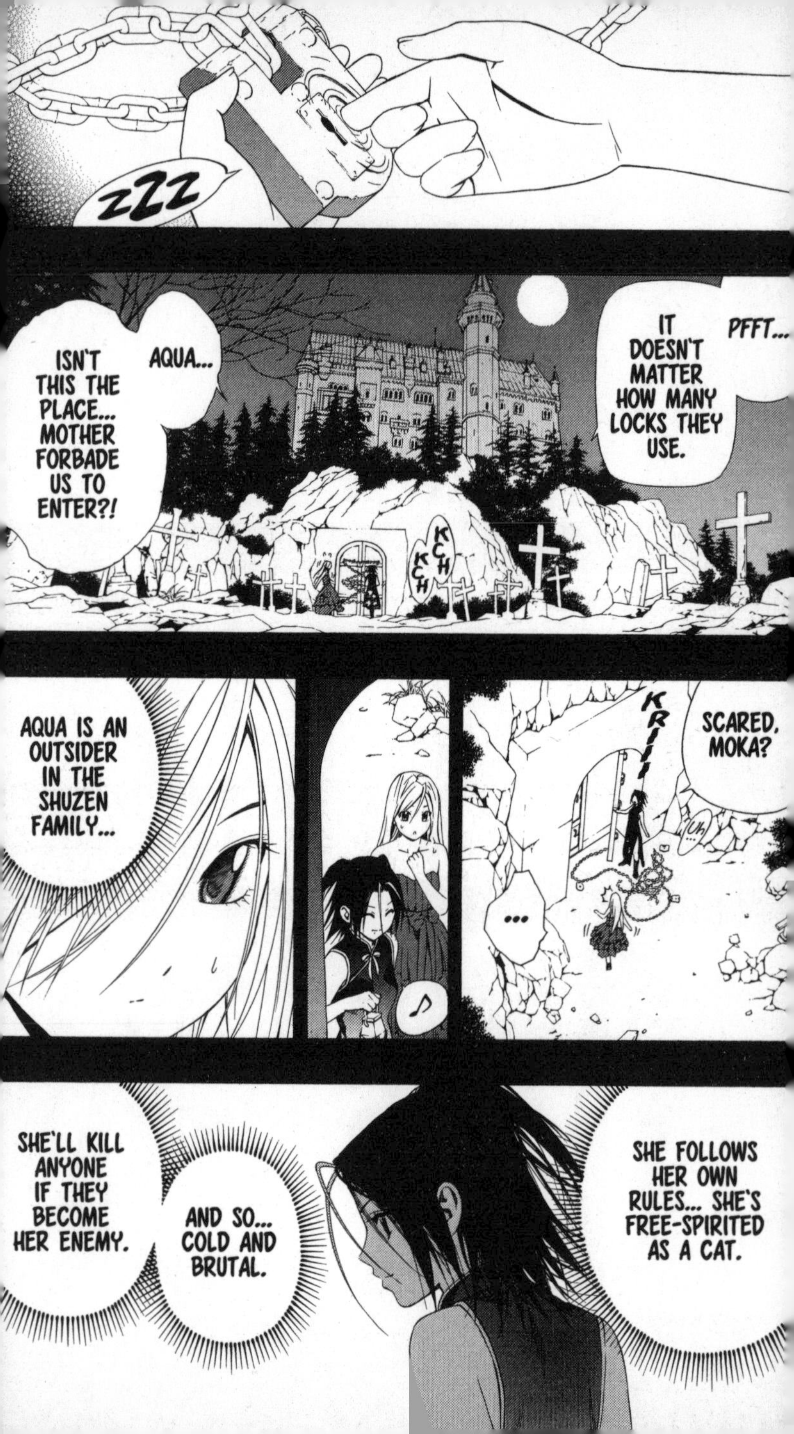
ZZZ
PFFT...
IT DOESN'T MATTER HOW MANY LOCKS THEY USE.
AQUA...
ISN'T THIS THE PLACE... MOTHER FORBADE US TO ENTER?!
KCH KCH
KRIII
SCARED, MOKA?
Uh...
...
♪
AQUA IS AN OUTSIDER IN THE SHUZEN FAMILY...
SHE FOLLOWS HER OWN RULES... SHE'S FREE-SPIRITED AS A CAT.
AND SO... COLD AND BRUTAL.
SHE'LL KILL ANYONE IF THEY BECOME HER ENEMY.

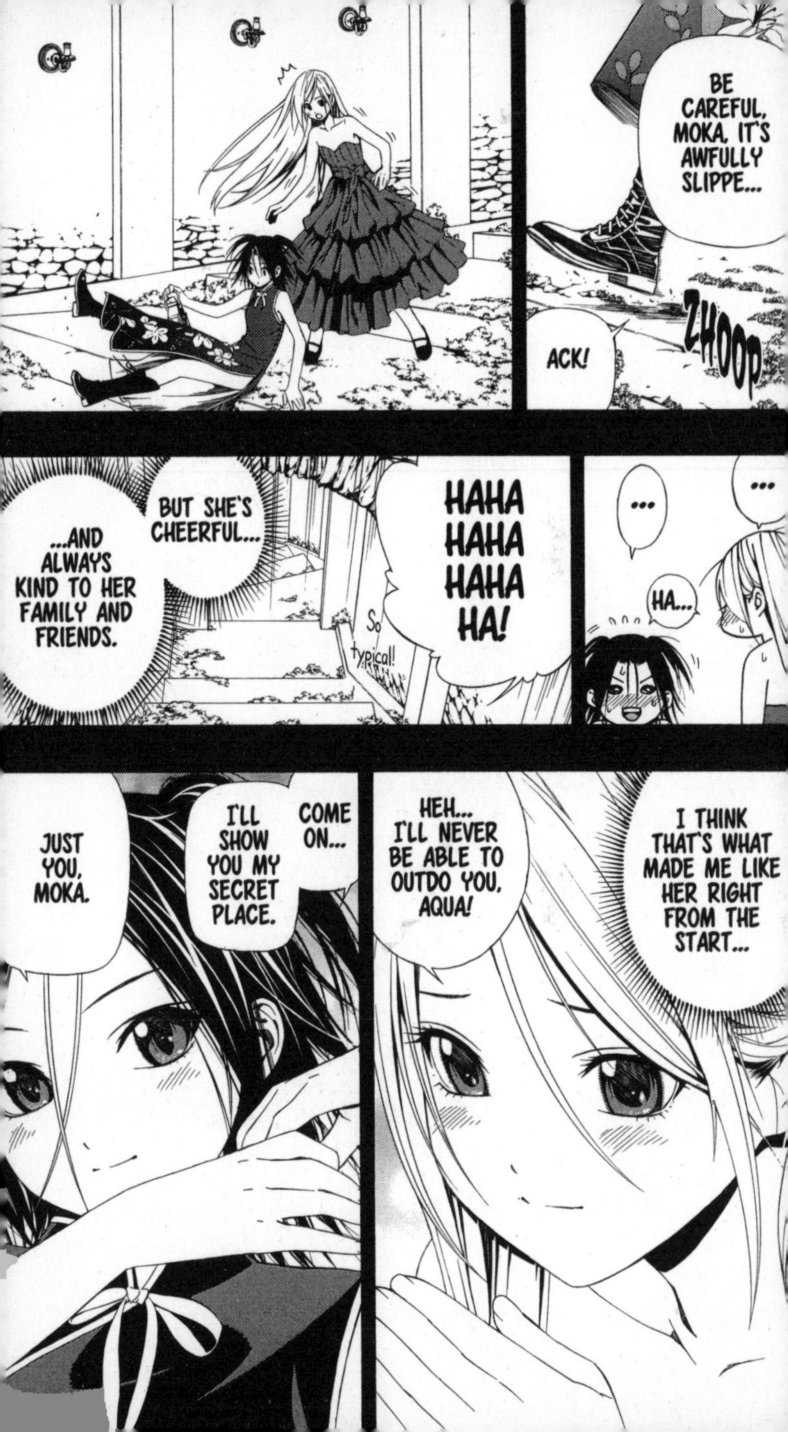
BE CAREFUL, MOKA, IT'S AWFULLY SLIPPE...
ZHOOP
ACK!
...
...
HA...
HAHA HAHA HAHA HA!
So typical!
BUT SHE'S CHEERFUL...
...AND ALWAYS KIND TO HER FAMILY AND FRIENDS.
I THINK THAT'S WHAT MADE ME LIKE HER RIGHT FROM THE START...
HEH... I'LL NEVER BE ABLE TO OUTDO YOU, AQUA!
COME ON...
I'LL SHOW YOU MY SECRET PLACE.
JUST YOU, MOKA.

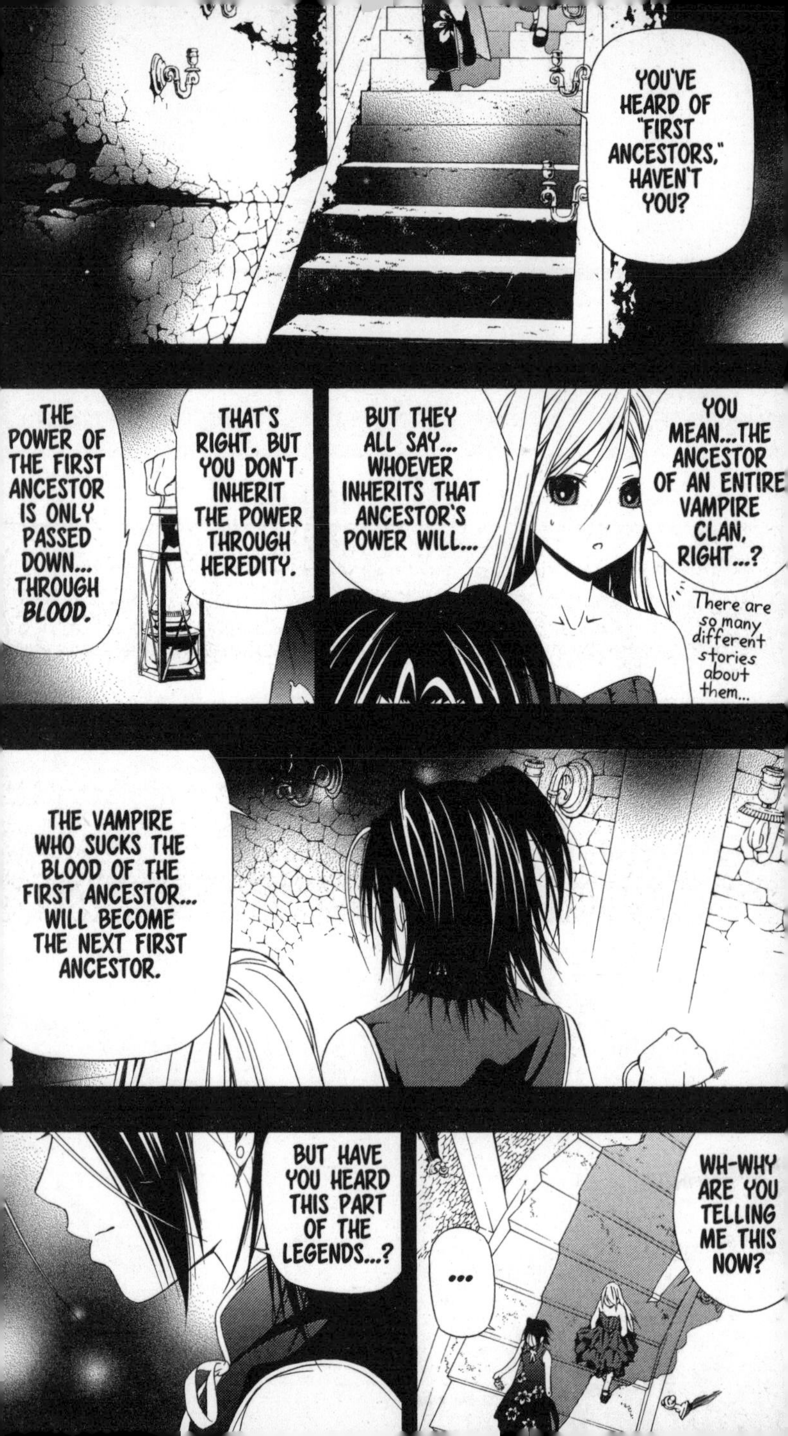
YOU'VE HEARD OF "FIRST ANCESTORS," HAVEN'T YOU?
YOU MEAN...THE ANCESTOR OF AN ENTIRE VAMPIRE CLAN, RIGHT...?
There are so many different stories about them...
BUT THEY ALL SAY... WHOEVER INHERITS THAT ANCESTOR'S POWER WILL...
THAT'S RIGHT. BUT YOU DON'T INHERIT THE POWER THROUGH HEREDITY.
THE POWER OF THE FIRST ANCESTOR IS ONLY PASSED DOWN... THROUGH BLOOD.
THE VAMPIRE WHO SUCKS THE BLOOD OF THE FIRST ANCESTOR... WILL BECOME THE NEXT FIRST ANCESTOR.
WH-WHY ARE YOU TELLING ME THIS NOW?
...
BUT HAVE YOU HEARD THIS PART OF THE LEGENDS...?

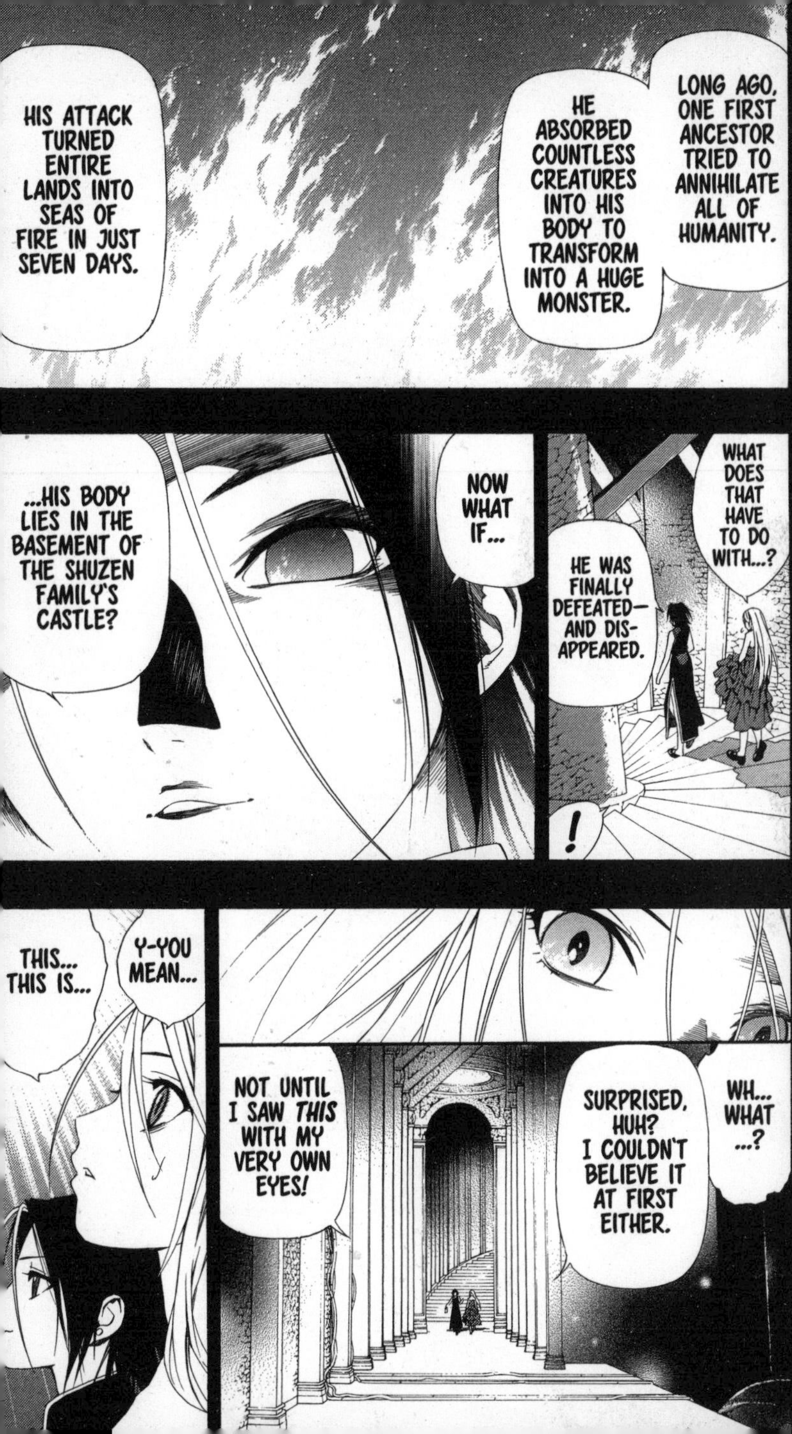
LONG AGO, ONE FIRST ANCESTOR TRIED TO ANNIHILATE ALL OF HUMANITY.
HE ABSORBED COUNTLESS CREATURES INTO HIS BODY TO TRANSFORM INTO A HUGE MONSTER.
HIS ATTACK TURNED ENTIRE LANDS INTO SEAS OF FIRE IN JUST SEVEN DAYS.
WHAT DOES THAT HAVE TO DO WITH...?
HE WAS FINALLY DEFEATED—AND DIS-APPEARED.
!
NOW WHAT IF...
...HIS BODY LIES IN THE BASEMENT OF THE SHUZEN FAMILY'S CASTLE?
Y-YOU MEAN...
THIS... THIS IS...
WH... WHAT ...?
SURPRISED, HUH? I COULDN'T BELIEVE IT AT FIRST EITHER.
NOT UNTIL I SAW *THIS* WITH MY VERY OWN EYES!

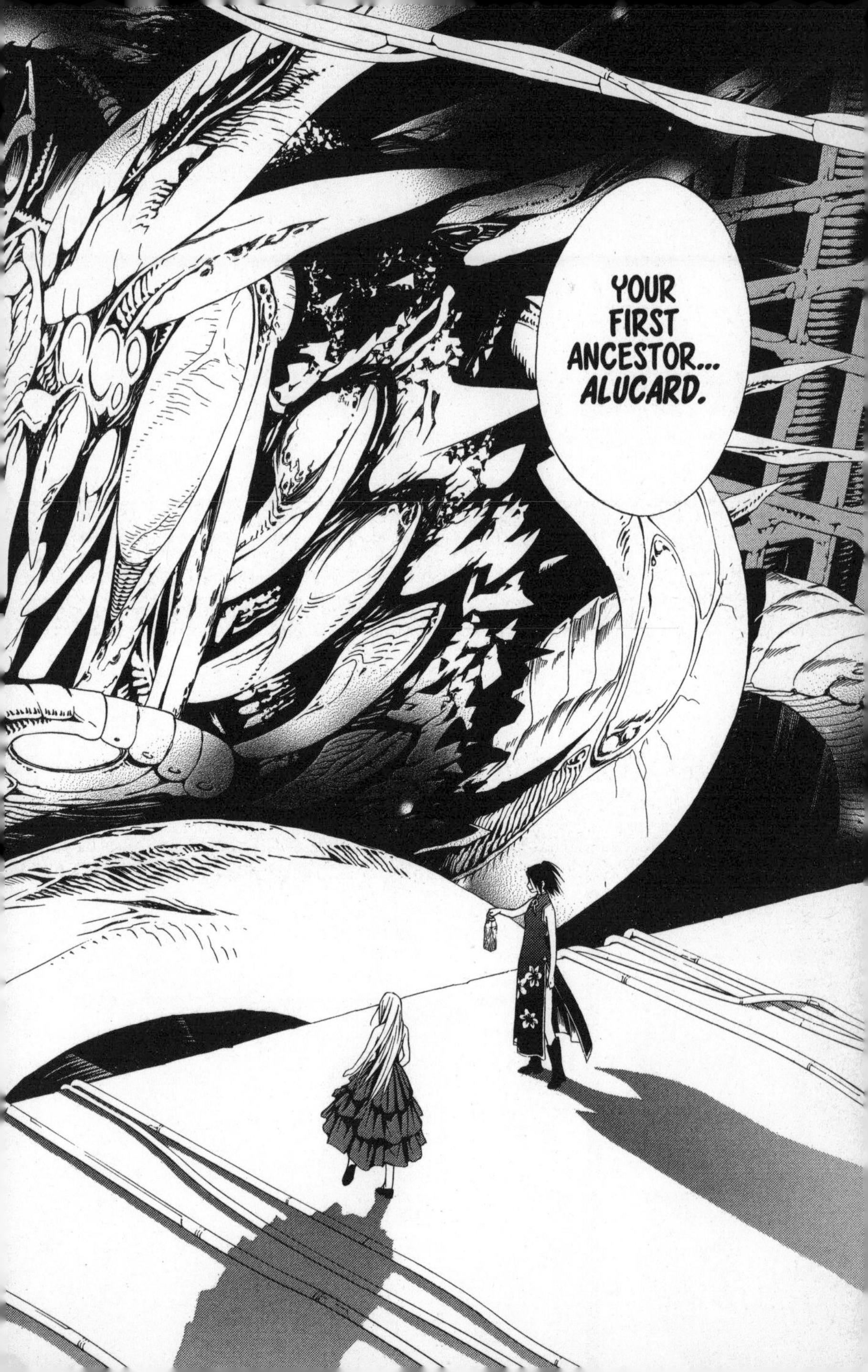
YOUR FIRST ANCESTOR... ALUCARD.

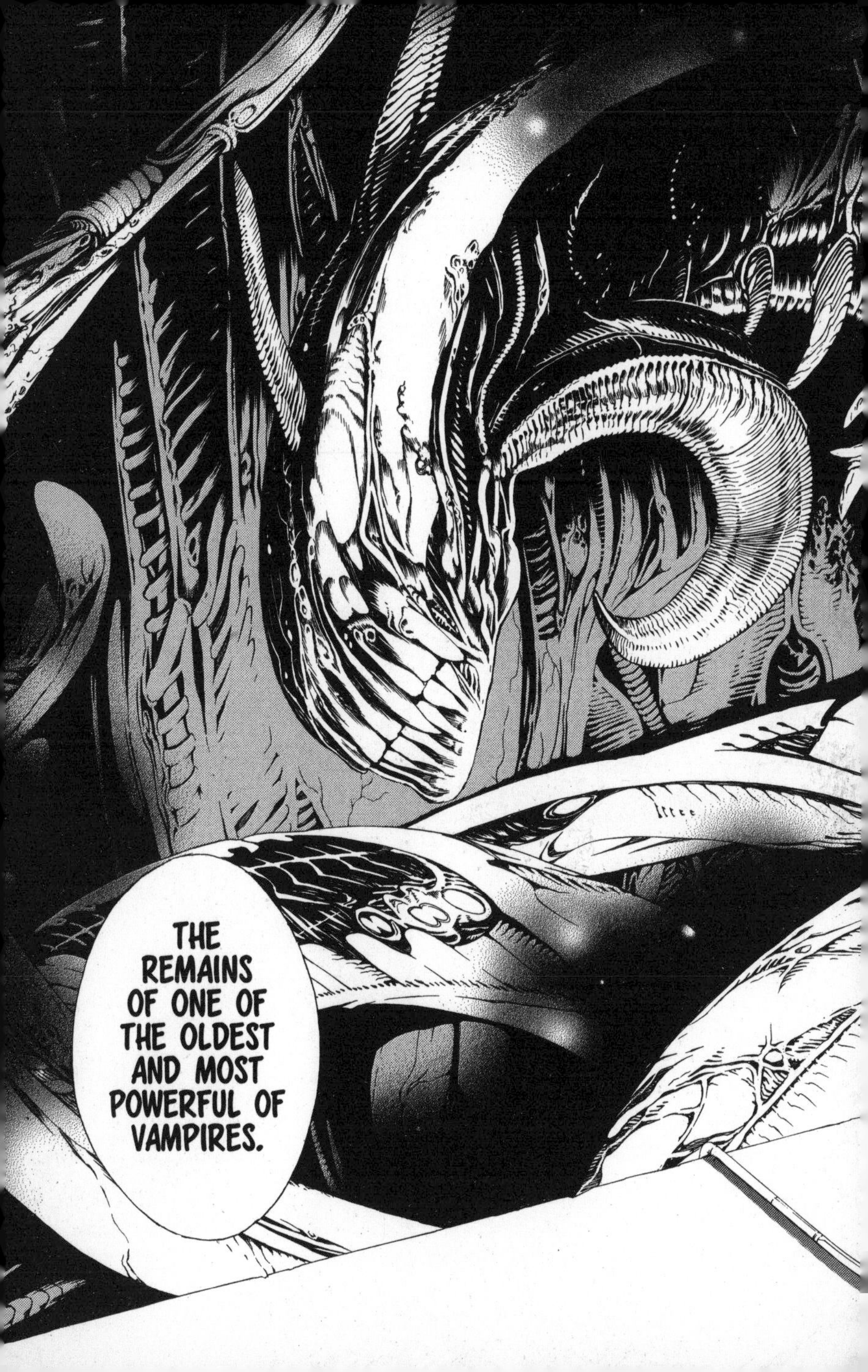
THE REMAINS OF ONE OF THE OLDEST AND MOST POWERFUL OF VAMPIRES.

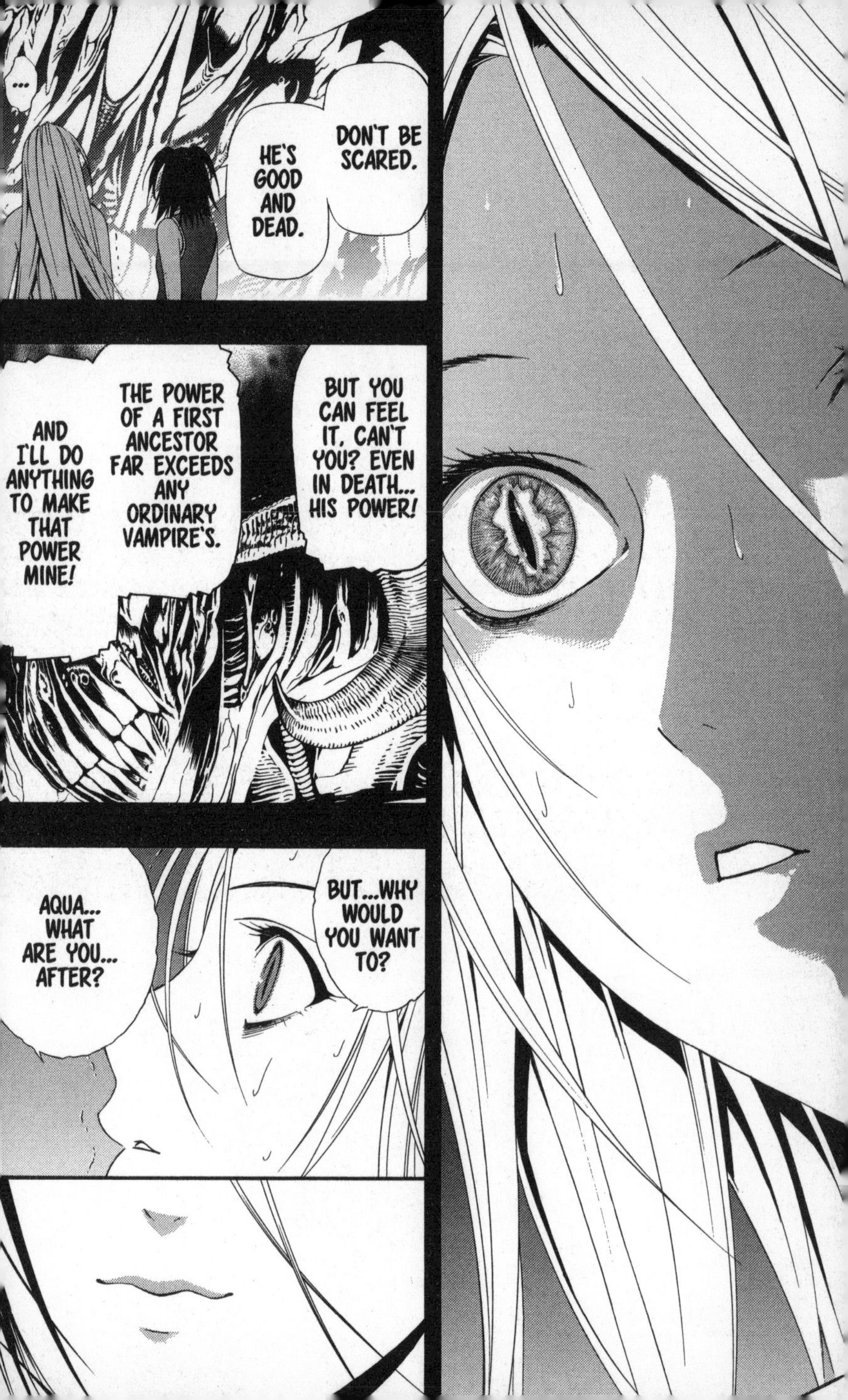
DON'T BE SCARED.
HE'S GOOD AND DEAD.
...
BUT YOU CAN FEEL IT, CAN'T YOU? EVEN IN DEATH... HIS POWER!
THE POWER OF A FIRST ANCESTOR FAR EXCEEDS ANY ORDINARY VAMPIRE'S.
AND I'LL DO ANYTHING TO MAKE THAT POWER MINE!
BUT...WHY WOULD YOU WANT TO?
AQUA... WHAT ARE YOU... AFTER?

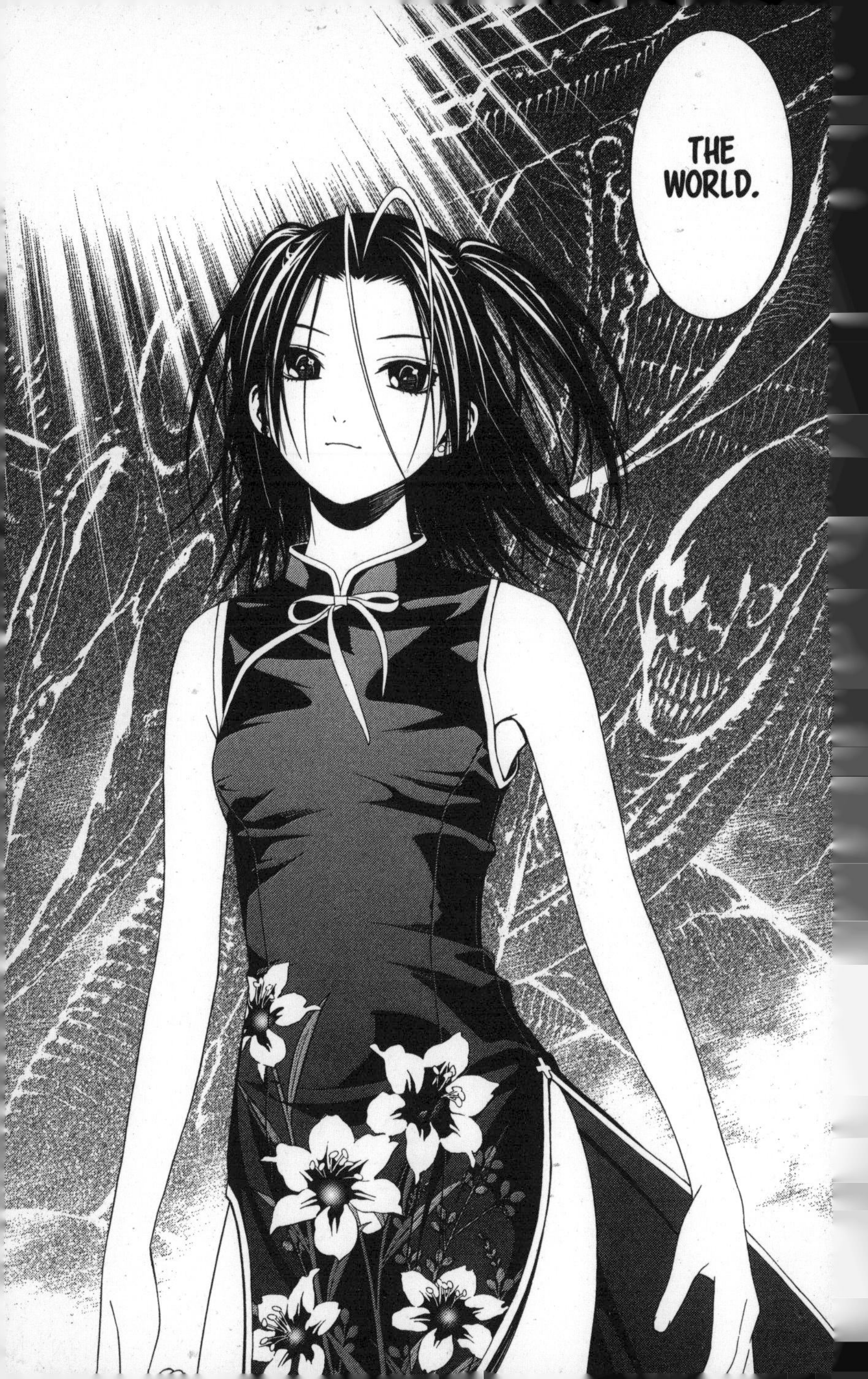
THE WORLD.

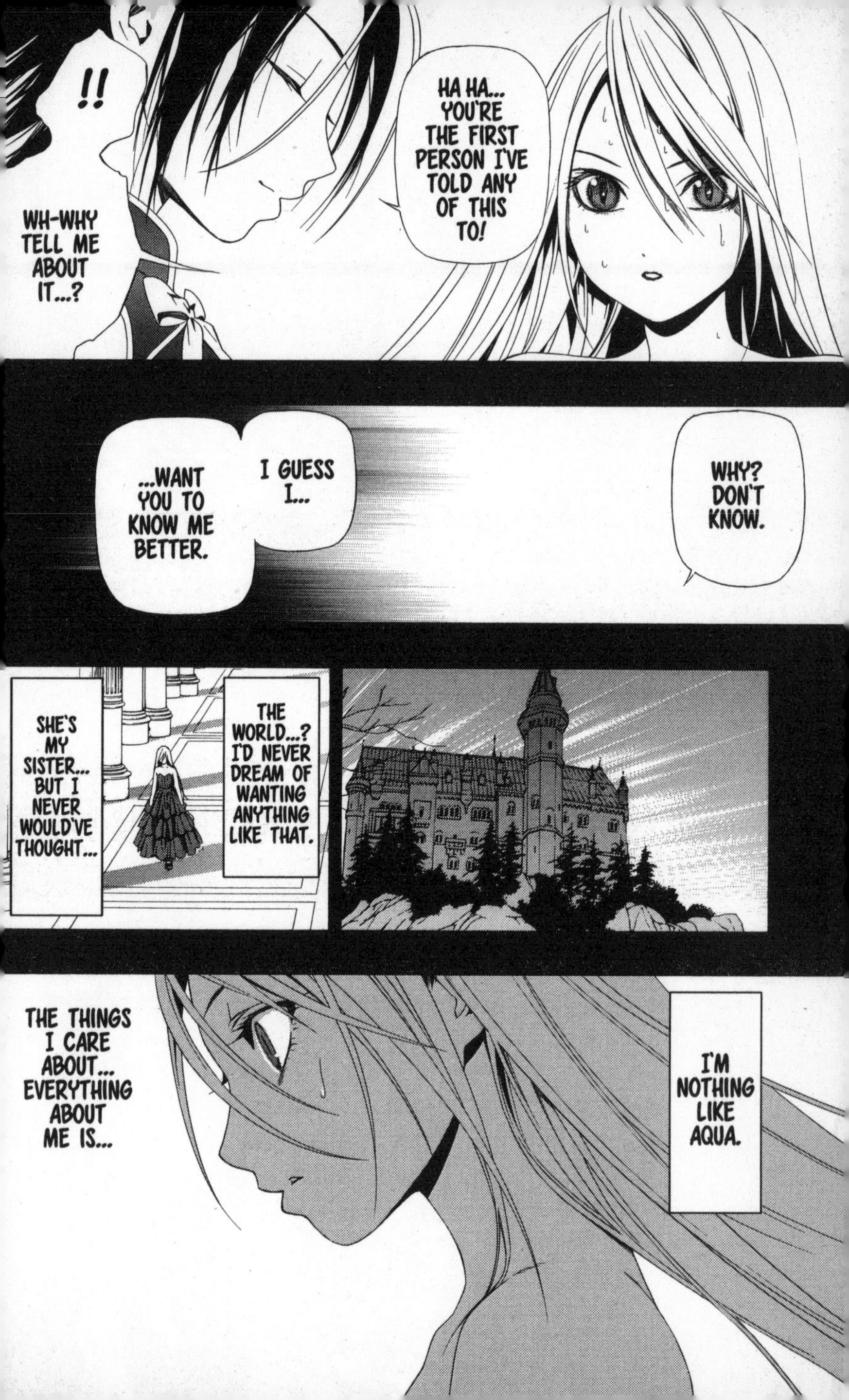
HA HA... YOU'RE THE FIRST PERSON I'VE TOLD ANY OF THIS TO!
!!
WH-WHY TELL ME ABOUT IT...?
WHY? DON'T KNOW.
I GUESS I...
...WANT YOU TO KNOW ME BETTER.
THE WORLD...? I'D NEVER DREAM OF WANTING ANYTHING LIKE THAT.
SHE'S MY SISTER... BUT I NEVER WOULD'VE THOUGHT...
I'M NOTHING LIKE AQUA.
THE THINGS I CARE ABOUT... EVERYTHING ABOUT ME IS...

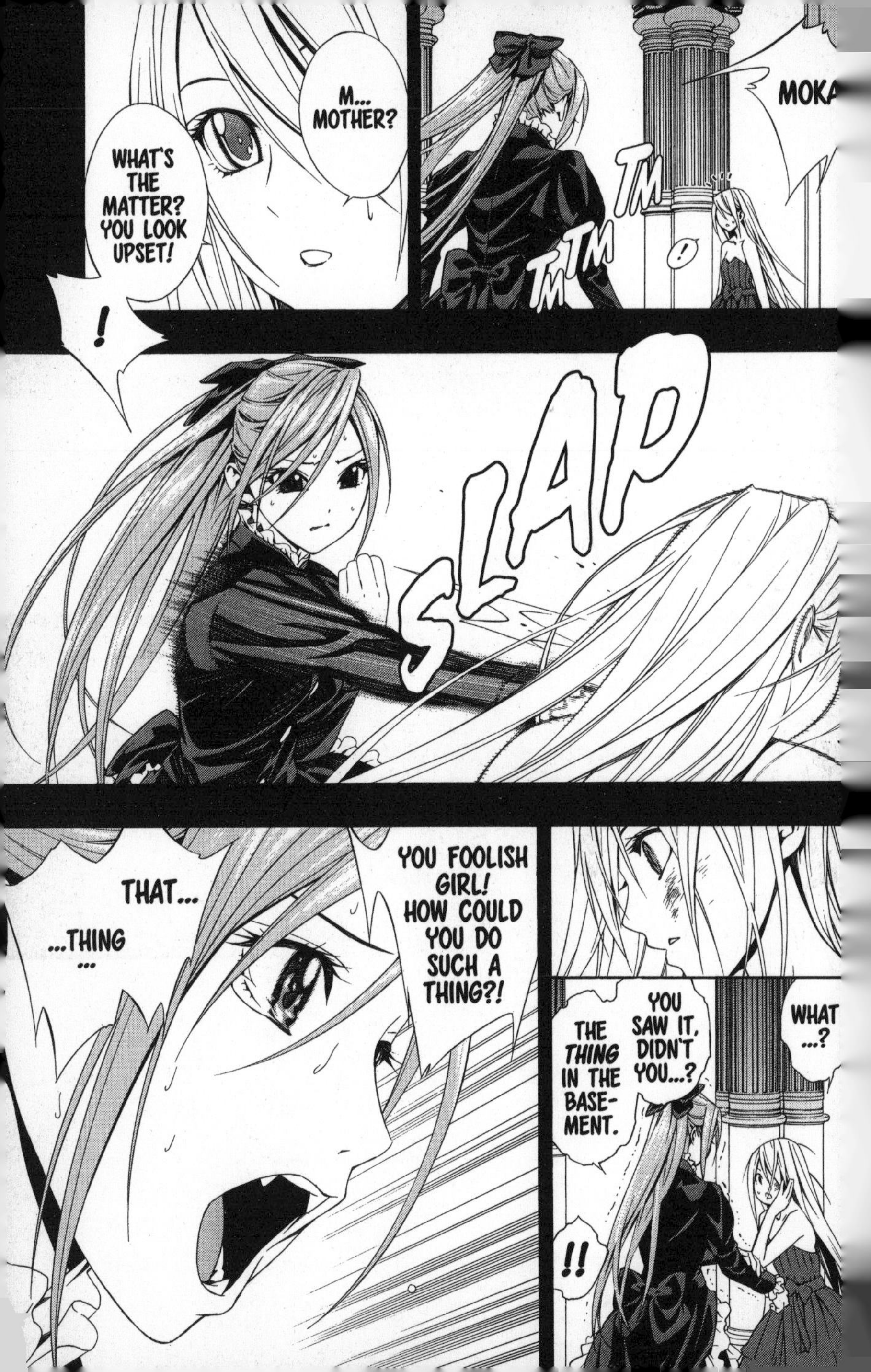
MOKA
TM TM TM TM
!
M... MOTHER?
WHAT'S THE MATTER? YOU LOOK UPSET!
!
SLAP
WHAT ...?
YOU SAW IT, DIDN'T YOU...?
THE *THING* IN THE BASE-MENT.
!!
YOU FOOLISH GIRL! HOW COULD YOU DO SUCH A THING?!
THAT...
...THING ...

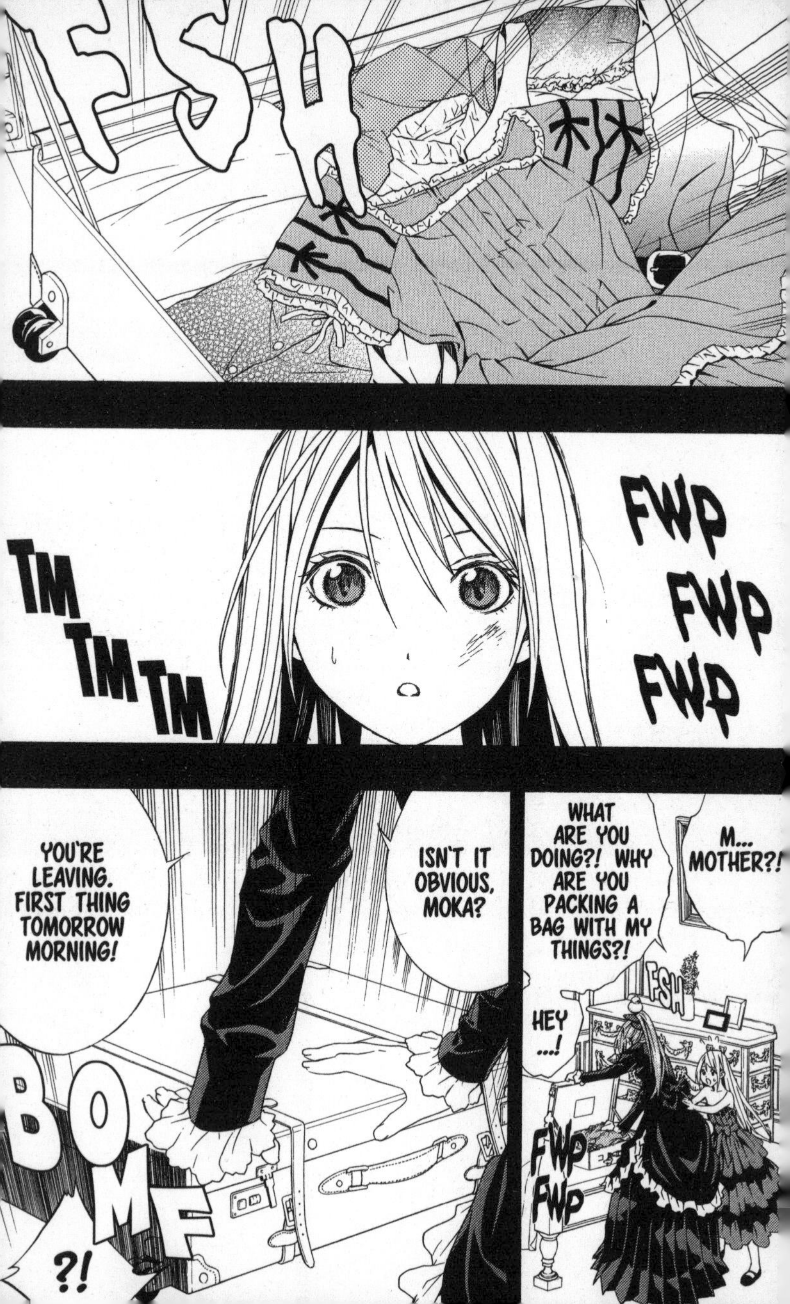
FSH
FWP FWP FWP
TM TM TM
M... MOTHER?!
WHAT ARE YOU DOING?! WHY ARE YOU PACKING A BAG WITH MY THINGS?!
FSH
HEY ...!
FWP FWP
ISN'T IT OBVIOUS, MOKA?
YOU'RE LEAVING. FIRST THING TOMORROW MORNING!
BOMF
?!

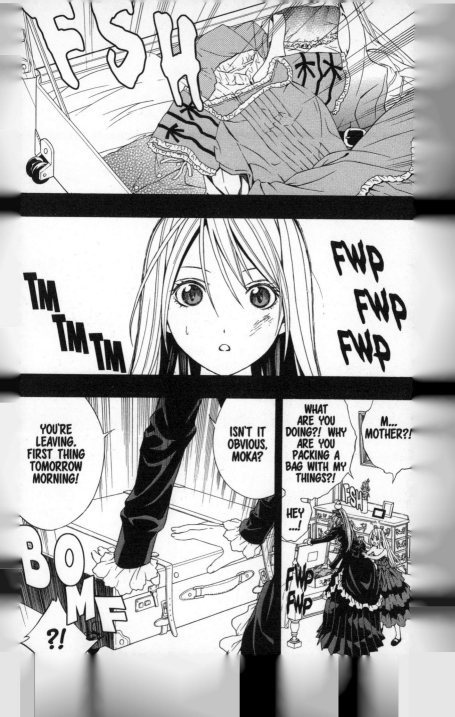

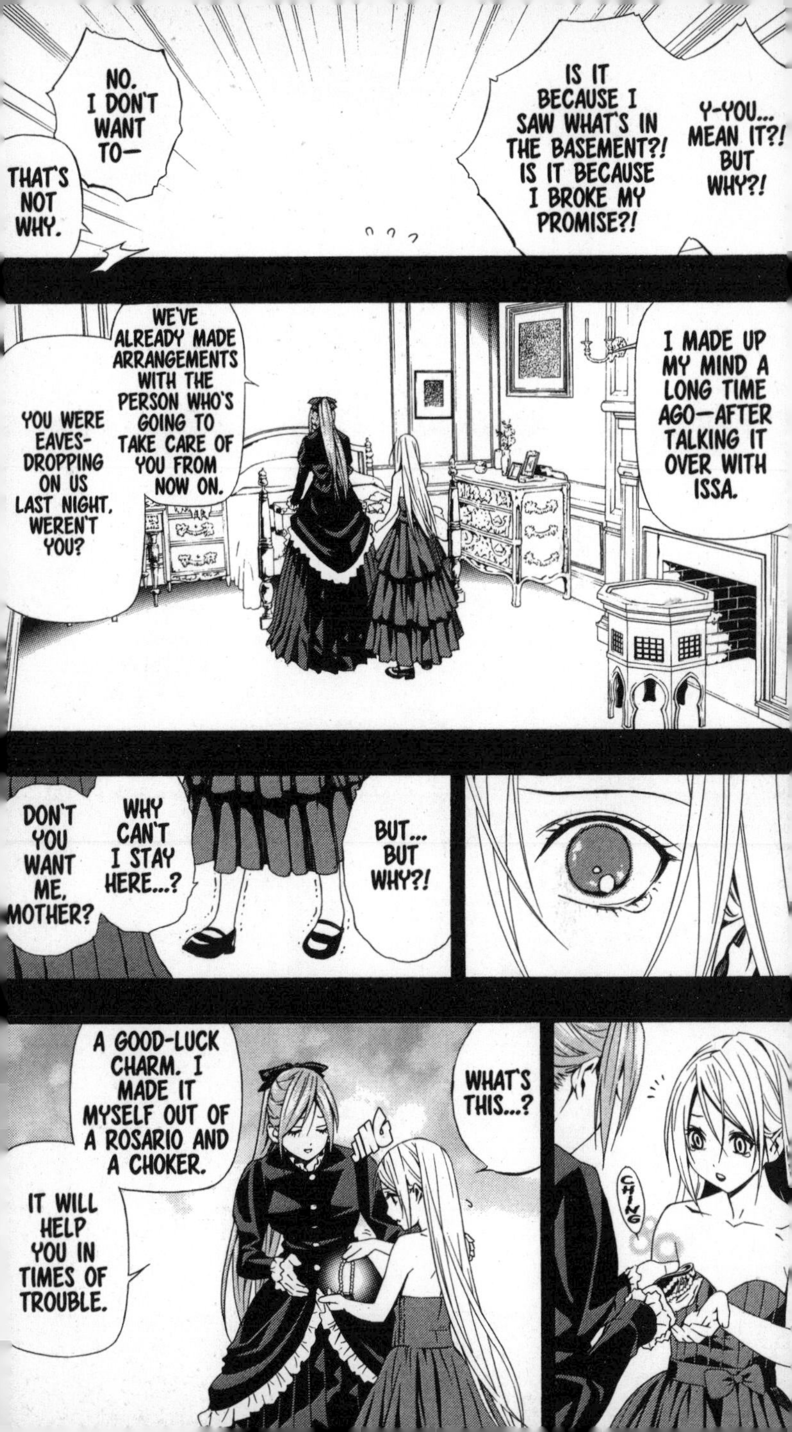
Y-YOU... MEAN IT?! BUT WHY?!
IS IT BECAUSE I SAW WHAT'S IN THE BASEMENT?! IS IT BECAUSE I BROKE MY PROMISE?!
NO. I DON'T WANT TO—
THAT'S NOT WHY.
I MADE UP MY MIND A LONG TIME AGO—AFTER TALKING IT OVER WITH ISSA.
WE'VE ALREADY MADE ARRANGEMENTS WITH THE PERSON WHO'S GOING TO TAKE CARE OF YOU FROM NOW ON.
YOU WERE EAVES-DROPPING ON US LAST NIGHT, WEREN'T YOU?
BUT... BUT WHY?!
WHY CAN'T I STAY HERE...?
DON'T YOU WANT ME, MOTHER?
CHING
WHAT'S THIS...?
A GOOD-LUCK CHARM. I MADE IT MYSELF OUT OF A ROSARIO AND A CHOKER.
IT WILL HELP YOU IN TIMES OF TROUBLE.

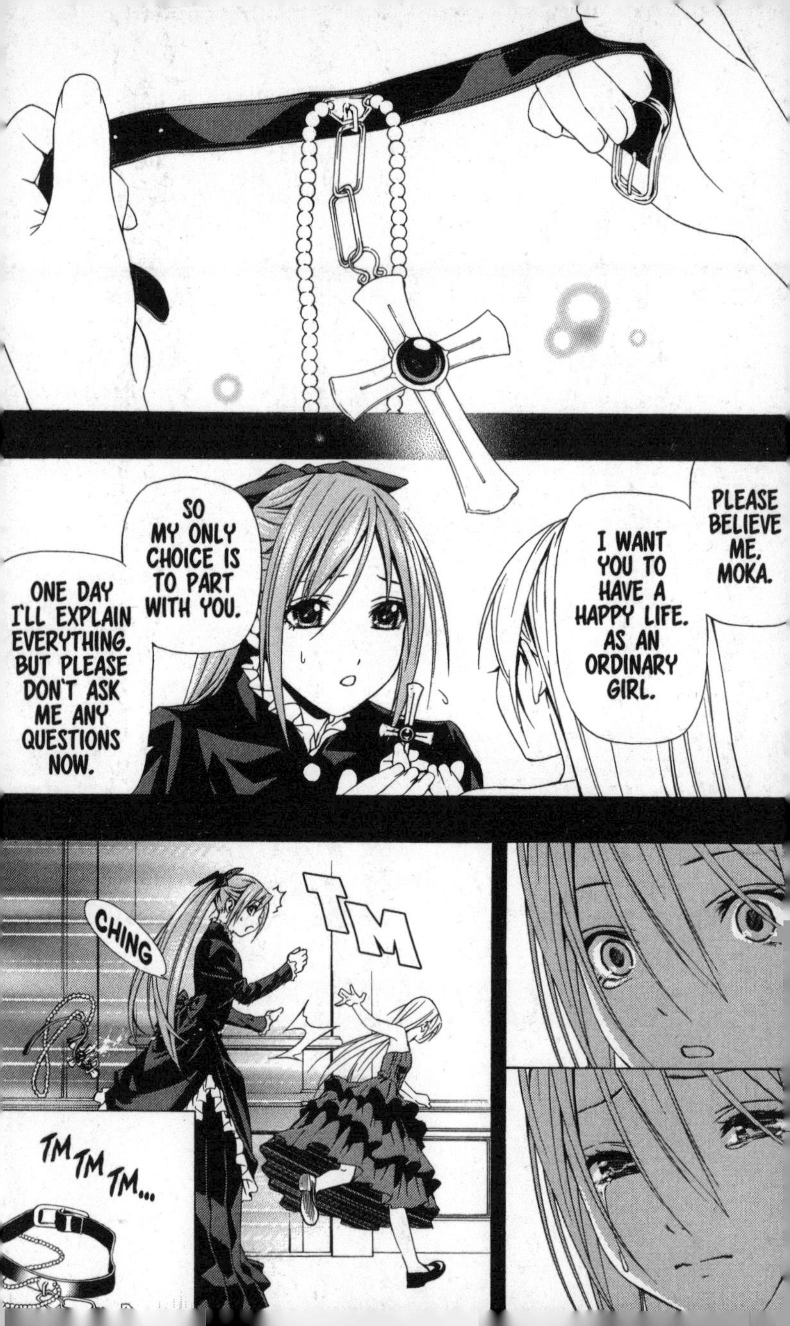
PLEASE BELIEVE ME, MOKA.
I WANT YOU TO HAVE A HAPPY LIFE. AS AN ORDINARY GIRL.
SO MY ONLY CHOICE IS TO PART WITH YOU.
ONE DAY I'LL EXPLAIN EVERYTHING. BUT PLEASE DON'T ASK ME ANY QUESTIONS NOW.
TM
CHING
TM TM TM...

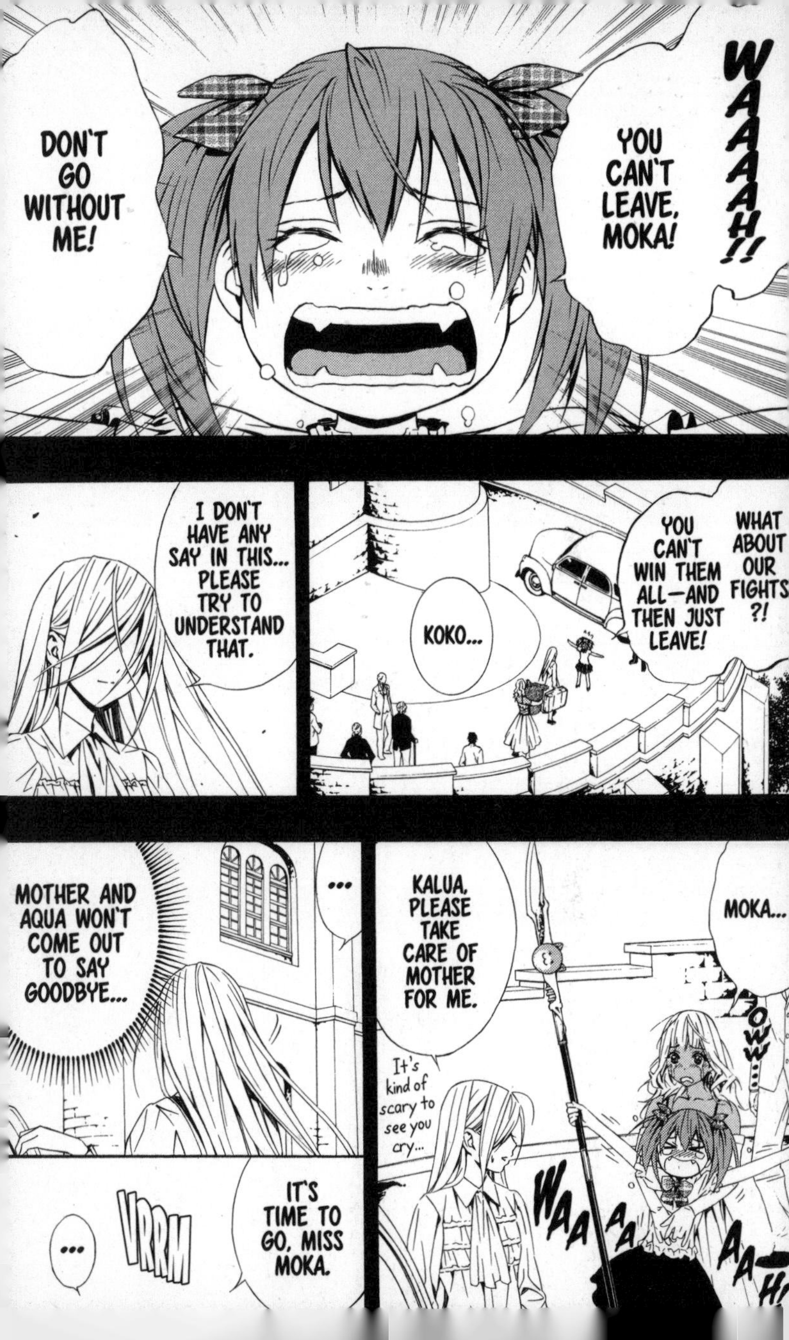
WAAAAAH!!
YOU CAN'T LEAVE, MOKA!
DON'T GO WITHOUT ME!
WHAT ABOUT OUR FIGHTS?!
YOU CAN'T WIN THEM ALL—AND THEN JUST LEAVE!
KOKO...
I DON'T HAVE ANY SAY IN THIS... PLEASE TRY TO UNDERSTAND THAT.
MOKA...
KALUA, PLEASE TAKE CARE OF MOTHER FOR ME.
OWW...
It's kind of scary to see you cry...
WAAAAAAH!
...
MOTHER AND AQUA WON'T COME OUT TO SAY GOODBYE...
IT'S TIME TO GO, MISS MOKA.
VRRM
...

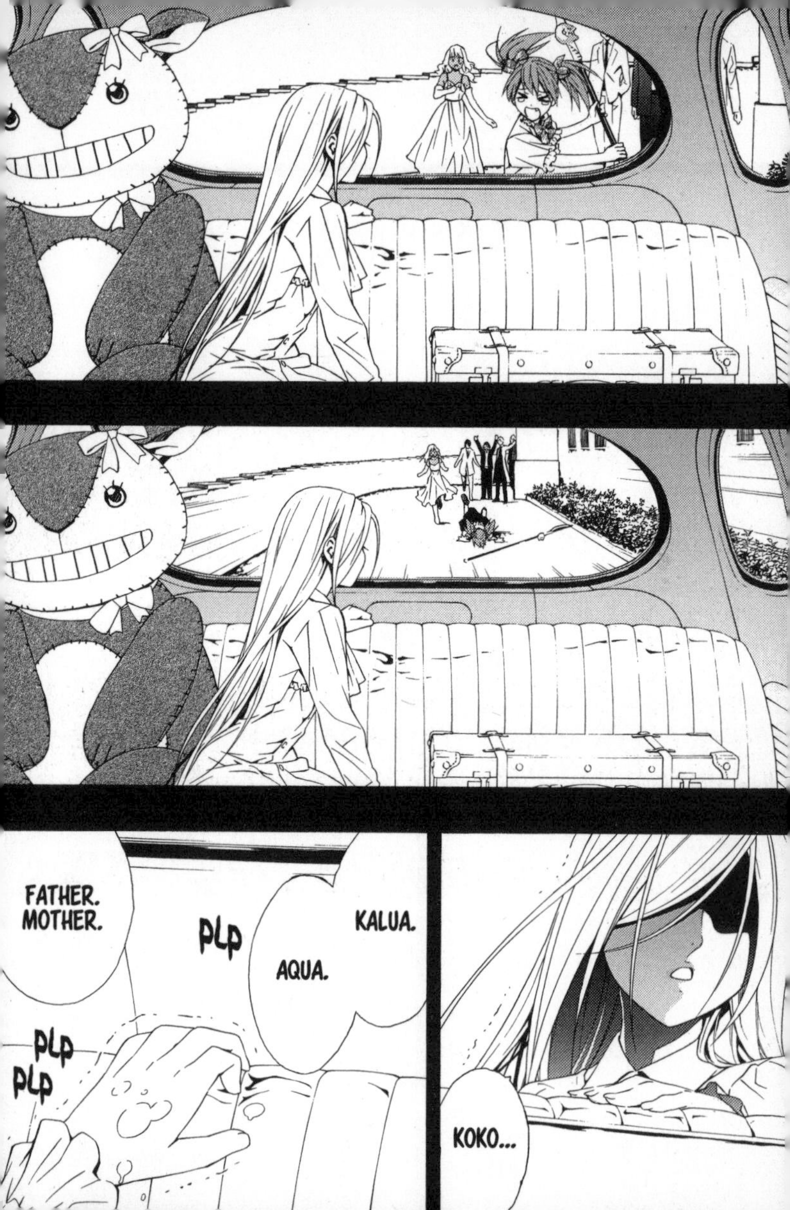
KOKO...
KALUA.
AQUA.
PLP
FATHER. MOTHER.
PLP
PLP

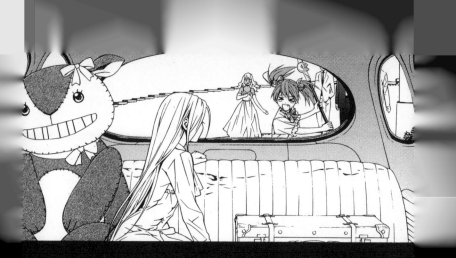

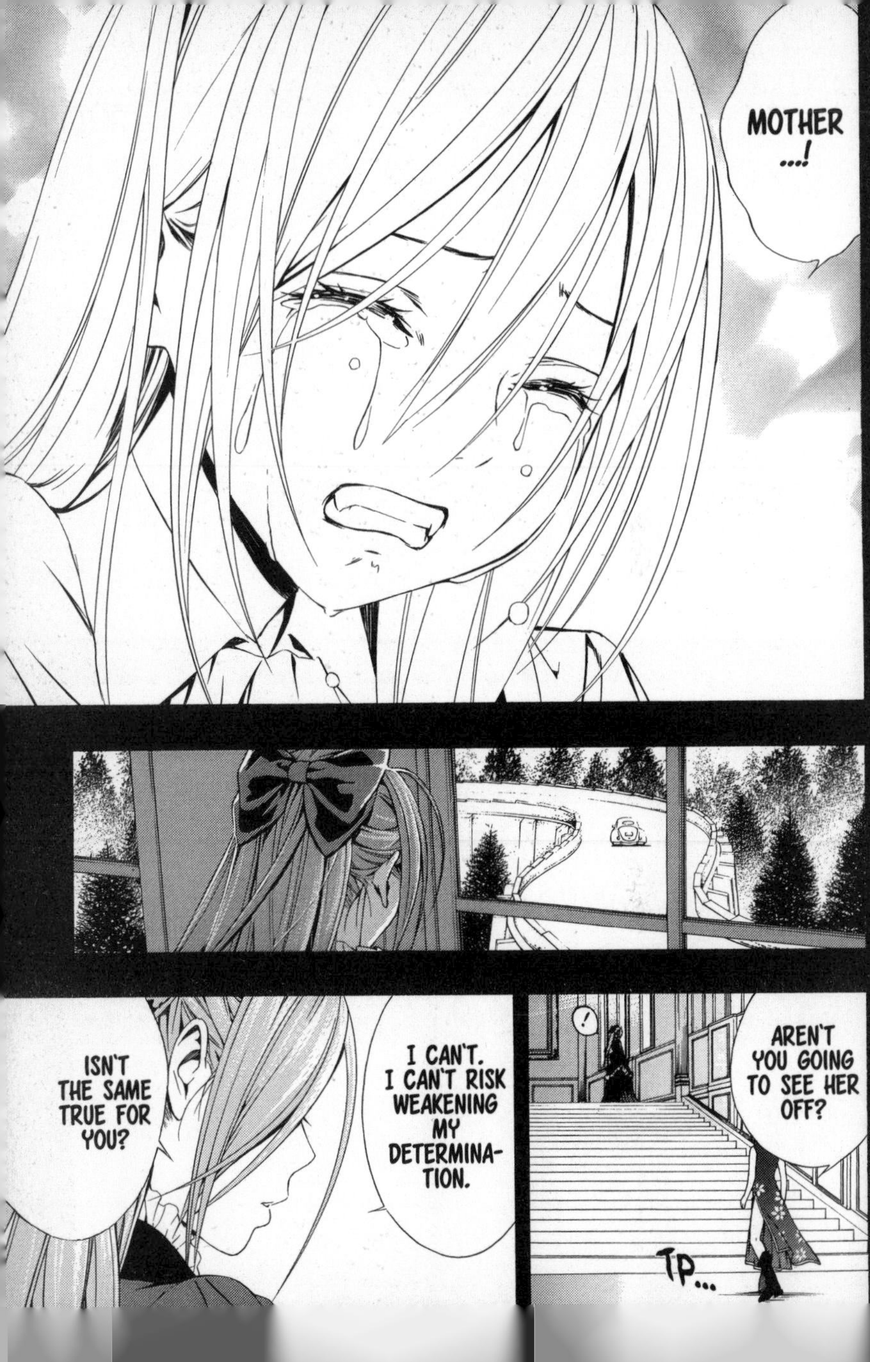
MOTHER ...!
!
AREN'T YOU GOING TO SEE HER OFF?
TP...
I CAN'T. I CAN'T RISK WEAKENING MY DETERMINATION.
ISN'T THE SAME TRUE FOR YOU?

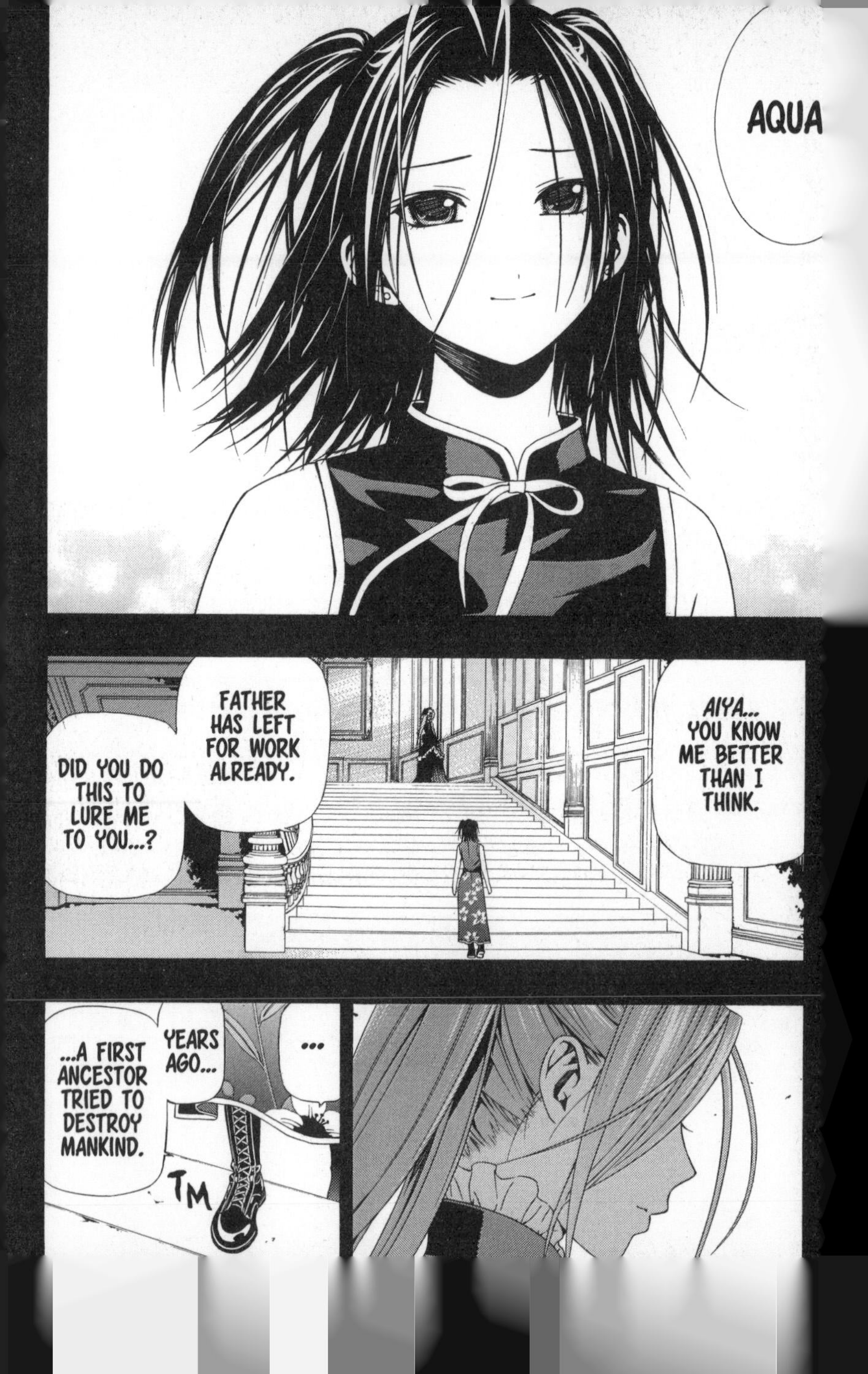
AQUA
AIYA... YOU KNOW ME BETTER THAN I THINK.
FATHER HAS LEFT FOR WORK ALREADY.
DID YOU DO THIS TO LURE ME TO YOU...?
...
YEARS AGO...
...A FIRST ANCESTOR TRIED TO DESTROY MANKIND.
TM

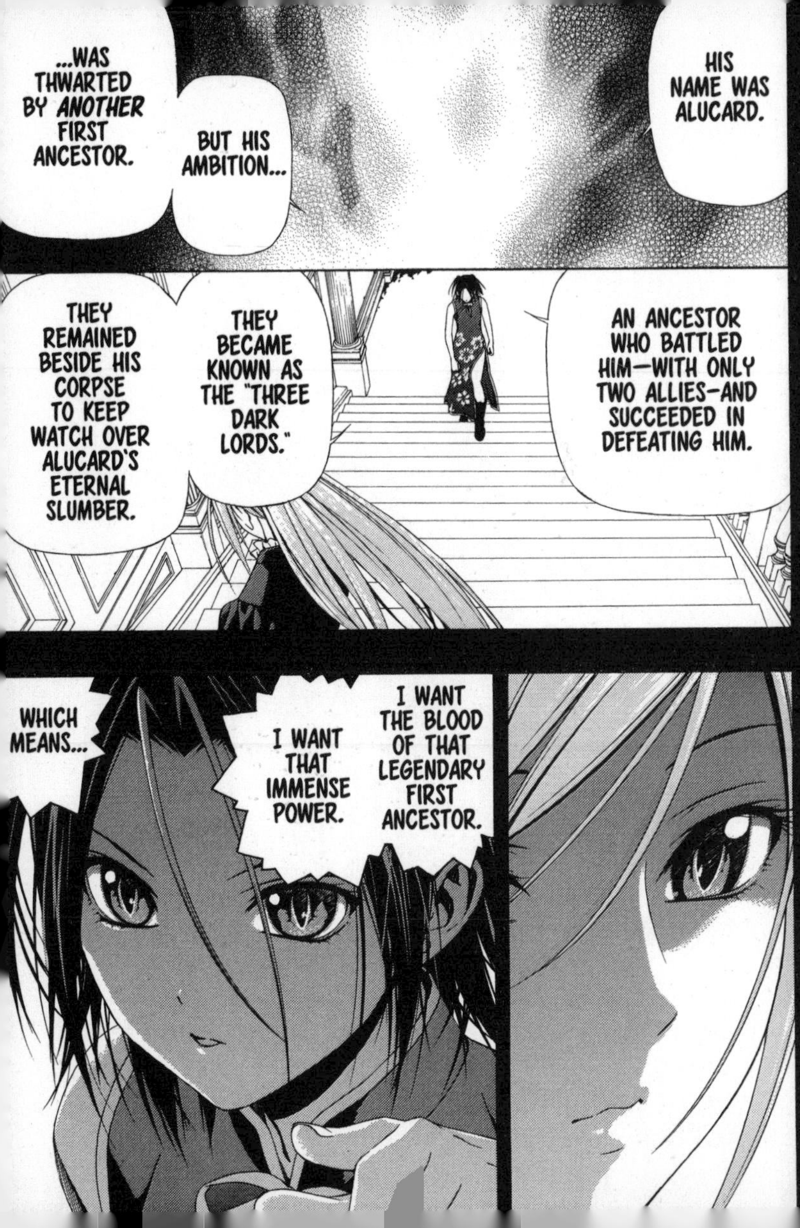
HIS NAME WAS ALUCARD.
BUT HIS AMBITION...
...WAS THWARTED BY ANOTHER FIRST ANCESTOR.
AN ANCESTOR WHO BATTLED HIM—WITH ONLY TWO ALLIES—AND SUCCEEDED IN DEFEATING HIM.
THEY BECAME KNOWN AS THE "THREE DARK LORDS."
THEY REMAINED BESIDE HIS CORPSE TO KEEP WATCH OVER ALUCARD'S ETERNAL SLUMBER.
I WANT THE BLOOD OF THAT LEGENDARY FIRST ANCESTOR.
I WANT THAT IMMENSE POWER.
WHICH MEANS...

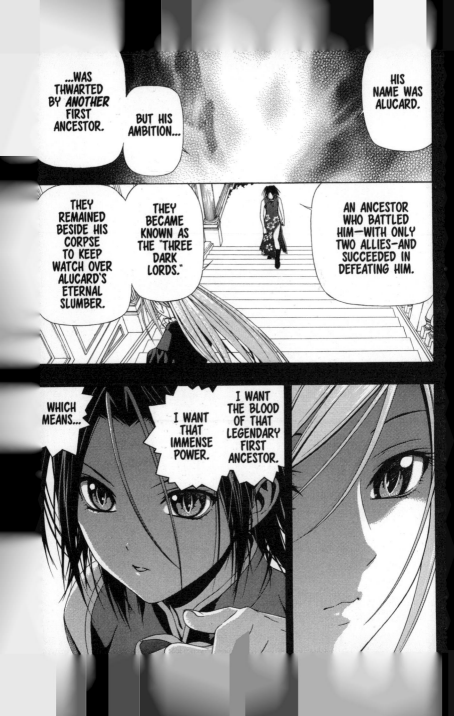

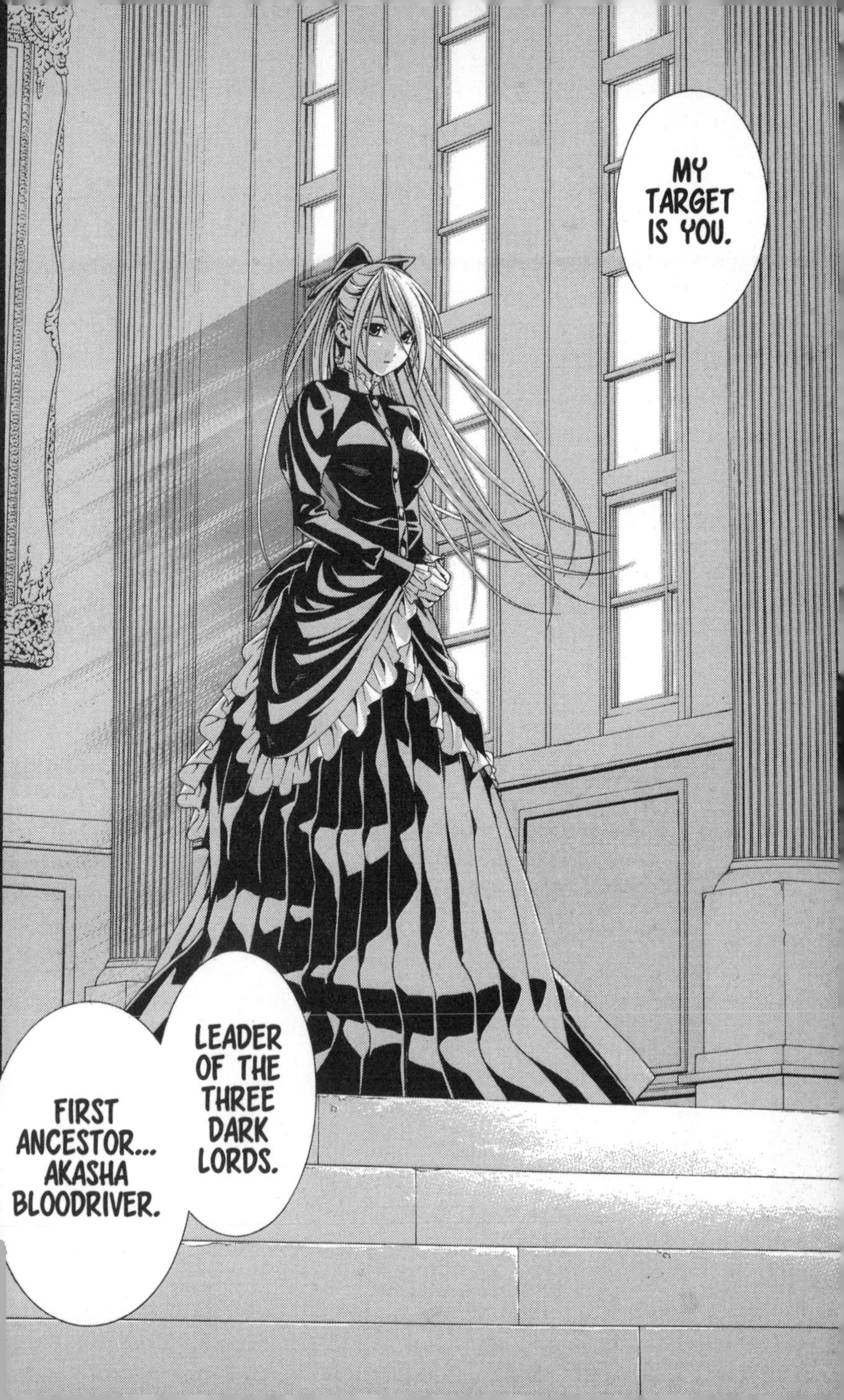
MY TARGET IS YOU.
LEADER OF THE THREE DARK LORDS.
FIRST ANCESTOR... AKASHA BLOODRIVER.

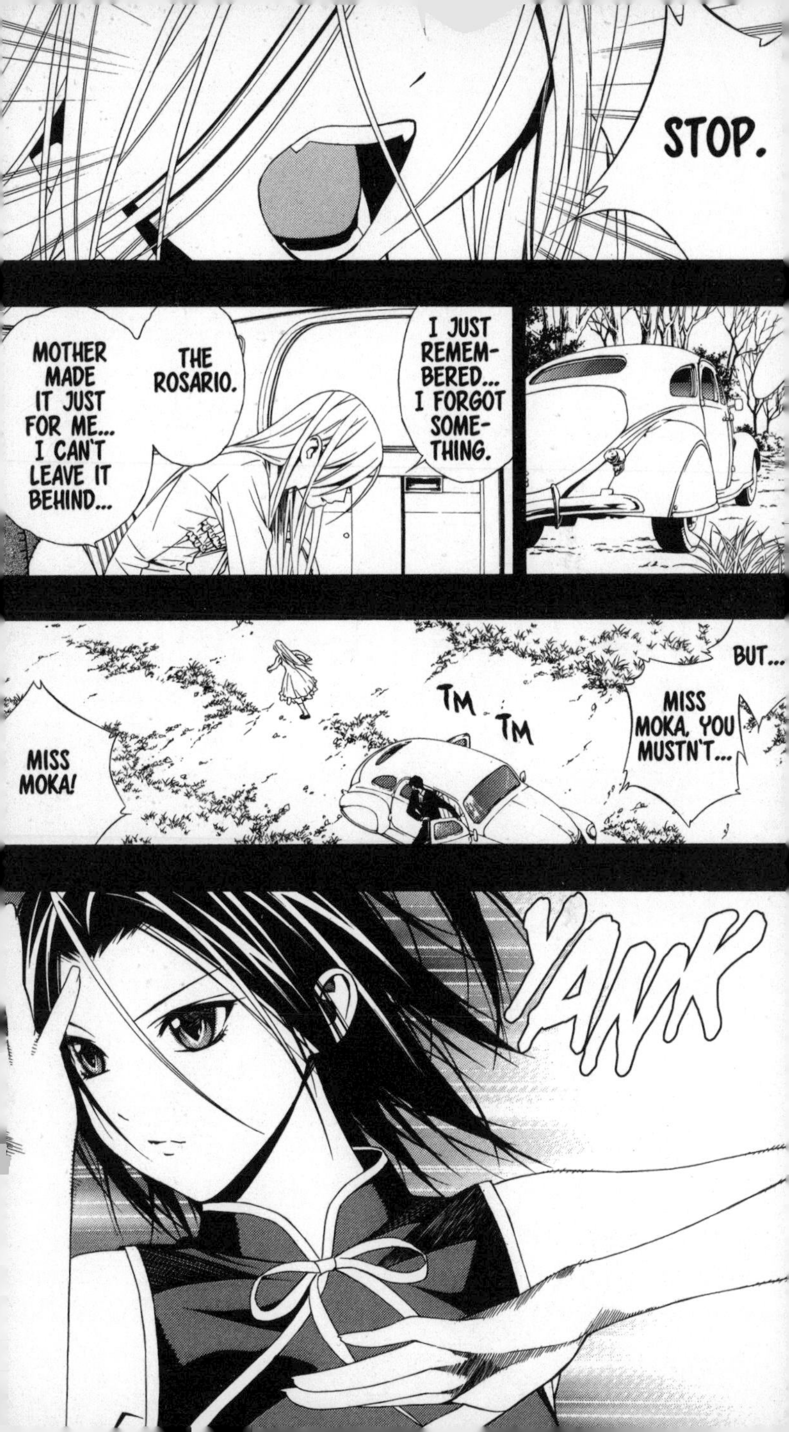
STOP.
I JUST REMEMBERED... I FORGOT SOMETHING.
THE ROSARIO.
MOTHER MADE IT JUST FOR ME... I CAN'T LEAVE IT BEHIND...
BUT...
MISS MOKA, YOU MUSTN'T...
TM TM
MISS MOKA!
YANK

# 32: Darkness Falls, a Star Is Born

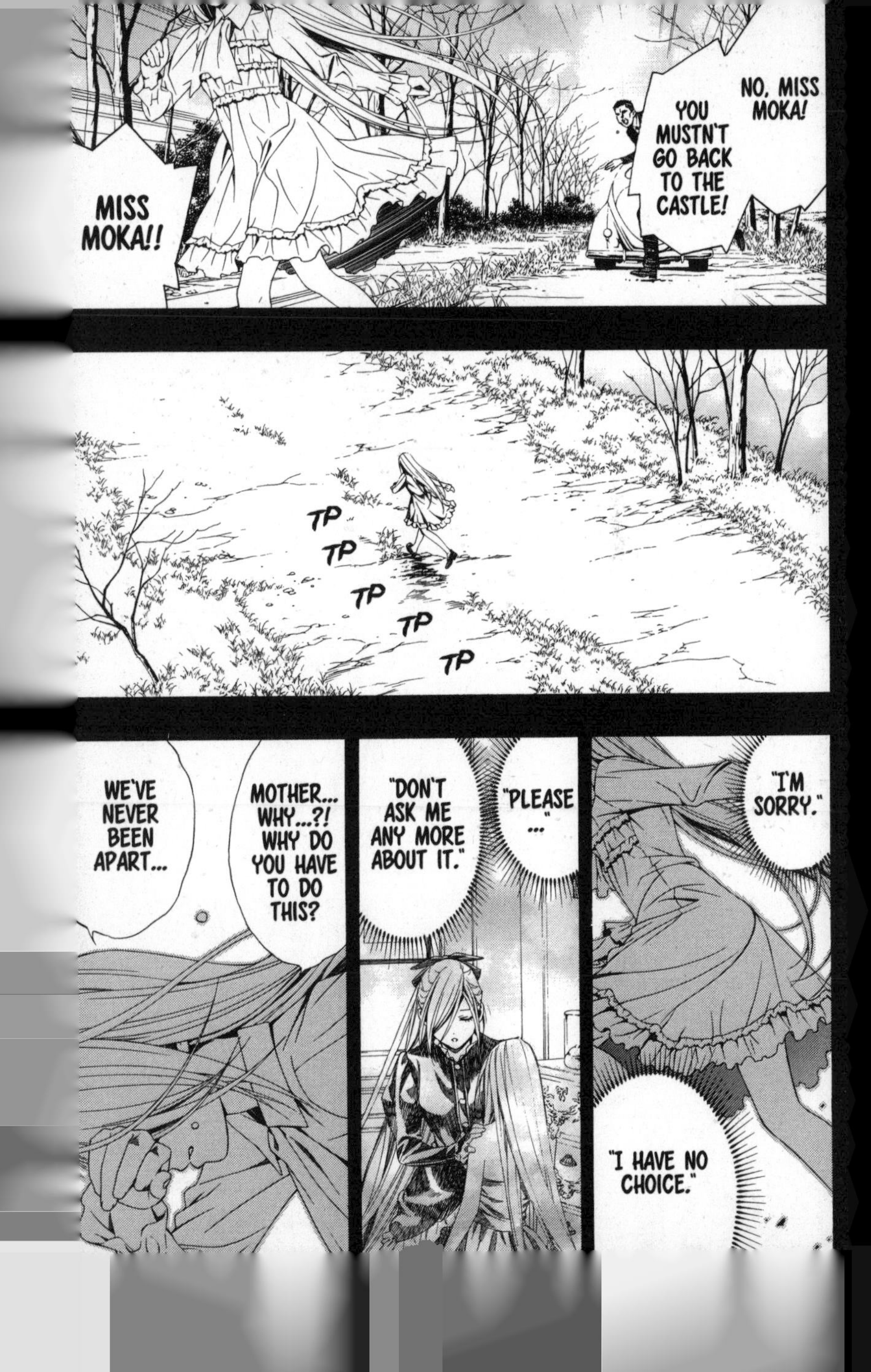
NO, MISS MOKA!
YOU MUSTN'T GO BACK TO THE CASTLE!
MISS MOKA!!
TP
TP
TP
TP
TP
"I'M SORRY."
"I HAVE NO CHOICE."
"PLEASE ..."
"DON'T ASK ME ANY MORE ABOUT IT."
MOTHER... WHY...?! WHY DO YOU HAVE TO DO THIS?
WE'VE NEVER BEEN APART...

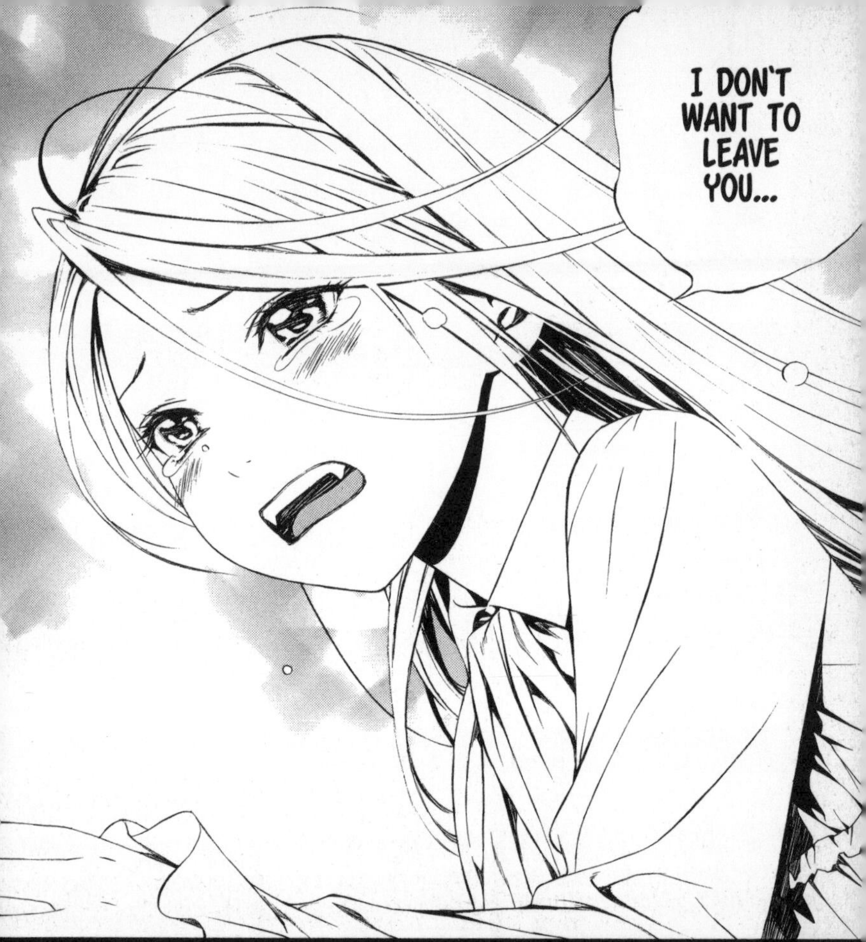
I DON'T WANT TO LEAVE YOU...

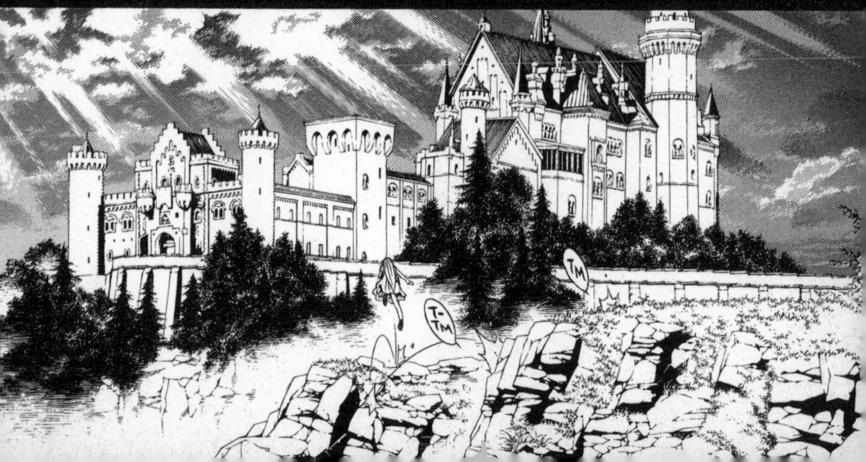
TM
T-TM

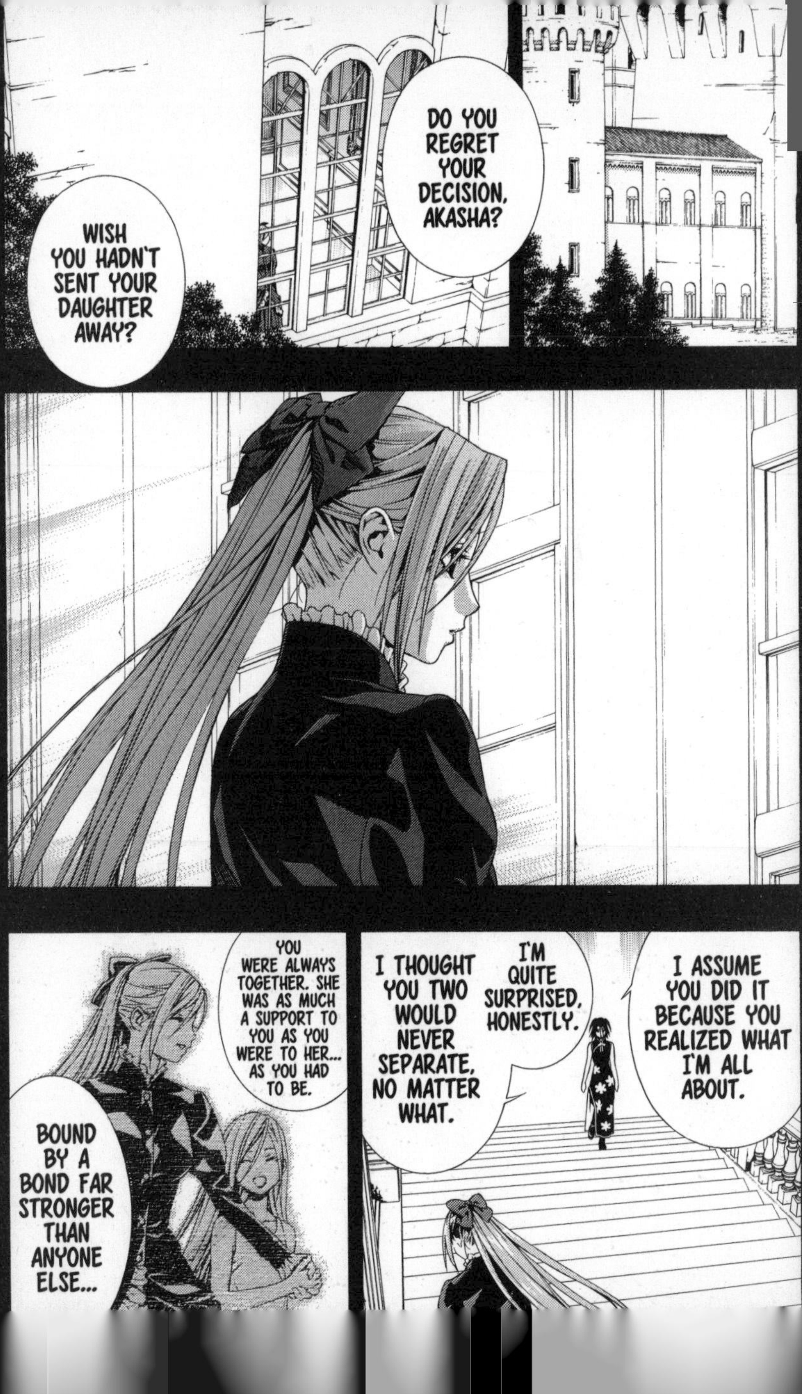
DO YOU REGRET YOUR DECISION, AKASHA?
WISH YOU HADN'T SENT YOUR DAUGHTER AWAY?
I ASSUME YOU DID IT BECAUSE YOU REALIZED WHAT I'M ALL ABOUT.
I'M QUITE SURPRISED, HONESTLY.
I THOUGHT YOU TWO WOULD NEVER SEPARATE, NO MATTER WHAT.
YOU WERE ALWAYS TOGETHER. SHE WAS AS MUCH A SUPPORT TO YOU AS YOU WERE TO HER... AS YOU HAD TO BE.
BOUND BY A BOND FAR STRONGER THAN ANYONE ELSE...

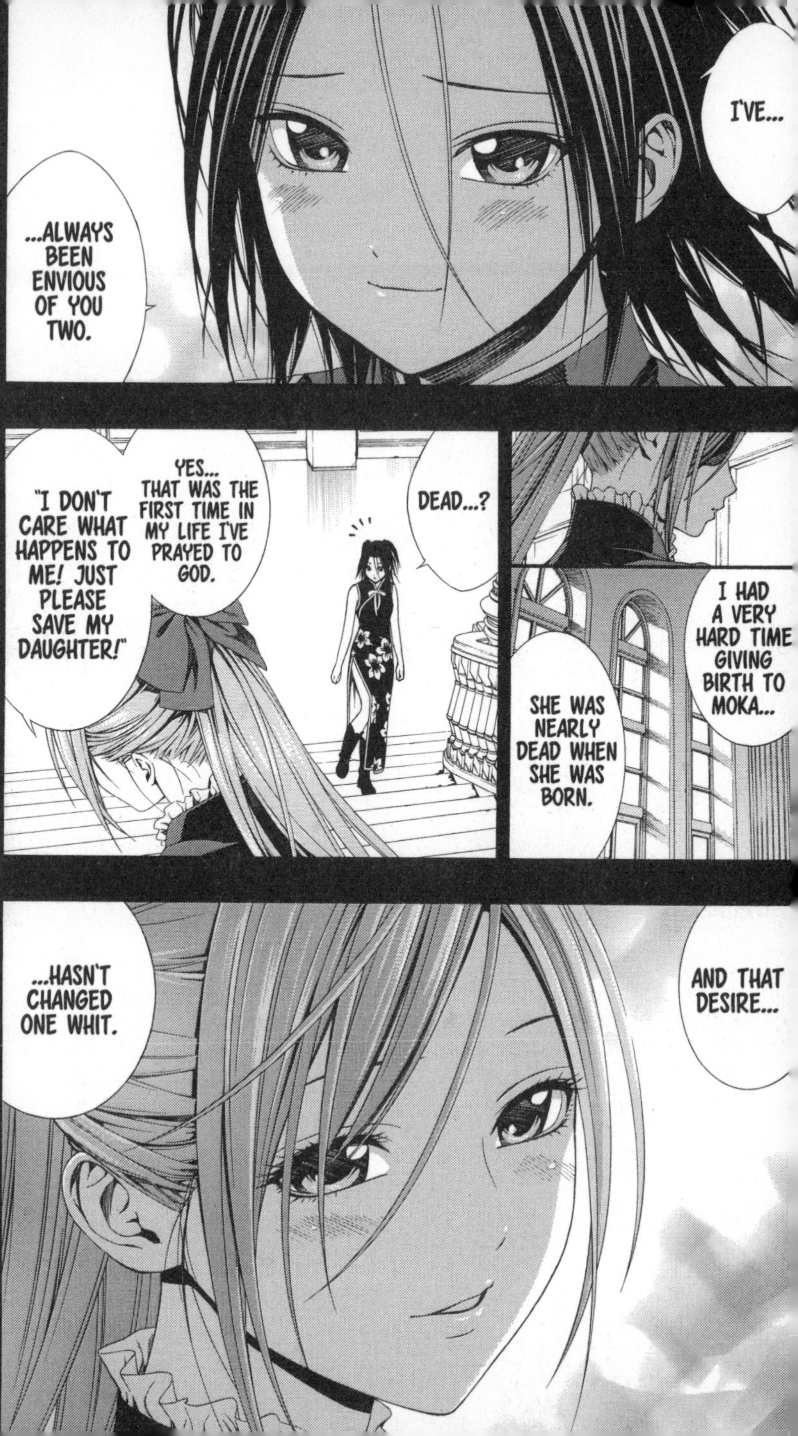
I'VE...
...ALWAYS BEEN ENVIOUS OF YOU TWO.
I HAD A VERY HARD TIME GIVING BIRTH TO MOKA...
SHE WAS NEARLY DEAD WHEN SHE WAS BORN.
DEAD...?
YES... THAT WAS THE FIRST TIME IN MY LIFE I'VE PRAYED TO GOD.
"I DON'T CARE WHAT HAPPENS TO ME! JUST PLEASE SAVE MY DAUGHTER!"
AND THAT DESIRE...
...HASN'T CHANGED ONE WHIT.

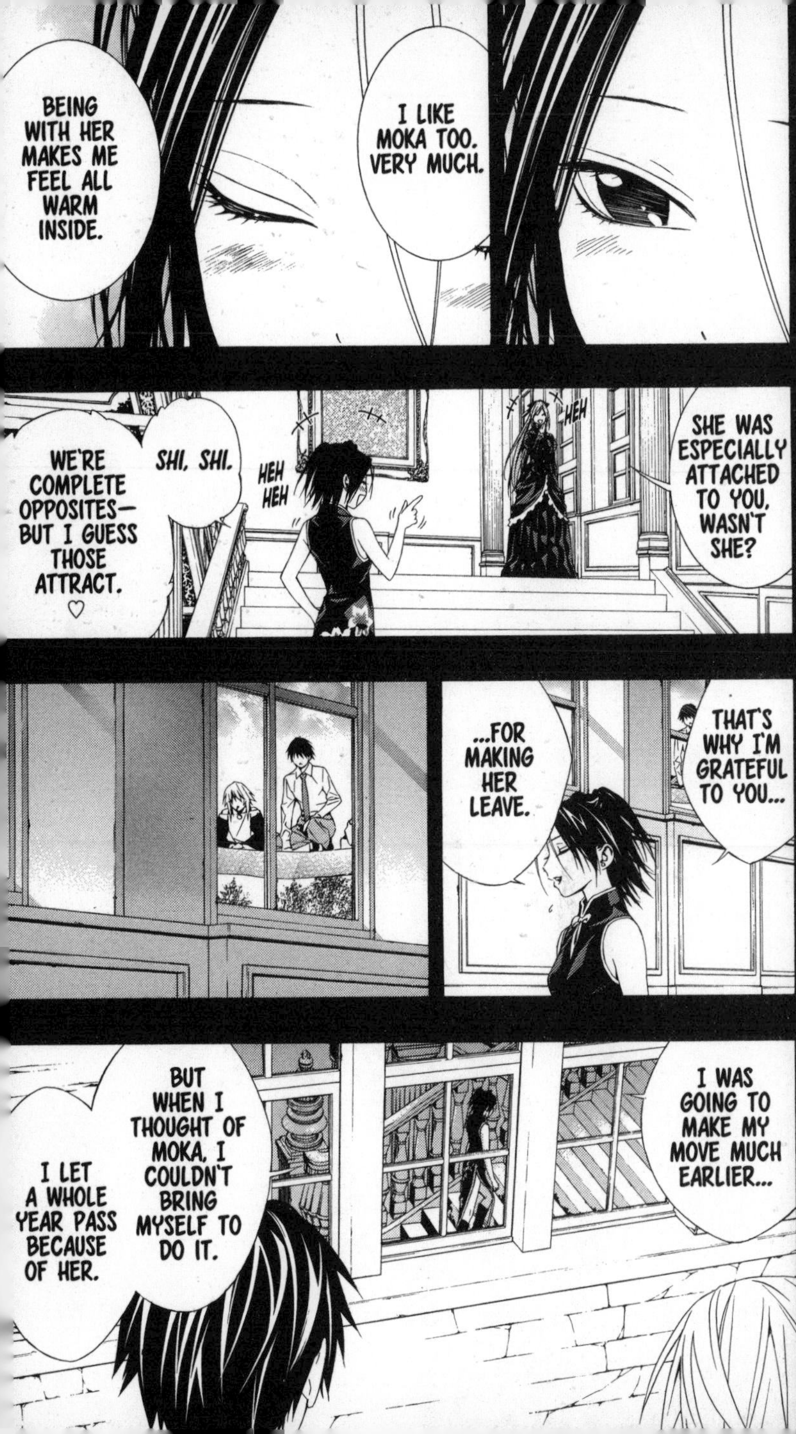
I LIKE MOKA TOO. VERY MUCH.
BEING WITH HER MAKES ME FEEL ALL WARM INSIDE.
SHE WAS ESPECIALLY ATTACHED TO YOU, WASN'T SHE?
HEH
HEH HEH
SHI, SHI.
WE'RE COMPLETE OPPOSITES— BUT I GUESS THOSE ATTRACT. ♡
THAT'S WHY I'M GRATEFUL TO YOU...
...FOR MAKING HER LEAVE.
I WAS GOING TO MAKE MY MOVE MUCH EARLIER...
BUT WHEN I THOUGHT OF MOKA, I COULDN'T BRING MYSELF TO DO IT.
I LET A WHOLE YEAR PASS BECAUSE OF HER.

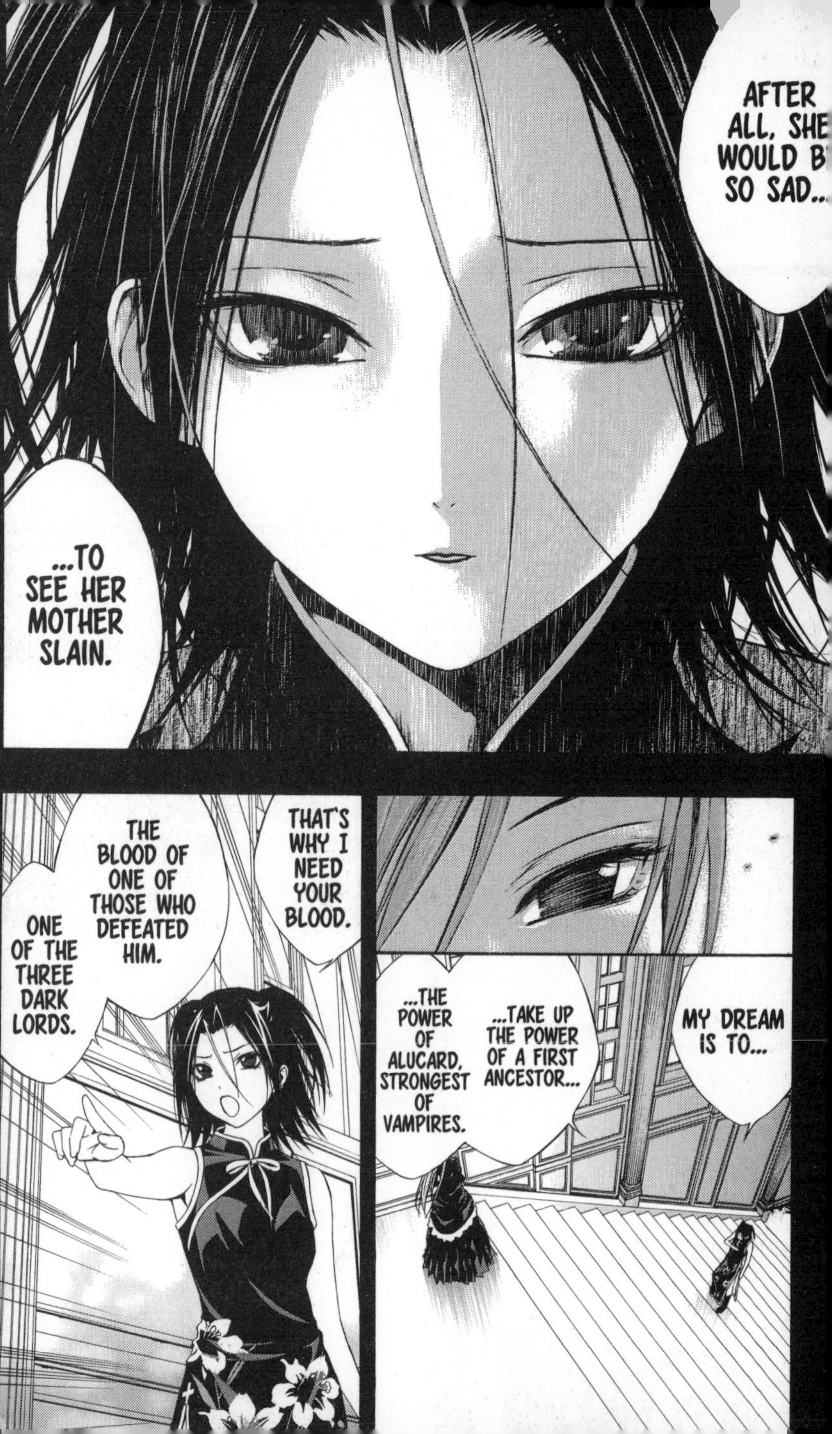
AFTER ALL, SHE WOULD B SO SAD...
...TO SEE HER MOTHER SLAIN.
MY DREAM IS TO...
...TAKE UP THE POWER OF A FIRST ANCESTOR...
...THE POWER OF ALUCARD, STRONGEST OF VAMPIRES.
THAT'S WHY I NEED YOUR BLOOD.
THE BLOOD OF ONE OF THOSE WHO DEFEATED HIM.
ONE OF THE THREE DARK LORDS.

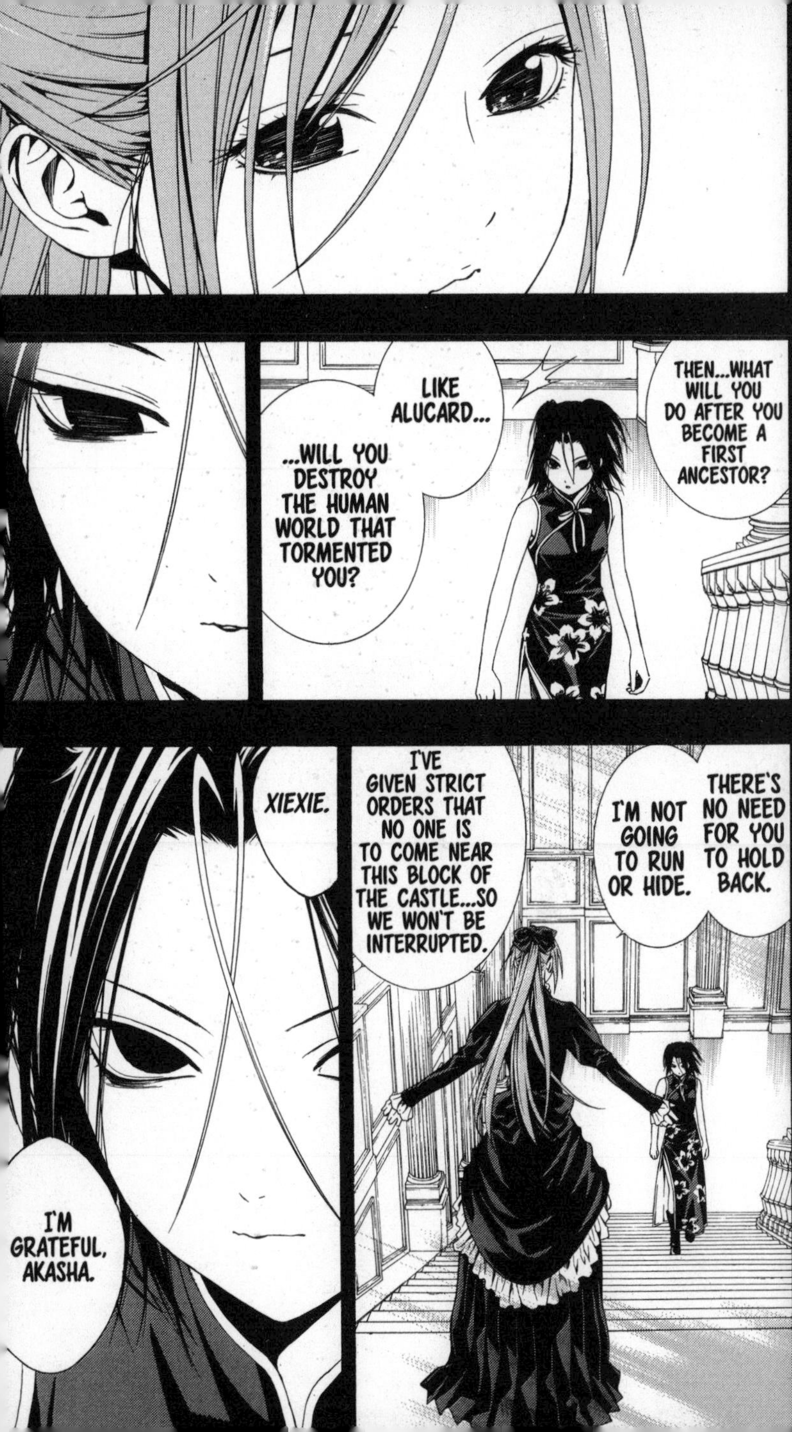
THEN...WHAT WILL YOU DO AFTER YOU BECOME A FIRST ANCESTOR?
LIKE ALUCARD...
...WILL YOU DESTROY THE HUMAN WORLD THAT TORMENTED YOU?
THERE'S NO NEED FOR YOU TO HOLD BACK.
I'M NOT GOING TO RUN OR HIDE.
I'VE GIVEN STRICT ORDERS THAT NO ONE IS TO COME NEAR THIS BLOCK OF THE CASTLE...SO WE WON'T BE INTERRUPTED.
XIEXIE.
I'M GRATEFUL, AKASHA.

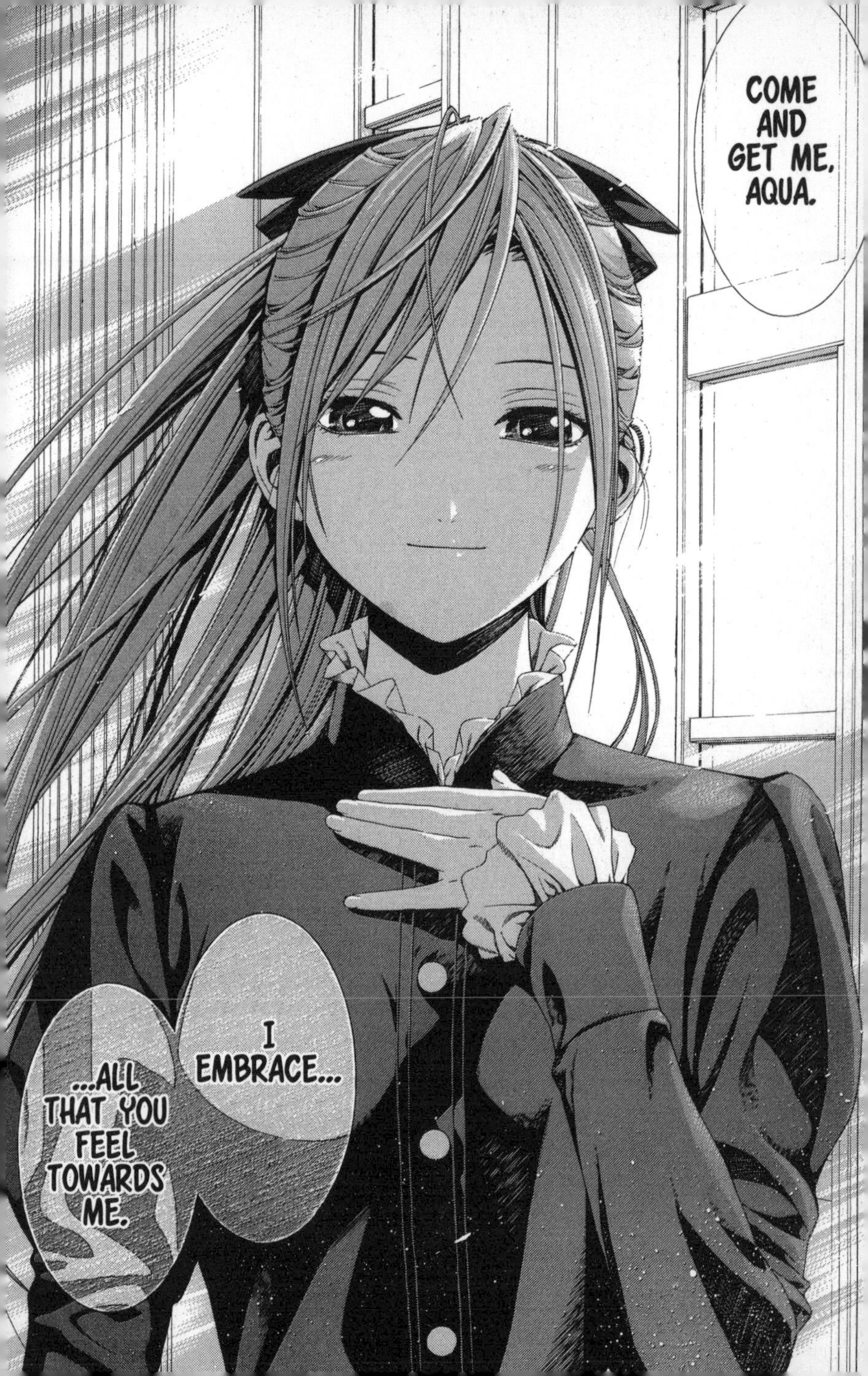
COME AND GET ME, AQUA.
I EMBRACE...
...ALL THAT YOU FEEL TOWARDS ME.

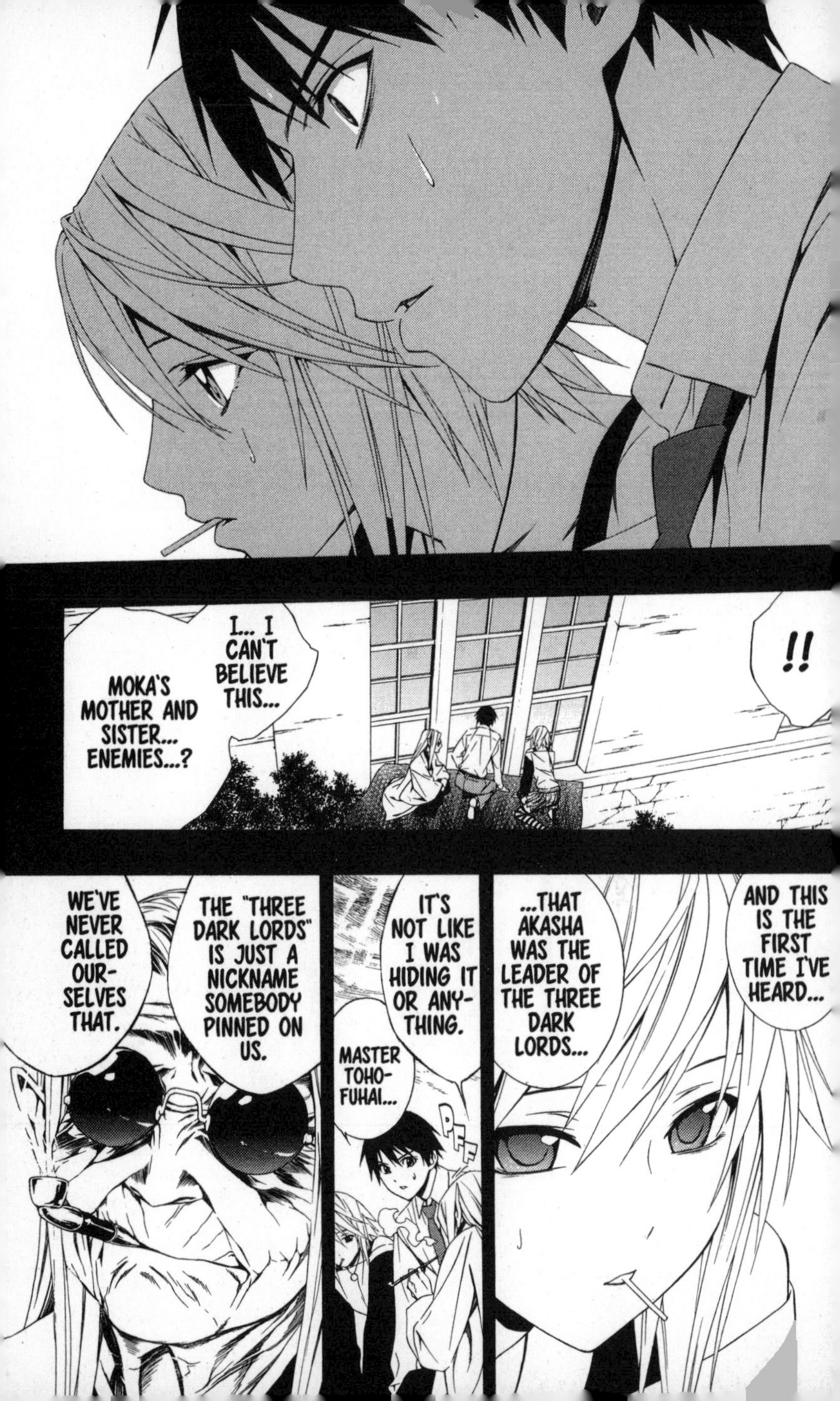
!!
I... I CAN'T BELIEVE THIS...
MOKA'S MOTHER AND SISTER... ENEMIES...?
AND THIS IS THE FIRST TIME I'VE HEARD...
...THAT AKASHA WAS THE LEADER OF THE THREE DARK LORDS...
IT'S NOT LIKE I WAS HIDING IT OR ANY-THING.
MASTER TOHO-FUHAI...
PFF
THE "THREE DARK LORDS" IS JUST A NICKNAME SOMEBODY PINNED ON US.
WE'VE NEVER CALLED OUR-SELVES THAT.

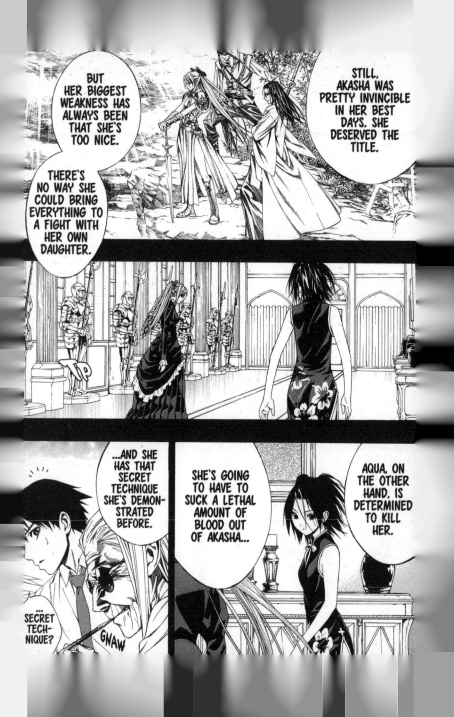

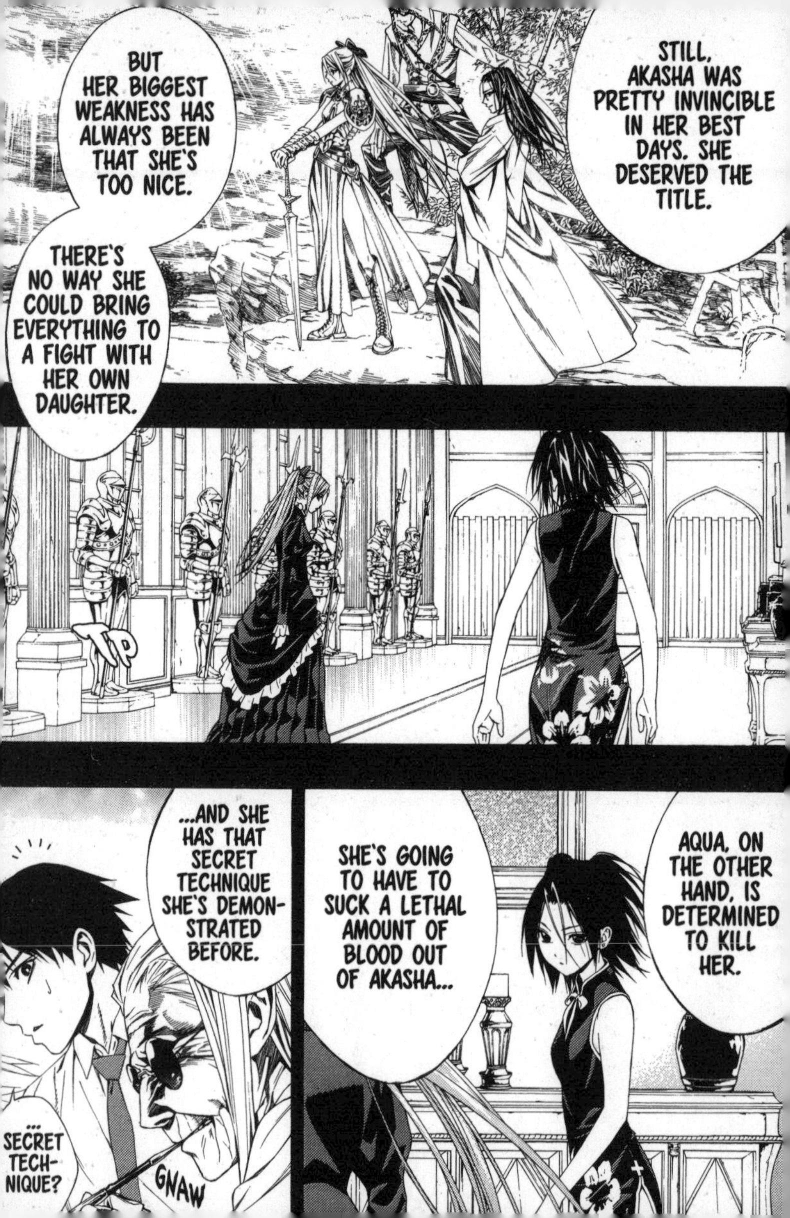
STILL, AKASHA WAS PRETTY INVINCIBLE IN HER BEST DAYS. SHE DESERVED THE TITLE.
BUT HER BIGGEST WEAKNESS HAS ALWAYS BEEN THAT SHE'S TOO NICE.
THERE'S NO WAY SHE COULD BRING EVERYTHING TO A FIGHT WITH HER OWN DAUGHTER.
TP
AQUA, ON THE OTHER HAND, IS DETERMINED TO KILL HER.
SHE'S GOING TO HAVE TO SUCK A LETHAL AMOUNT OF BLOOD OUT OF AKASHA...
...AND SHE HAS THAT SECRET TECHNIQUE SHE'S DEMON-STRATED BEFORE.
GNAW
... SECRET TECH-NIQUE?

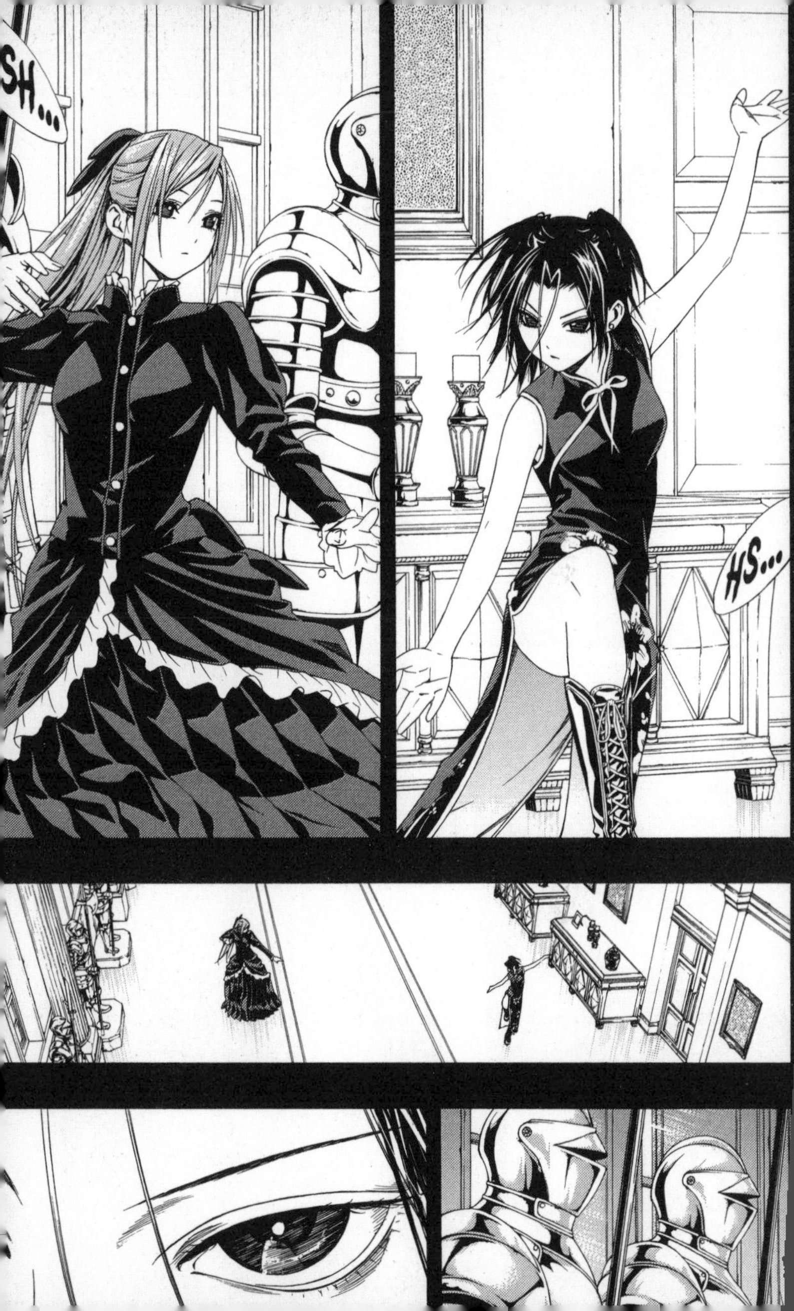
HS...
SH...

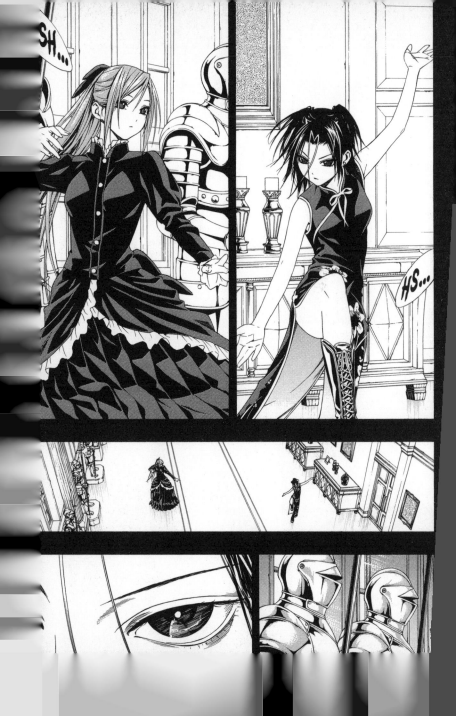

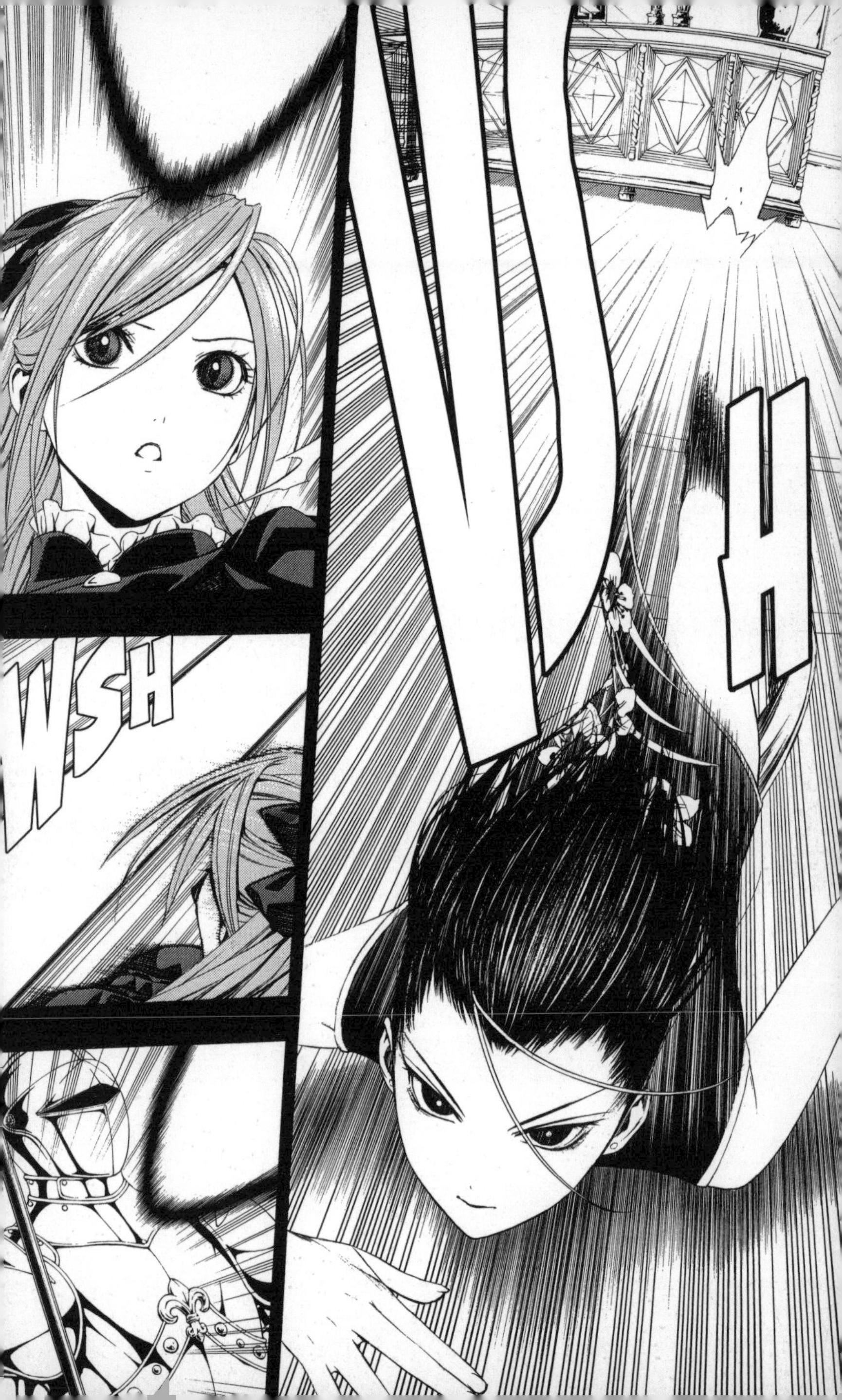
WSH

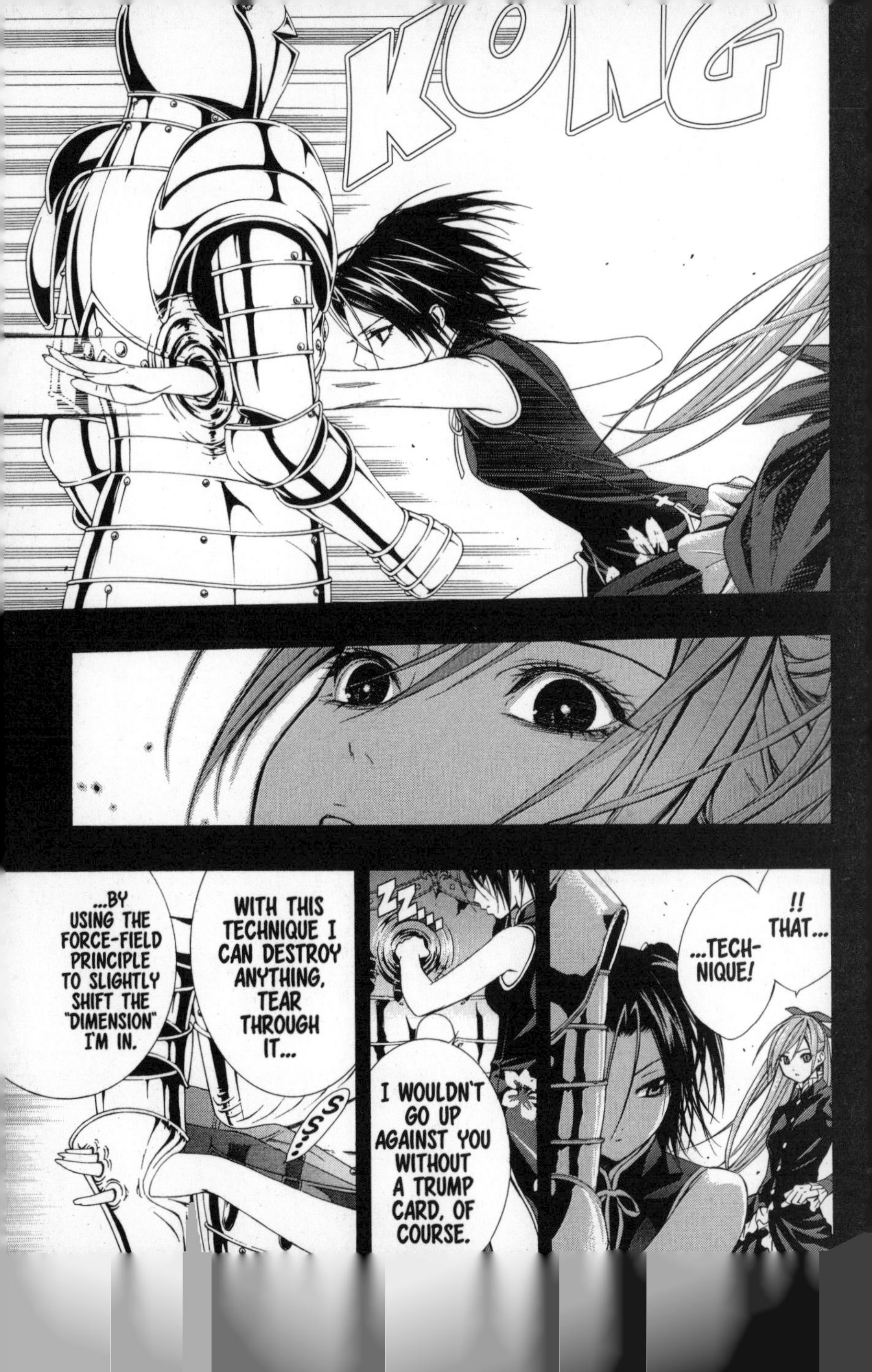
KONG
!! THAT...
...TECHNIQUE!
I WOULDN'T GO UP AGAINST YOU WITHOUT A TRUMP CARD, OF COURSE.
WITH THIS TECHNIQUE I CAN DESTROY ANYTHING, TEAR THROUGH IT...
...BY USING THE FORCE-FIELD PRINCIPLE TO SLIGHTLY SHIFT THE "DIMENSION" I'M IN.

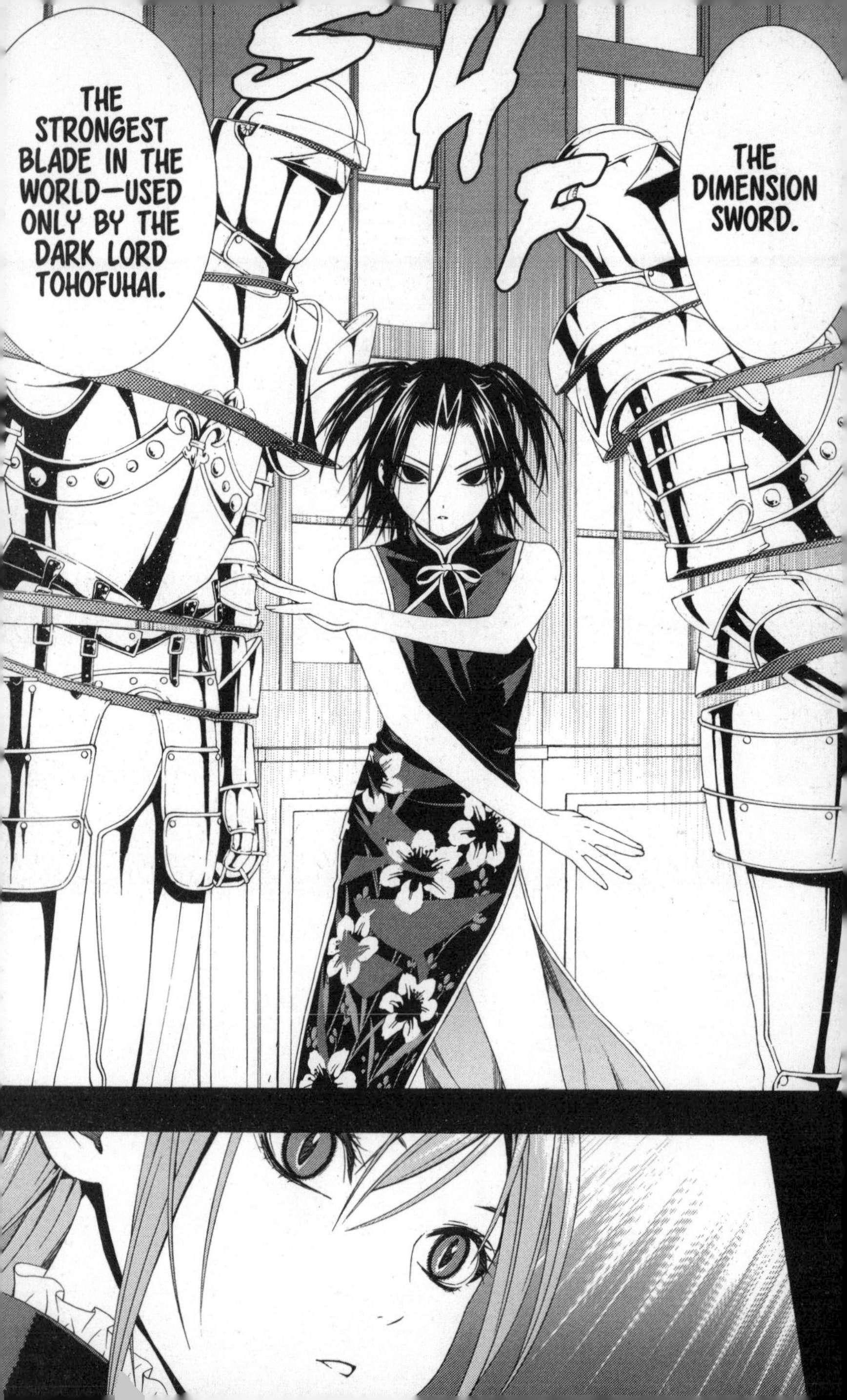
THE DIMENSION SWORD.
THE STRONGEST BLADE IN THE WORLD—USED ONLY BY THE DARK LORD TOHOFUHAI.

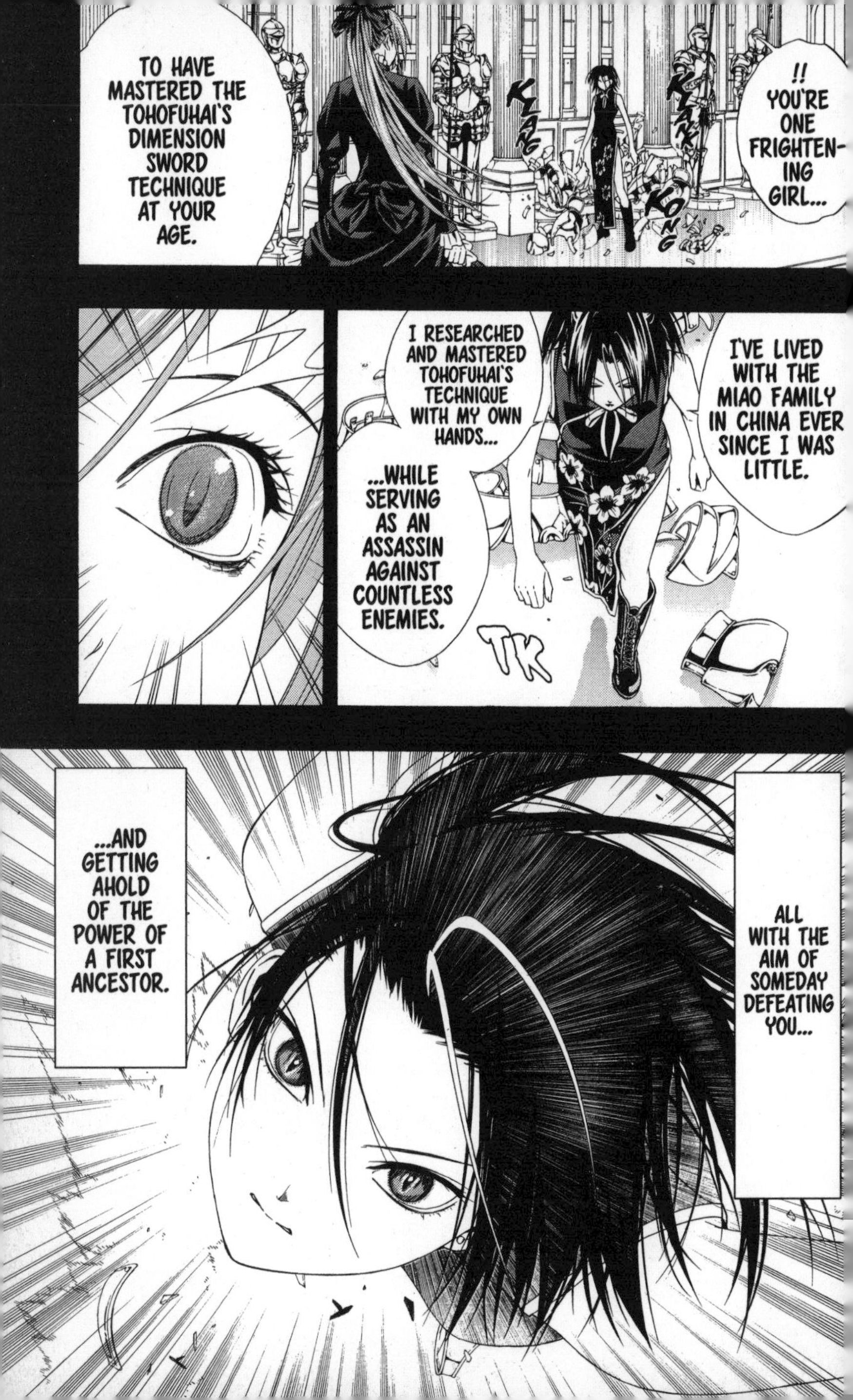
!! YOU'RE ONE FRIGHTENING GIRL...
KLANK
KONG
KLANG
TO HAVE MASTERED THE TOHOFUHAI'S DIMENSION SWORD TECHNIQUE AT YOUR AGE.
I'VE LIVED WITH THE MIAO FAMILY IN CHINA EVER SINCE I WAS LITTLE.
I RESEARCHED AND MASTERED TOHOFUHAI'S TECHNIQUE WITH MY OWN HANDS...
...WHILE SERVING AS AN ASSASSIN AGAINST COUNTLESS ENEMIES.
TK
ALL WITH THE AIM OF SOMEDAY DEFEATING YOU...
...AND GETTING AHOLD OF THE POWER OF A FIRST ANCESTOR.

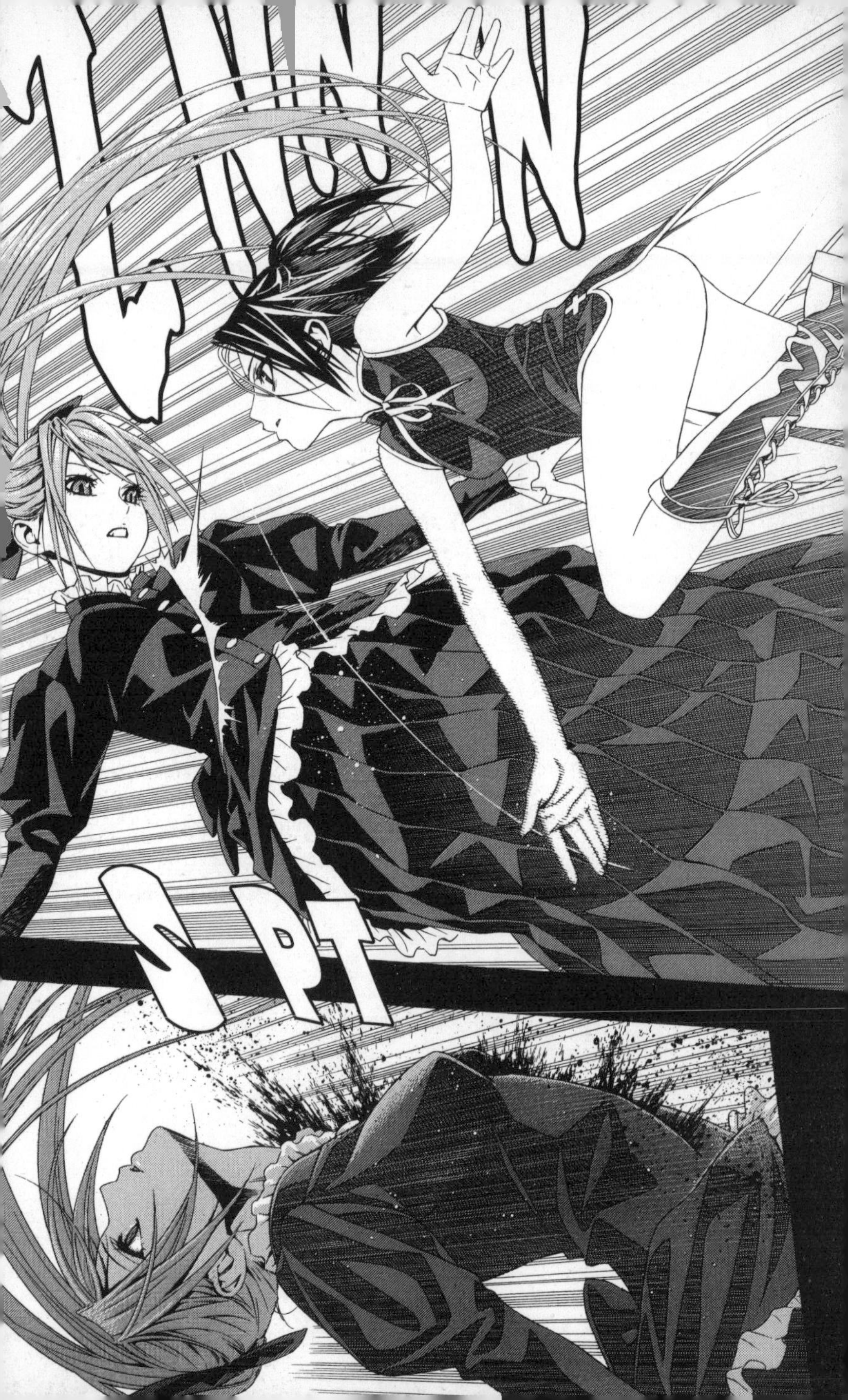
SPT

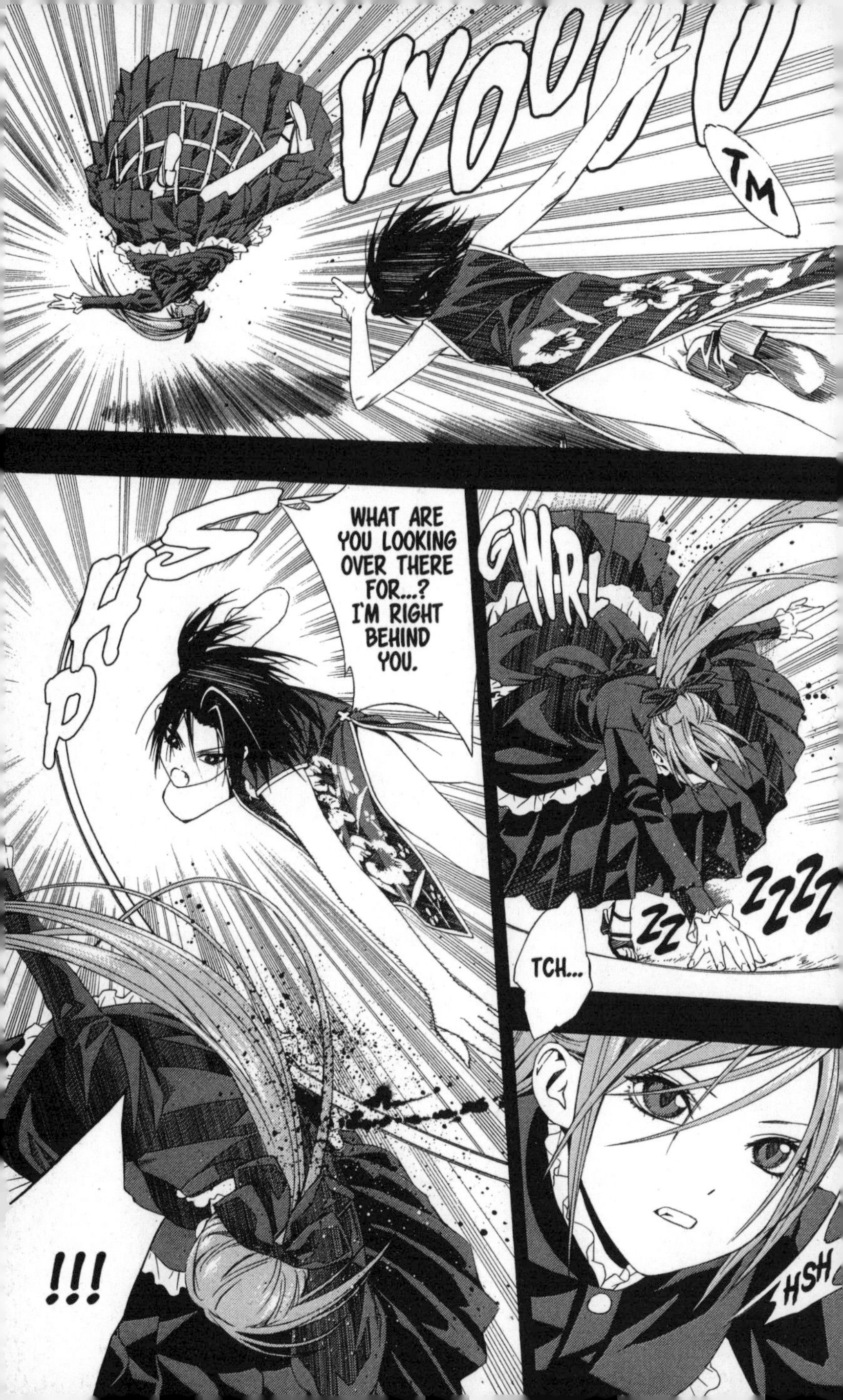
VYOOOO
TM
GWRL
ZZZZ
ZZ
TCH...
HSH
PHSS
WHAT ARE YOU LOOKING OVER THERE FOR...? I'M RIGHT BEHIND YOU.
!!!

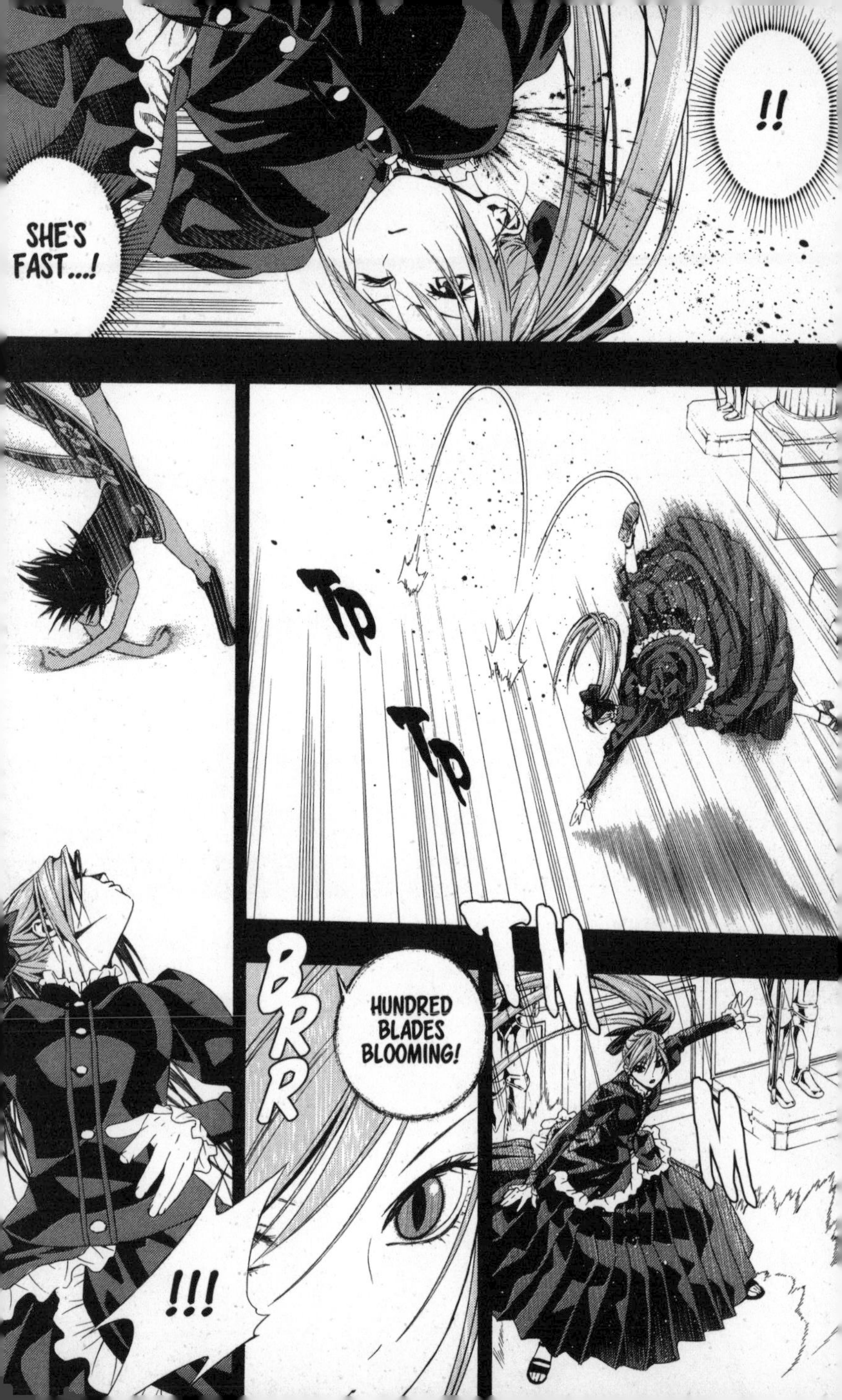
!!
SHE'S FAST...!
TP
TP
TMM
BRR
HUNDRED BLADES BLOOMING!
!!!

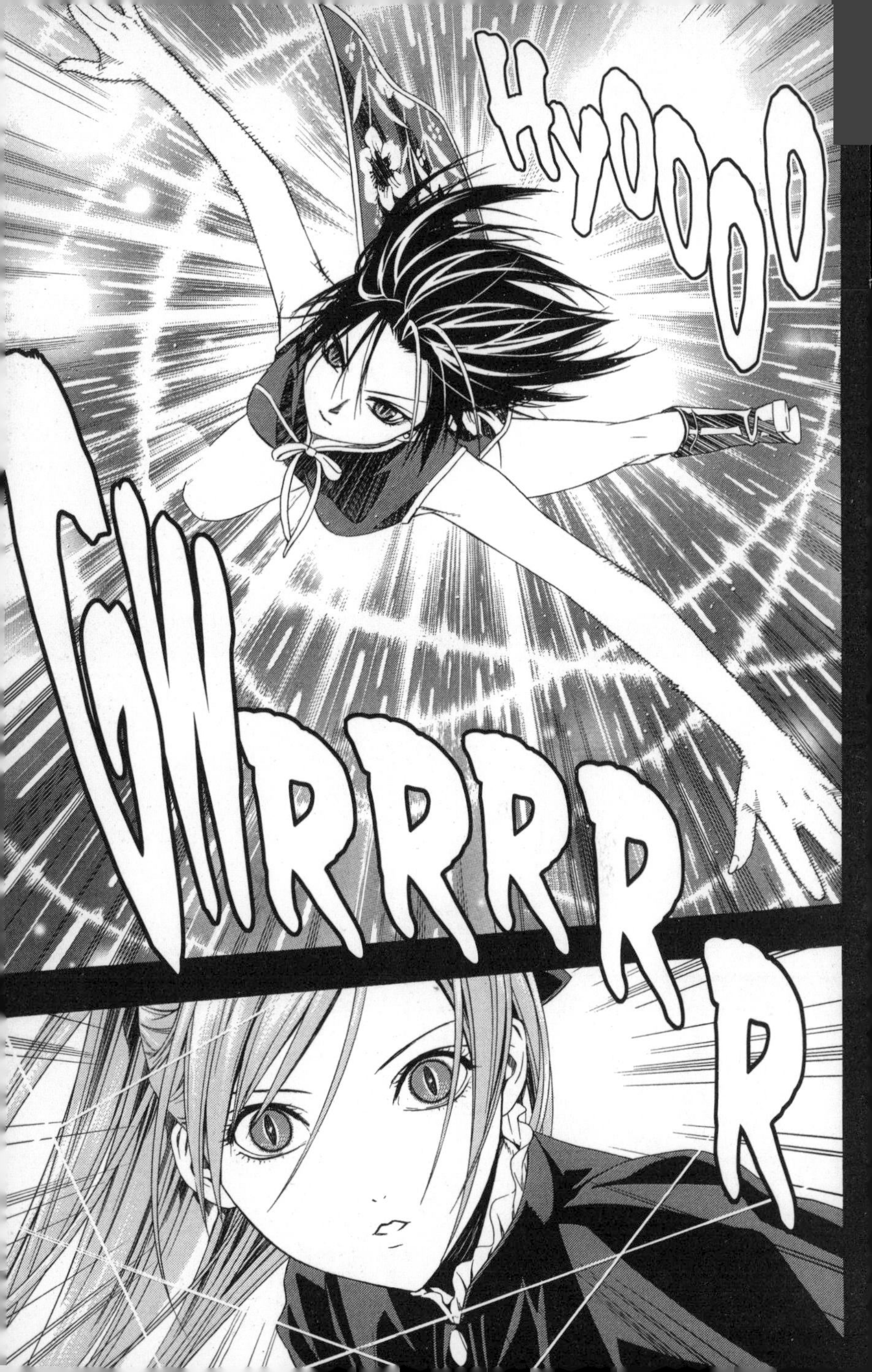
HYOOOOO
GWRRRRRRR

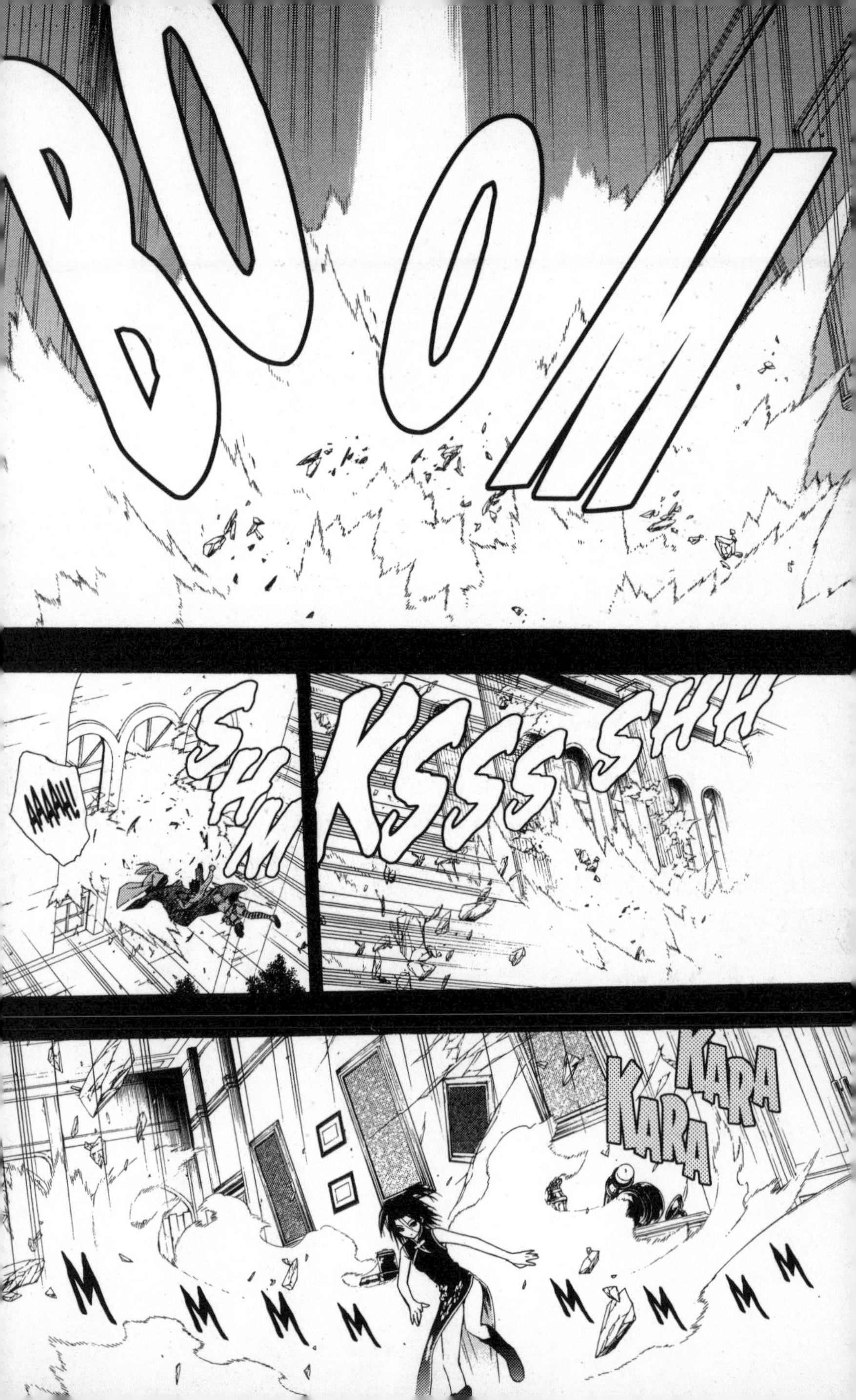
BOOM
KSSSSSHH
SHM
AAAAH!
KARA KARA
MMMM MMMM

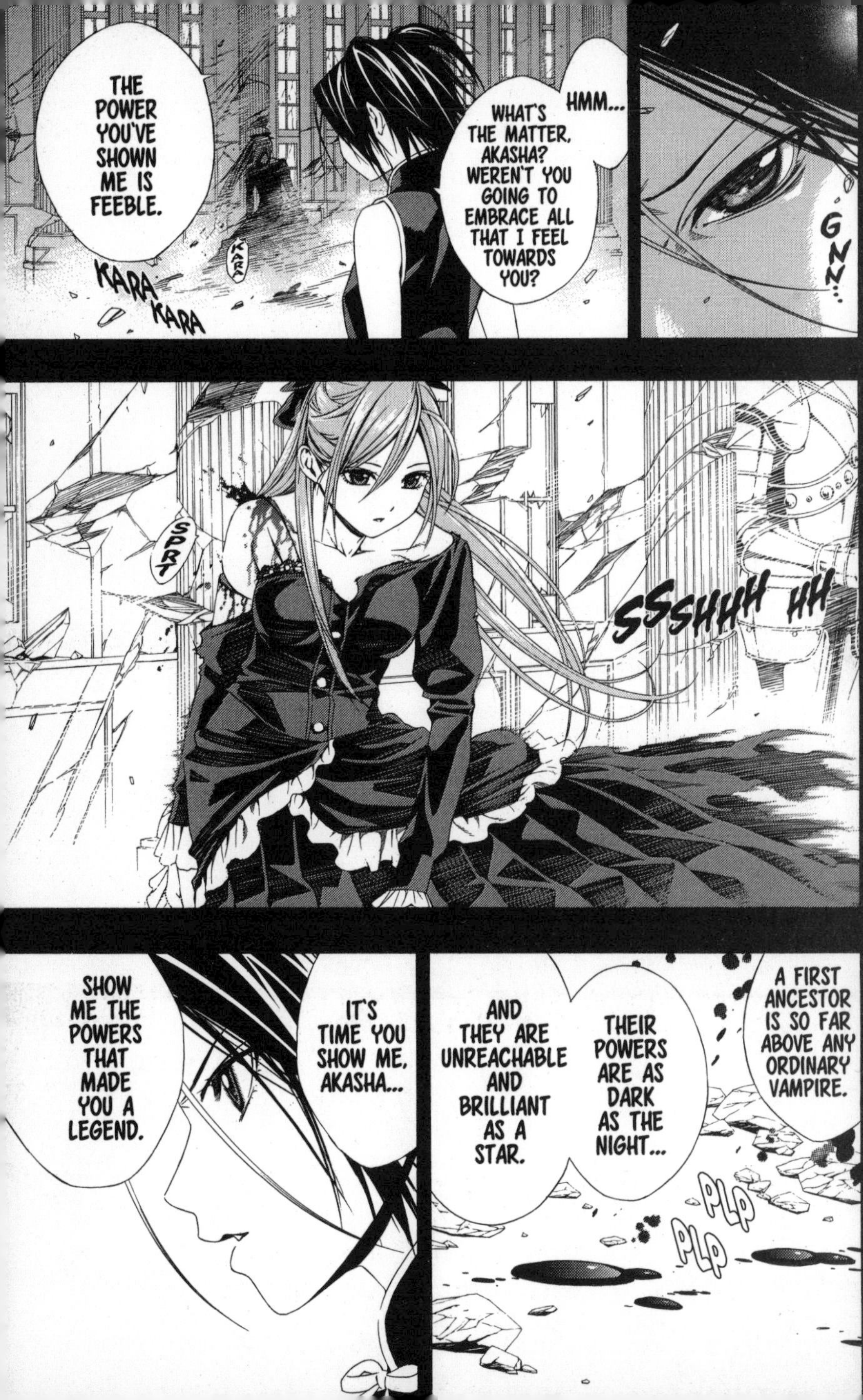
GNN...
HMM...
WHAT'S THE MATTER, AKASHA? WEREN'T YOU GOING TO EMBRACE ALL THAT I FEEL TOWARDS YOU?
THE POWER YOU'VE SHOWN ME IS FEEBLE.
KARA
KARA KARA
SSSHHH HH
SPRT
A FIRST ANCESTOR IS SO FAR ABOVE ANY ORDINARY VAMPIRE.
THEIR POWERS ARE AS DARK AS THE NIGHT...
AND THEY ARE UNREACHABLE AND BRILLIANT AS A STAR.
PLP
PLP
IT'S TIME YOU SHOW ME, AKASHA...
SHOW ME THE POWERS THAT MADE YOU A LEGEND.

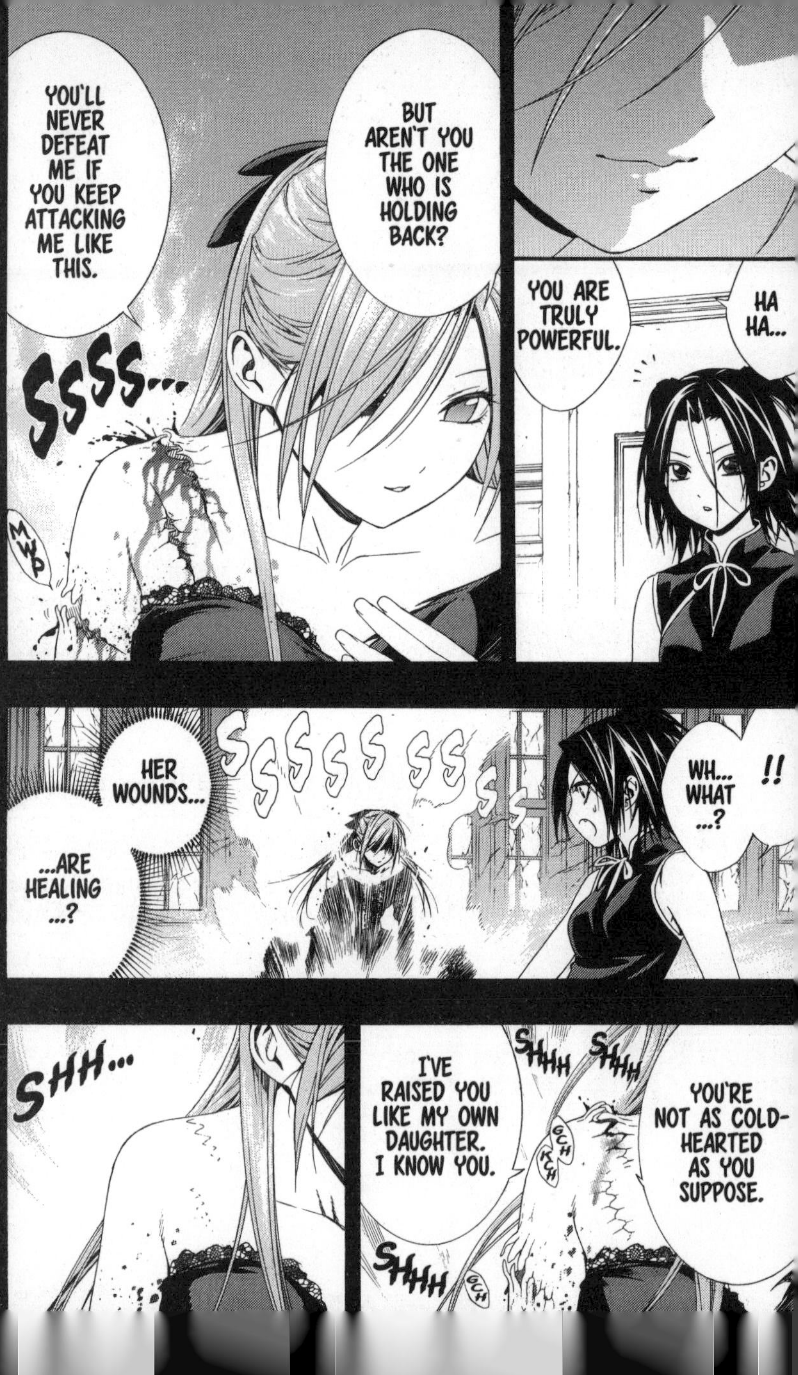
HA HA...
YOU ARE TRULY POWERFUL.
BUT AREN'T YOU THE ONE WHO IS HOLDING BACK?
YOU'LL NEVER DEFEAT ME IF YOU KEEP ATTACKING ME LIKE THIS.
SSSS...
MWP
!!
WH... WHAT ...?
SSSSSSSSS
HER WOUNDS...
...ARE HEALING ...?
SHHH
SHHH
YOU'RE NOT AS COLD-HEARTED AS YOU SUPPOSE.
GCH
KCH
I'VE RAISED YOU LIKE MY OWN DAUGHTER. I KNOW YOU.
SHHH
GCH
SHH...

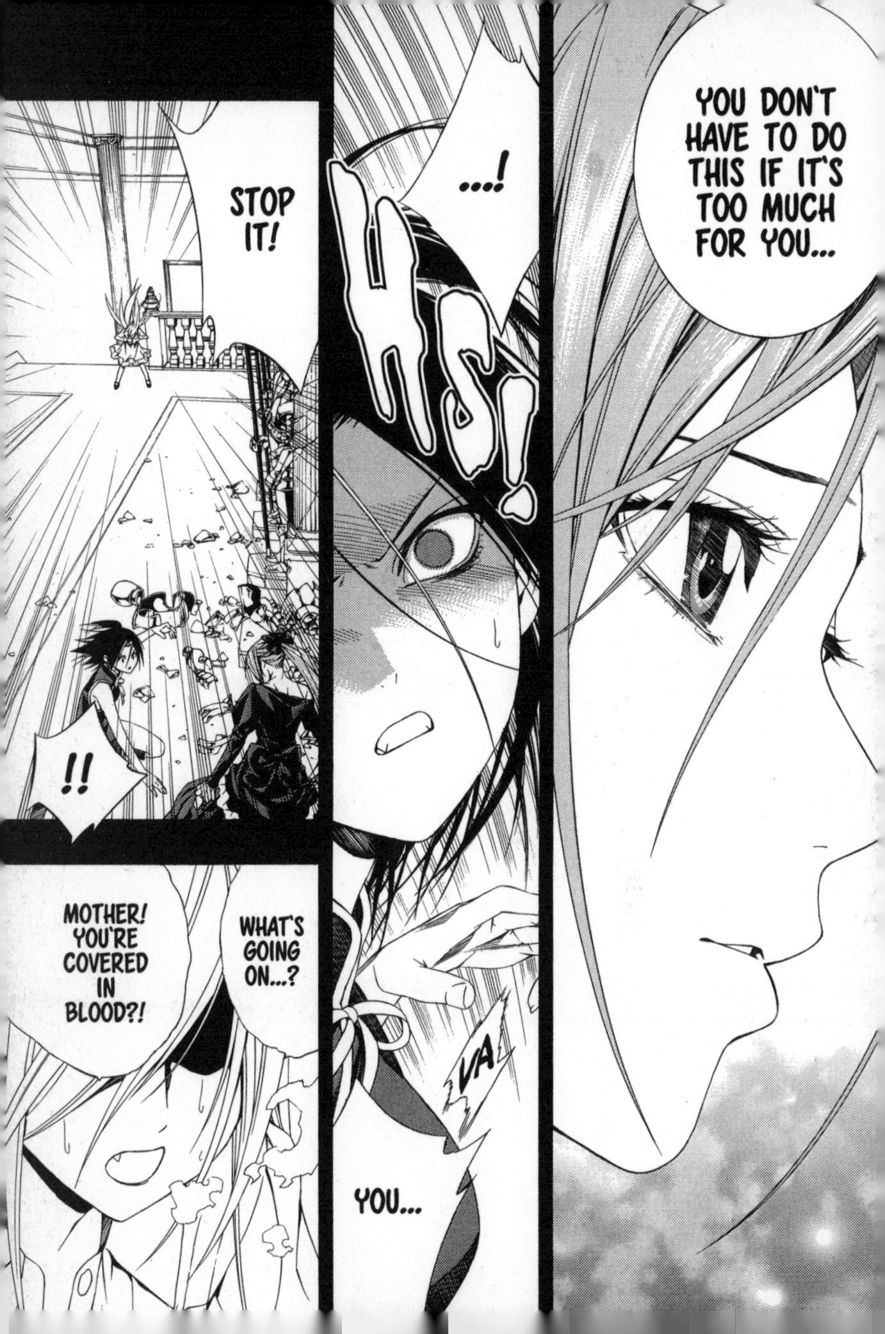
YOU DON'T HAVE TO DO THIS IF IT'S TOO MUCH FOR YOU...
...!
HS!
VA
YOU...
STOP IT!
!!
WHAT'S GOING ON...?
MOTHER! YOU'RE COVERED IN BLOOD?!

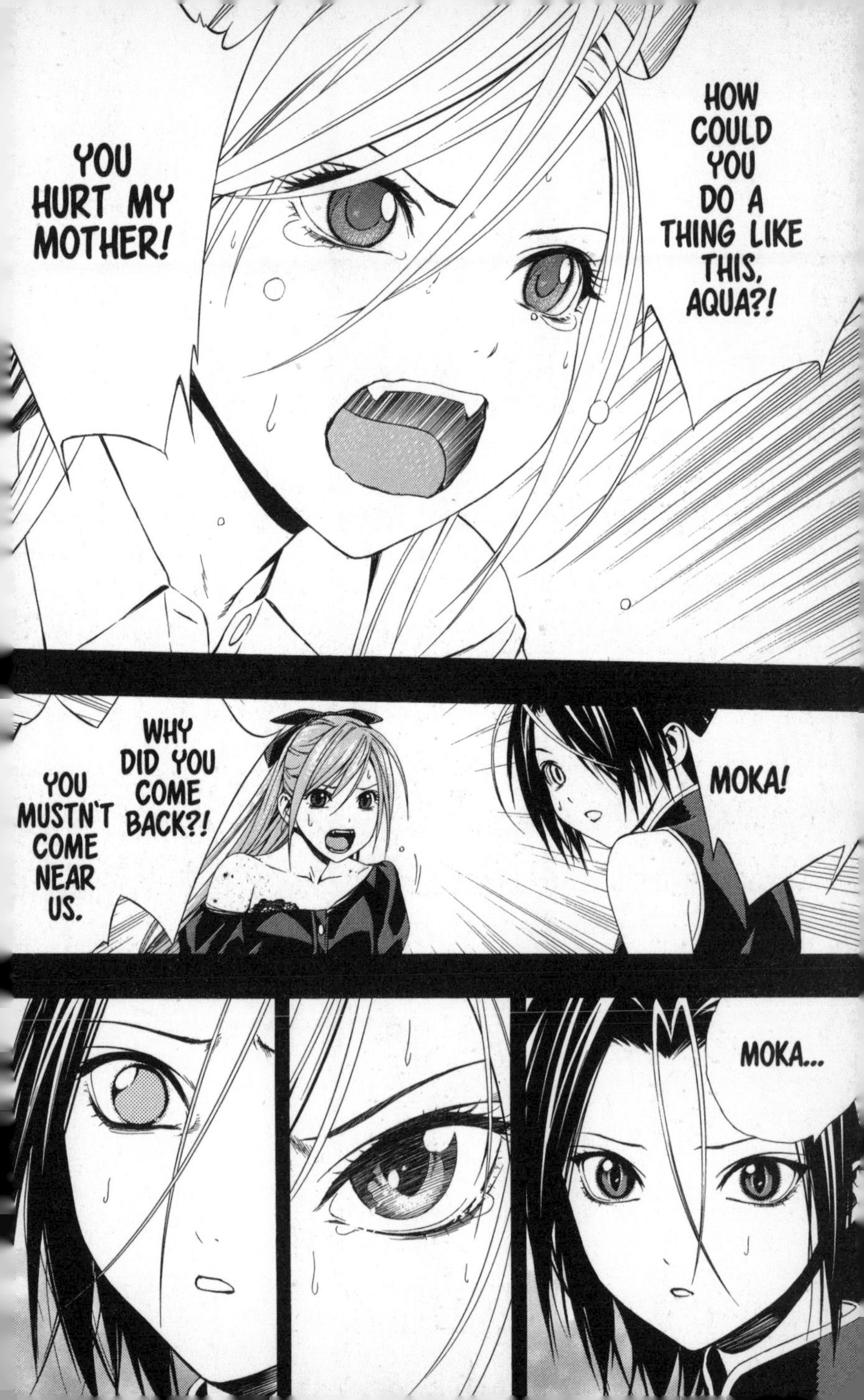
HOW COULD YOU DO A THING LIKE THIS, AQUA?!
YOU HURT MY MOTHER!
MOKA!
WHY DID YOU COME BACK?!
YOU MUSTN'T COME NEAR US.
MOKA...

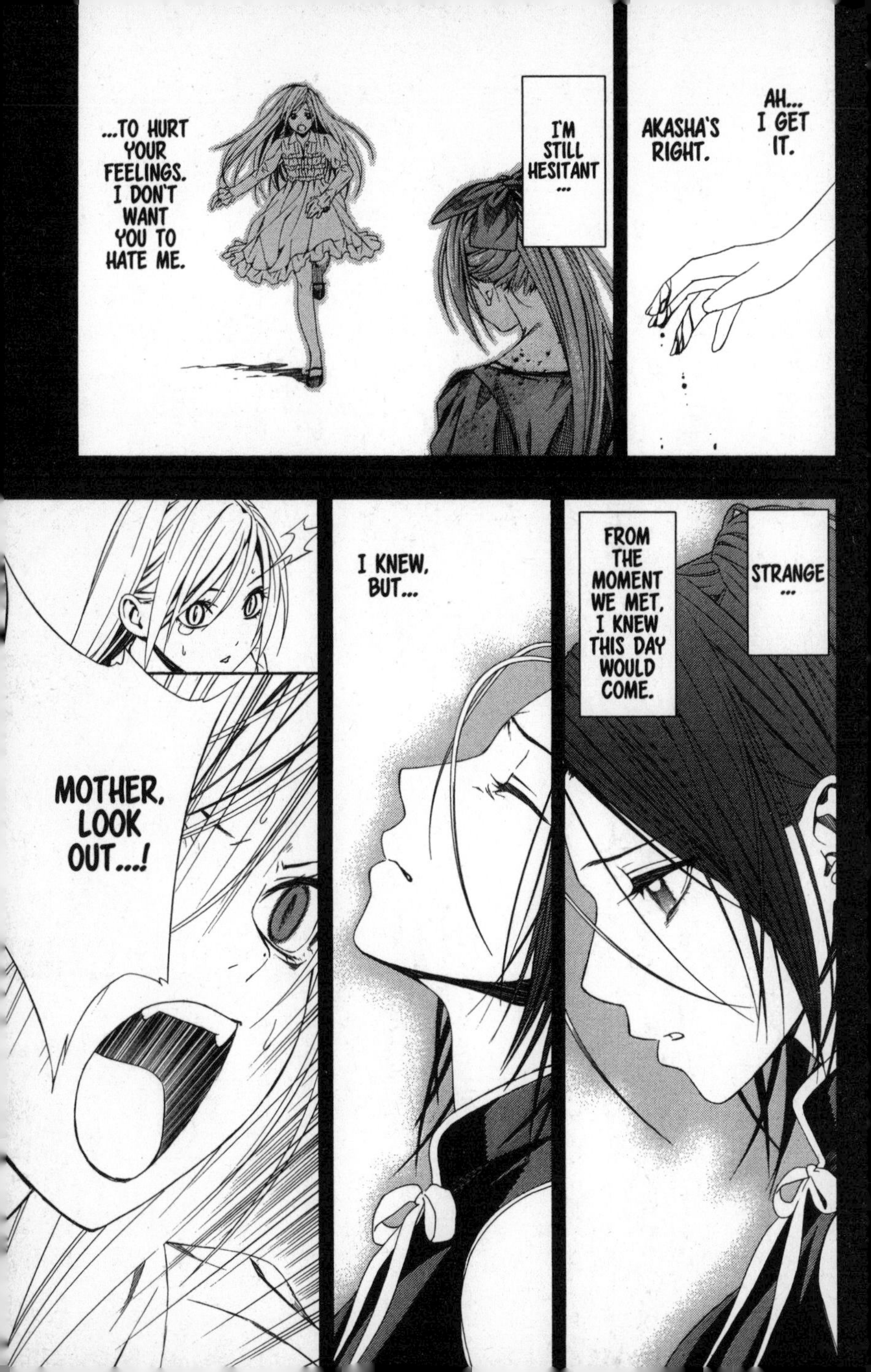
AH... I GET IT.
AKASHA'S RIGHT.
I'M STILL HESITANT...
...TO HURT YOUR FEELINGS. I DON'T WANT YOU TO HATE ME.
STRANGE...
FROM THE MOMENT WE MET, I KNEW THIS DAY WOULD COME.
I KNEW, BUT...
MOTHER, LOOK OUT...!

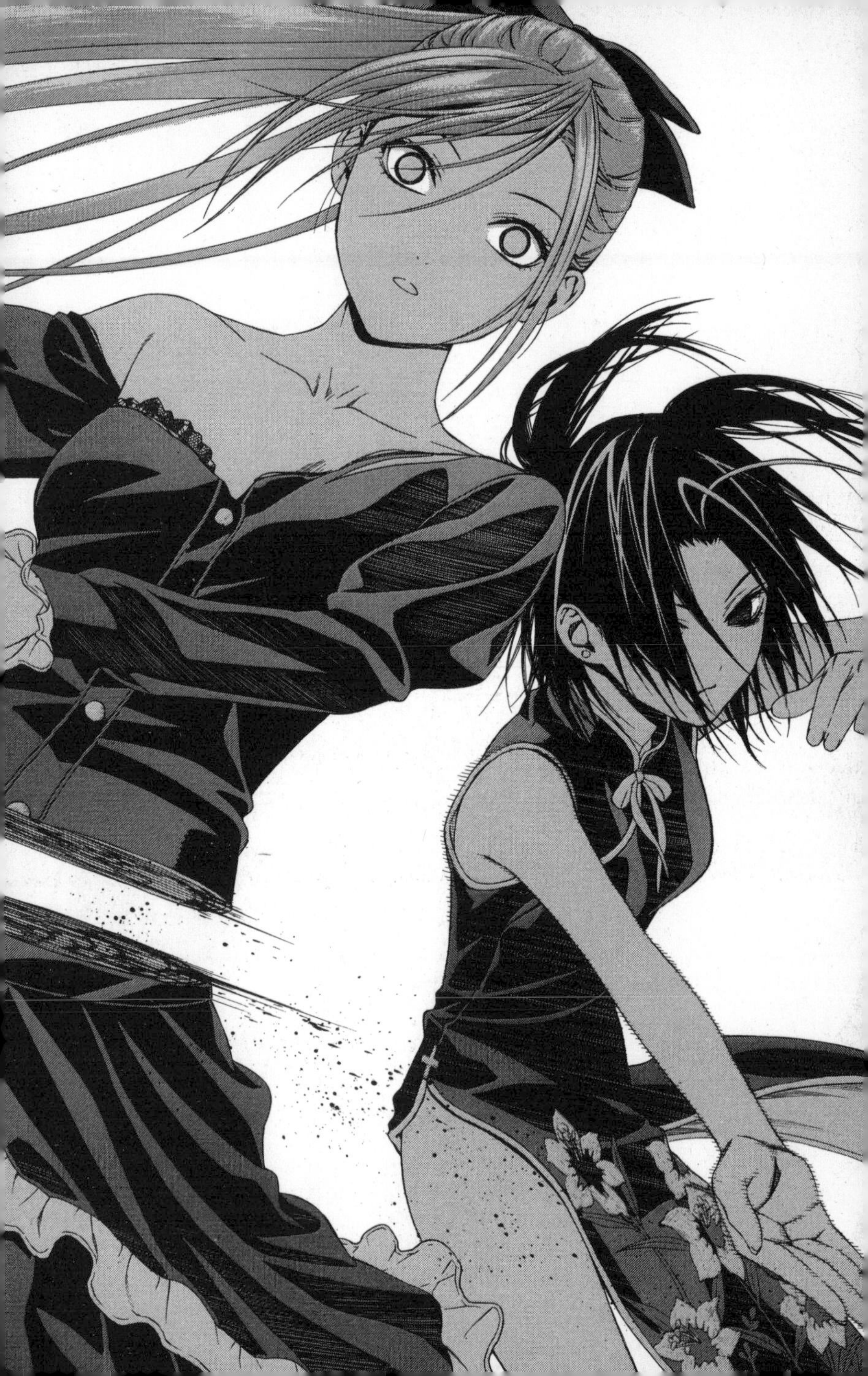

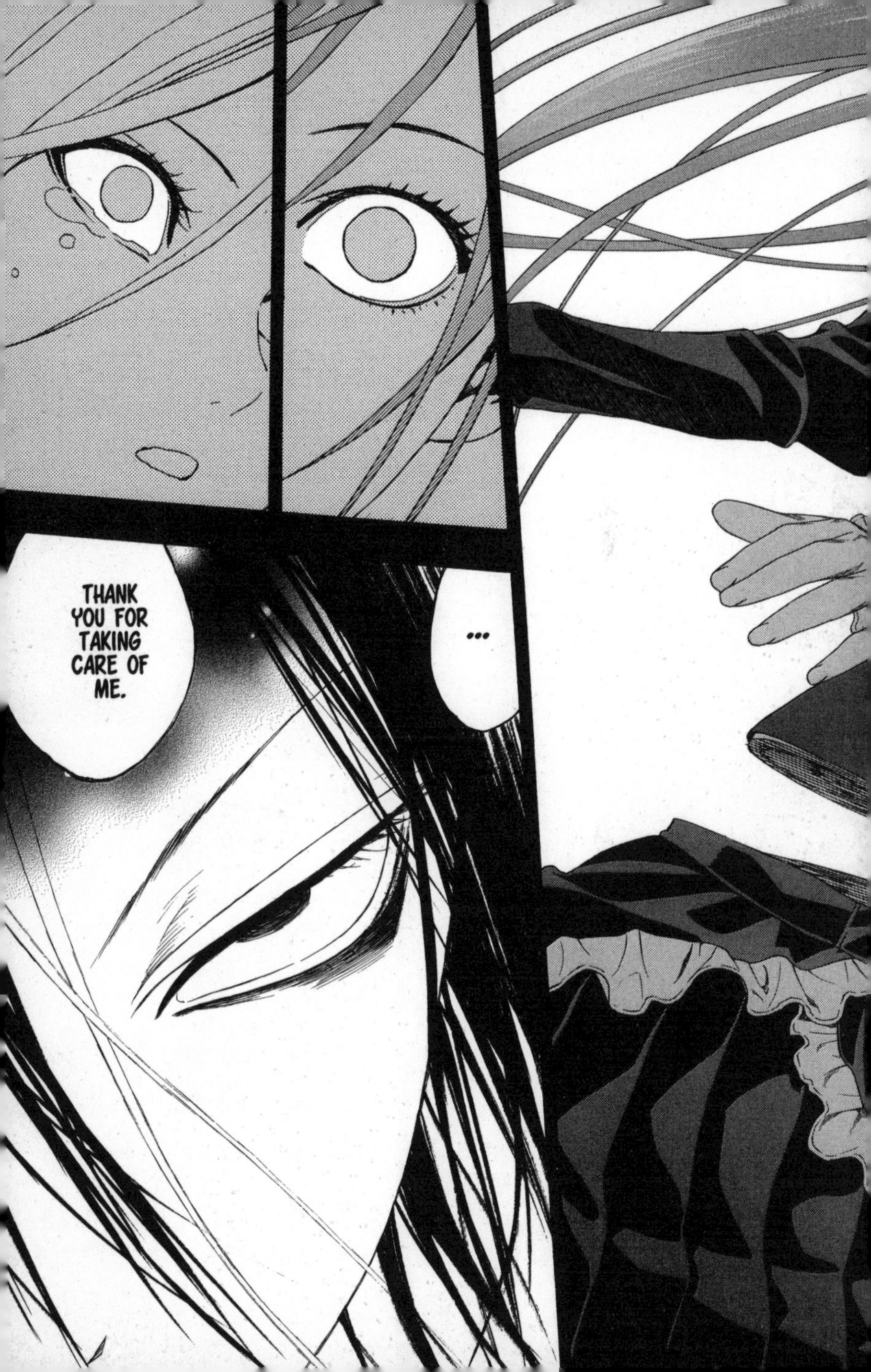
...
THANK YOU FOR TAKING CARE OF ME.

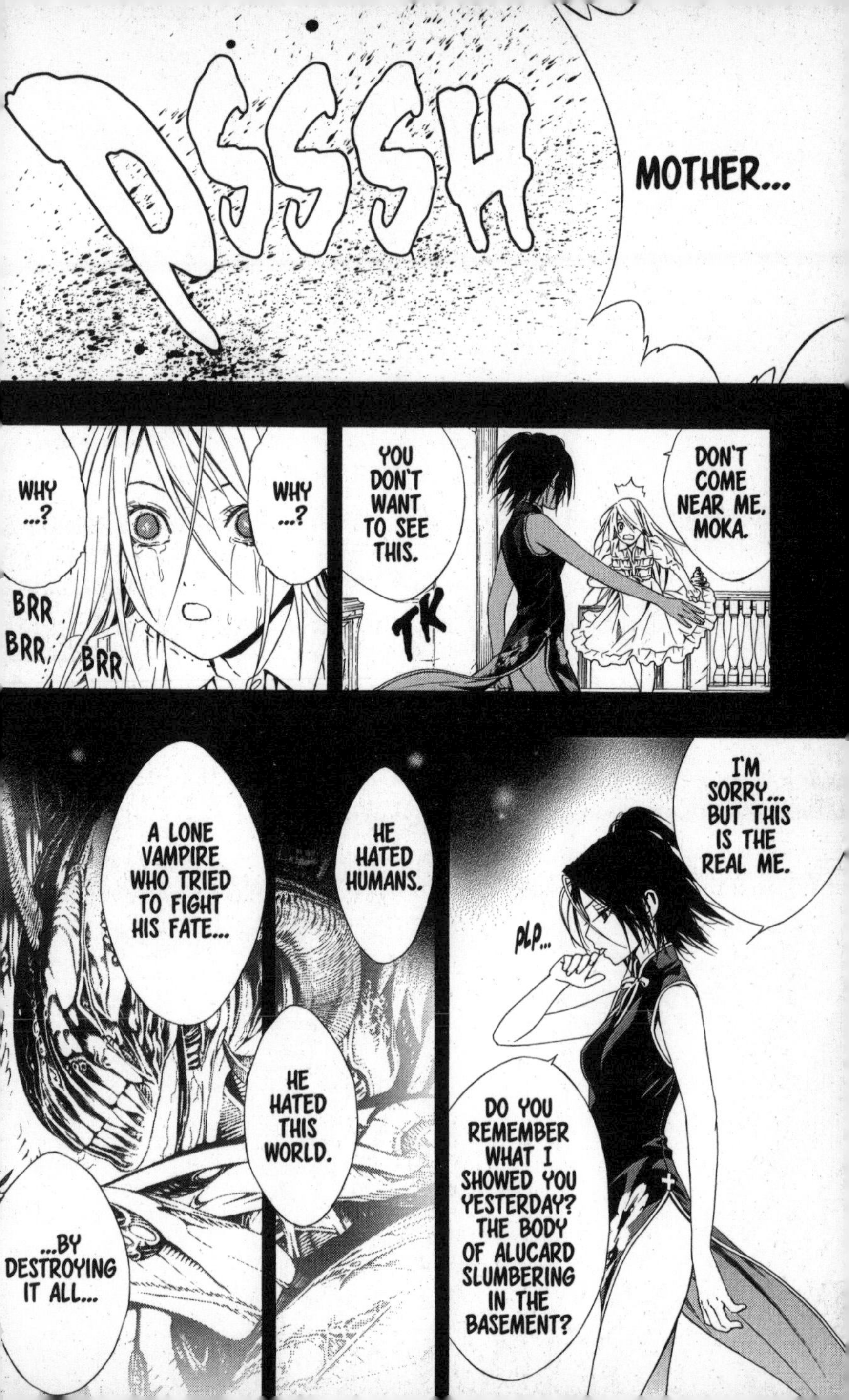
MOTHER...
PSSSH
DON'T COME NEAR ME, MOKA.
YOU DON'T WANT TO SEE THIS.
TK
WHY ...?
WHY ...?
BRR BRR BRR
I'M SORRY... BUT THIS IS THE REAL ME.
PLP...
DO YOU REMEMBER WHAT I SHOWED YOU YESTERDAY? THE BODY OF ALUCARD SLUMBERING IN THE BASEMENT?
HE HATED HUMANS.
A LONE VAMPIRE WHO TRIED TO FIGHT HIS FATE...
HE HATED THIS WORLD.
...BY DESTROYING IT ALL...

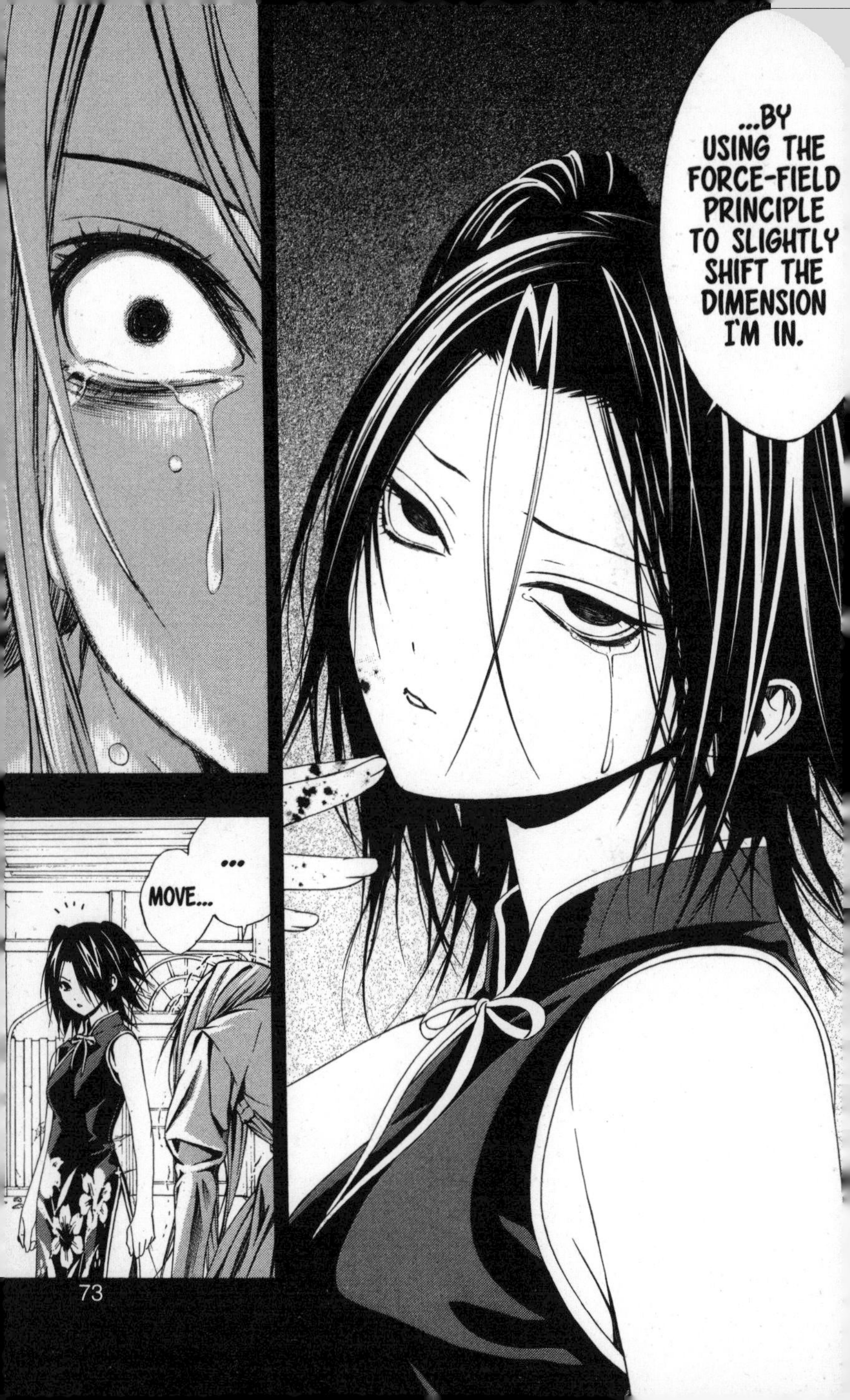
...BY USING THE FORCE-FIELD PRINCIPLE TO SLIGHTLY SHIFT THE DIMENSION I'M IN.
... MOVE...

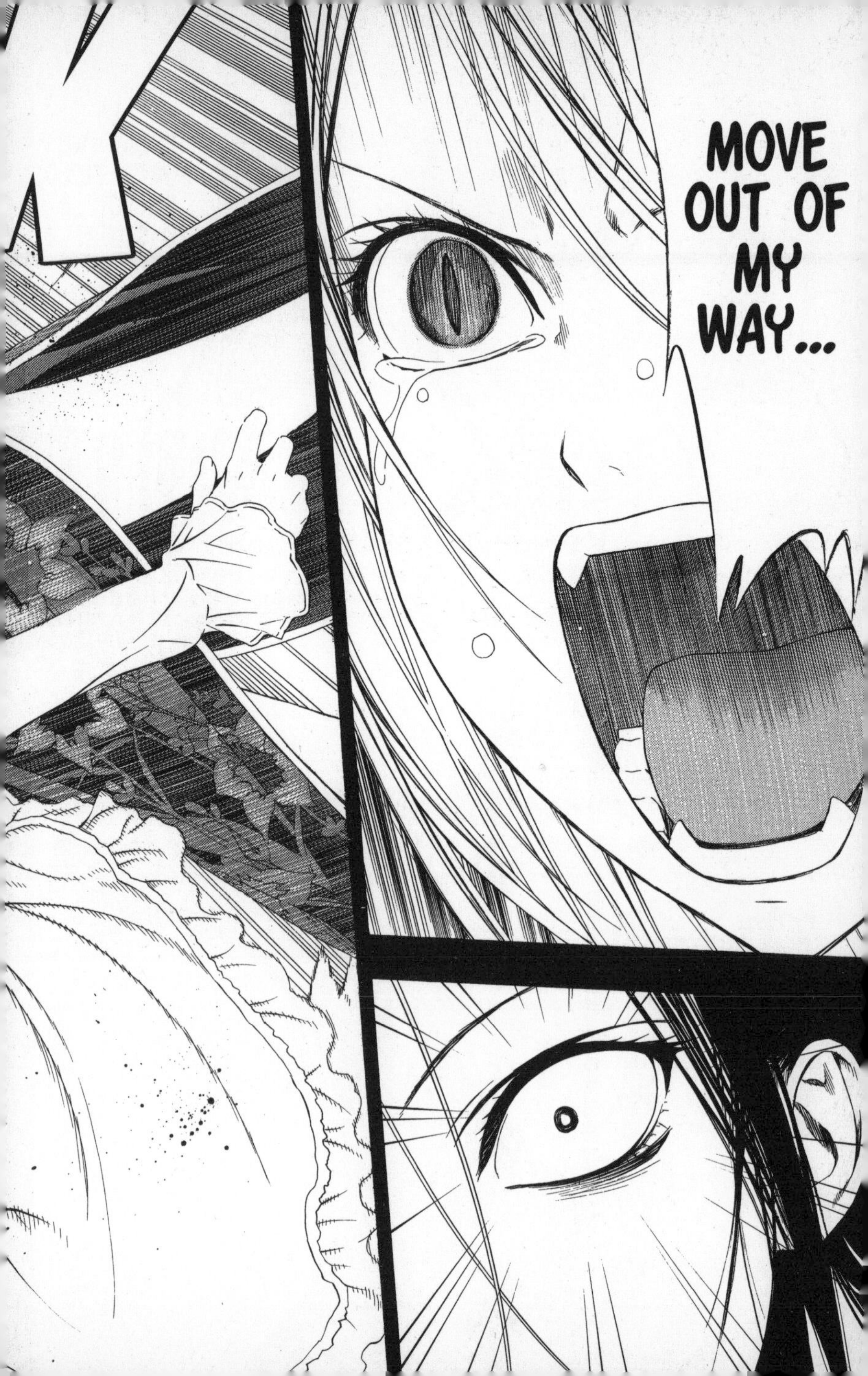
MOVE OUT OF MY WAY...

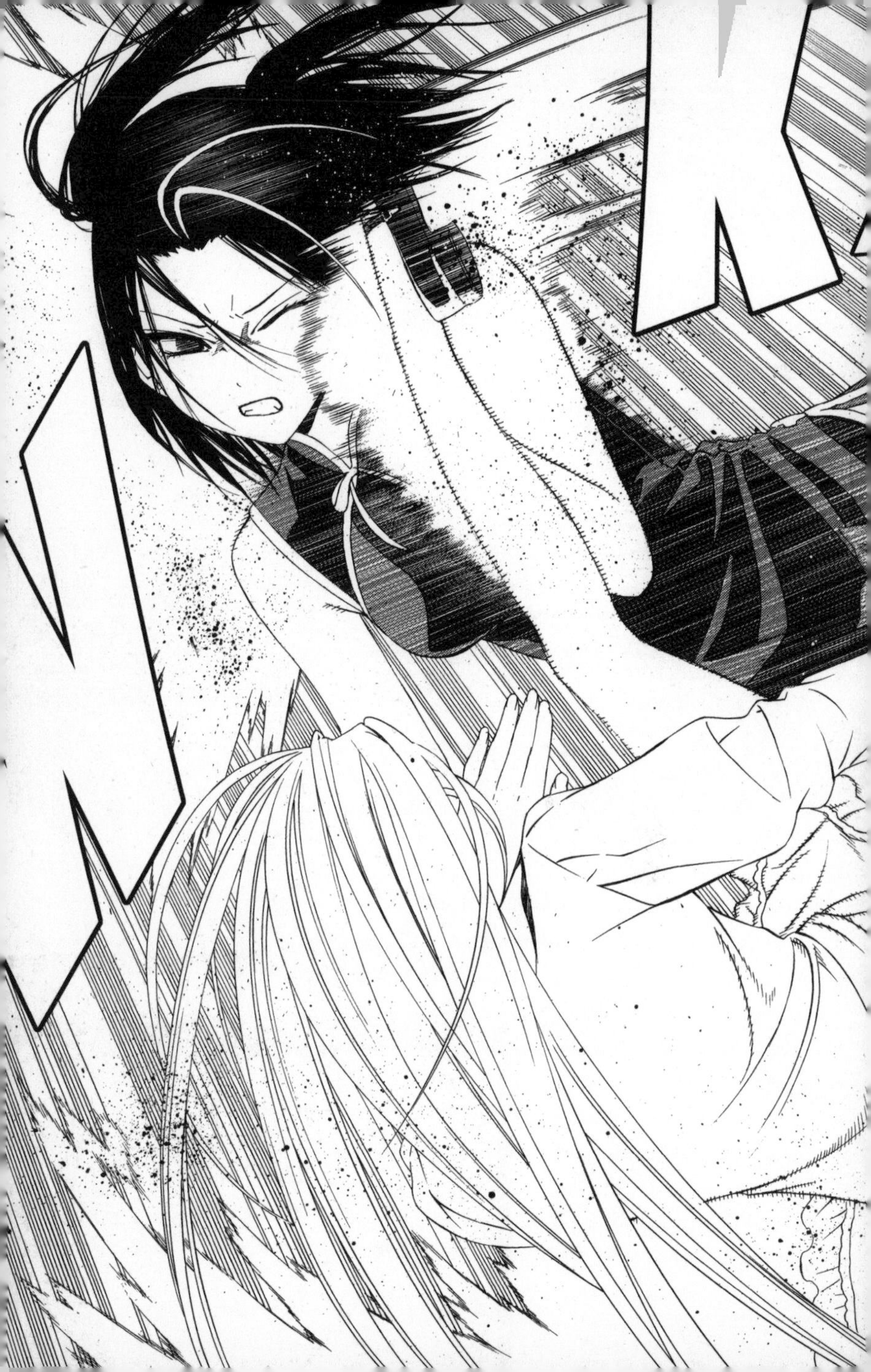

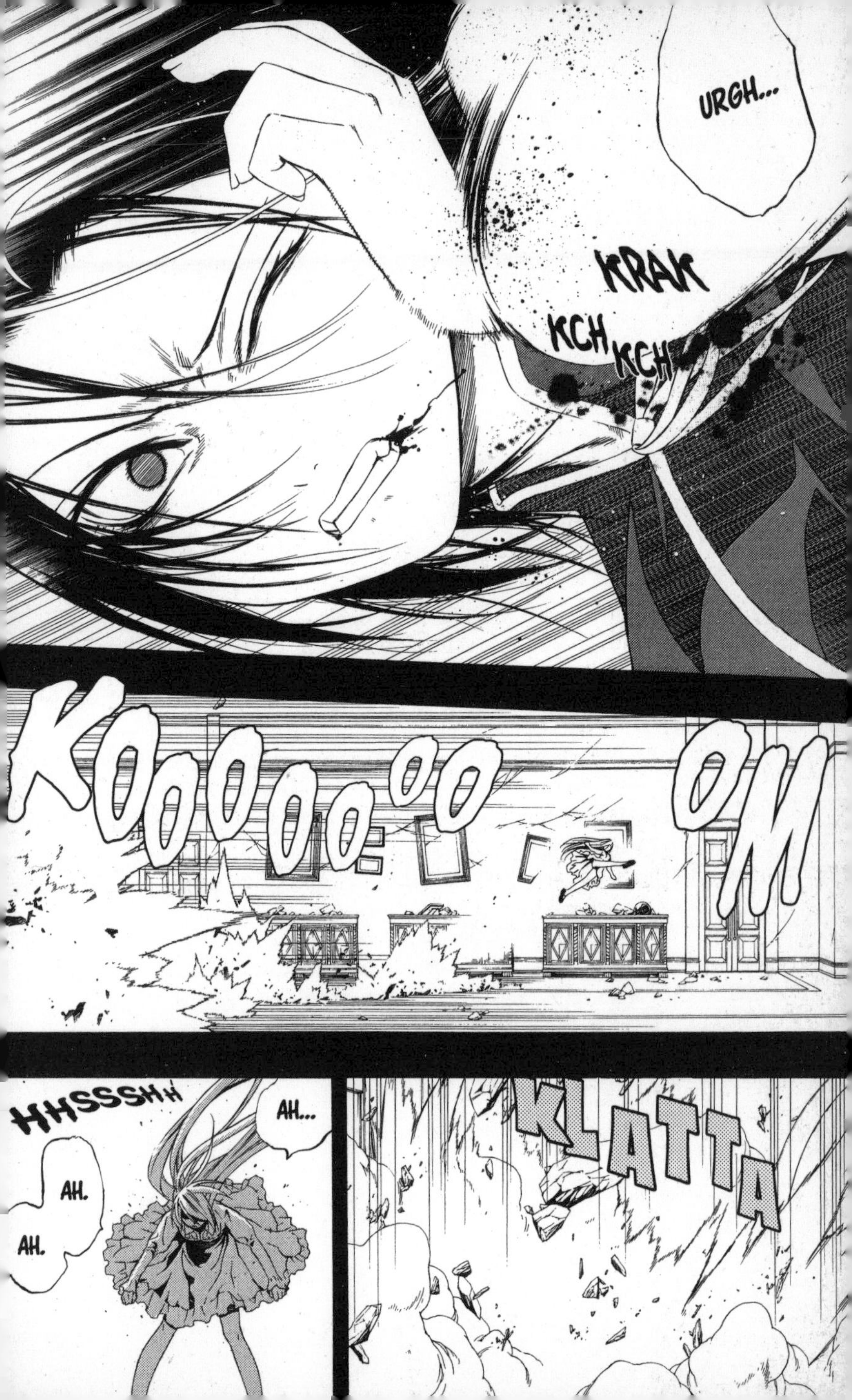

URGH...
KRAK
KCH KCH
KOOOOOOOOOOOM
KLATTA
AH...
HHSSSHH
AH.
AH.

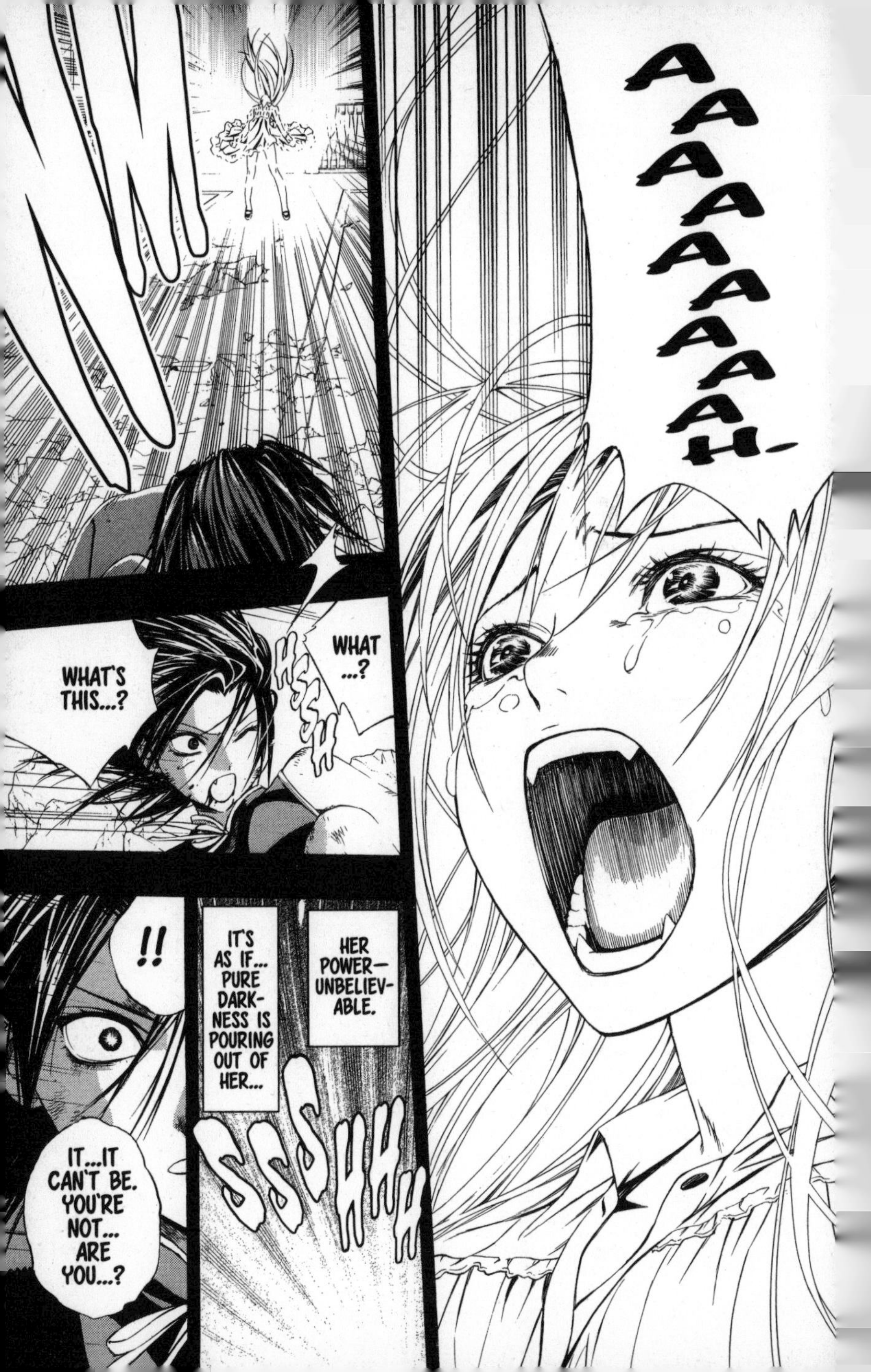
AAAAAAAAAH-
WHAT ...?
HSSH
WHAT'S THIS...?
HER POWER—UNBELIEVABLE.
IT'S AS IF... PURE DARKNESS IS POURING OUT OF HER...
!!
SSSHHH
IT...IT CAN'T BE. YOU'RE NOT... ARE YOU...?

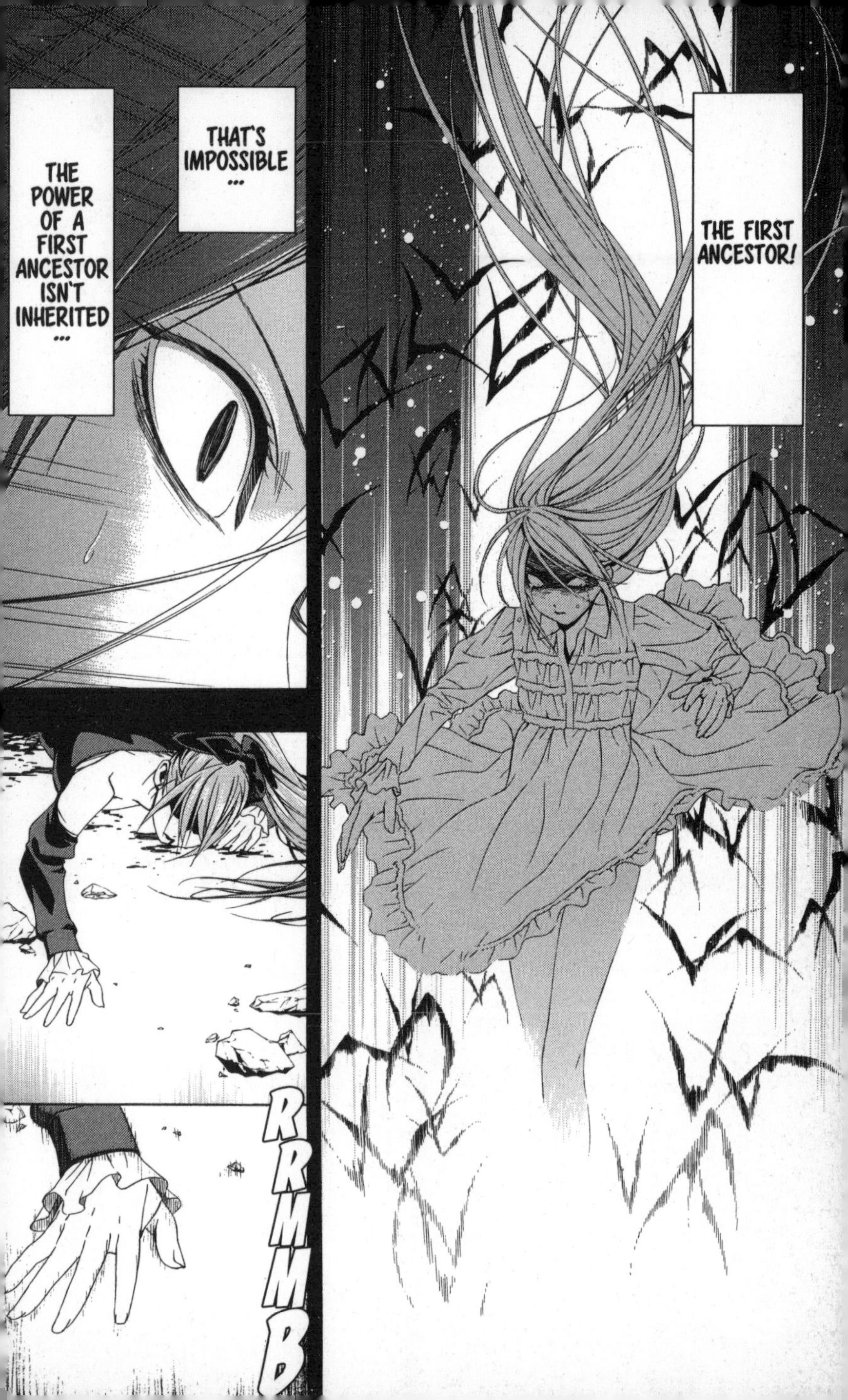
THE FIRST ANCESTOR!
THAT'S IMPOSSIBLE ...
THE POWER OF A FIRST ANCESTOR ISN'T INHERITED ...
RRMMB

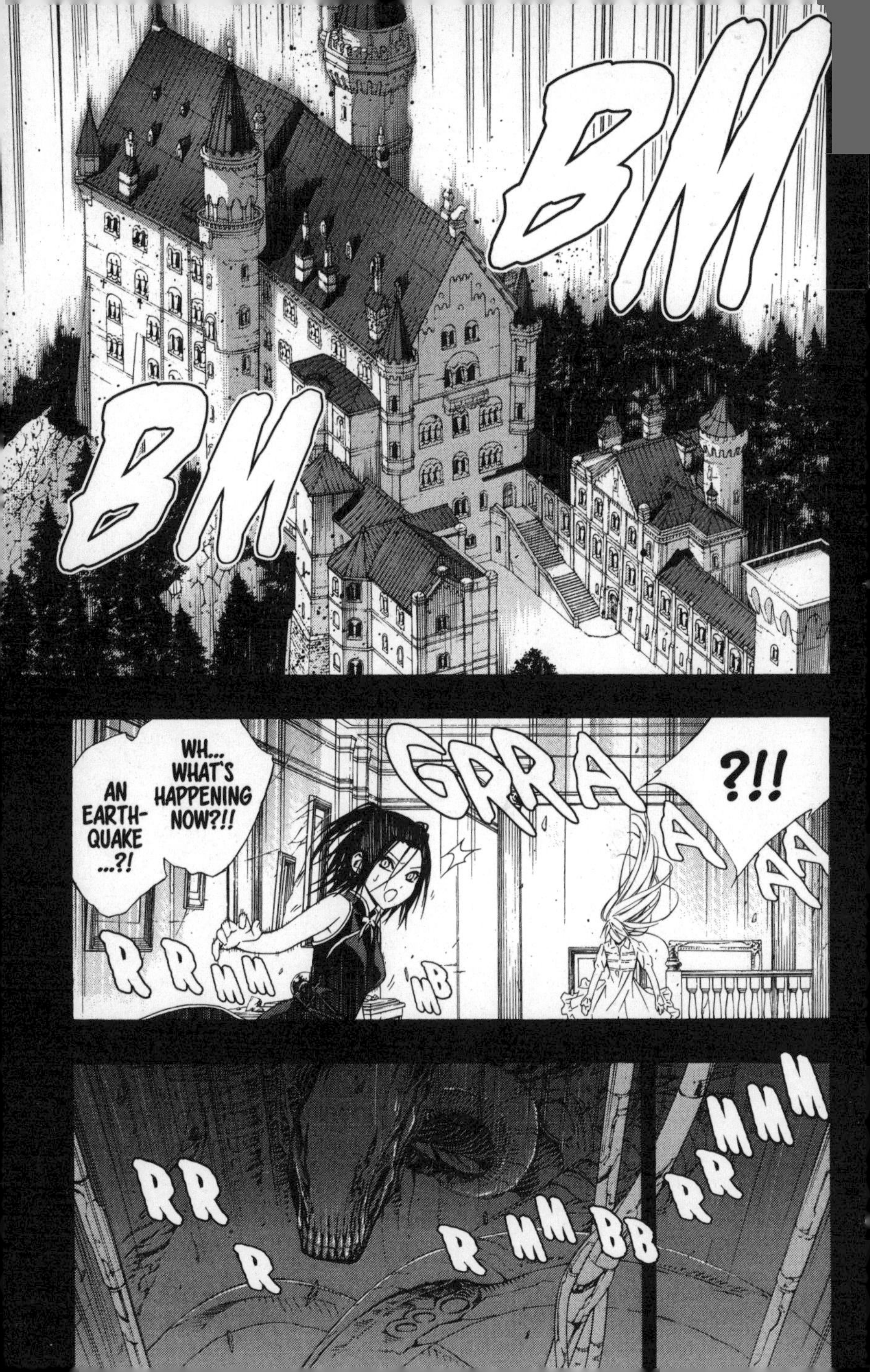
BM
BM
?!!
GRRAAAA
WH... WHAT'S HAPPENING NOW?!!
AN EARTH-QUAKE ...?!
RRMMMB
RRMMMM
RR R RMMBB

# 33: Treasure

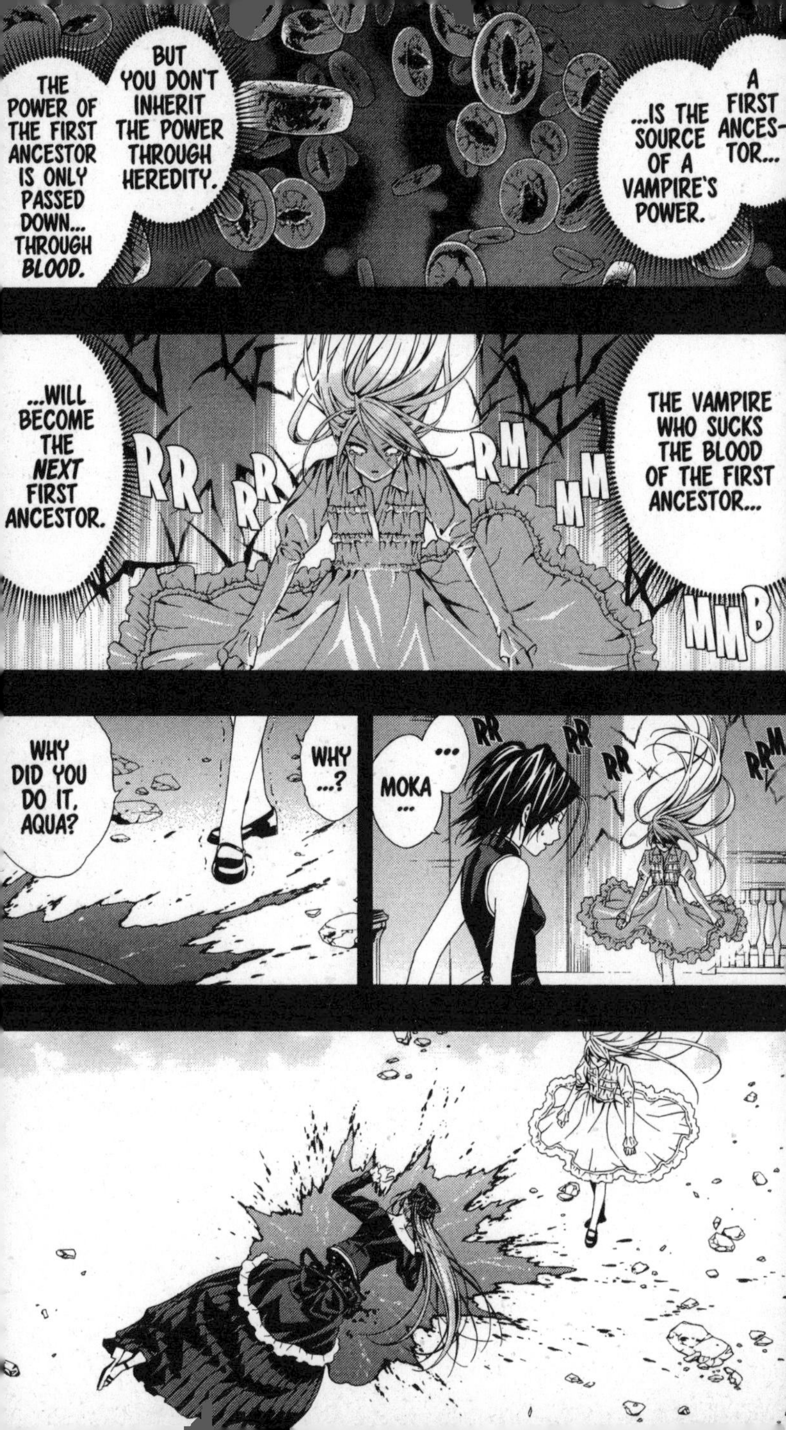
A FIRST ANCESTOR...
...IS THE SOURCE OF A VAMPIRE'S POWER.
BUT YOU DON'T INHERIT THE POWER THROUGH HEREDITY.
THE POWER OF THE FIRST ANCESTOR IS ONLY PASSED DOWN... THROUGH BLOOD.
THE VAMPIRE WHO SUCKS THE BLOOD OF THE FIRST ANCESTOR...
...WILL BECOME THE *NEXT* FIRST ANCESTOR.
RR RRR RM MMM MMB
RR RR RR RRM
... MOKA ...
WHY ...?
WHY DID YOU DO IT, AQUA?

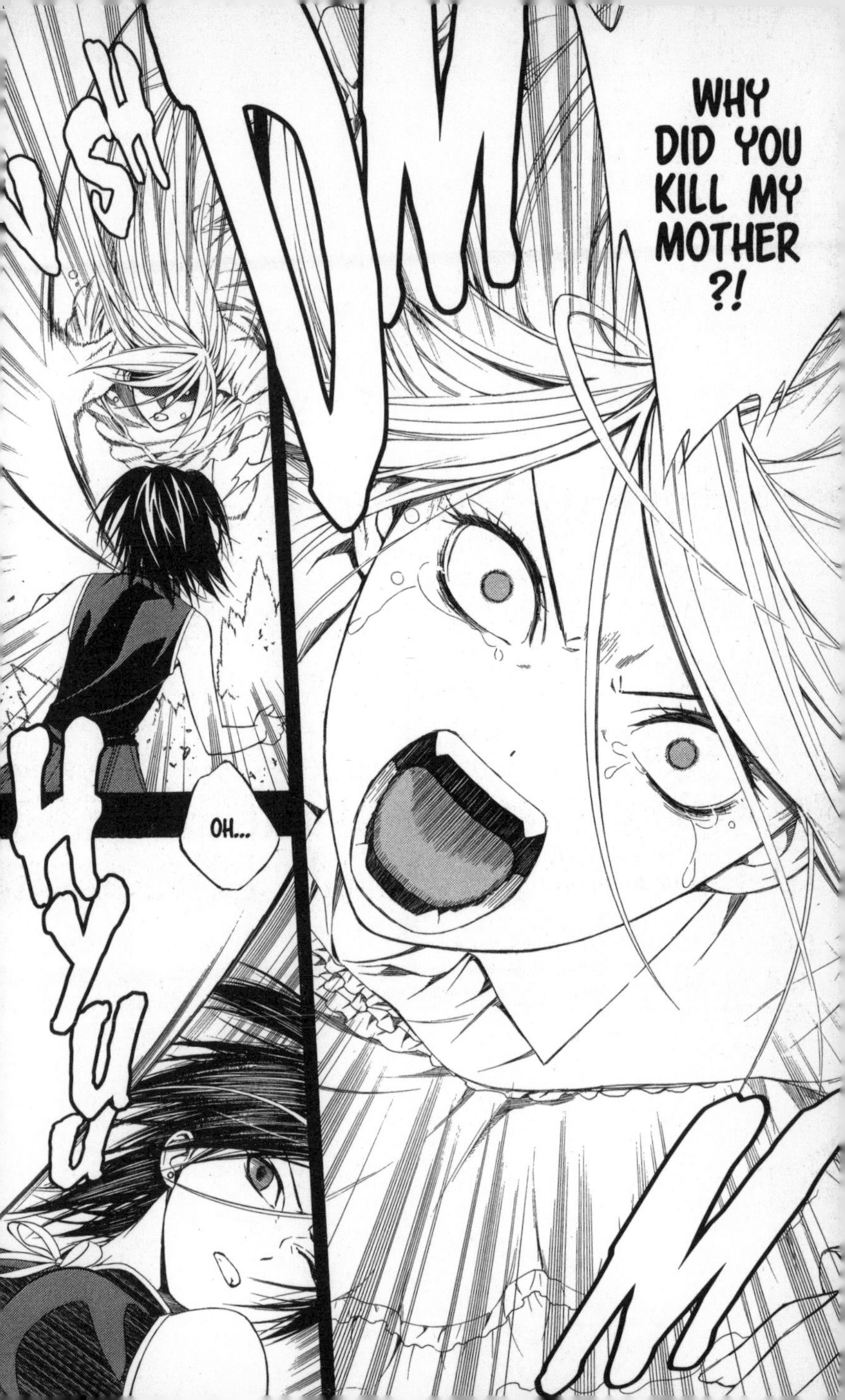
WHY DID YOU KILL MY MOTHER ?!
OH...

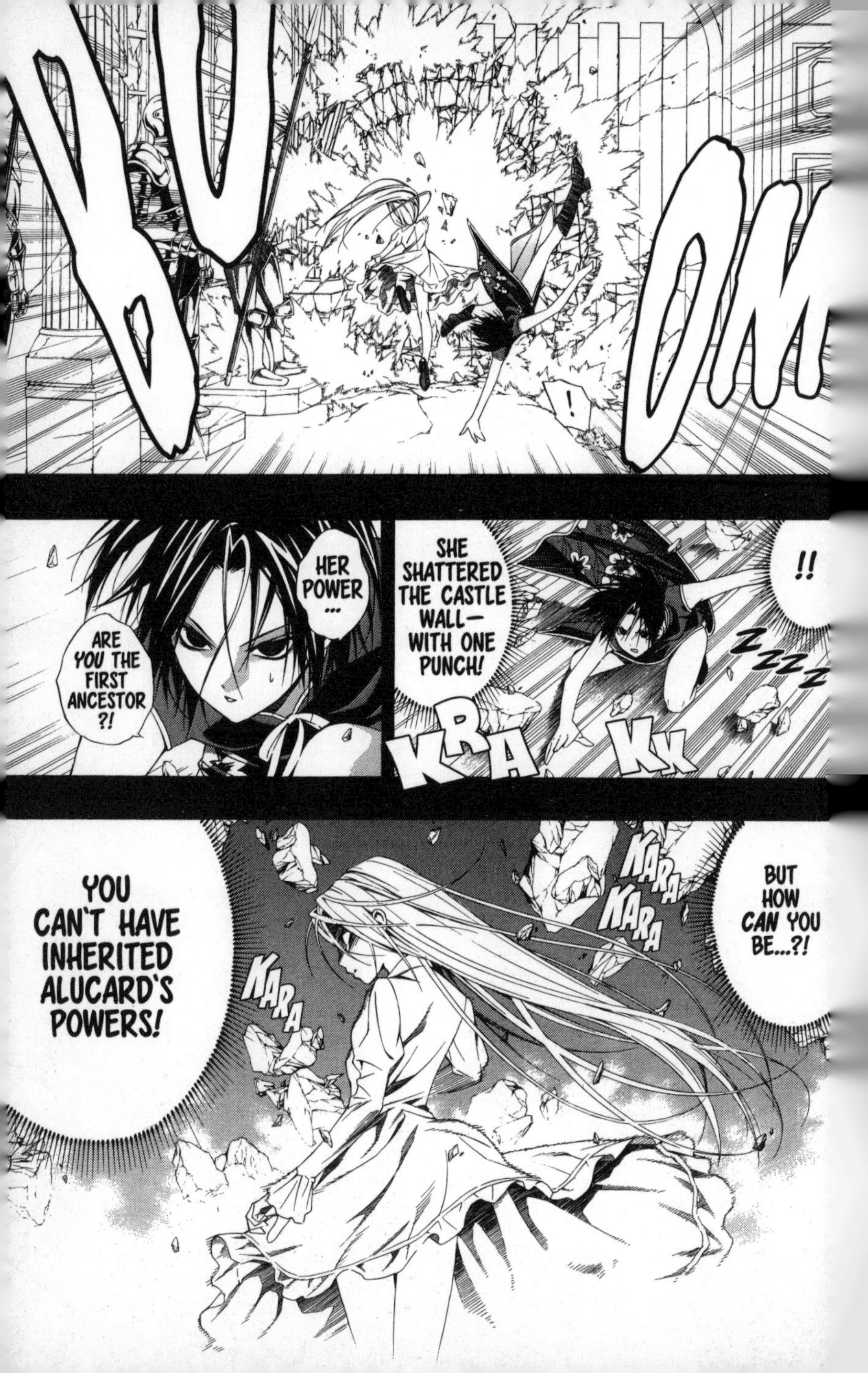
!
!!
SHE SHATTERED THE CASTLE WALL—WITH ONE PUNCH!
KRAKK
HER POWER...
ARE YOU THE FIRST ANCESTOR?!
BUT HOW CAN YOU BE...?!
KARA KARA
KARA
YOU CAN'T HAVE INHERITED ALUCARD'S POWERS!

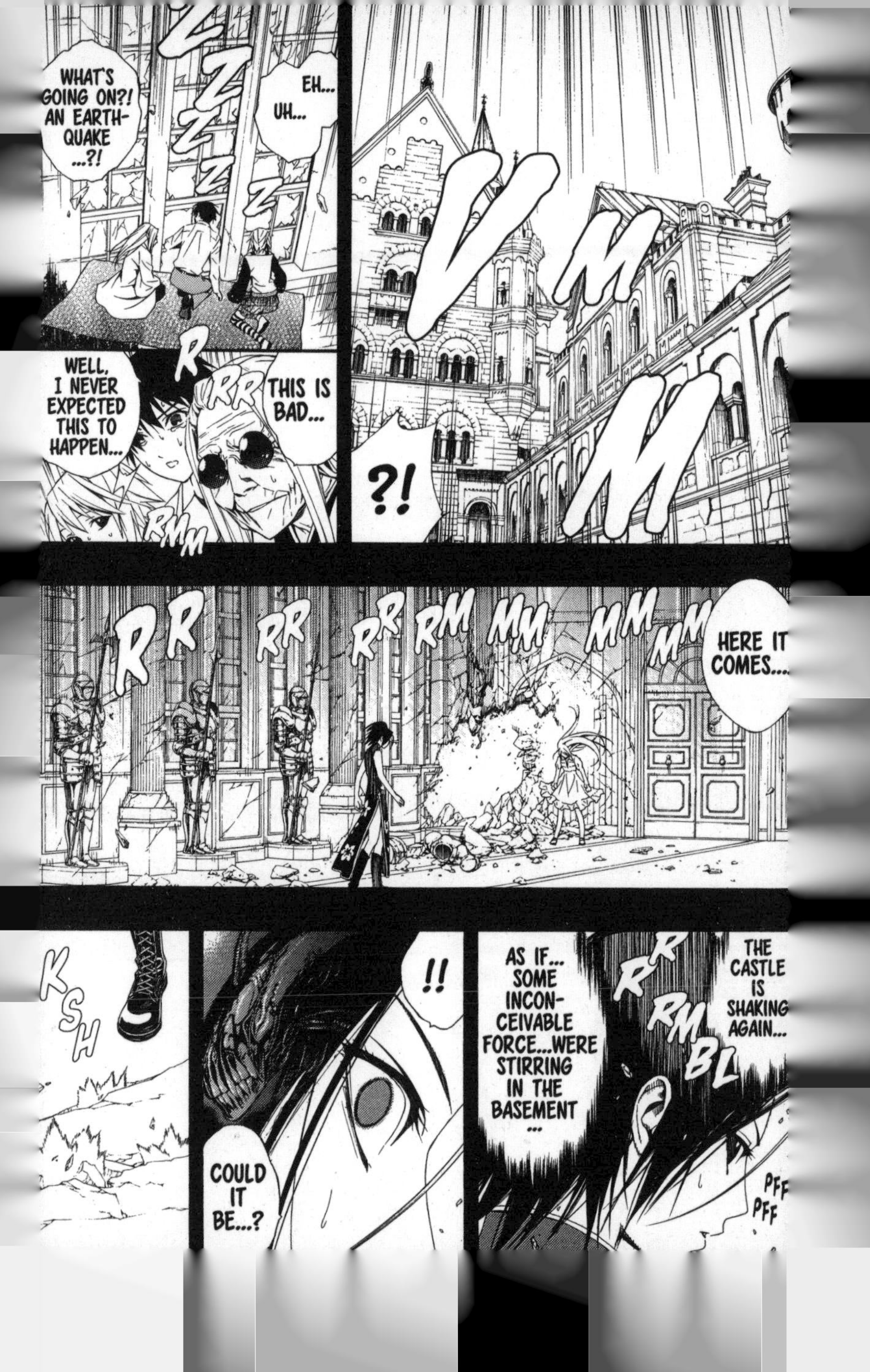
VMMM
?!
EH... UH...
WHAT'S GOING ON?! AN EARTHQUAKE ...?!
ZZZZZZ
THIS IS BAD...
WELL, I NEVER EXPECTED THIS TO HAPPEN...
RRR
RMM
HERE IT COMES....
RR RR RR RM MM MM MM
THE CASTLE IS SHAKING AGAIN...
RRRMBL
AS IF... SOME INCONCEIVABLE FORCE...WERE STIRRING IN THE BASEMENT ...
PFF PFF
!!
COULD IT BE...?
KSH

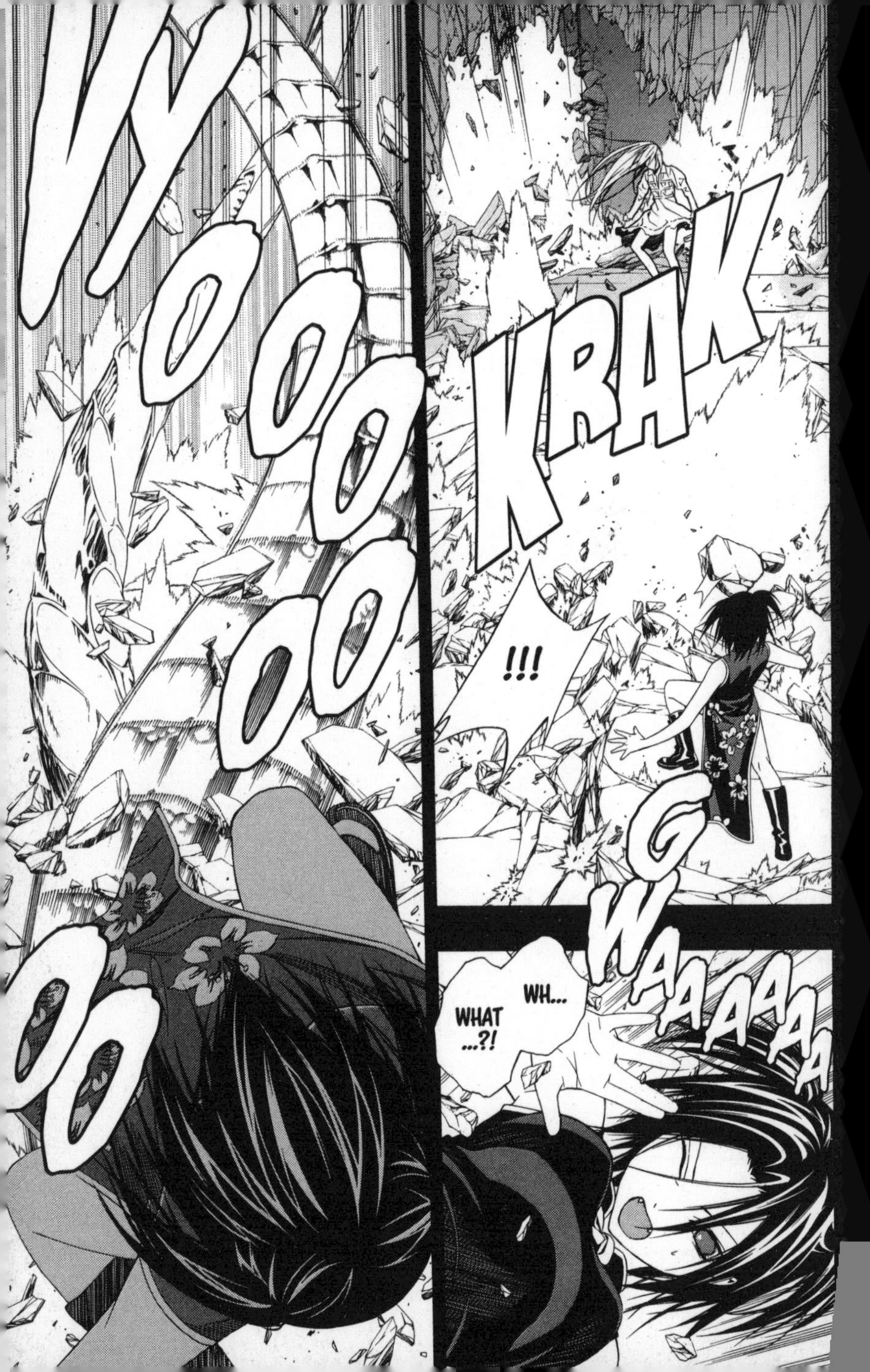
KRAK
!!!
GWAAAAAA
WH...
WHAT ...?!
VYOOOOOOO

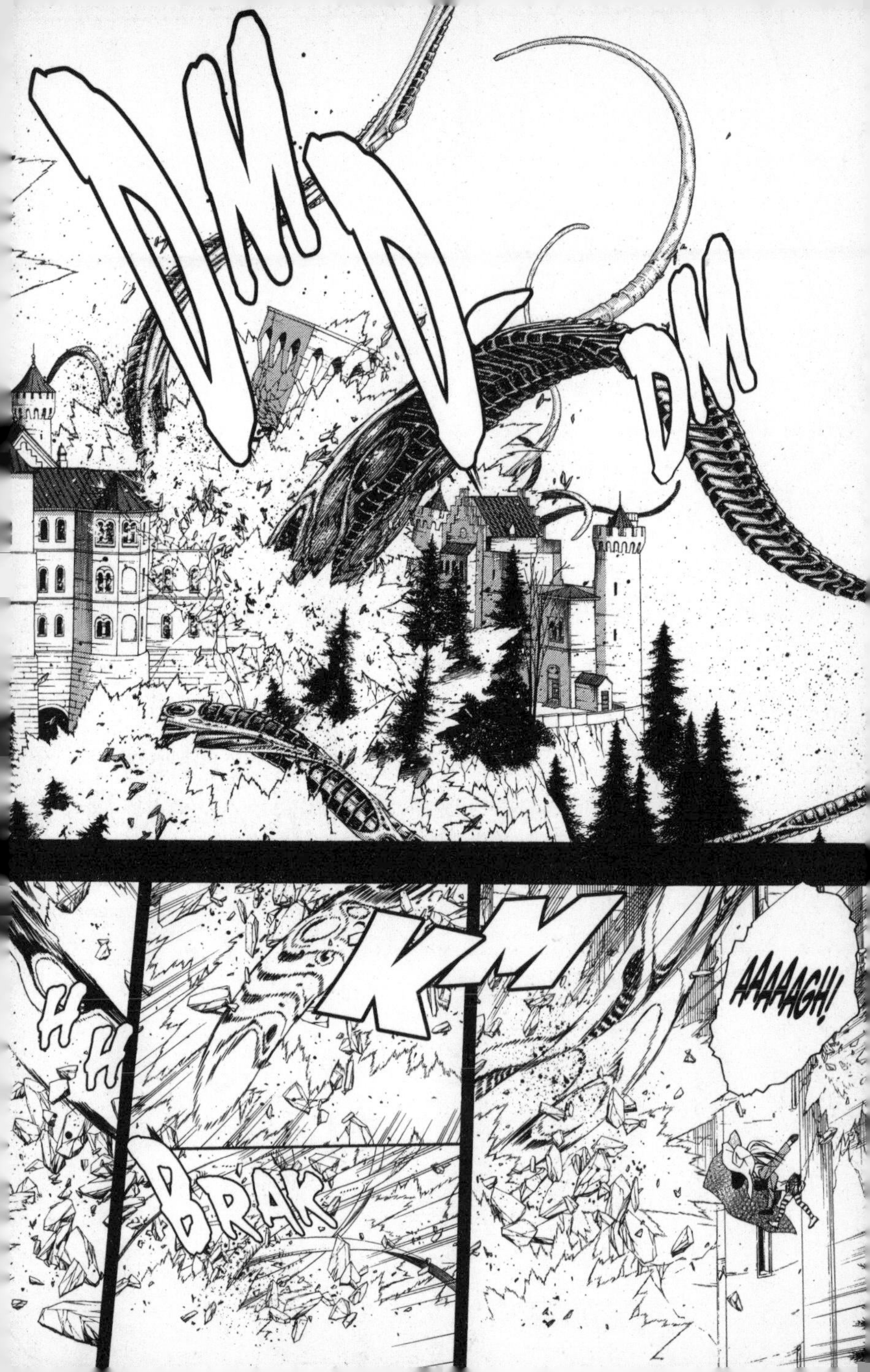

DMD
DM
AAAAGH!
KM
HH
BRAK

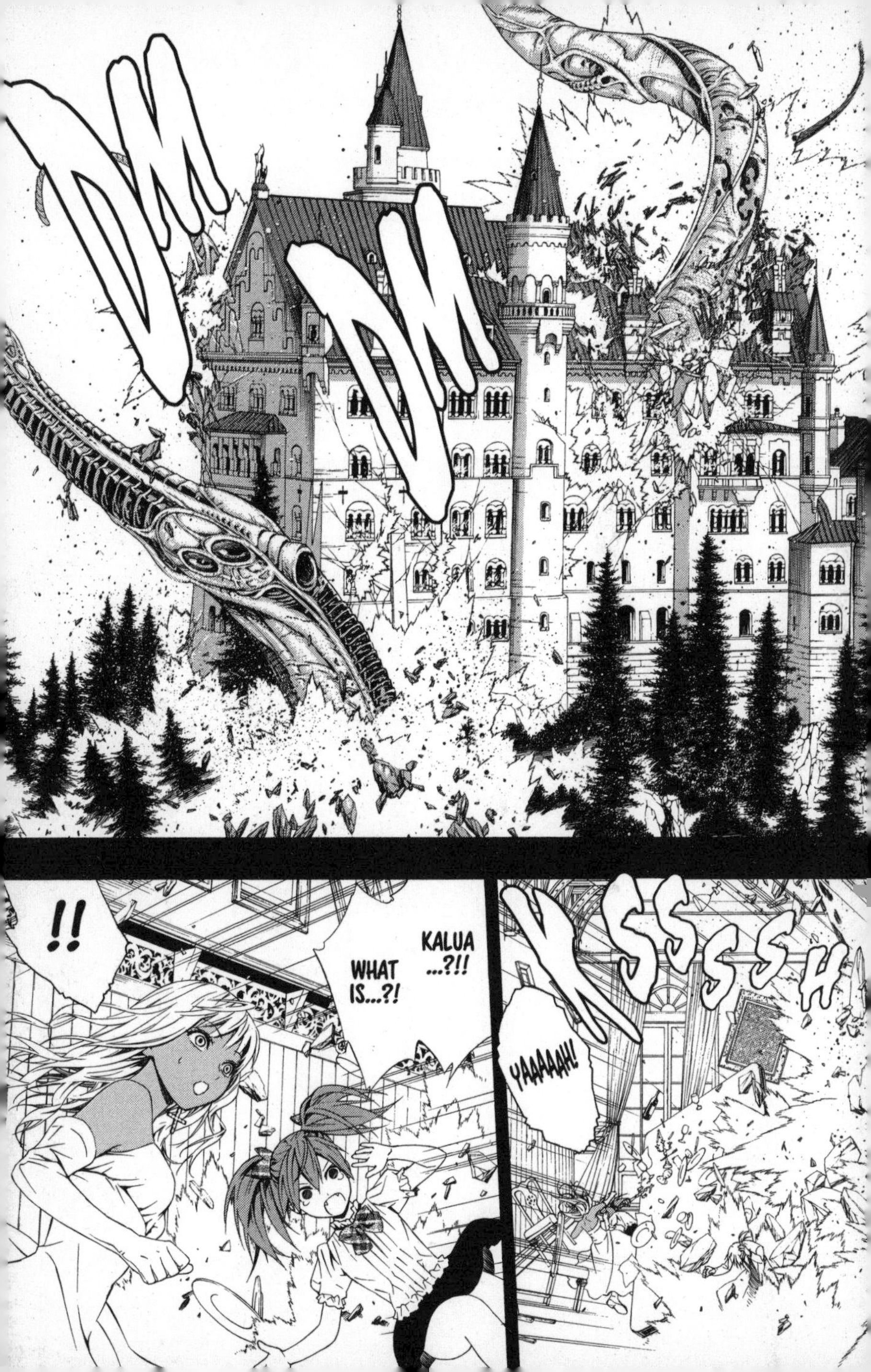
DM
DM
WSSSSH
YAAAAAH!
KALUA ...?!!
WHAT IS...?!
!!

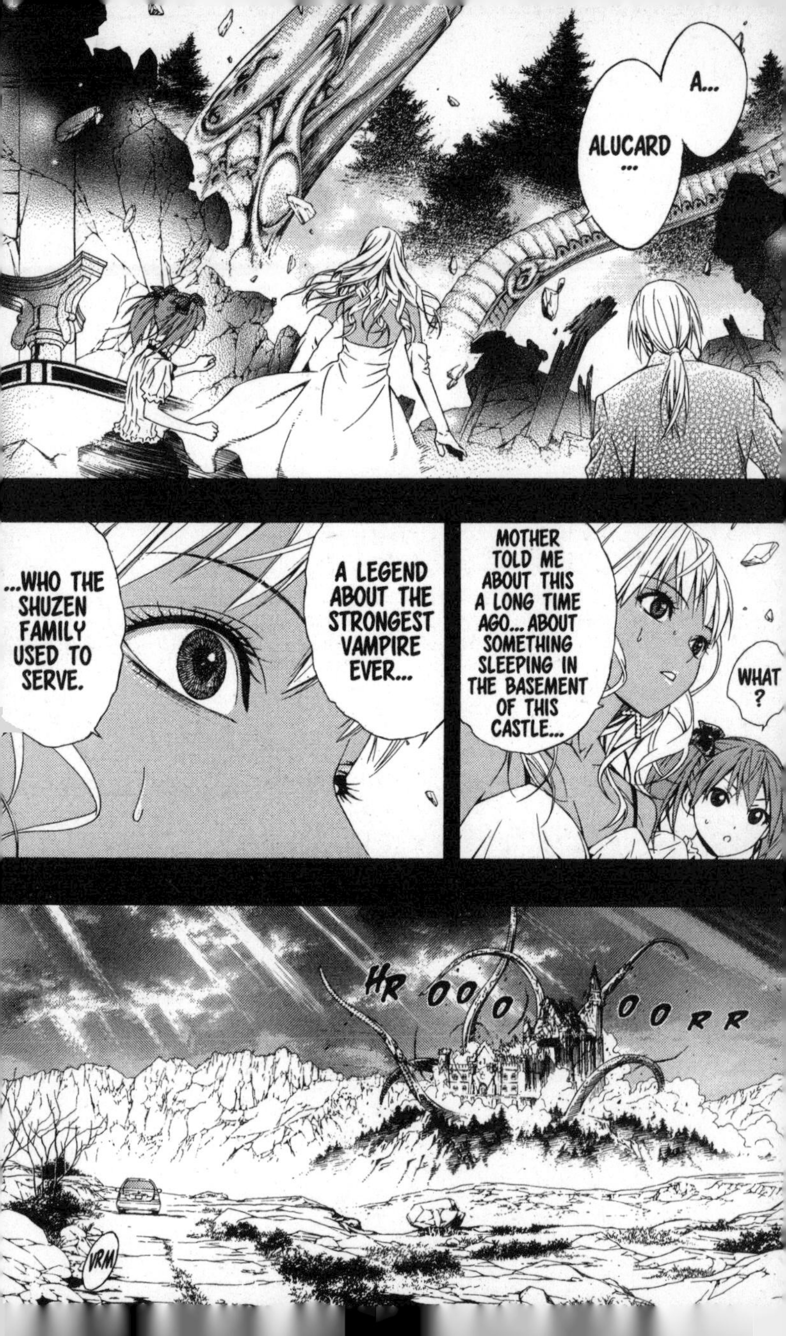
A...
ALUCARD...
MOTHER TOLD ME ABOUT THIS A LONG TIME AGO... ABOUT SOMETHING SLEEPING IN THE BASEMENT OF THIS CASTLE...
WHAT?
A LEGEND ABOUT THE STRONGEST VAMPIRE EVER...
...WHO THE SHUZEN FAMILY USED TO SERVE.
HROOOOOORR
VRM

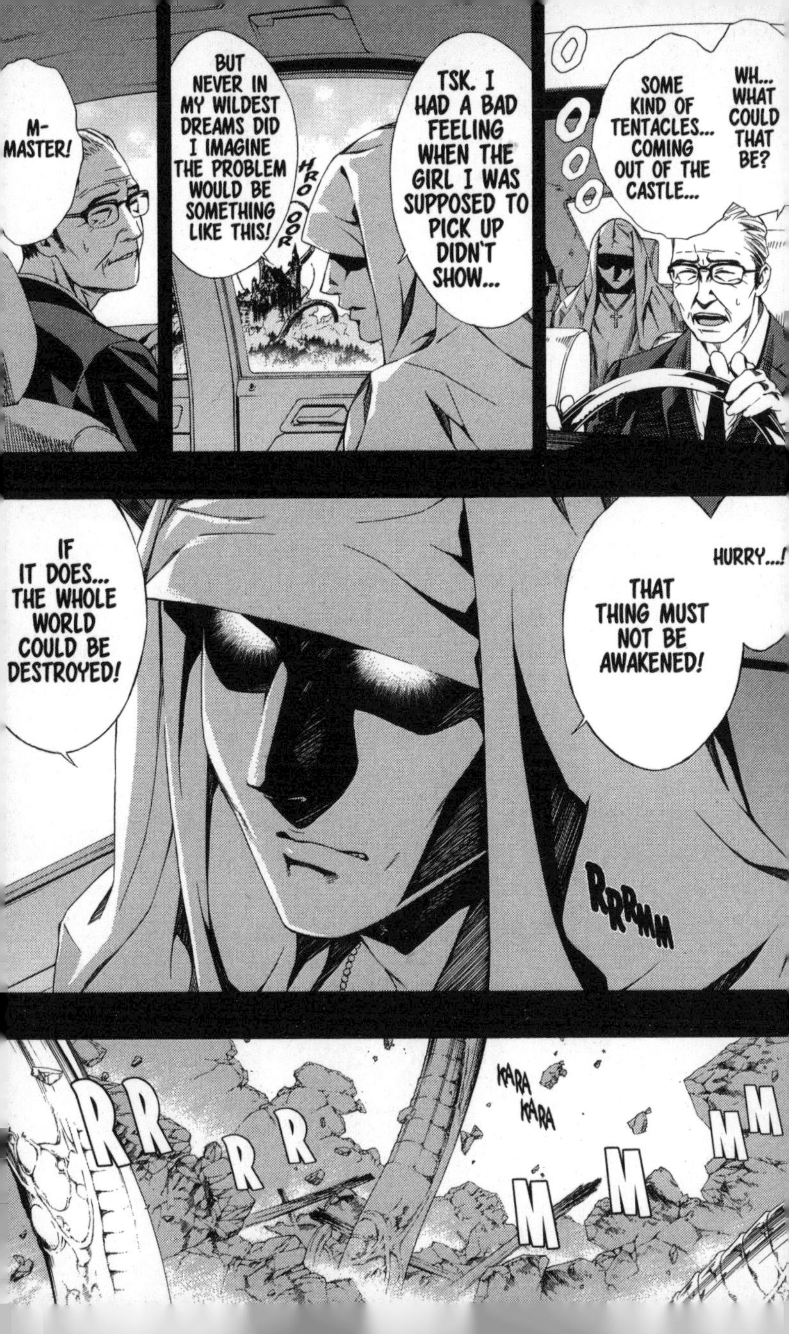
WH... WHAT COULD THAT BE?
SOME KIND OF TENTACLES... COMING OUT OF THE CASTLE...
TSK. I HAD A BAD FEELING WHEN THE GIRL I WAS SUPPOSED TO PICK UP DIDN'T SHOW...
HROOOOR
BUT NEVER IN MY WILDEST DREAMS DID I IMAGINE THE PROBLEM WOULD BE SOMETHING LIKE THIS!
M-MASTER!
HURRY...!
THAT THING MUST NOT BE AWAKENED!
IF IT DOES... THE WHOLE WORLD COULD BE DESTROYED!
RRRMM
KARA KARA
RRRRMMMM

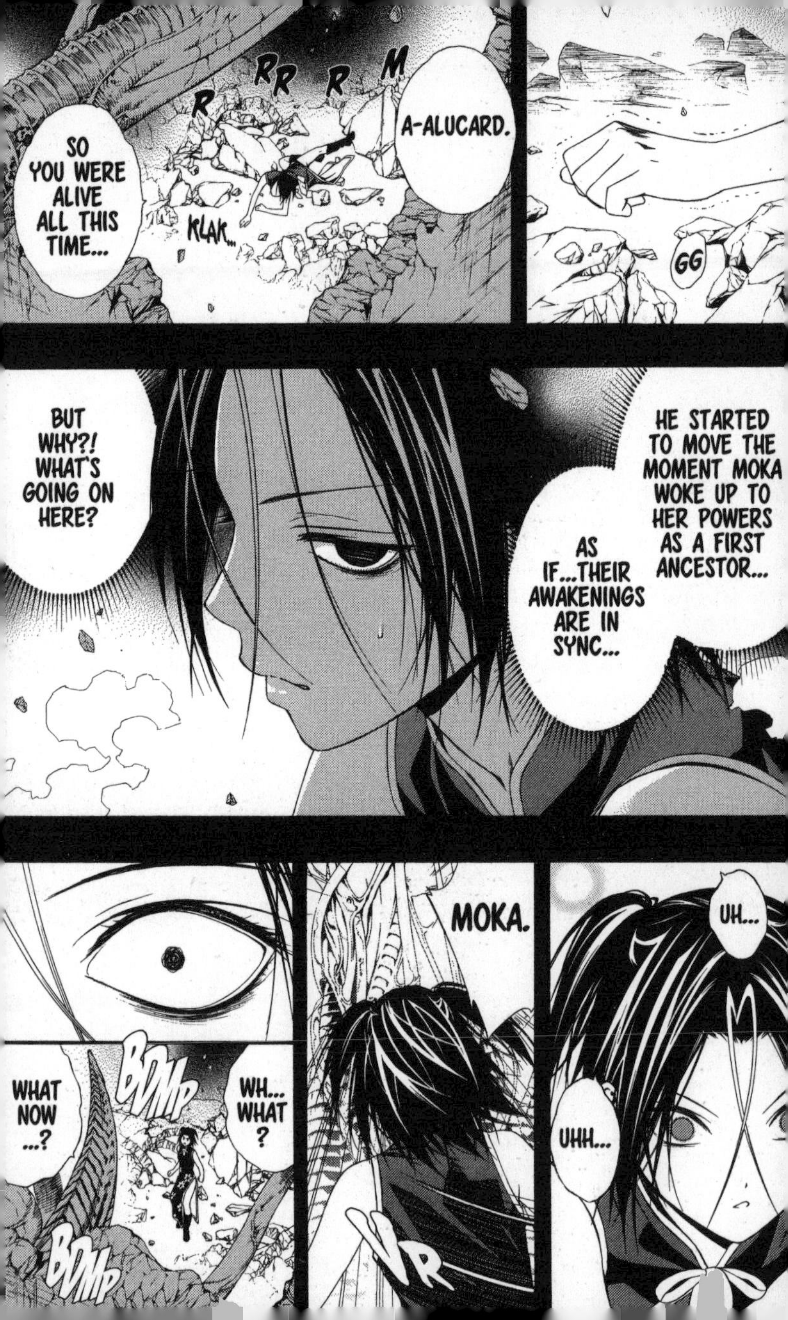
GG
A-ALUCARD.
RRRRM
SO YOU WERE ALIVE ALL THIS TIME...
KLAK...
HE STARTED TO MOVE THE MOMENT MOKA WOKE UP TO HER POWERS AS A FIRST ANCESTOR...
AS IF...THEIR AWAKENINGS ARE IN SYNC...
BUT WHY?! WHAT'S GOING ON HERE?
UH...
UHH...
MOKA.
VR
WH... WHAT?
BDMP
WHAT NOW...?
BDMP

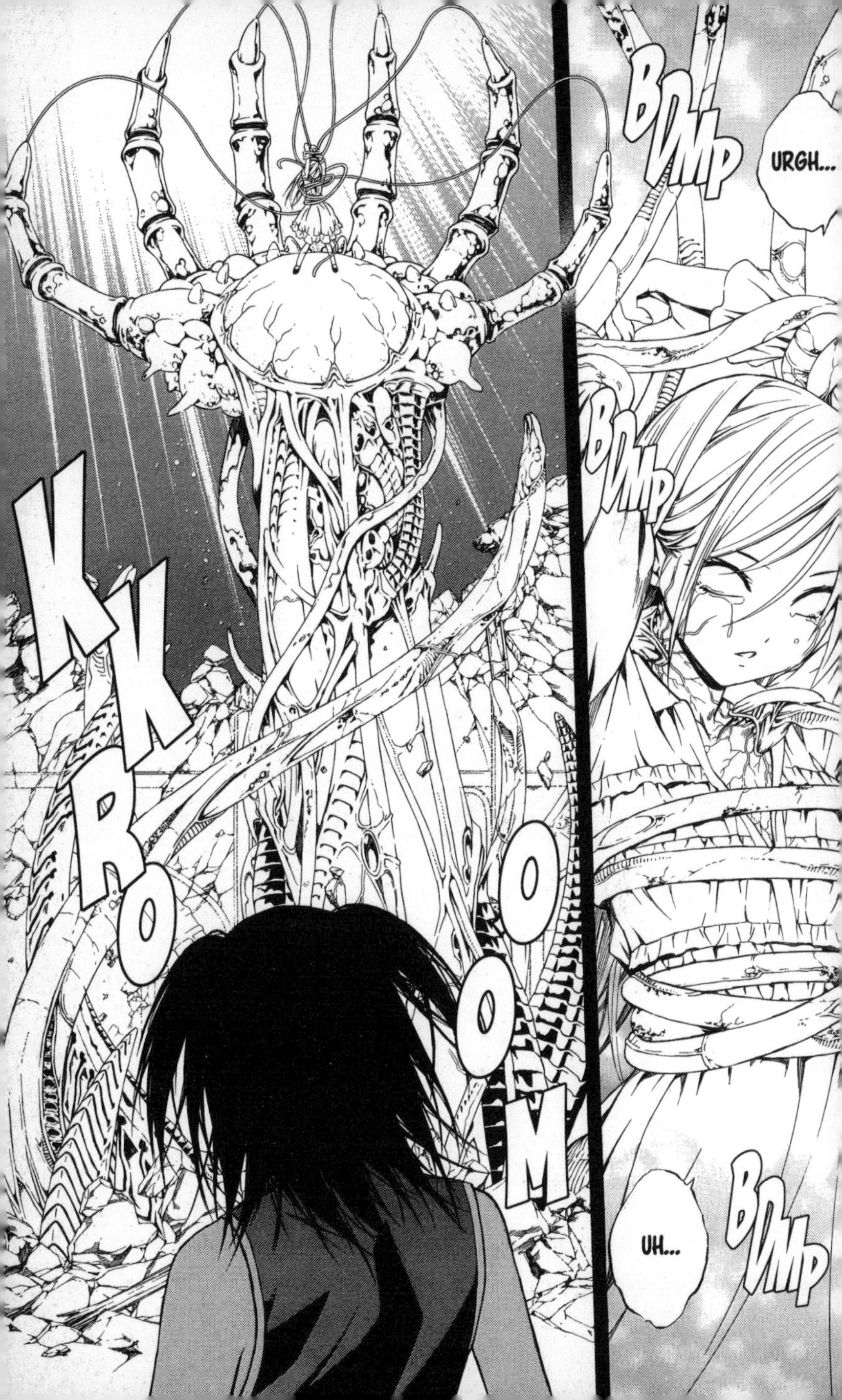
BUMP
URGH...
BUMP
UH...
BUMP
KKROOOM

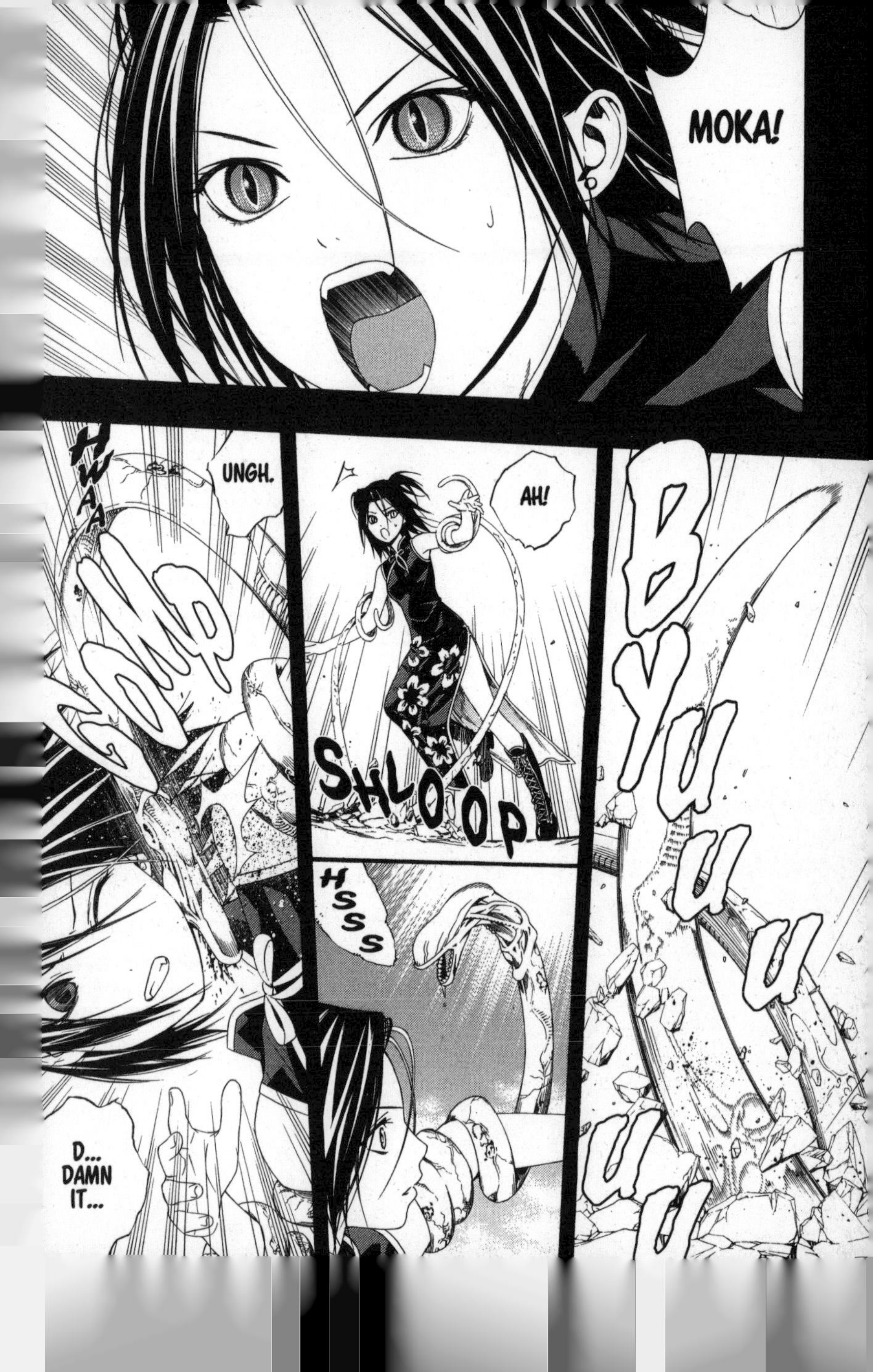
MOKA!
BYUUUUU
AH!
SHLOOP
HSSS
HWAA
UNGH.
GOMP
D... DAMN IT...

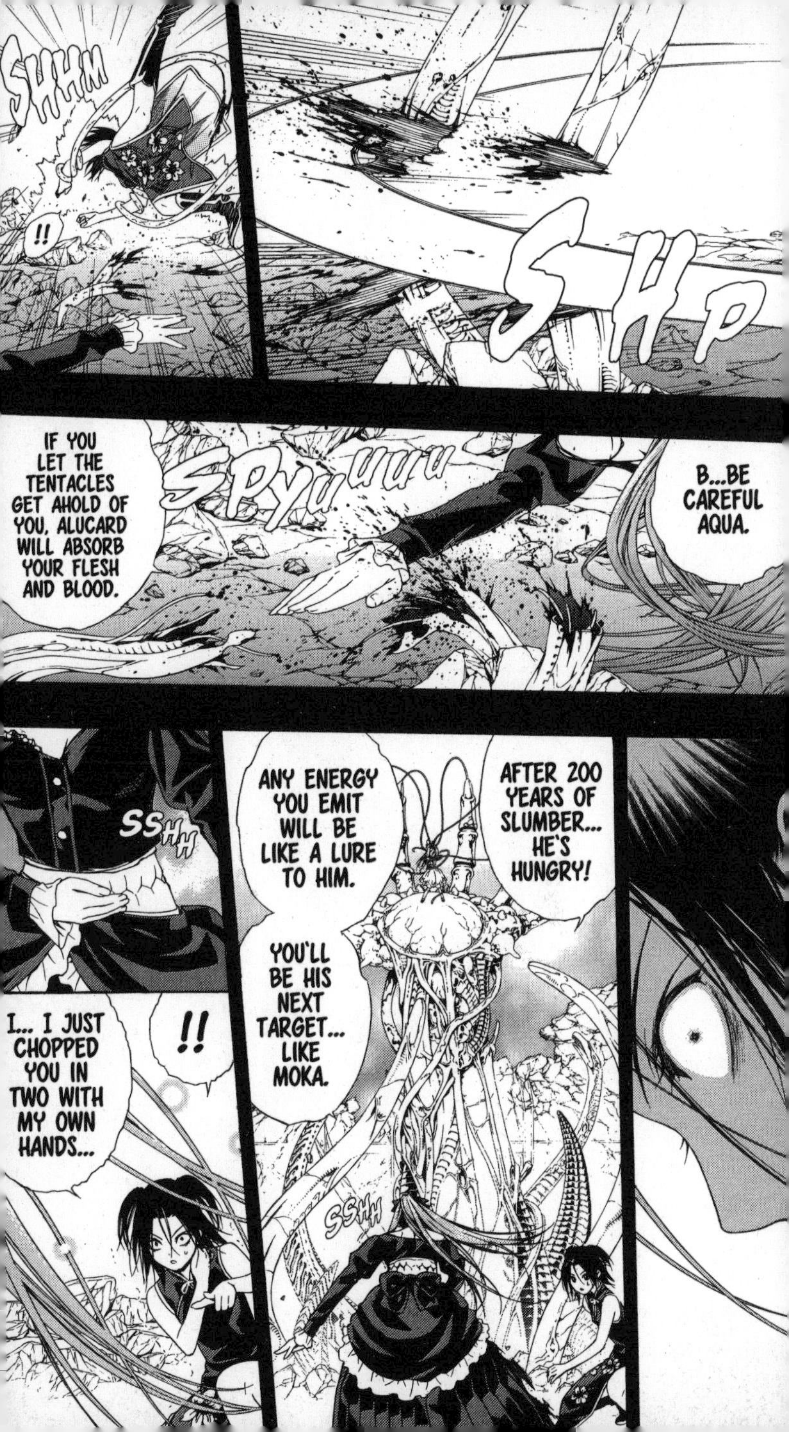
SHP
SHHM
!!
B...BE CAREFUL AQUA.
SPYUUUU
IF YOU LET THE TENTACLES GET AHOLD OF YOU, ALUCARD WILL ABSORB YOUR FLESH AND BLOOD.
AFTER 200 YEARS OF SLUMBER... HE'S HUNGRY!
ANY ENERGY YOU EMIT WILL BE LIKE A LURE TO HIM.
YOU'LL BE HIS NEXT TARGET... LIKE MOKA.
SSHH
SSHH
!!
I... I JUST CHOPPED YOU IN TWO WITH MY OWN HANDS...

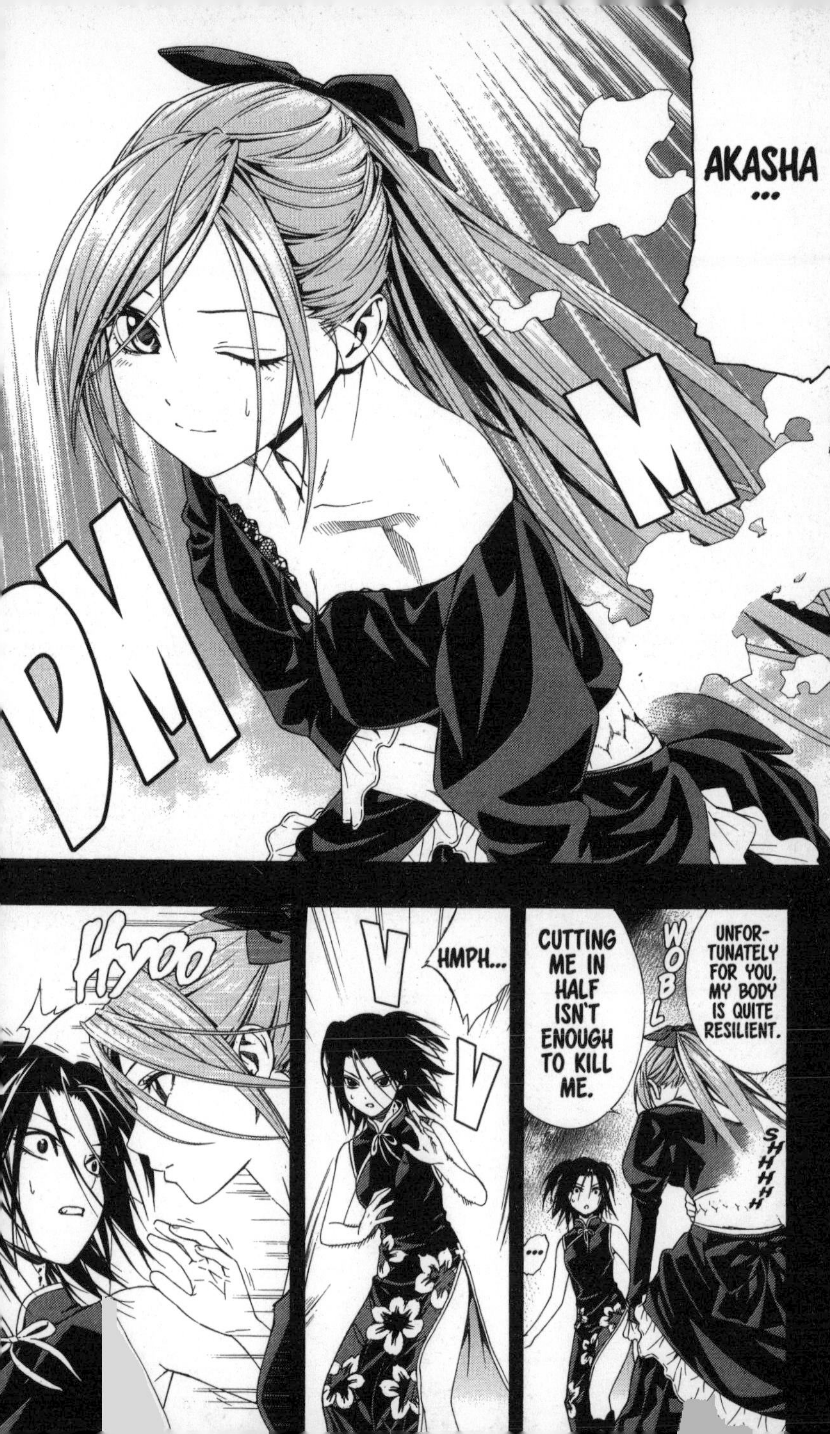
AKASHA
...
DM
M
UNFOR-TUNATELY FOR YOU, MY BODY IS QUITE RESILIENT.
WOBL
CUTTING ME IN HALF ISN'T ENOUGH TO KILL ME.
SHHHHHH
...
HMPH...
V
V
Hyoo

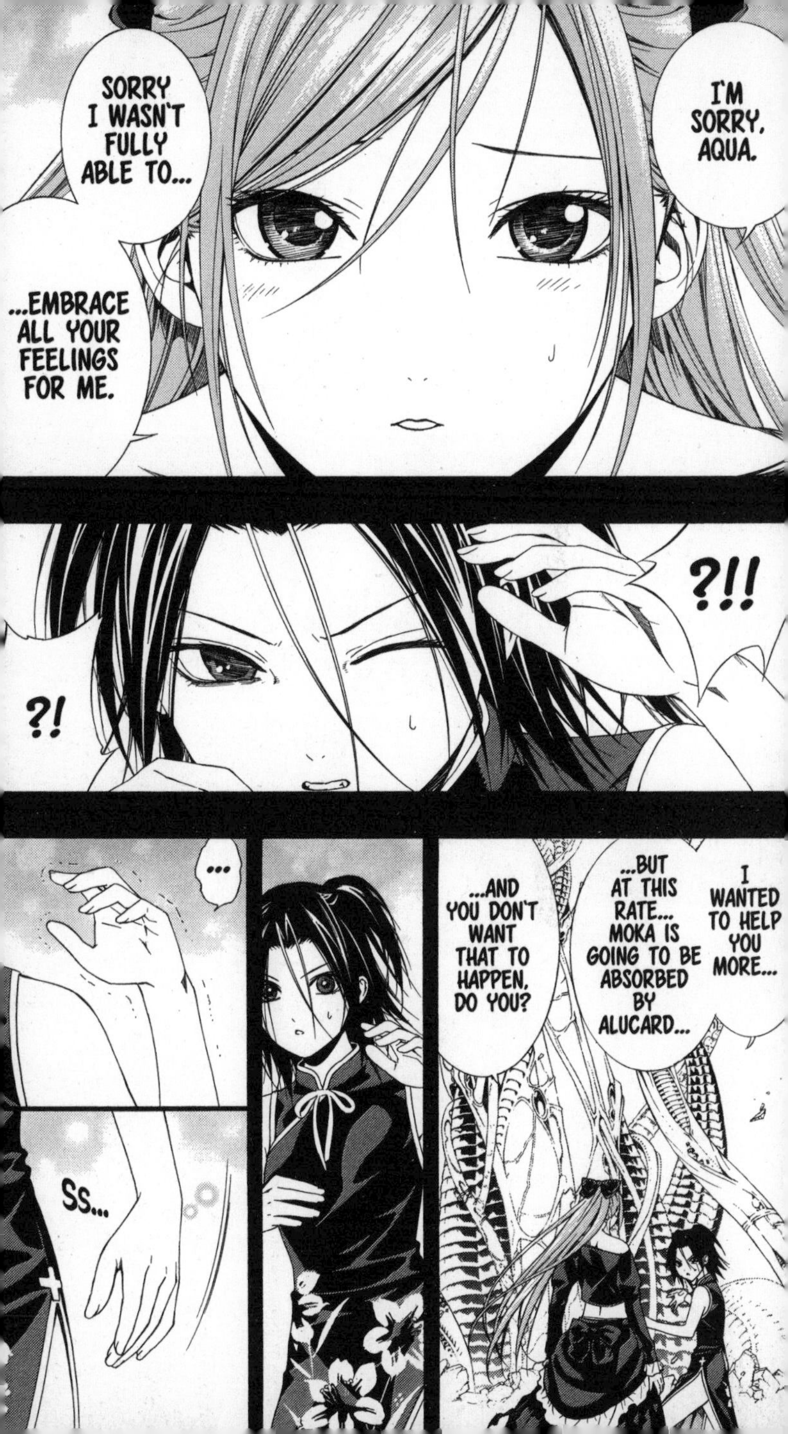
I'M SORRY, AQUA.
SORRY I WASN'T FULLY ABLE TO...
...EMBRACE ALL YOUR FEELINGS FOR ME.
?!!
?!
I WANTED TO HELP YOU MORE...
...BUT AT THIS RATE... MOKA IS GOING TO BE ABSORBED BY ALUCARD...
...AND YOU DON'T WANT THAT TO HAPPEN, DO YOU?
...
SS...

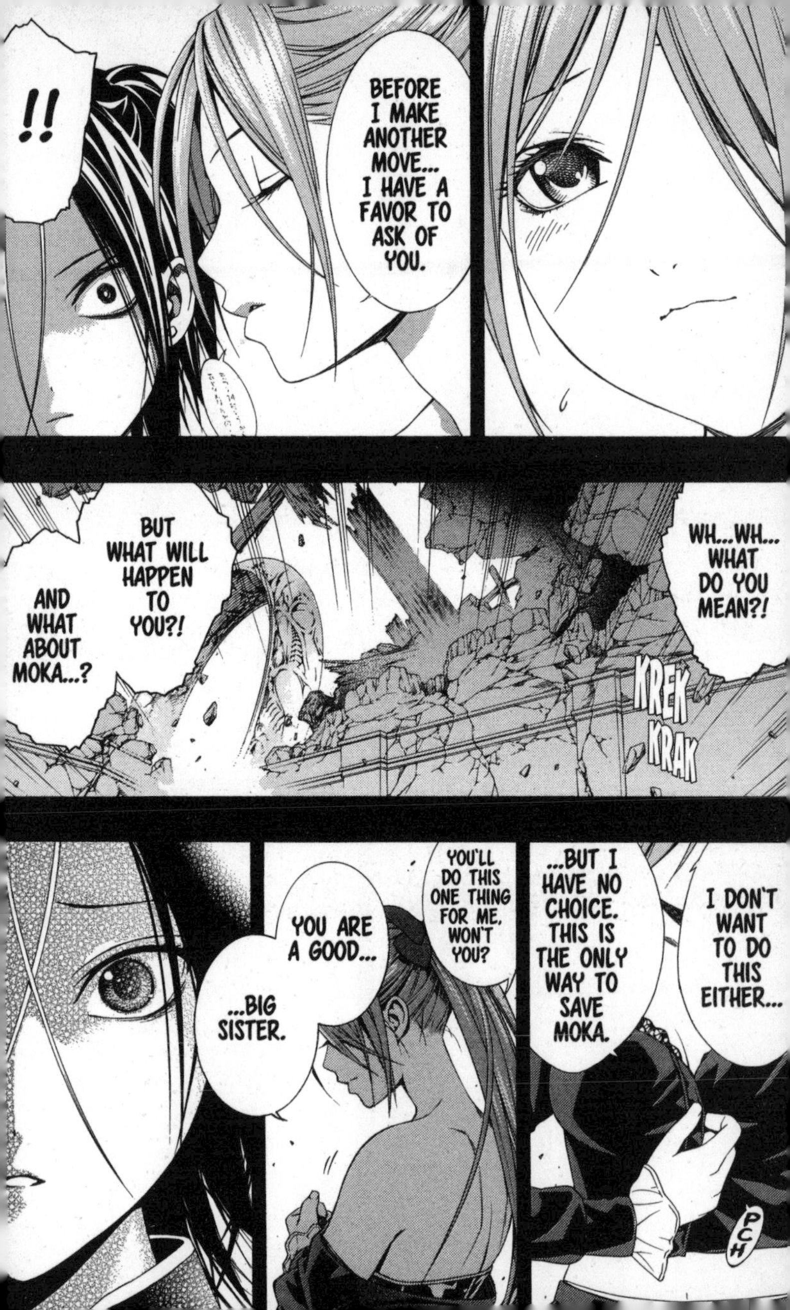
BEFORE I MAKE ANOTHER MOVE... I HAVE A FAVOR TO ASK OF YOU.
!!
WH...WH... WHAT DO YOU MEAN?!
KREK KRAK
BUT WHAT WILL HAPPEN TO YOU?!
AND WHAT ABOUT MOKA...?
I DON'T WANT TO DO THIS EITHER...
...BUT I HAVE NO CHOICE. THIS IS THE ONLY WAY TO SAVE MOKA.
PCH
YOU'LL DO THIS ONE THING FOR ME, WON'T YOU?
YOU ARE A GOOD...
...BIG SISTER.

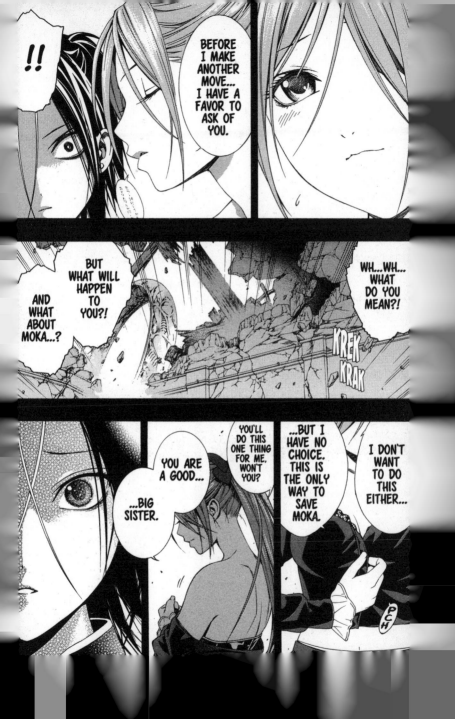

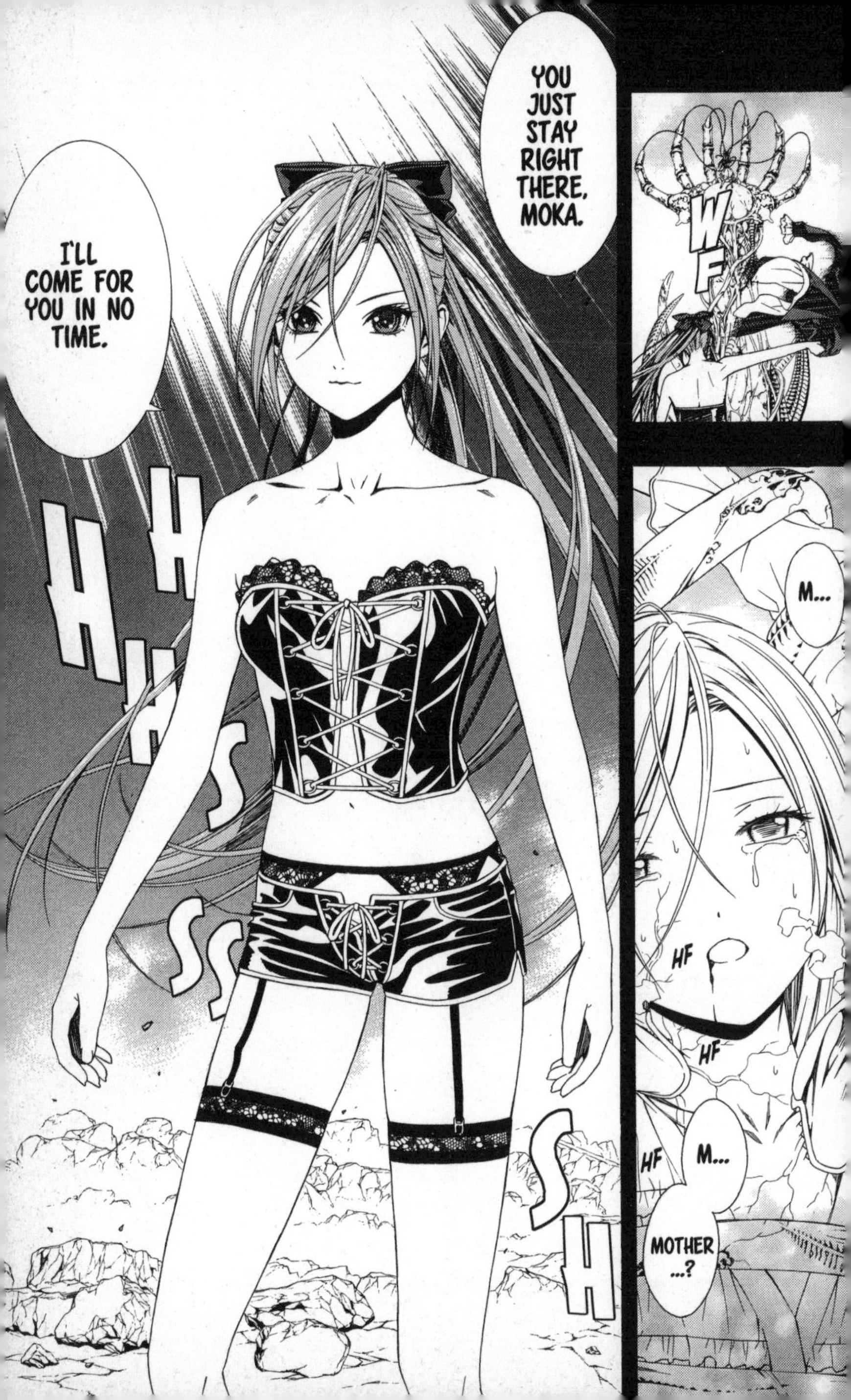
WF
M...
HF
HF
HF
M...
MOTHER ...?
YOU JUST STAY RIGHT THERE, MOKA.
I'LL COME FOR YOU IN NO TIME.
HHH
SSS
SSH

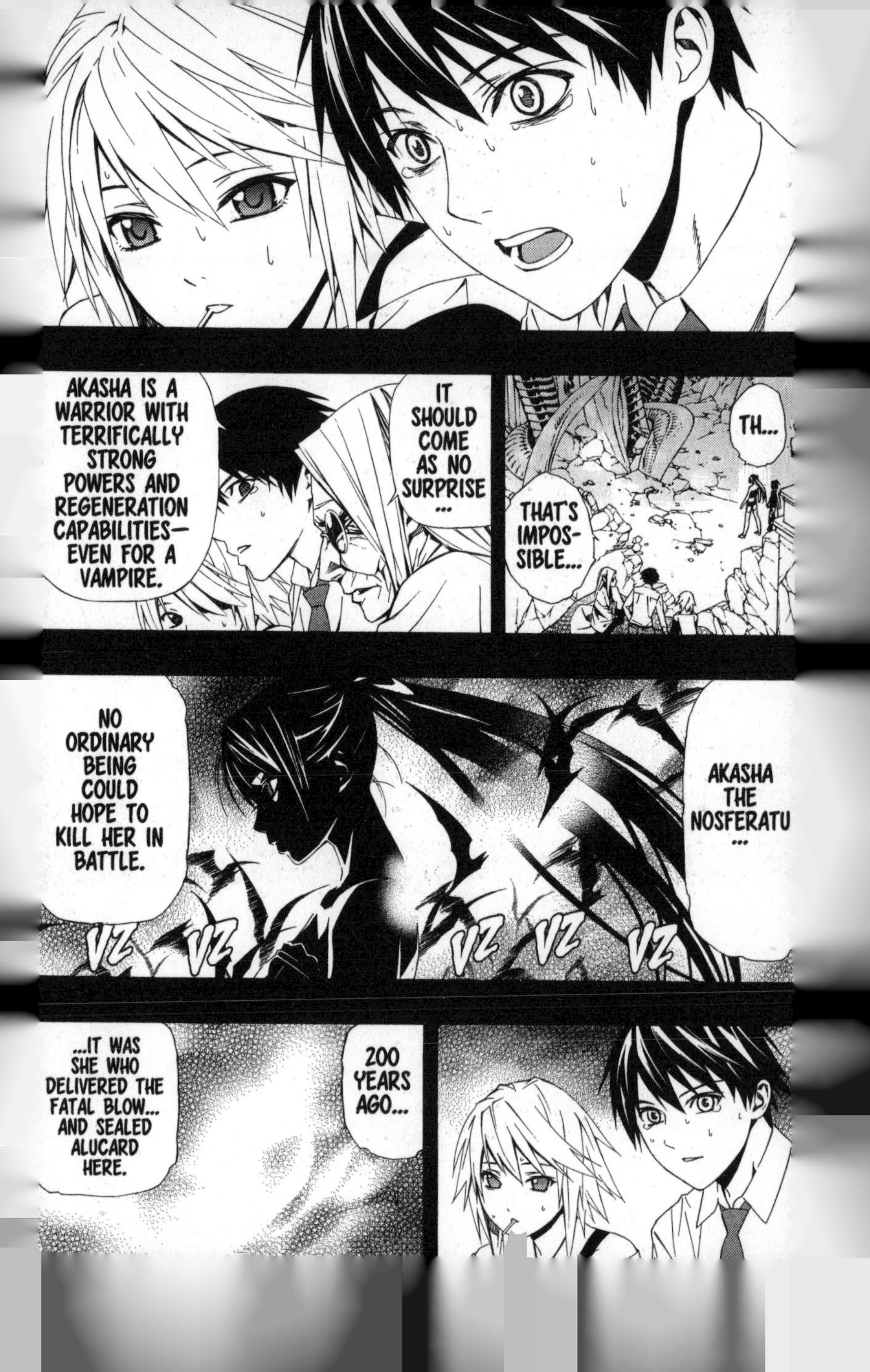
TH...
THAT'S IMPOSSIBLE...
IT SHOULD COME AS NO SURPRISE ...
AKASHA IS A WARRIOR WITH TERRIFICALLY STRONG POWERS AND REGENERATION CAPABILITIES— EVEN FOR A VAMPIRE.
AKASHA THE NOSFERATU ...
NO ORDINARY BEING COULD HOPE TO KILL HER IN BATTLE.
VZ VZ VZ VZ VZ
200 YEARS AGO...
...IT WAS SHE WHO DELIVERED THE FATAL BLOW... AND SEALED ALUCARD HERE.

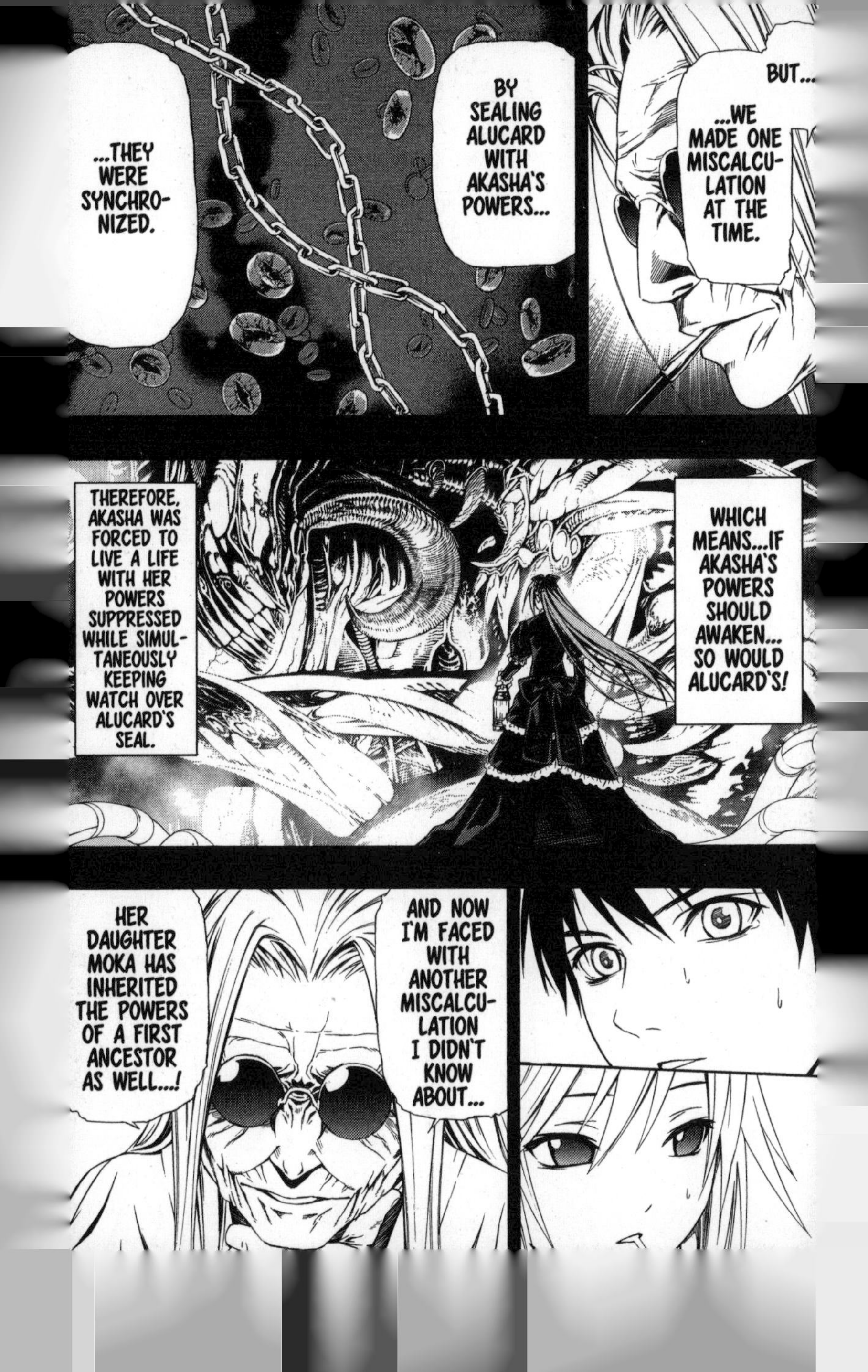
BUT...
...WE MADE ONE MISCALCULATION AT THE TIME.
BY SEALING ALUCARD WITH AKASHA'S POWERS...
...THEY WERE SYNCHRONIZED.
WHICH MEANS...IF AKASHA'S POWERS SHOULD AWAKEN... SO WOULD ALUCARD'S!
THEREFORE, AKASHA WAS FORCED TO LIVE A LIFE WITH HER POWERS SUPPRESSED WHILE SIMULTANEOUSLY KEEPING WATCH OVER ALUCARD'S SEAL.
AND NOW I'M FACED WITH ANOTHER MISCALCULATION I DIDN'T KNOW ABOUT...
HER DAUGHTER MOKA HAS INHERITED THE POWERS OF A FIRST ANCESTOR AS WELL...!

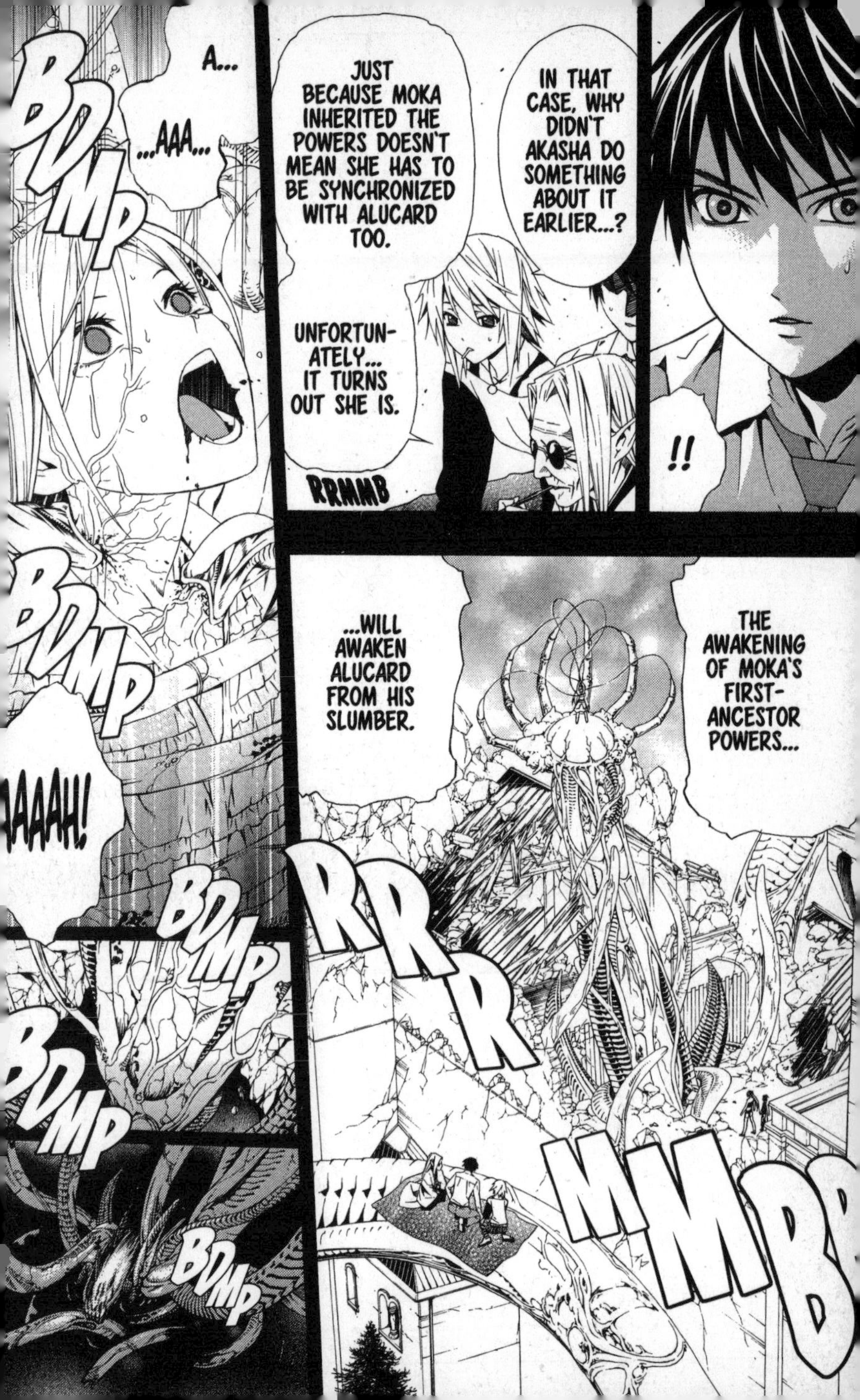
!!
IN THAT CASE, WHY DIDN'T AKASHA DO SOMETHING ABOUT IT EARLIER...?
JUST BECAUSE MOKA INHERITED THE POWERS DOESN'T MEAN SHE HAS TO BE SYNCHRONIZED WITH ALUCARD TOO.
UNFORTUN-ATELY... IT TURNS OUT SHE IS.
RRMMB
THE AWAKENING OF MOKA'S FIRST-ANCESTOR POWERS...
...WILL AWAKEN ALUCARD FROM HIS SLUMBER.
RRR
MMMB
A...
...AAA...
BDMP
BDMP
AAAAH!
BDMP
BDMP
BDMP

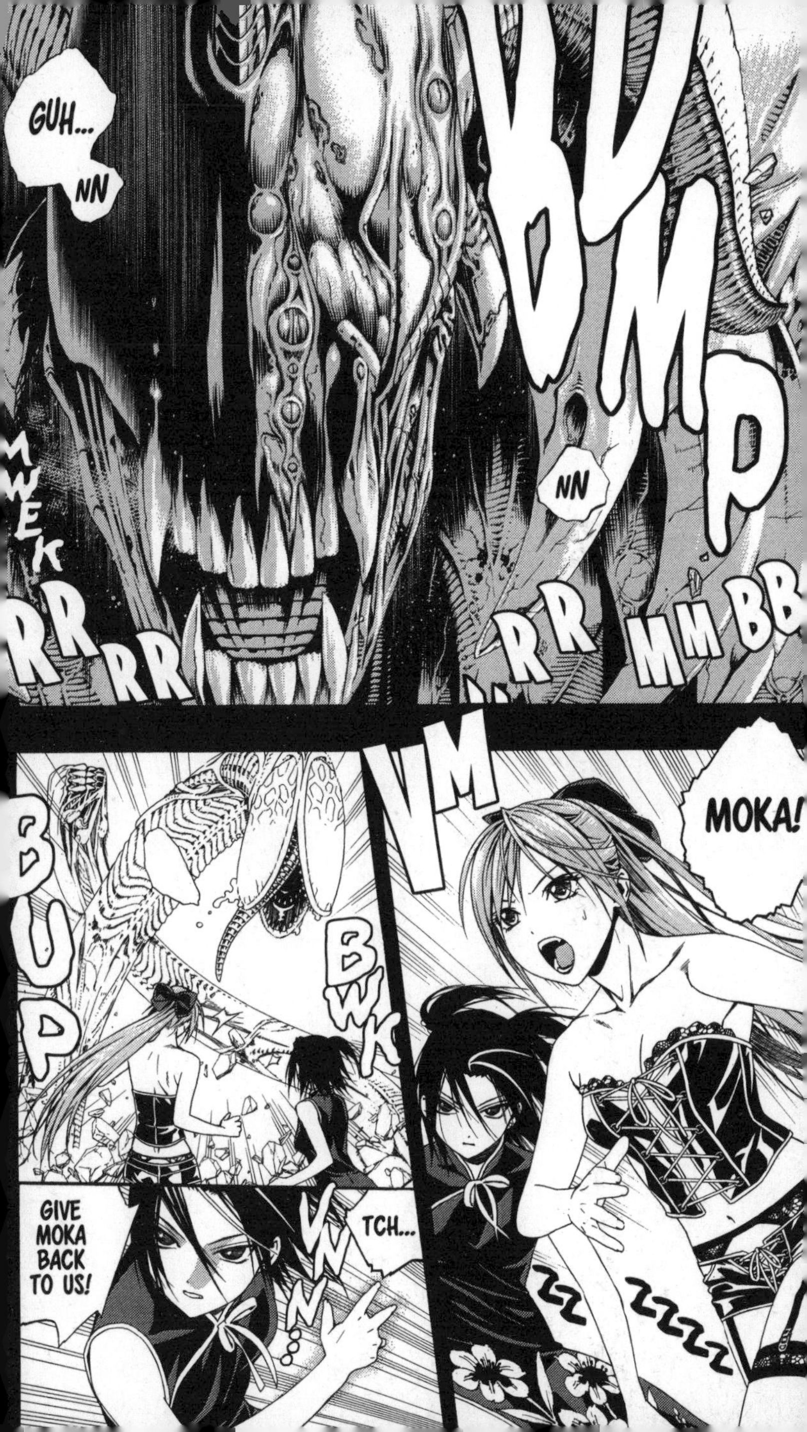
NN
RR MM BB
GUH...
NN
RRRR
VM
MOKA!
ZZZ
ZZZZZ
TCH...
GIVE MOKA BACK TO US!

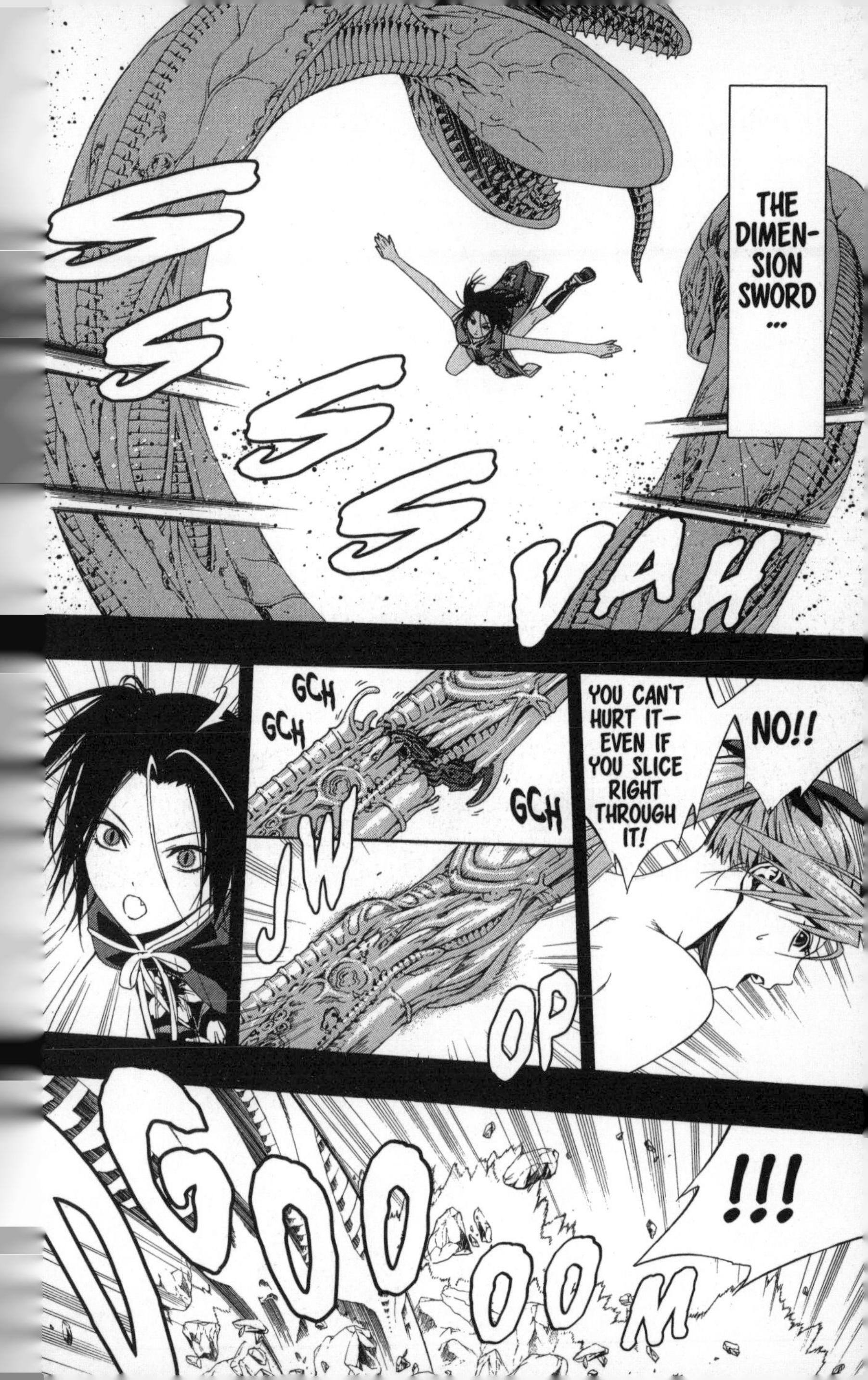
THE DIMEN-SION SWORD...
SSSSVAH
NO!!
YOU CAN'T HURT IT— EVEN IF YOU SLICE RIGHT THROUGH IT!
GCH GCH
GCH
JWOP
GOOOOOM
!!!

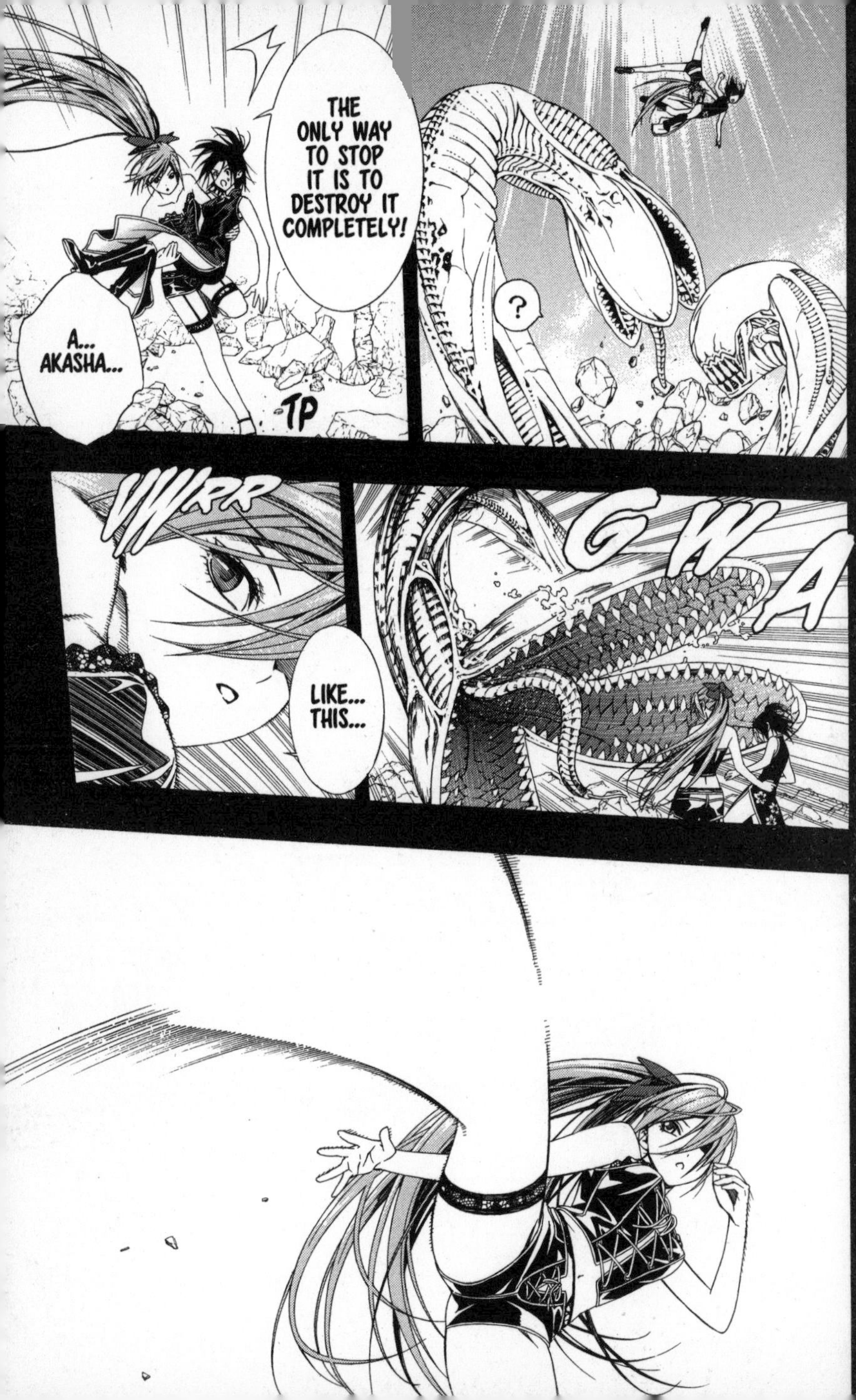
?
THE ONLY WAY TO STOP IT IS TO DESTROY IT COMPLETELY!
A... AKASHA...
TP
GWA
VWRR
LIKE... THIS...

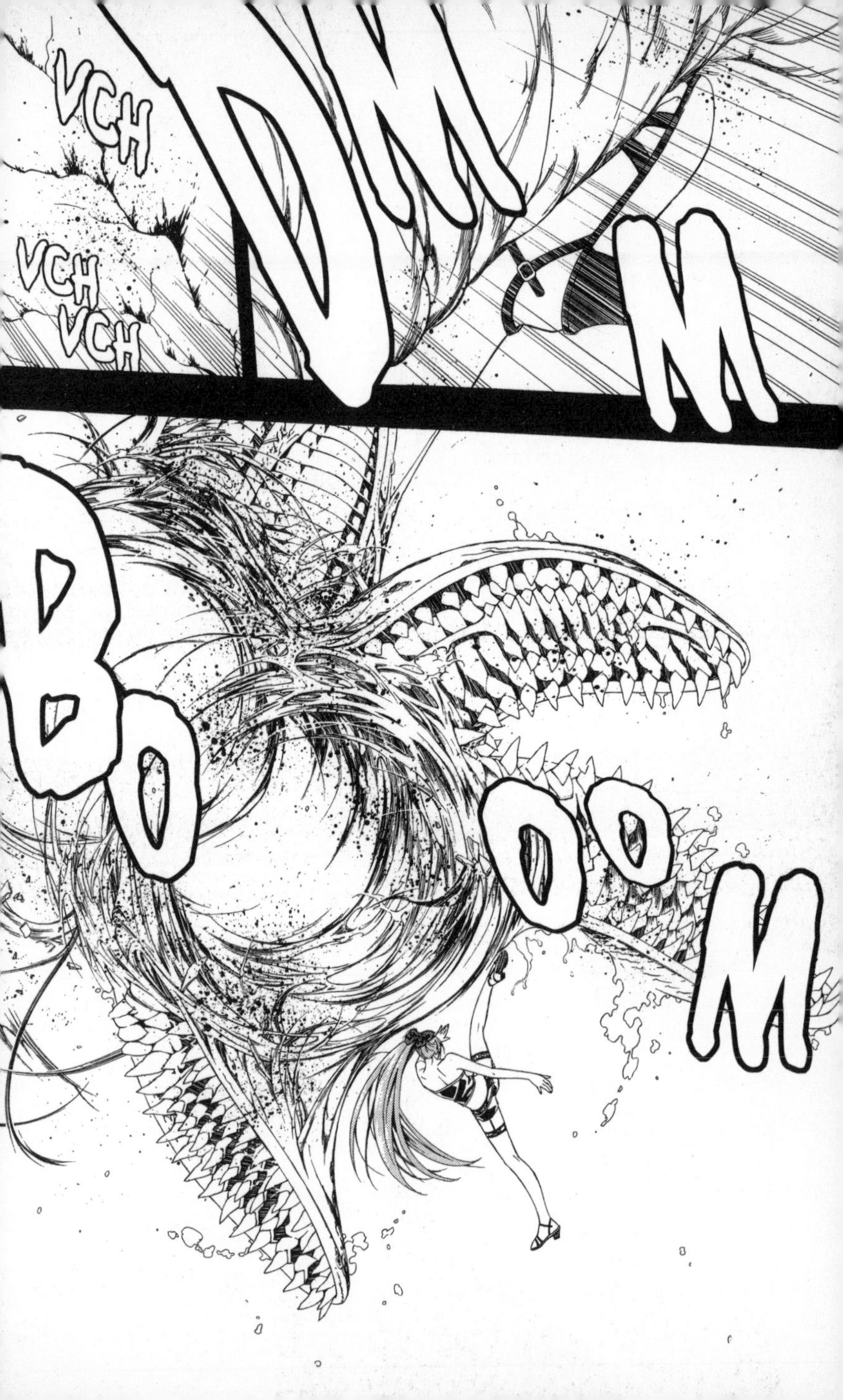
DMM
VCH
VCH
VCH
BOOOM

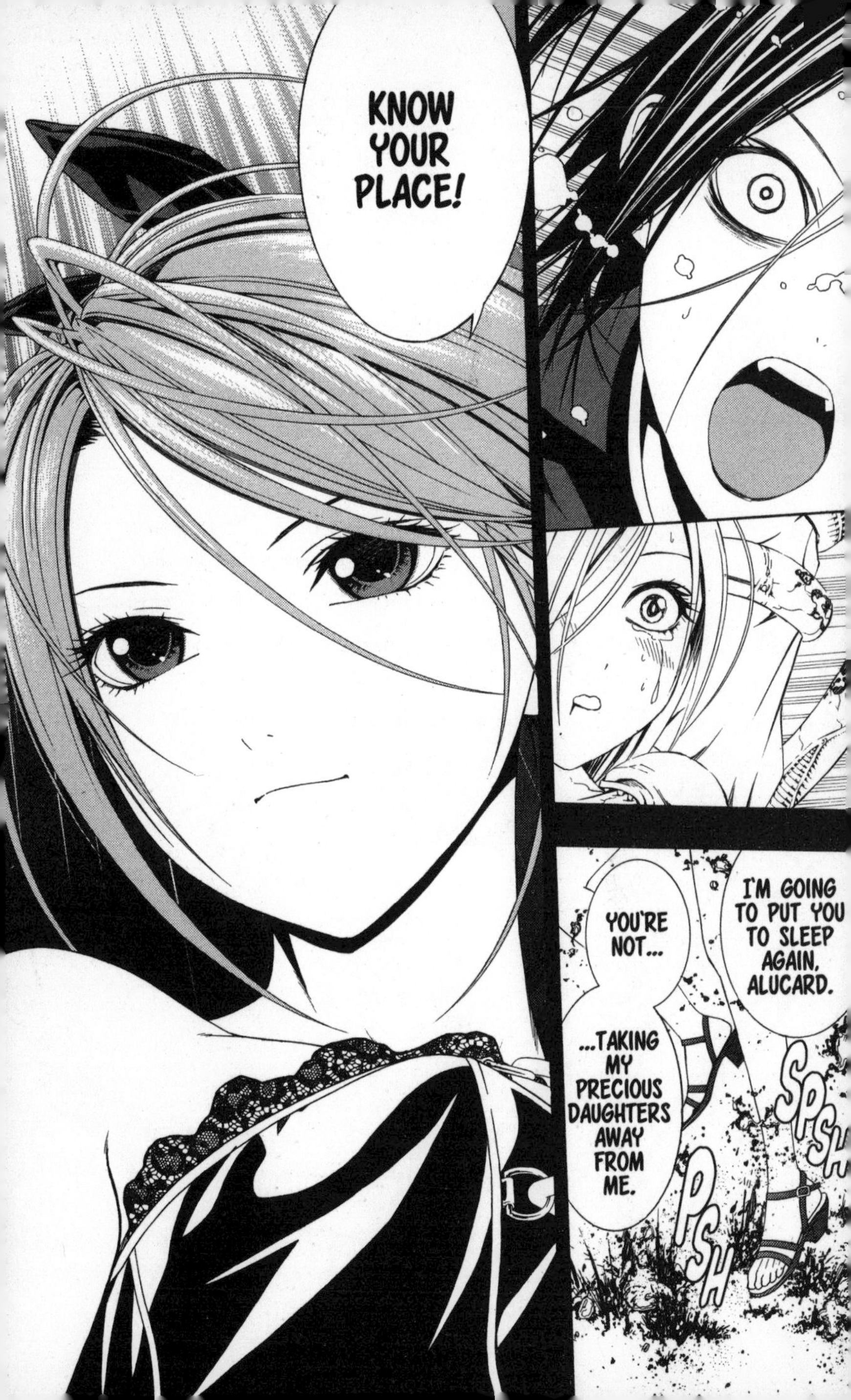
I'M GOING TO PUT YOU TO SLEEP AGAIN, ALUCARD.
YOU'RE NOT...
...TAKING MY PRECIOUS DAUGHTERS AWAY FROM ME.
SPSH
PSH
KNOW YOUR PLACE!

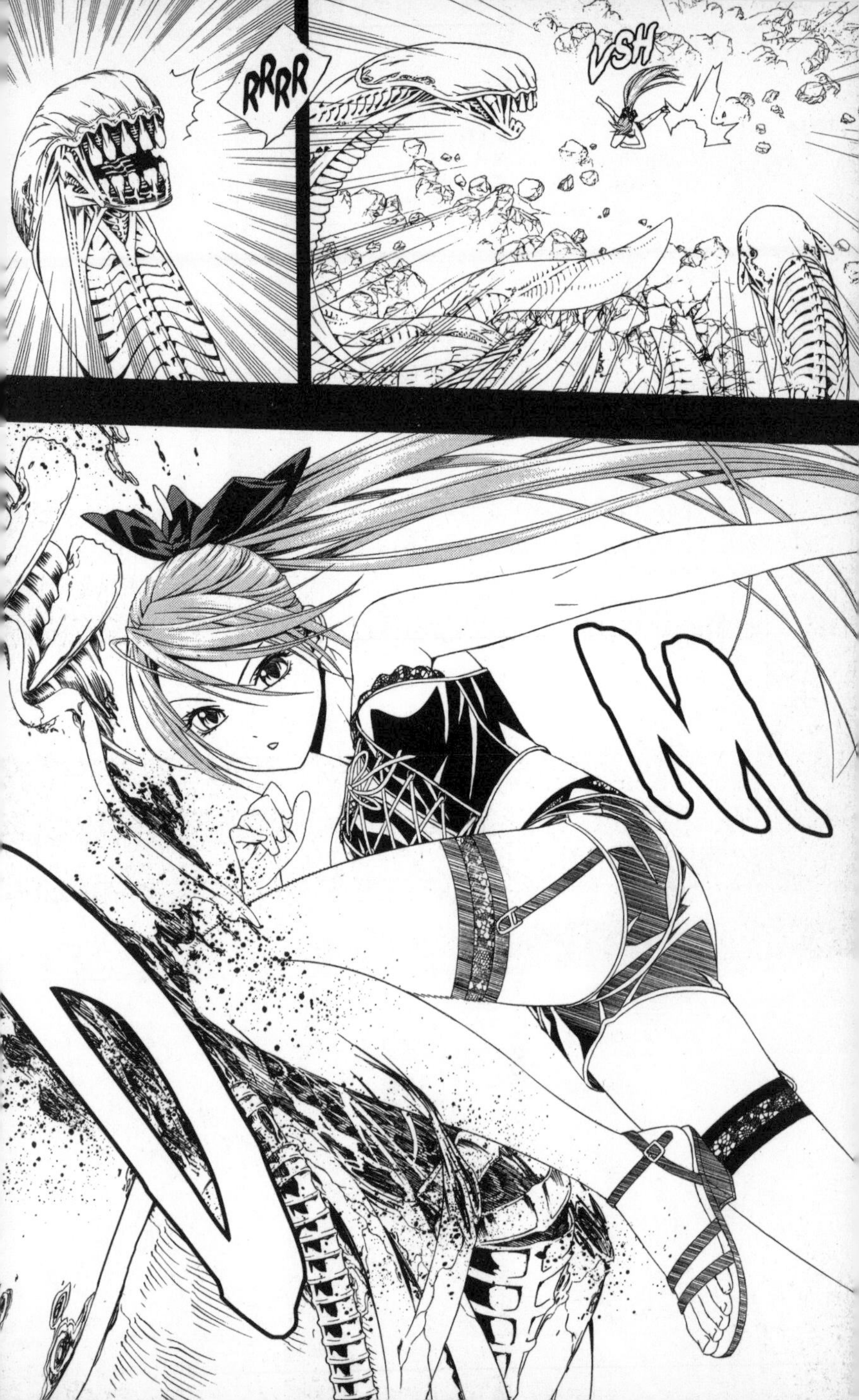
VSH
RRRR
M

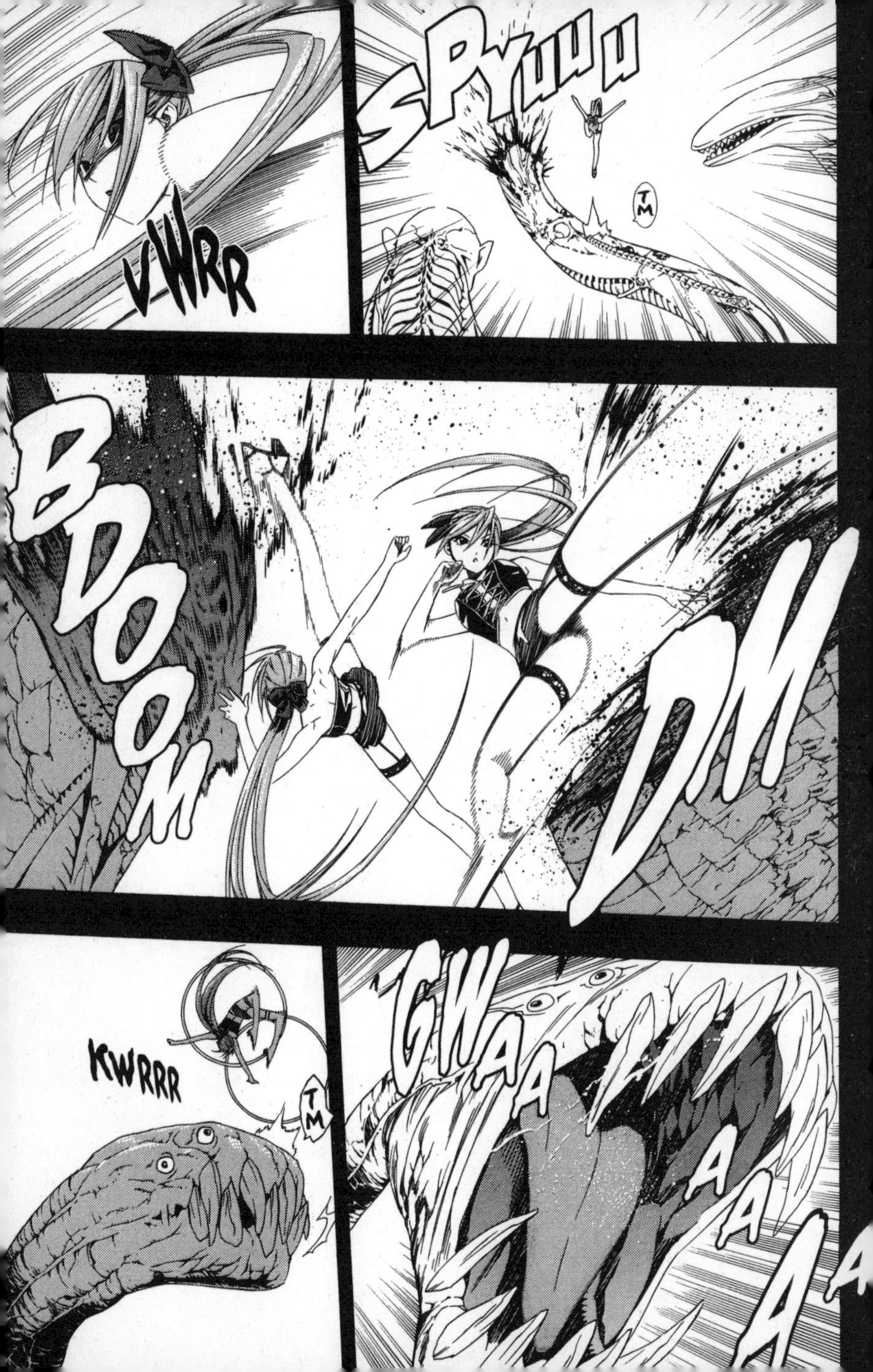
SPYUUU
TM
VWRR
DM
BDOOM
GWAAAAAAA
KWRRR
TM

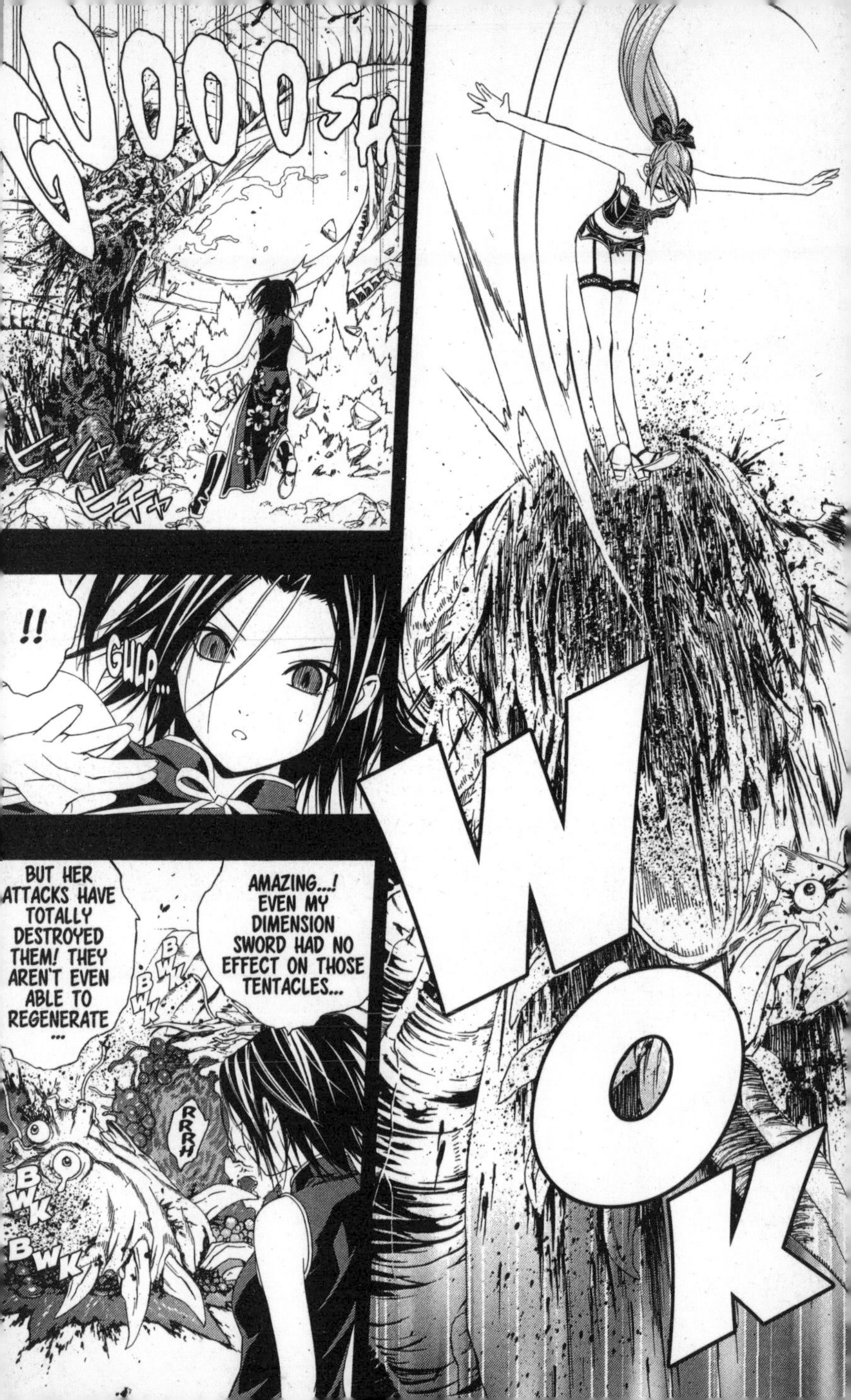
WOK
GOOOOSH
ビチャ
ビチャ
!!
GULP...
AMAZING...! EVEN MY DIMENSION SWORD HAD NO EFFECT ON THOSE TENTACLES...
BUT HER ATTACKS HAVE TOTALLY DESTROYED THEM! THEY AREN'T EVEN ABLE TO REGENERATE ...
BWK BWK
RRRH
BWK
BWK

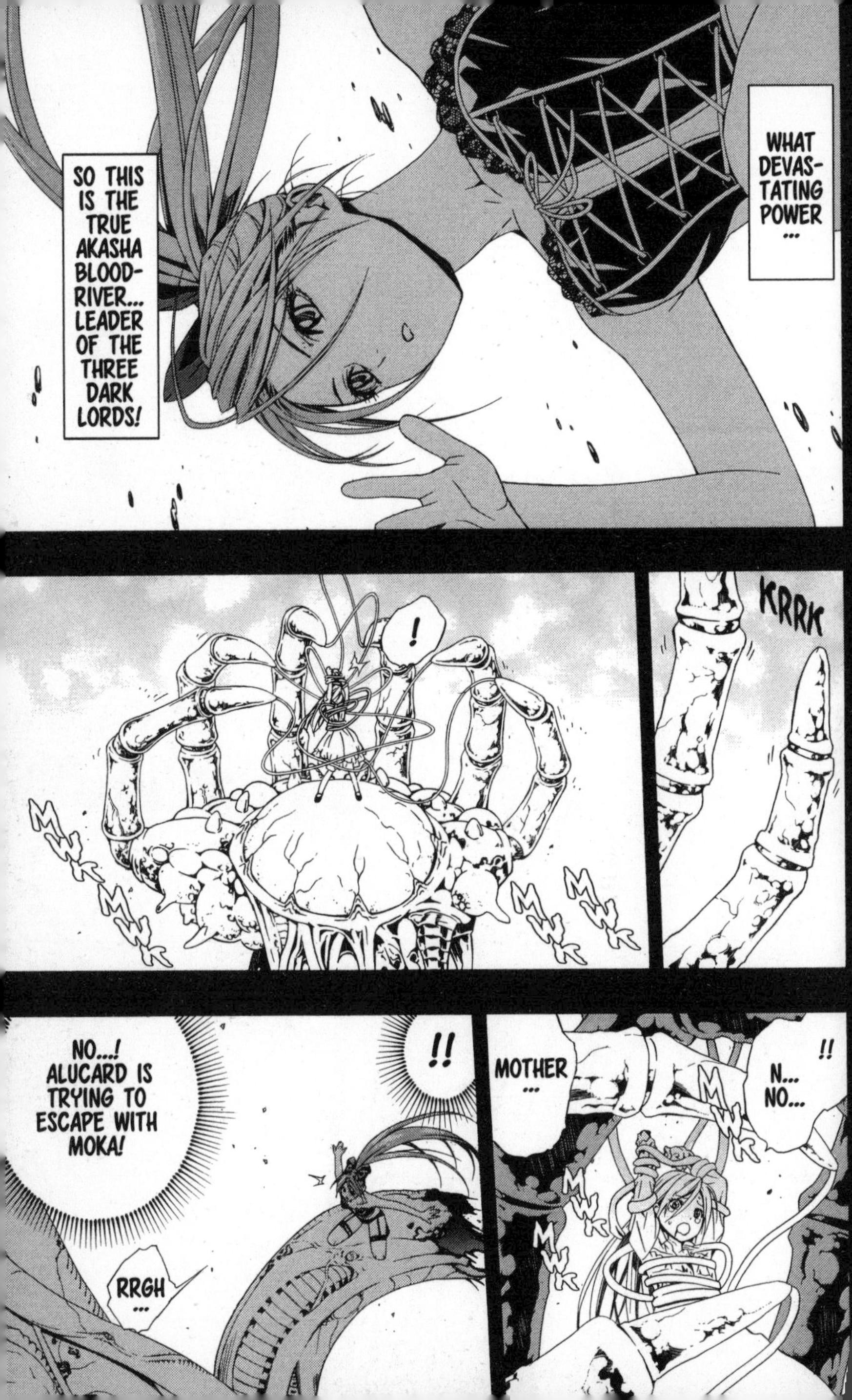
WHAT DEVAS-TATING POWER...
SO THIS IS THE TRUE AKASHA BLOOD-RIVER... LEADER OF THE THREE DARK LORDS!
KRRK
!
MWK
MWK
MWK
MWK
!!
N... NO...
MWK
MOTHER...
MWK
MWK
!!
NO...! ALUCARD IS TRYING TO ESCAPE WITH MOKA!
RRGH...

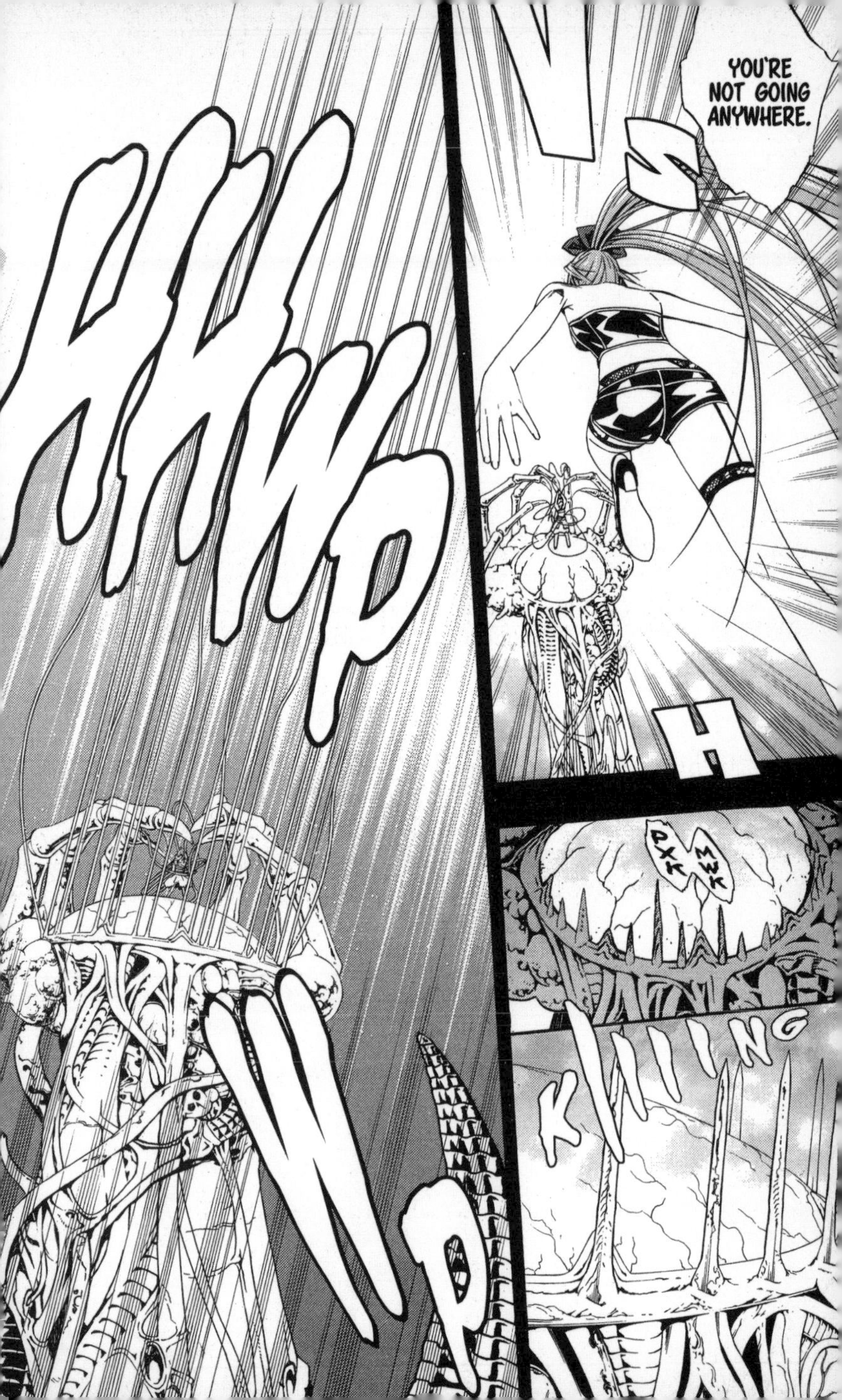
YOU'RE NOT GOING ANYWHERE.
S
H
PXK
MWK
KIIING
HHWP
WP

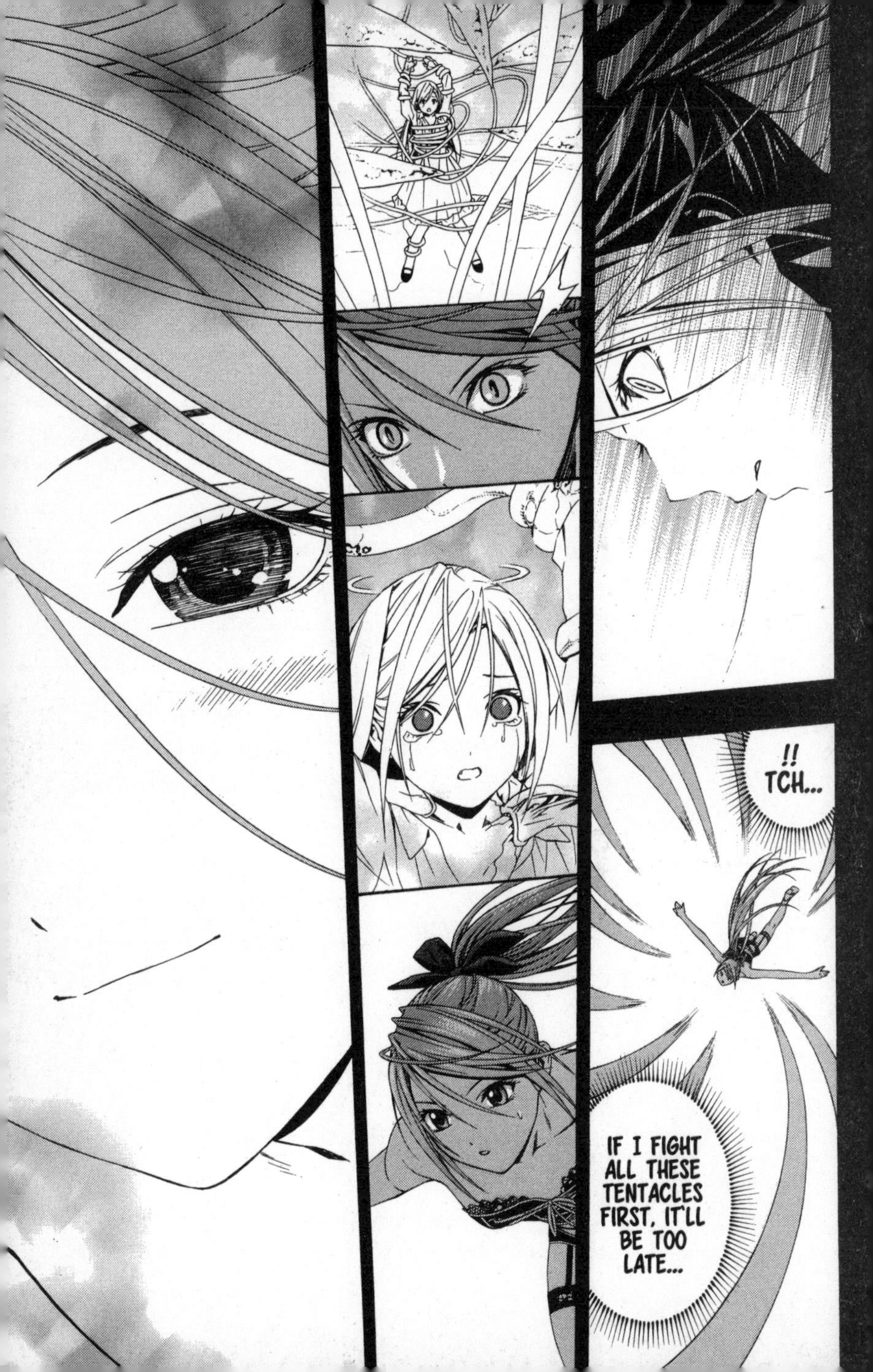
!!
TCH...
IF I FIGHT ALL THESE TENTACLES FIRST, IT'LL BE TOO LATE...

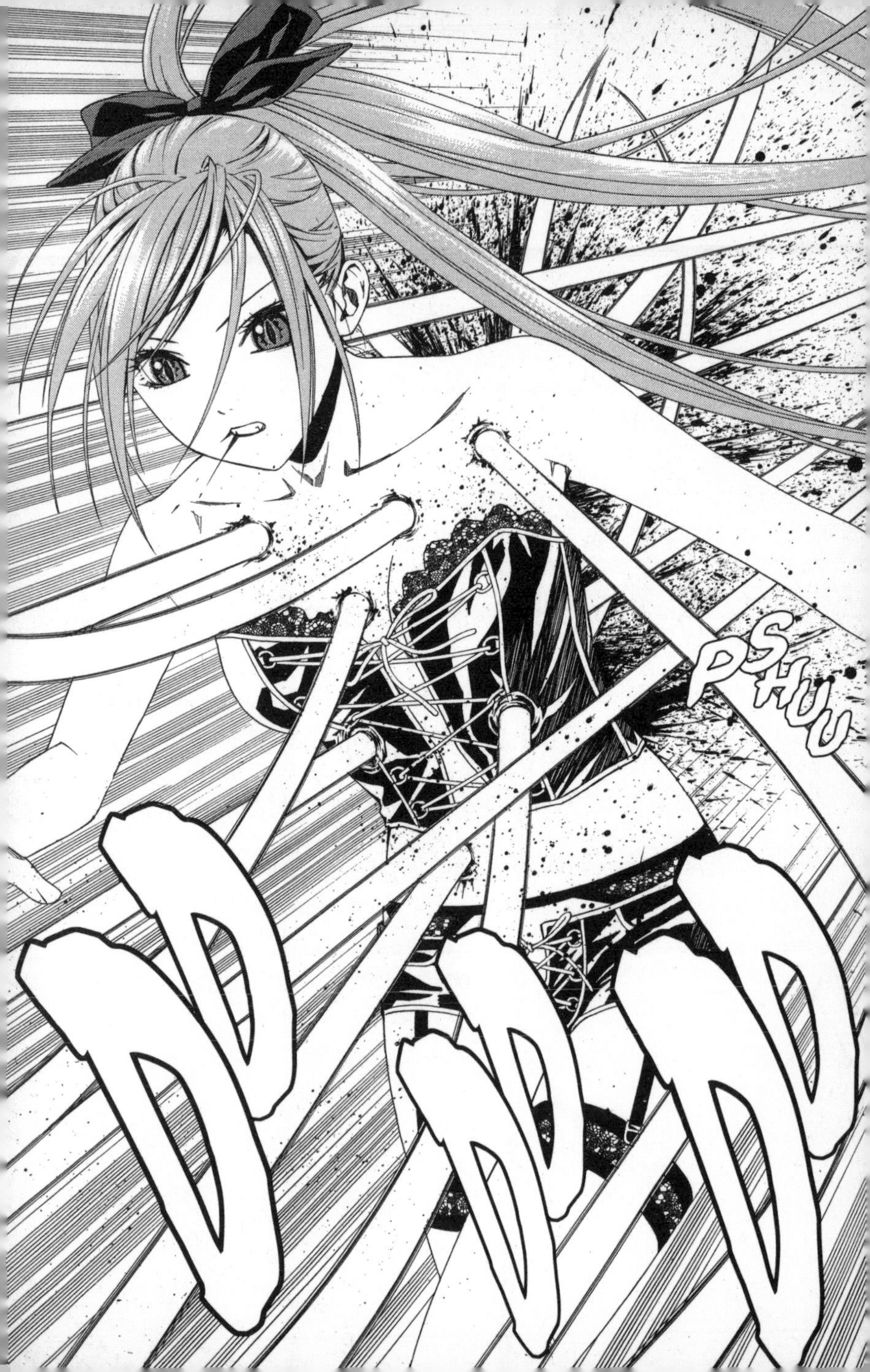
PSHUU

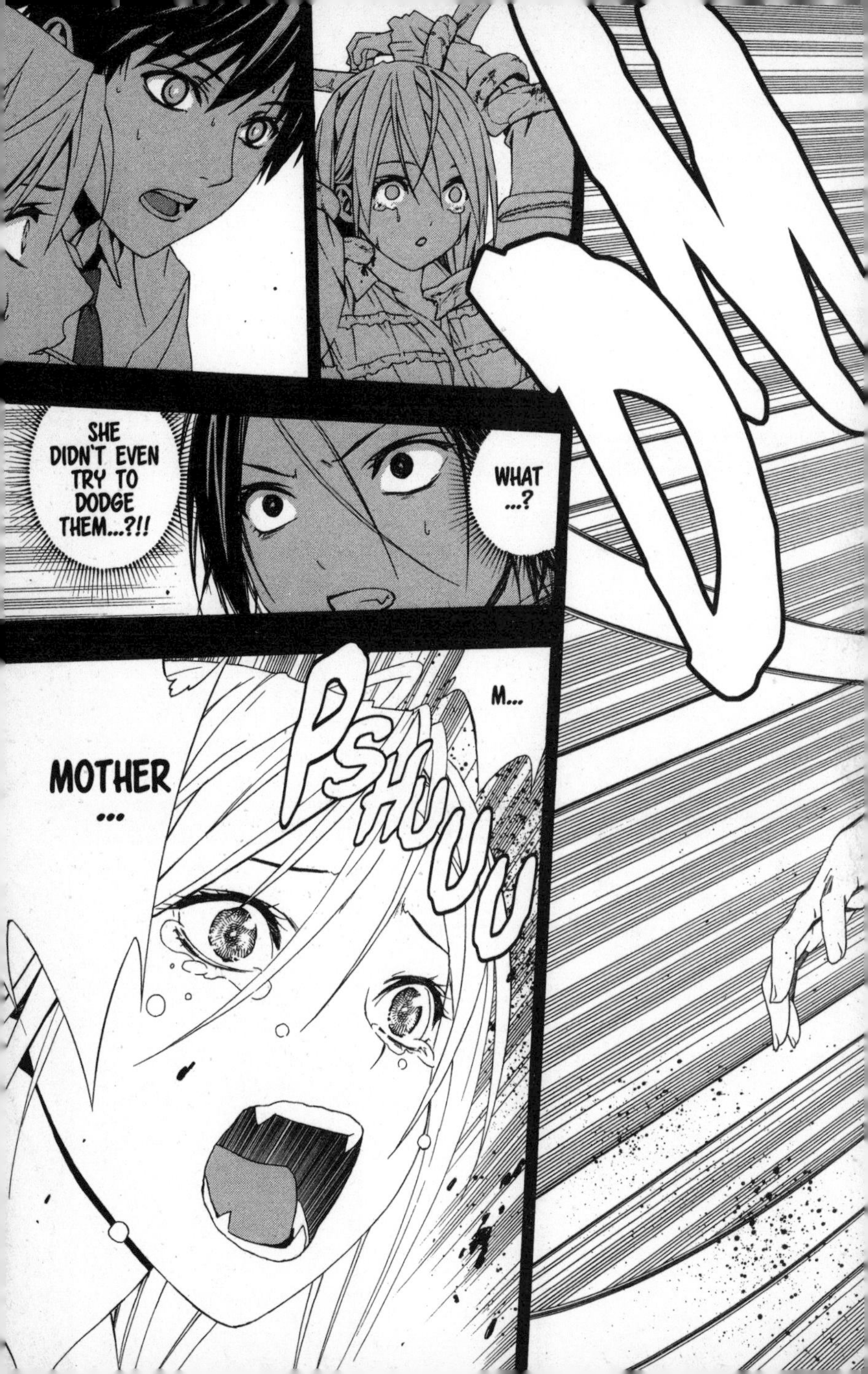
WHAT ...?
SHE DIDN'T EVEN TRY TO DODGE THEM...?!!
M...
PSHUUU
MOTHER ...

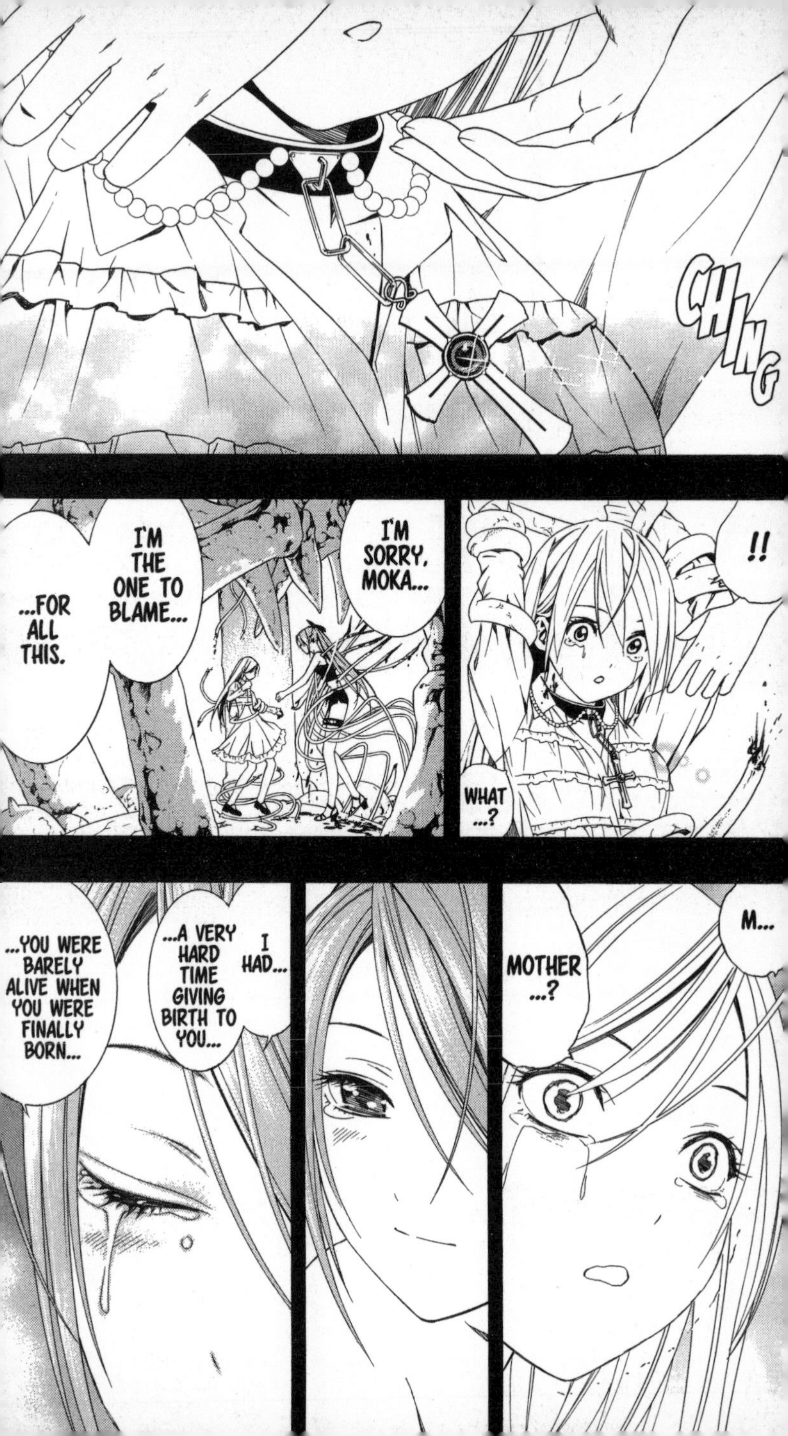
CHING
!!
WHAT ...?
I'M SORRY, MOKA...
I'M THE ONE TO BLAME...
...FOR ALL THIS.
M...
MOTHER ...?
I HAD...
...A VERY HARD TIME GIVING BIRTH TO YOU...
...YOU WERE BARELY ALIVE WHEN YOU WERE FINALLY BORN...

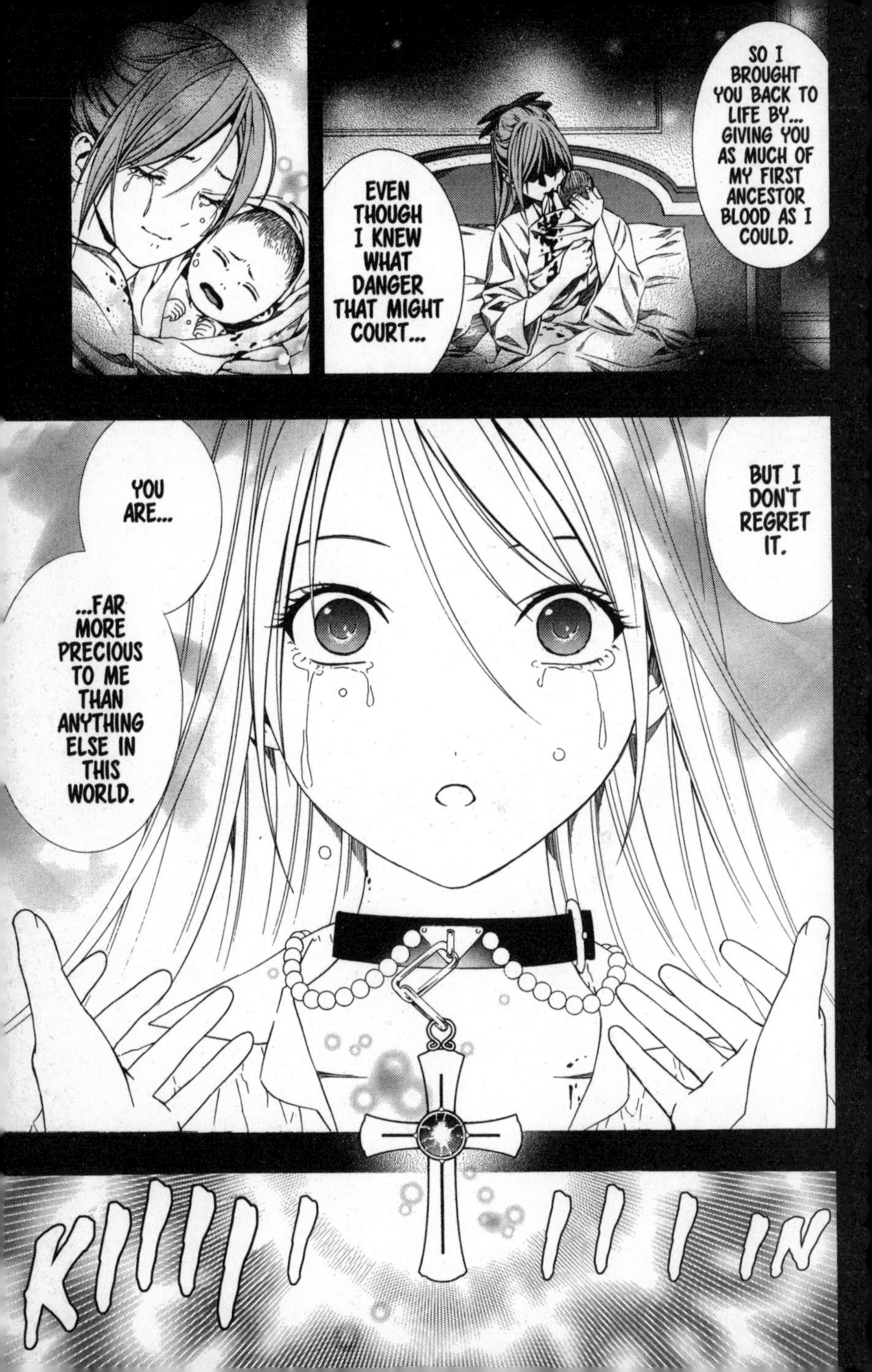
SO I BROUGHT YOU BACK TO LIFE BY... GIVING YOU AS MUCH OF MY FIRST ANCESTOR BLOOD AS I COULD.
EVEN THOUGH I KNEW WHAT DANGER THAT MIGHT COURT...
BUT I DON'T REGRET IT.
YOU ARE...
...FAR MORE PRECIOUS TO ME THAN ANYTHING ELSE IN THIS WORLD.
KIIIII I I I I IN

# 34: The Secret of the Seal

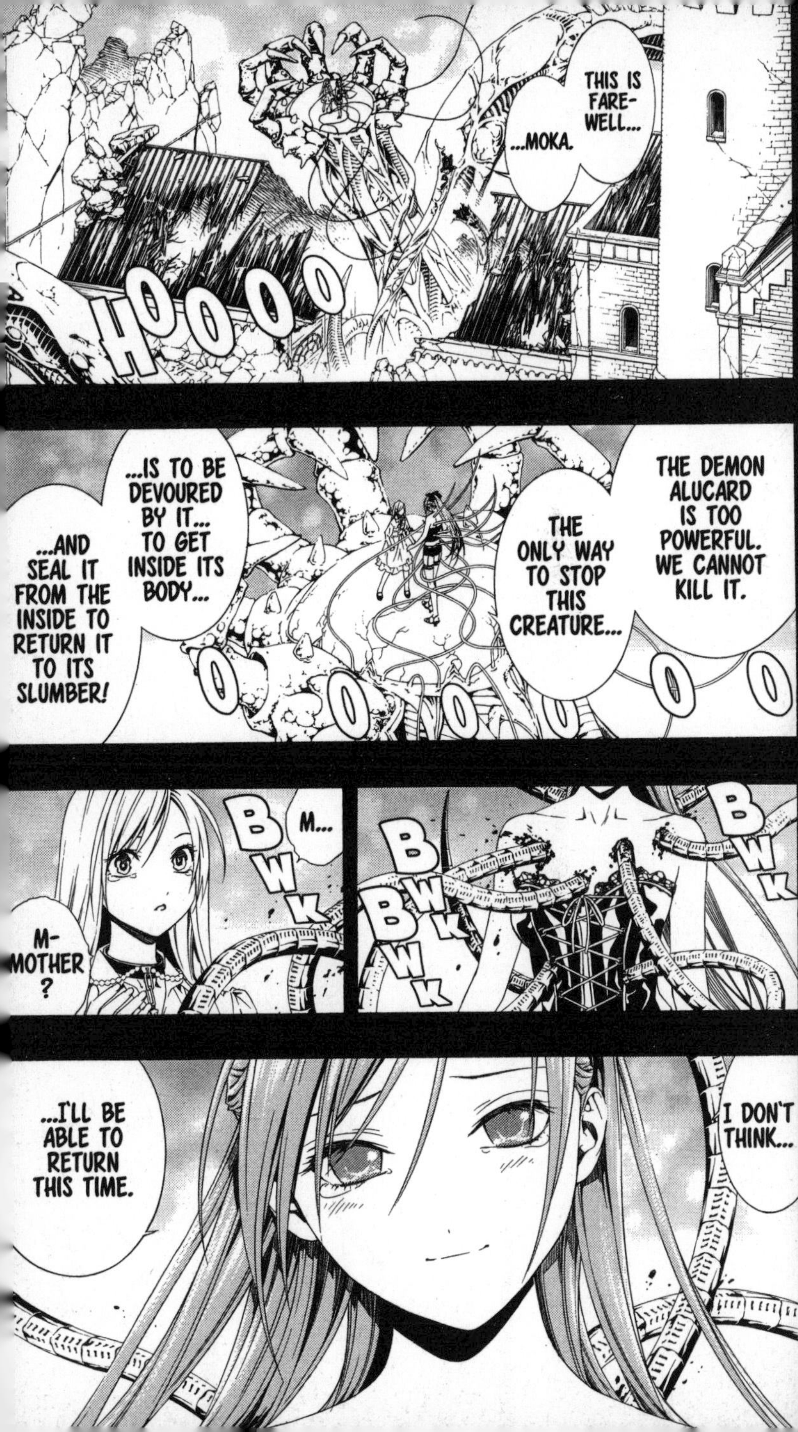
THIS IS FAREWELL...
...MOKA.
HOOOO
THE DEMON ALUCARD IS TOO POWERFUL. WE CANNOT KILL IT.
THE ONLY WAY TO STOP THIS CREATURE...
...IS TO BE DEVOURED BY IT... TO GET INSIDE ITS BODY...
...AND SEAL IT FROM THE INSIDE TO RETURN IT TO ITS SLUMBER!
OOOOOO
BWK
BWK
BWK
BWK
M...
BWK
M-MOTHER?
I DON'T THINK...
...I'LL BE ABLE TO RETURN THIS TIME.

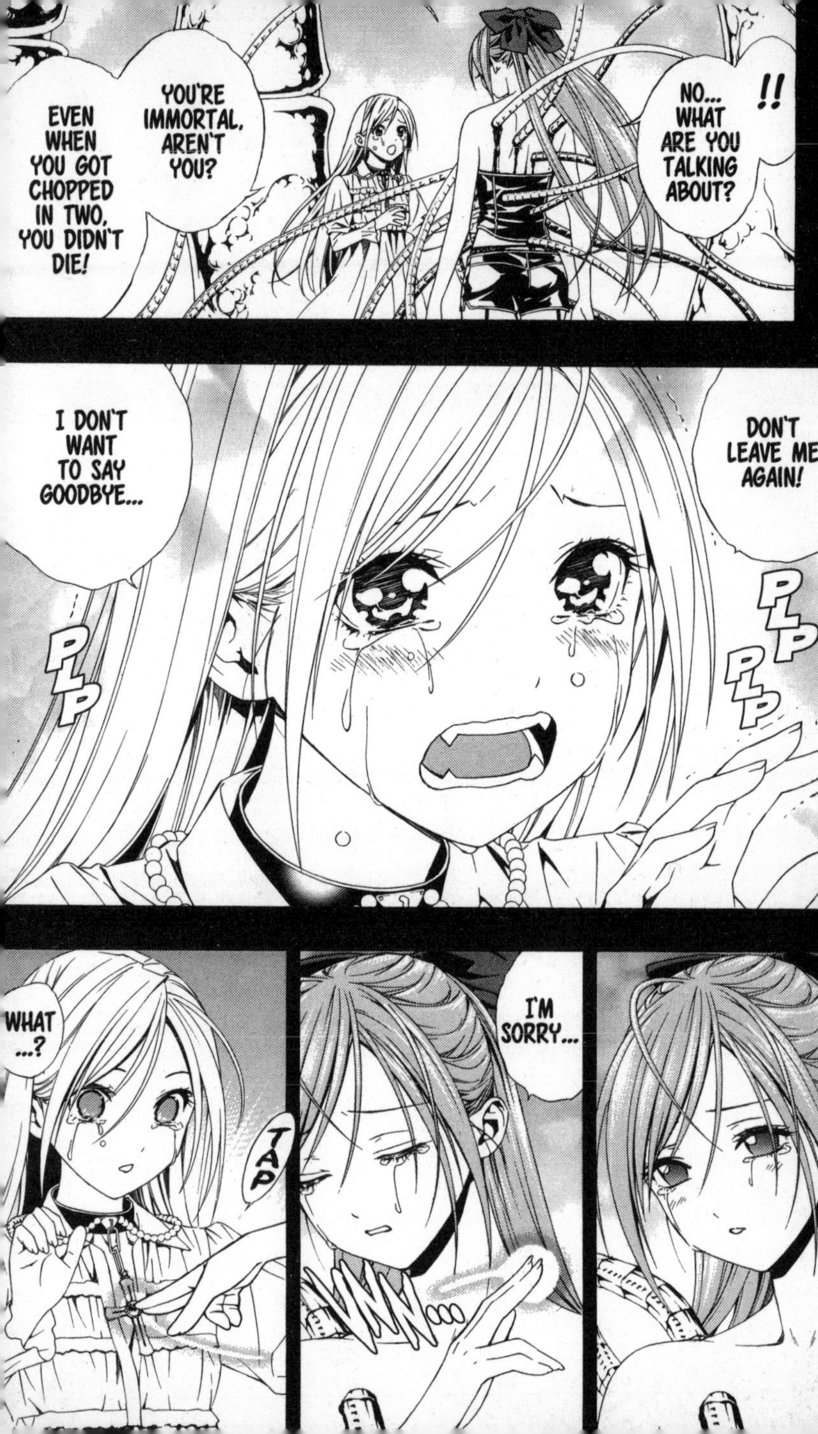
!!
NO... WHAT ARE YOU TALKING ABOUT?
YOU'RE IMMORTAL, AREN'T YOU?
EVEN WHEN YOU GOT CHOPPED IN TWO, YOU DIDN'T DIE!
DON'T LEAVE ME AGAIN!
PLP
PLP
I DON'T WANT TO SAY GOODBYE...
PLP
I'M SORRY...
WHAT ...?
TAP

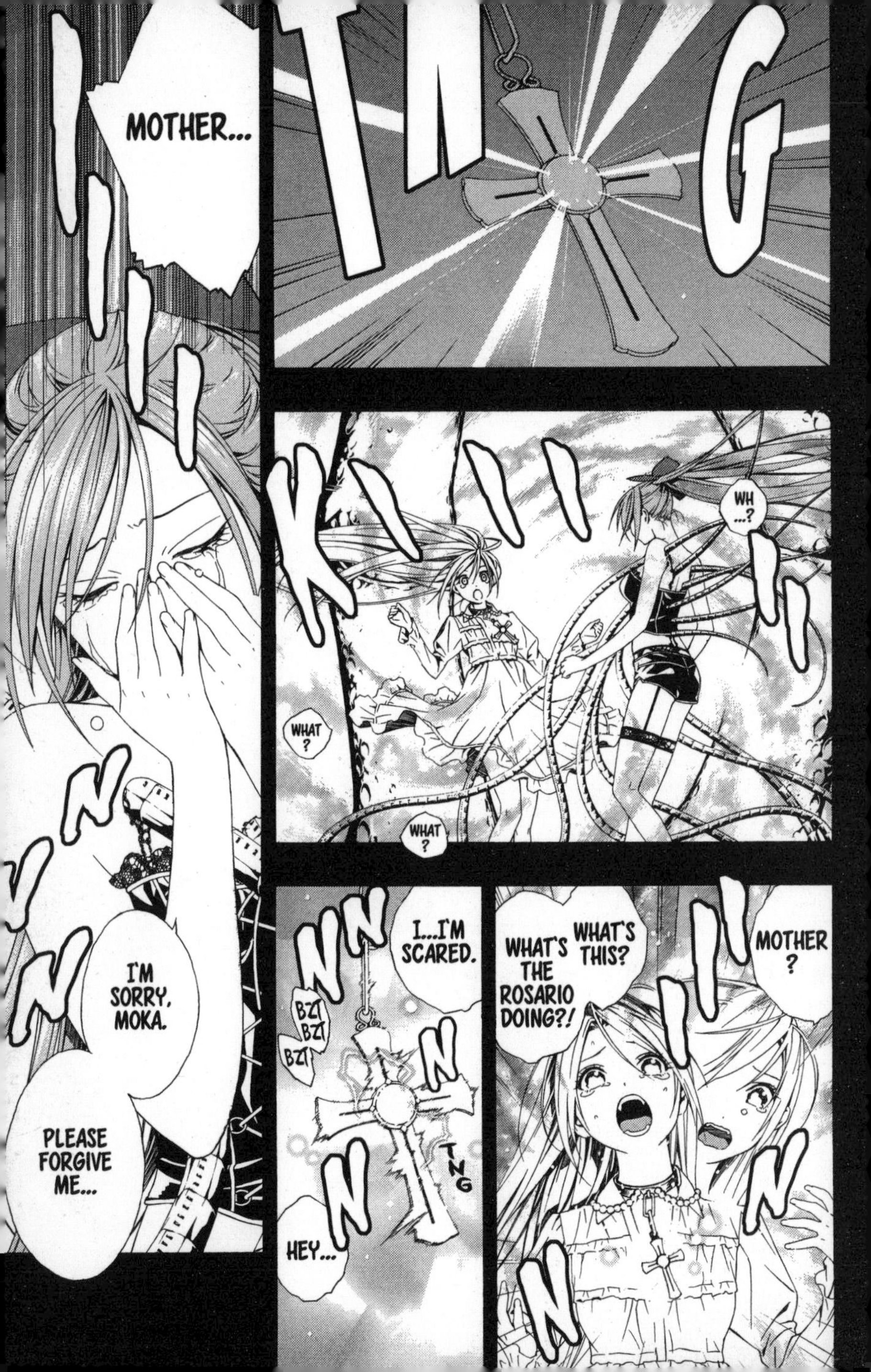
TNG
WH ...?
WHAT ?
WHAT ?
MOTHER ?
WHAT'S THIS?
WHAT'S THE ROSARIO DOING?!
I...I'M SCARED.
BZT BZT BZT
TNG
HEY...
MOTHER...
I'M SORRY, MOKA.
PLEASE FORGIVE ME...

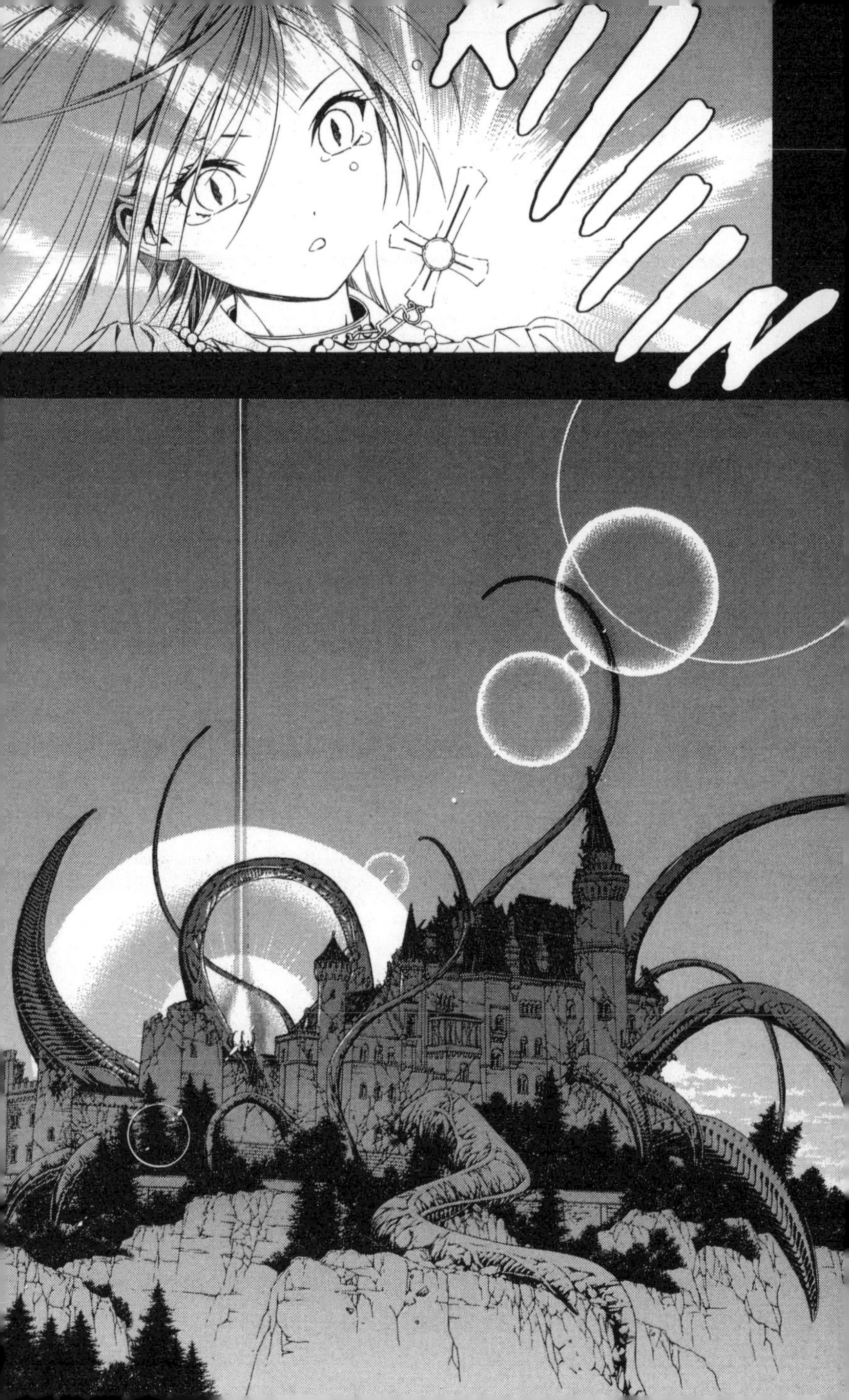

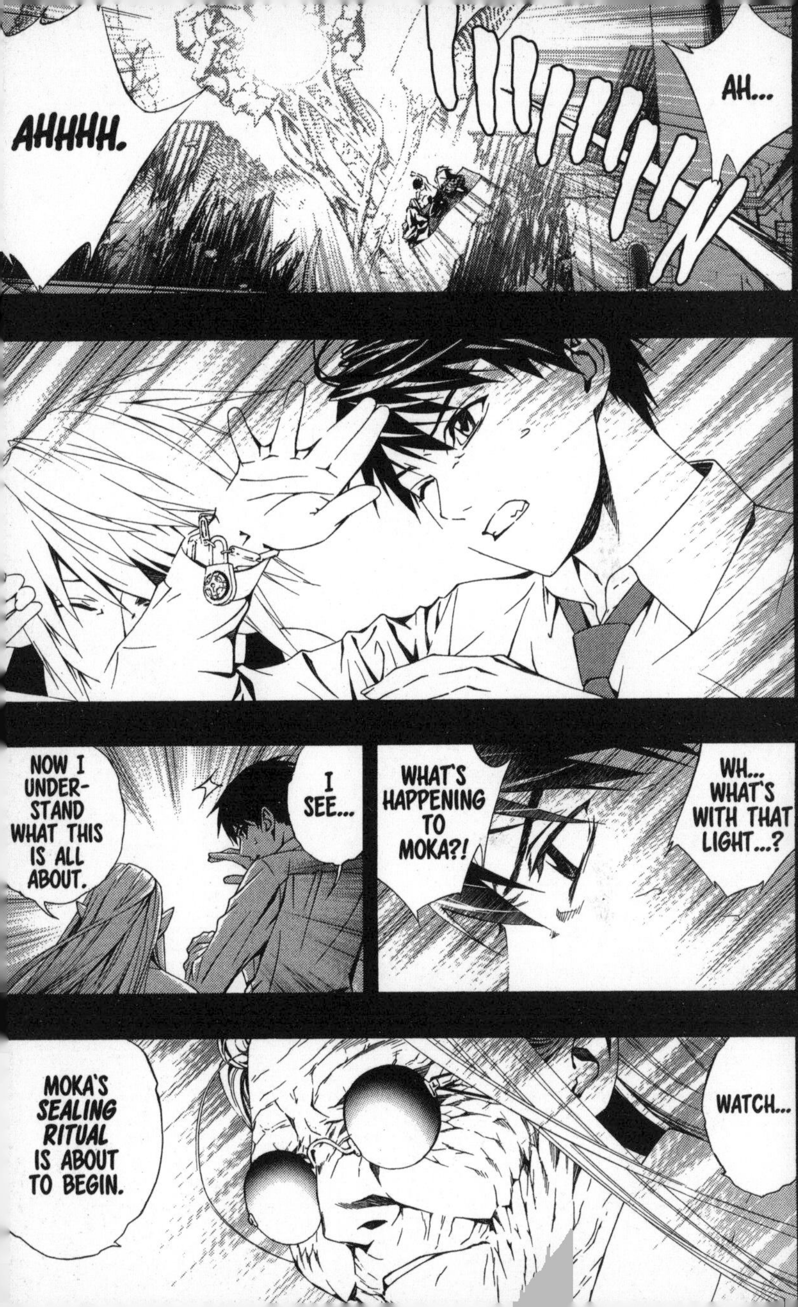
AH...
AHHHH.
WH... WHAT'S WITH THAT LIGHT...?
WHAT'S HAPPENING TO MOKA?!
I SEE...
NOW I UNDER-STAND WHAT THIS IS ALL ABOUT.
WATCH...
MOKA'S SEALING RITUAL IS ABOUT TO BEGIN.

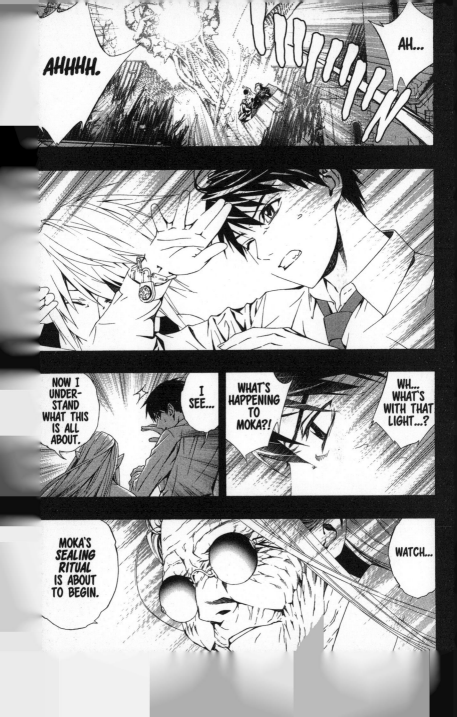

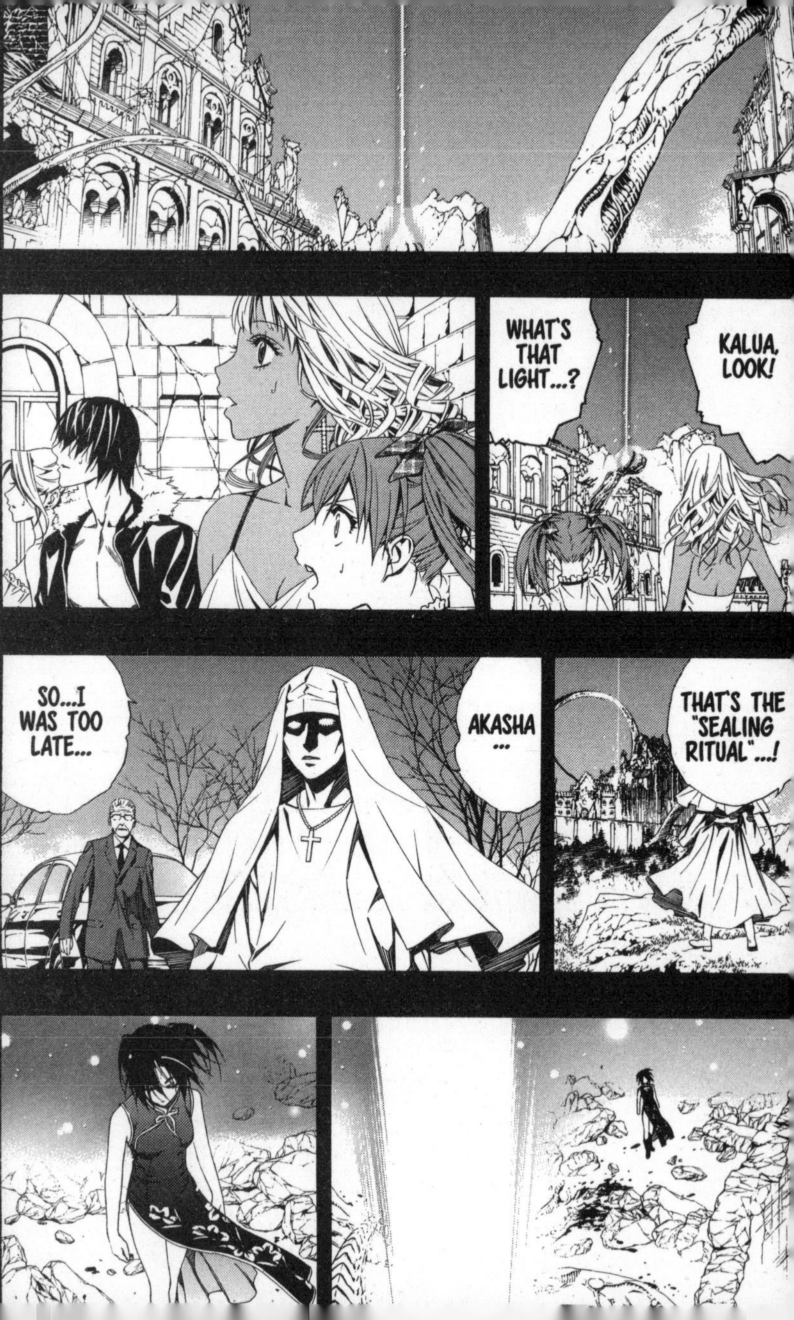
KALUA, LOOK!
WHAT'S THAT LIGHT...?
THAT'S THE "SEALING RITUAL"...!
AKASHA ...
SO...I WAS TOO LATE...

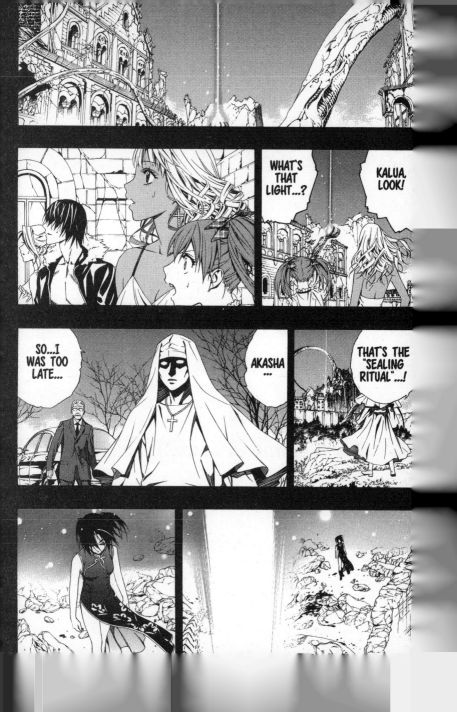

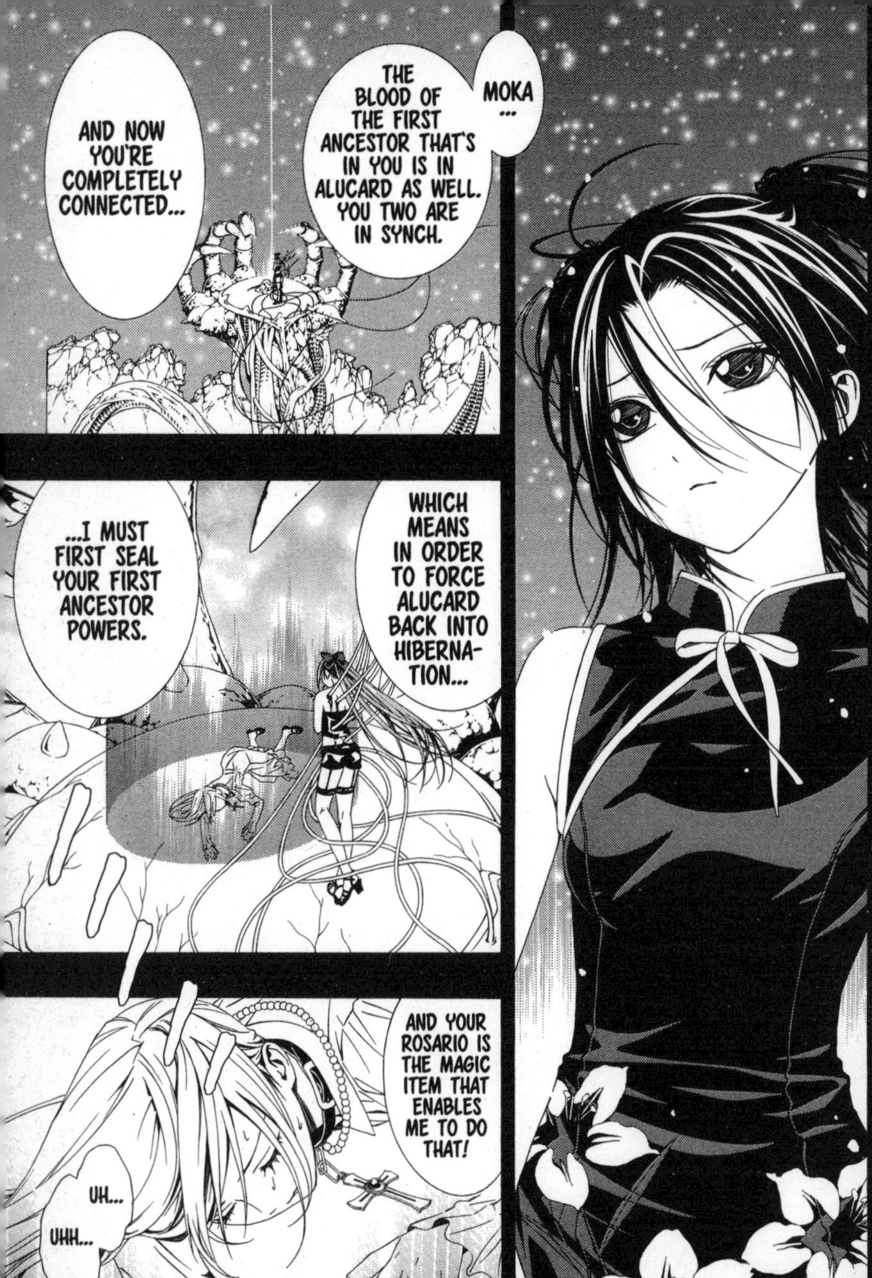
MOKA...
THE BLOOD OF THE FIRST ANCESTOR THAT'S IN YOU IS IN ALUCARD AS WELL. YOU TWO ARE IN SYNCH.
AND NOW YOU'RE COMPLETELY CONNECTED...
WHICH MEANS IN ORDER TO FORCE ALUCARD BACK INTO HIBERNA-TION...
...I MUST FIRST SEAL YOUR FIRST ANCESTOR POWERS.
AND YOUR ROSARIO IS THE MAGIC ITEM THAT ENABLES ME TO DO THAT!
UH...
UHH...

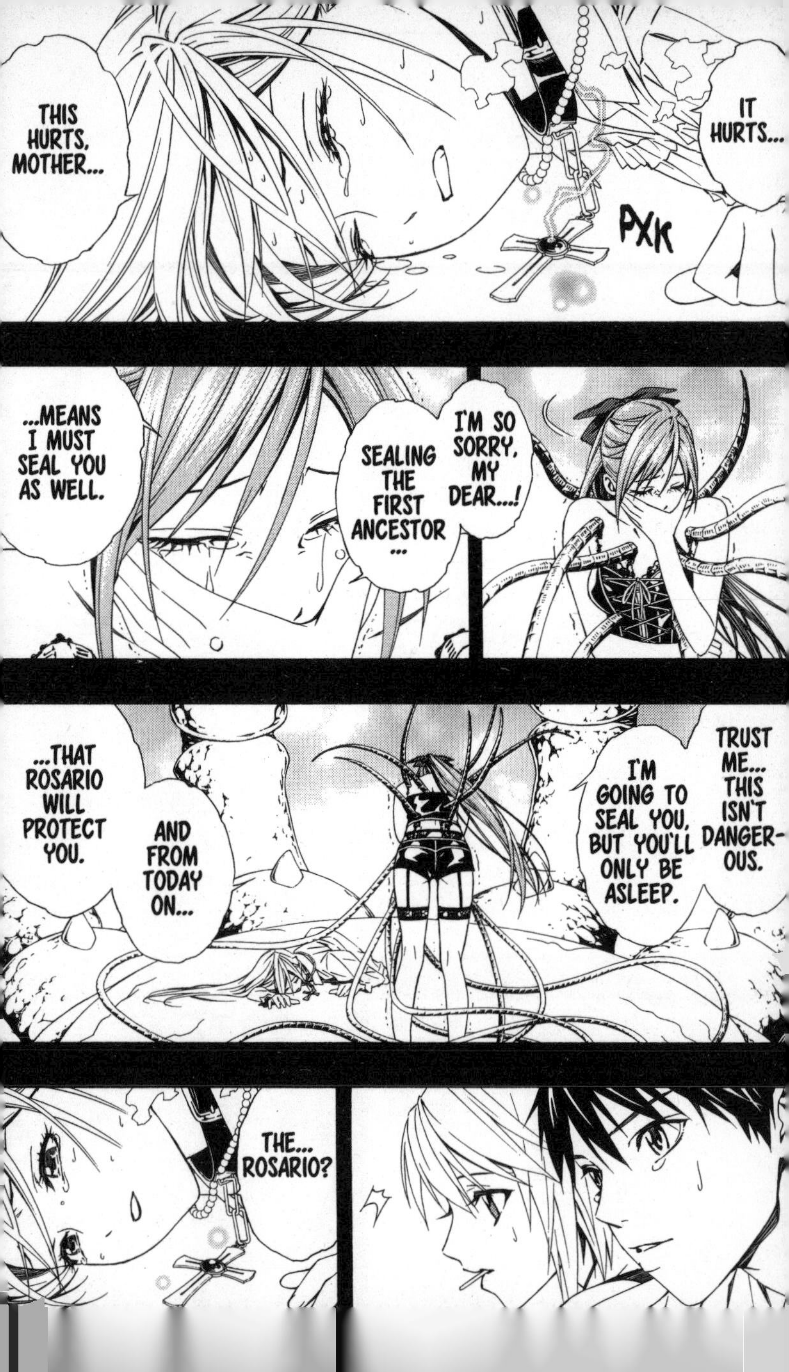
IT HURTS...
PXK
THIS HURTS, MOTHER...
I'M SO SORRY, MY DEAR...!
SEALING THE FIRST ANCESTOR...
...MEANS I MUST SEAL YOU AS WELL.
TRUST ME... THIS ISN'T DANGER-OUS.
I'M GOING TO SEAL YOU, BUT YOU'LL ONLY BE ASLEEP.
AND FROM TODAY ON...
...THAT ROSARIO WILL PROTECT YOU.
THE... ROSARIO?

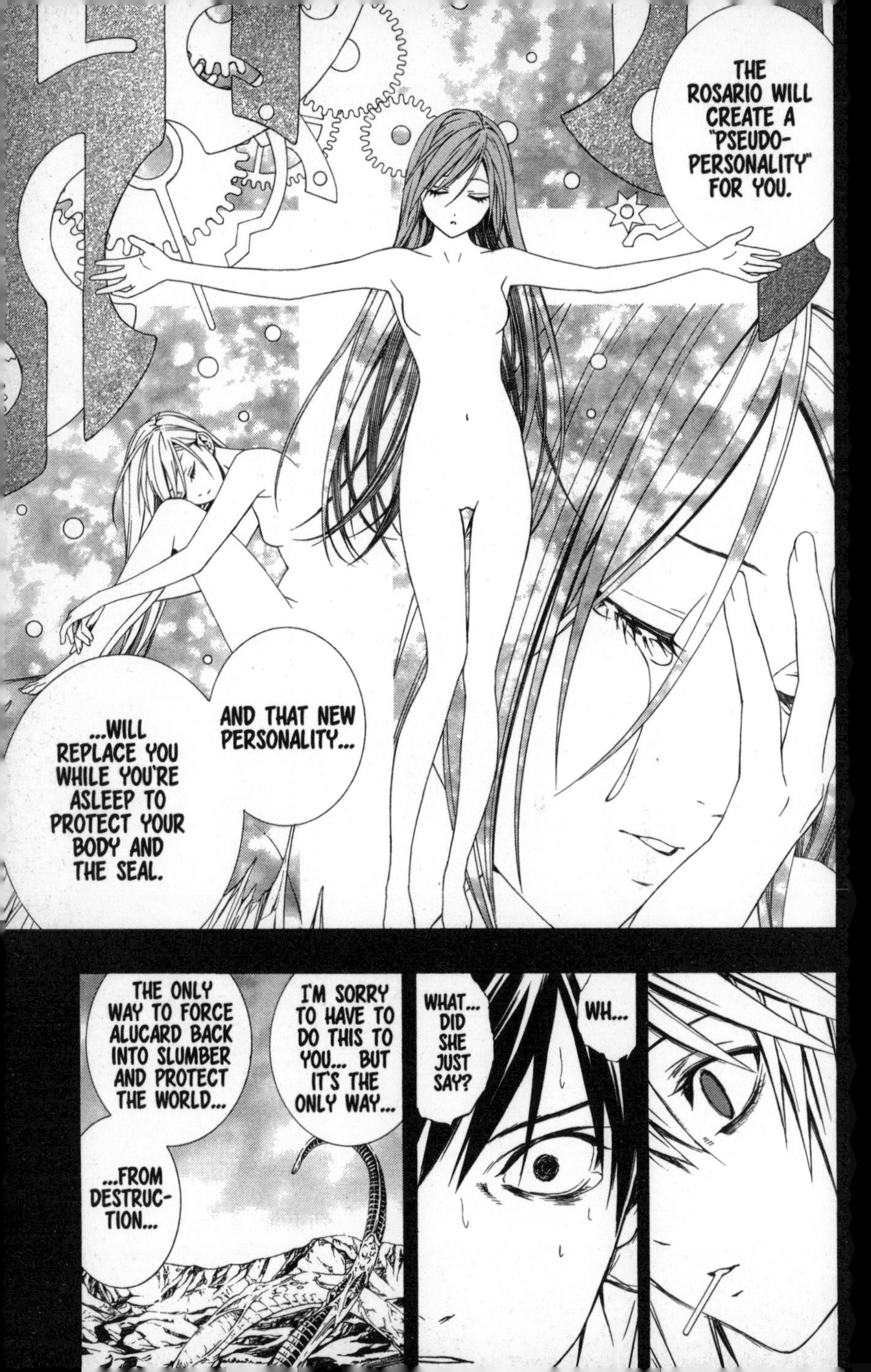
THE ROSARIO WILL CREATE A "PSEUDO-PERSONALITY" FOR YOU.
AND THAT NEW PERSONALITY...
...WILL REPLACE YOU WHILE YOU'RE ASLEEP TO PROTECT YOUR BODY AND THE SEAL.
WH...
WHAT... DID SHE JUST SAY?
I'M SORRY TO HAVE TO DO THIS TO YOU... BUT IT'S THE ONLY WAY...
THE ONLY WAY TO FORCE ALUCARD BACK INTO SLUMBER AND PROTECT THE WORLD...
...FROM DESTRUC-TION...

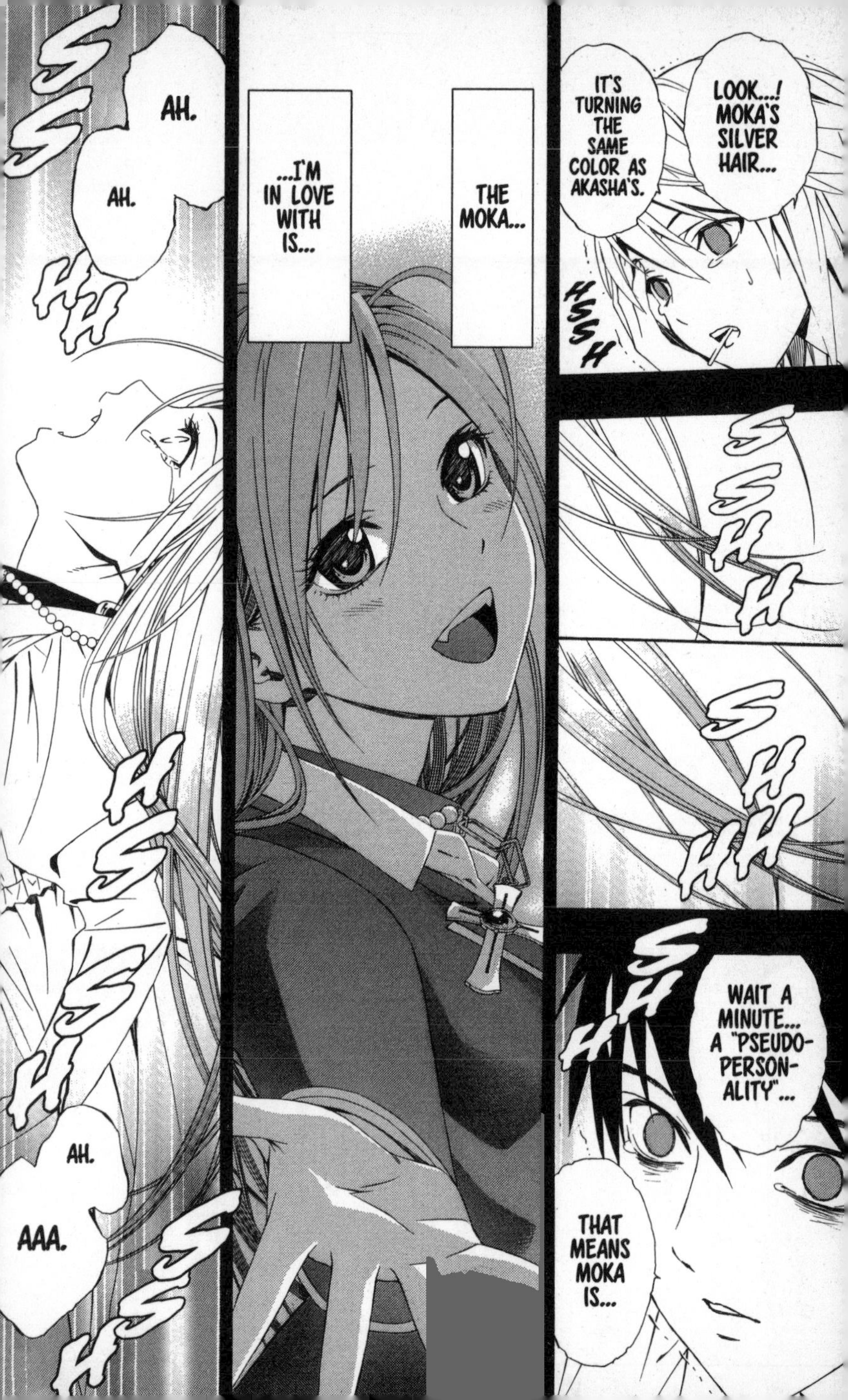
LOOK...! MOKA'S SILVER HAIR...
IT'S TURNING THE SAME COLOR AS AKASHA'S.
HSSH
SSHHH
SSHHH
SHHH
WAIT A MINUTE... A "PSEUDO-PERSONALITY"...
THAT MEANS MOKA IS...
THE MOKA...
...I'M IN LOVE WITH IS...
SSS
AH.
AH.
HHH
HSSH
SHSH
AH.
AAA.
SSHS

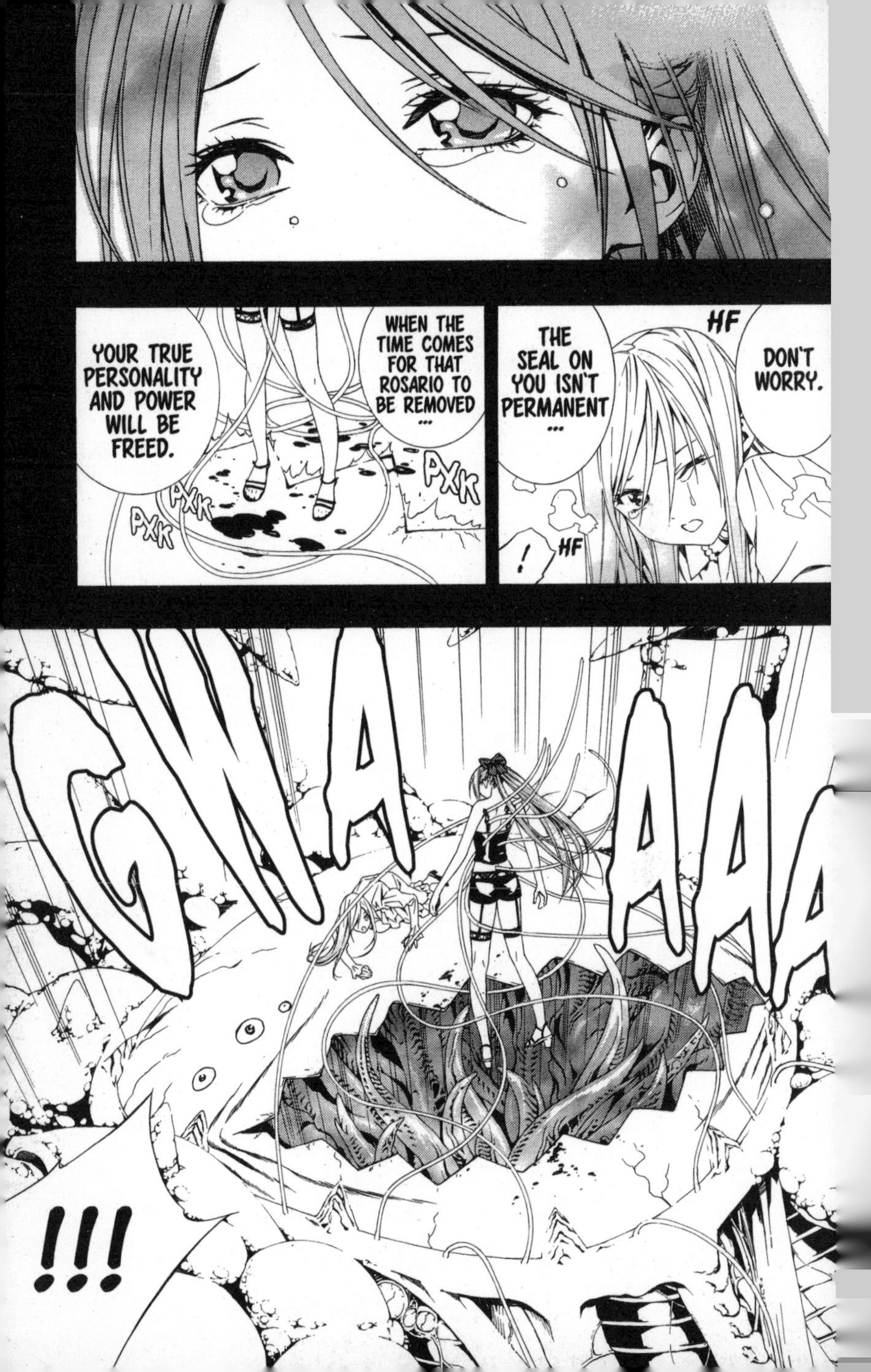
HF
DON'T WORRY.
THE SEAL ON YOU ISN'T PERMANENT ...
!
HF
WHEN THE TIME COMES FOR THAT ROSARIO TO BE REMOVED ...
YOUR TRUE PERSONALITY AND POWER WILL BE FREED.
PXK
PXK
PXK
GWAAA
!!!

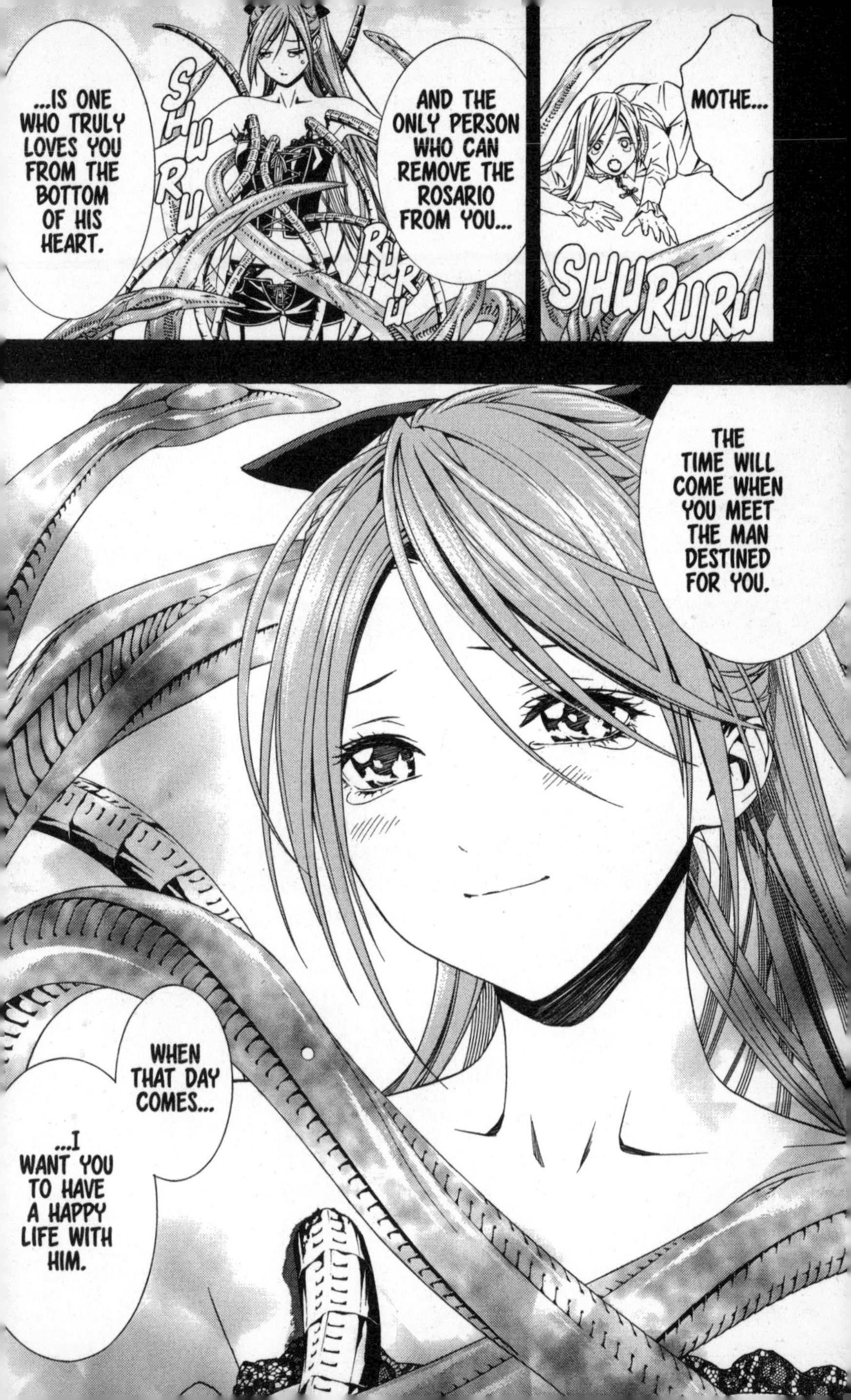
MOTHE...
SHURURU
AND THE ONLY PERSON WHO CAN REMOVE THE ROSARIO FROM YOU...
...IS ONE WHO TRULY LOVES YOU FROM THE BOTTOM OF HIS HEART.
SHURURU
THE TIME WILL COME WHEN YOU MEET THE MAN DESTINED FOR YOU.
WHEN THAT DAY COMES...
...I WANT YOU TO HAVE A HAPPY LIFE WITH HIM.

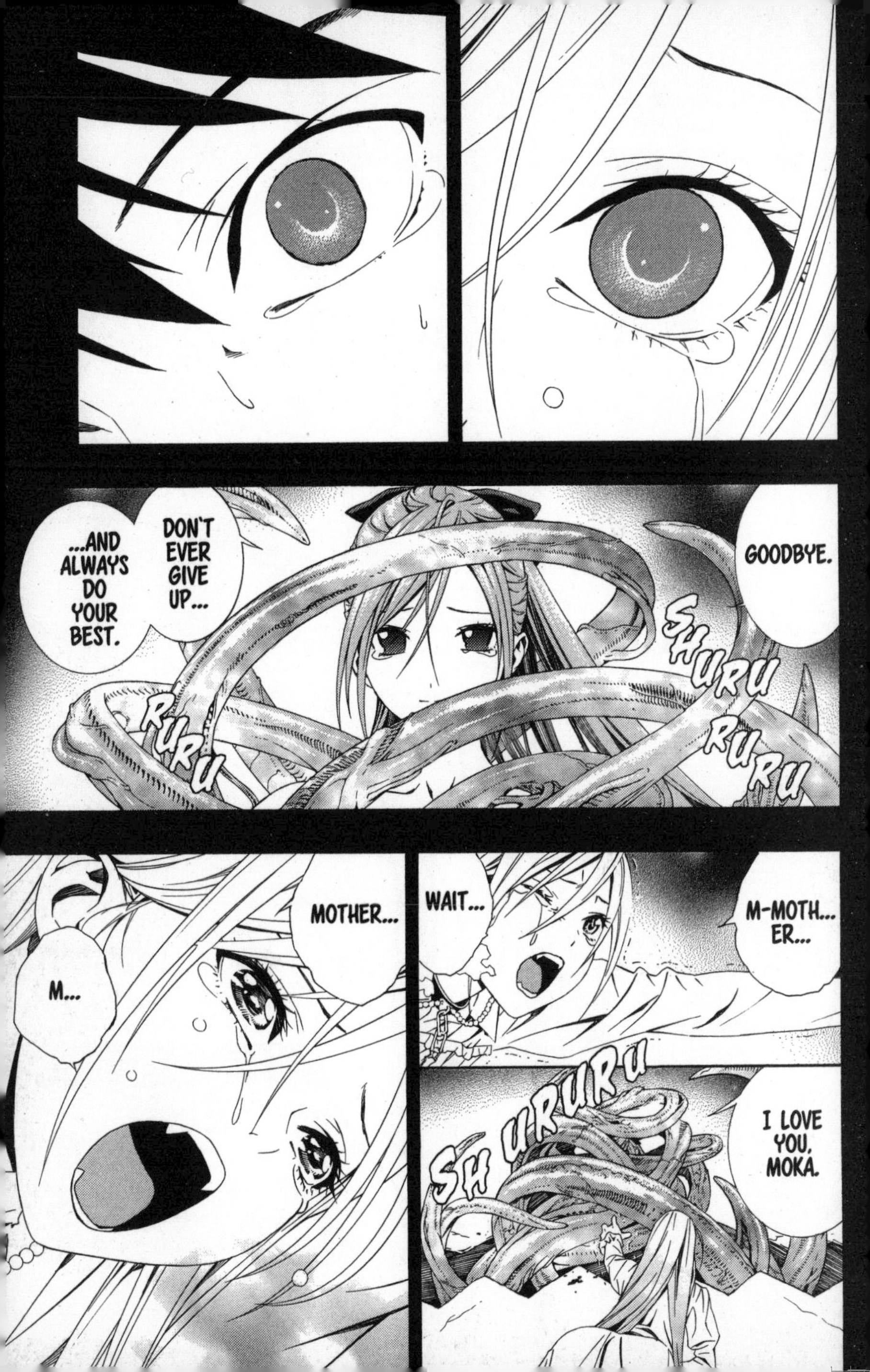
GOODBYE.
SHURU RURU
DON'T EVER GIVE UP...
...AND ALWAYS DO YOUR BEST.
RURU
M-MOTH... ER...
WAIT...
I LOVE YOU, MOKA.
SHURURURU
MOTHER...
M...

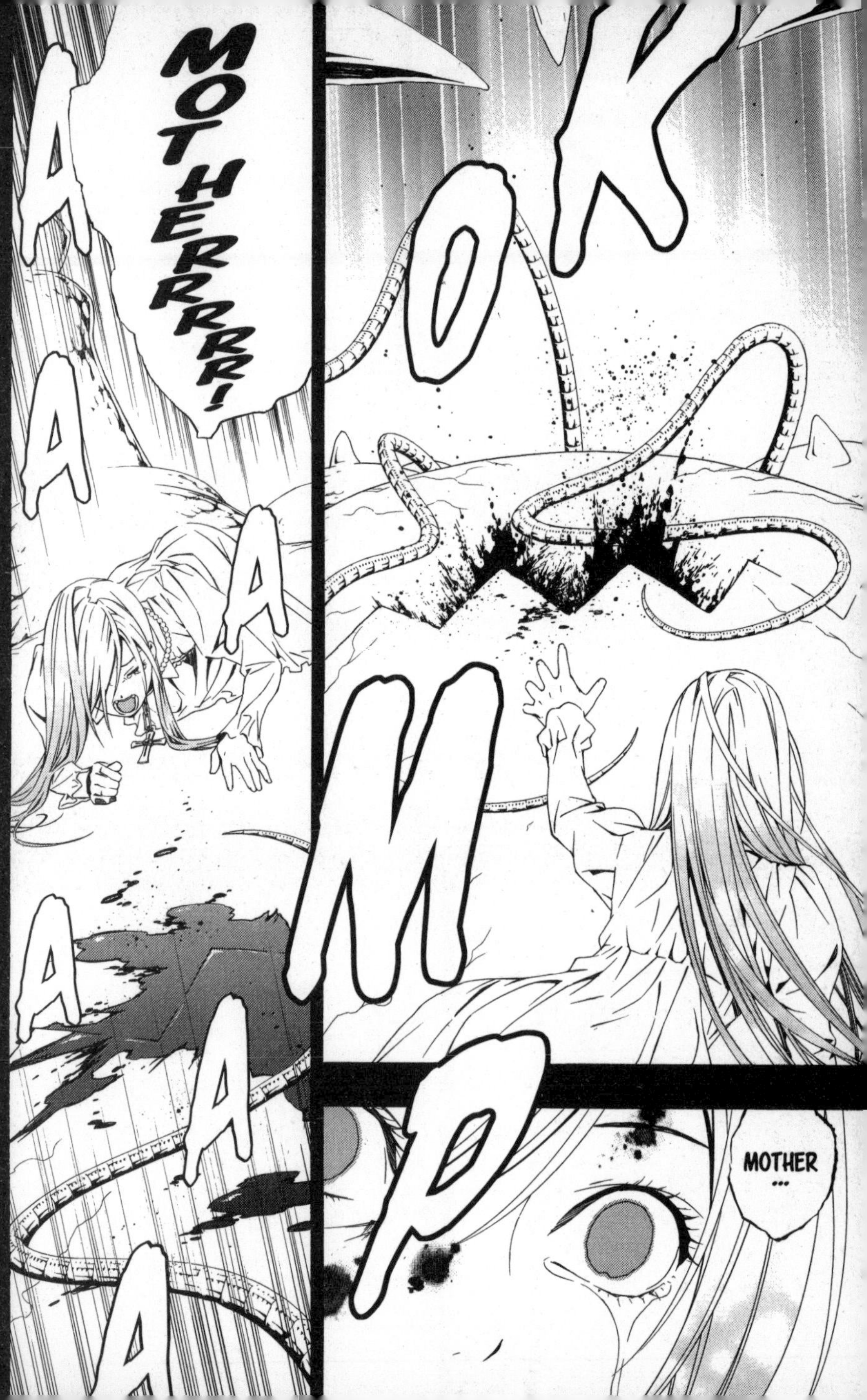

KOMP
MOTHER ...
MOTHERRRRR!
AAAAAA

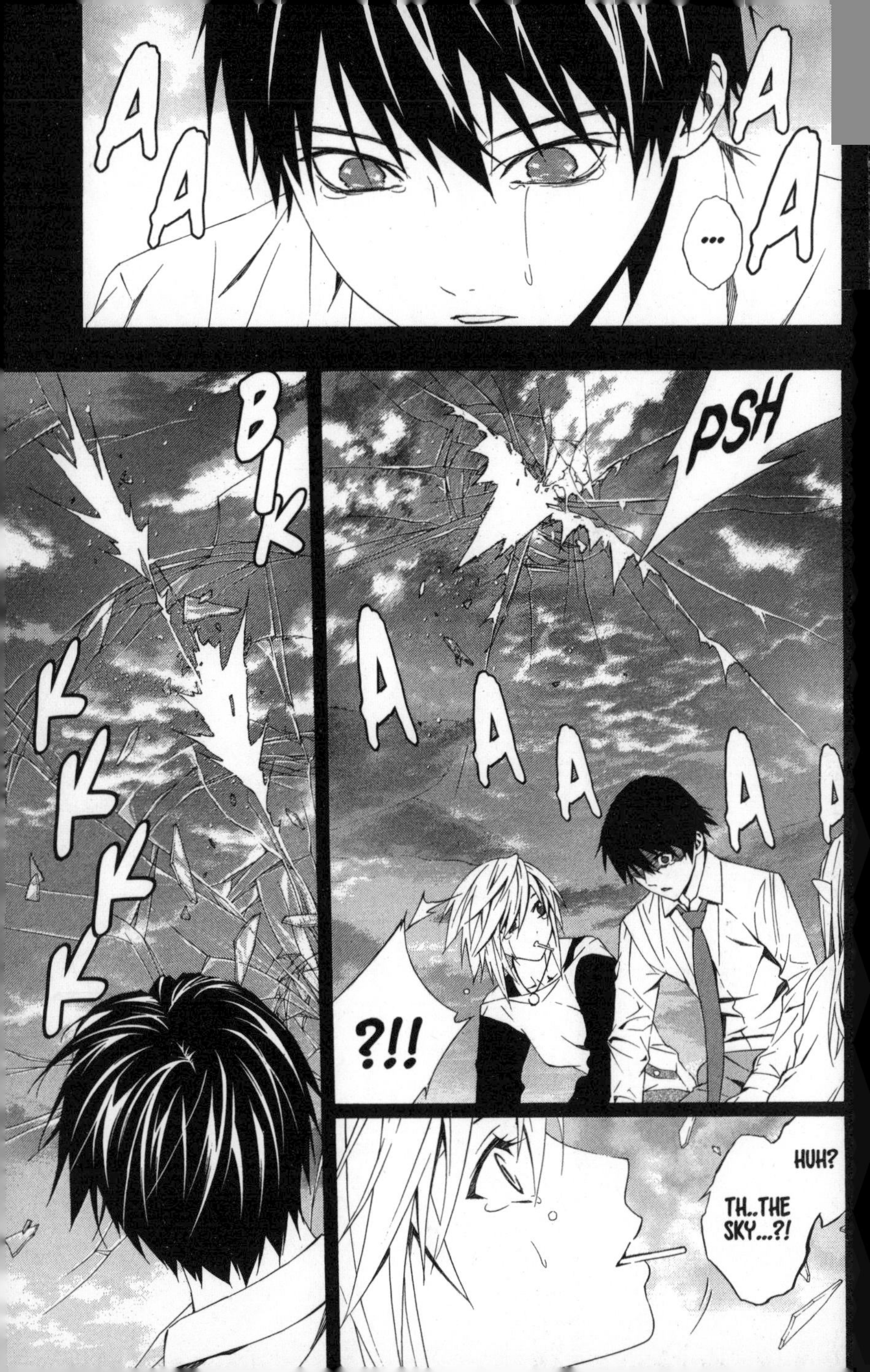
AAA
...
AA
PSH
AAAAA
?!!
HUH?
TH..THE SKY...?!
BIK
KKKKK

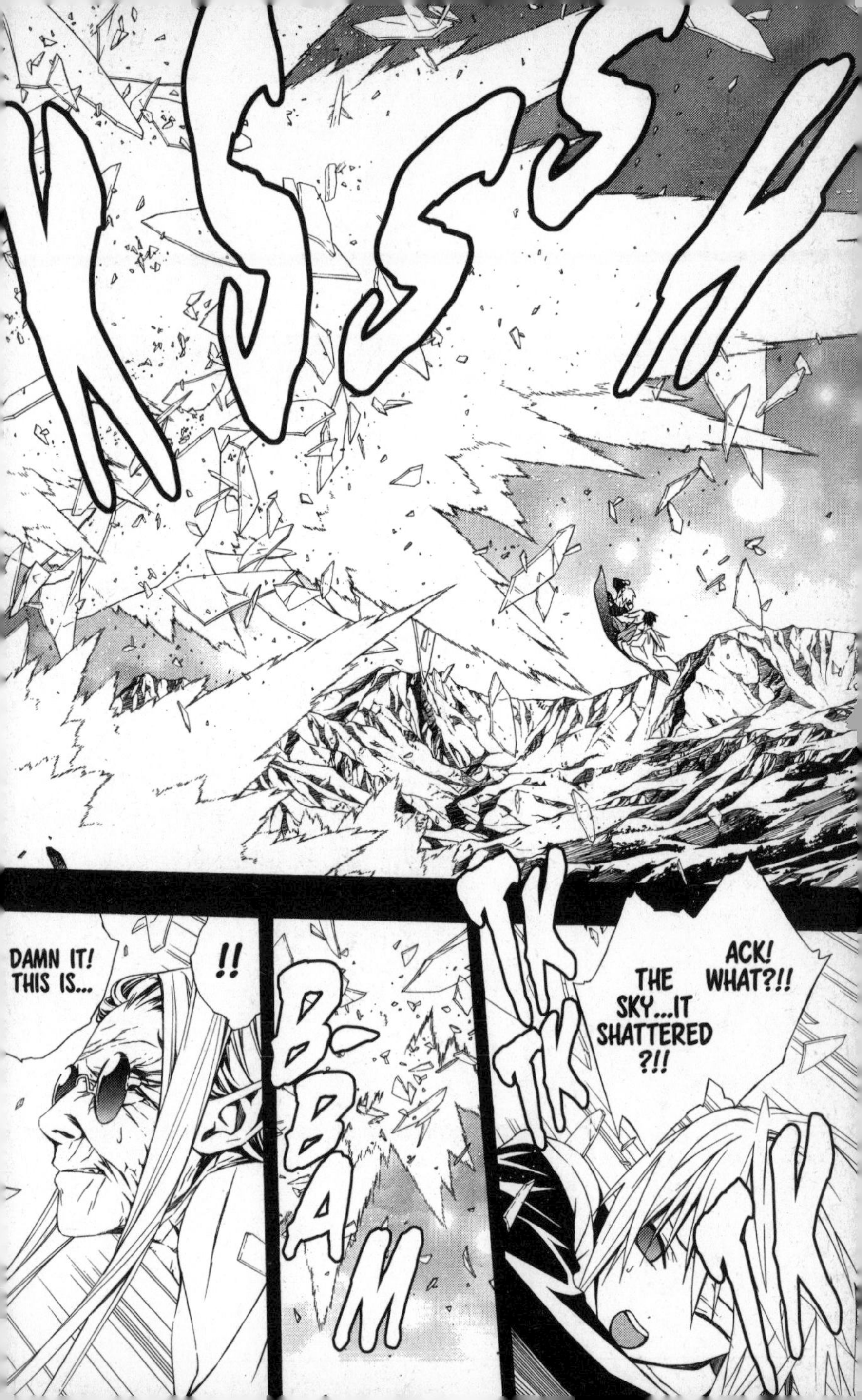
KSSSH
ACK! WHAT?!!
THE SKY...IT SHATTERED?!!
TK
TK
TK
B-BAM
!!
DAMN IT! THIS IS...

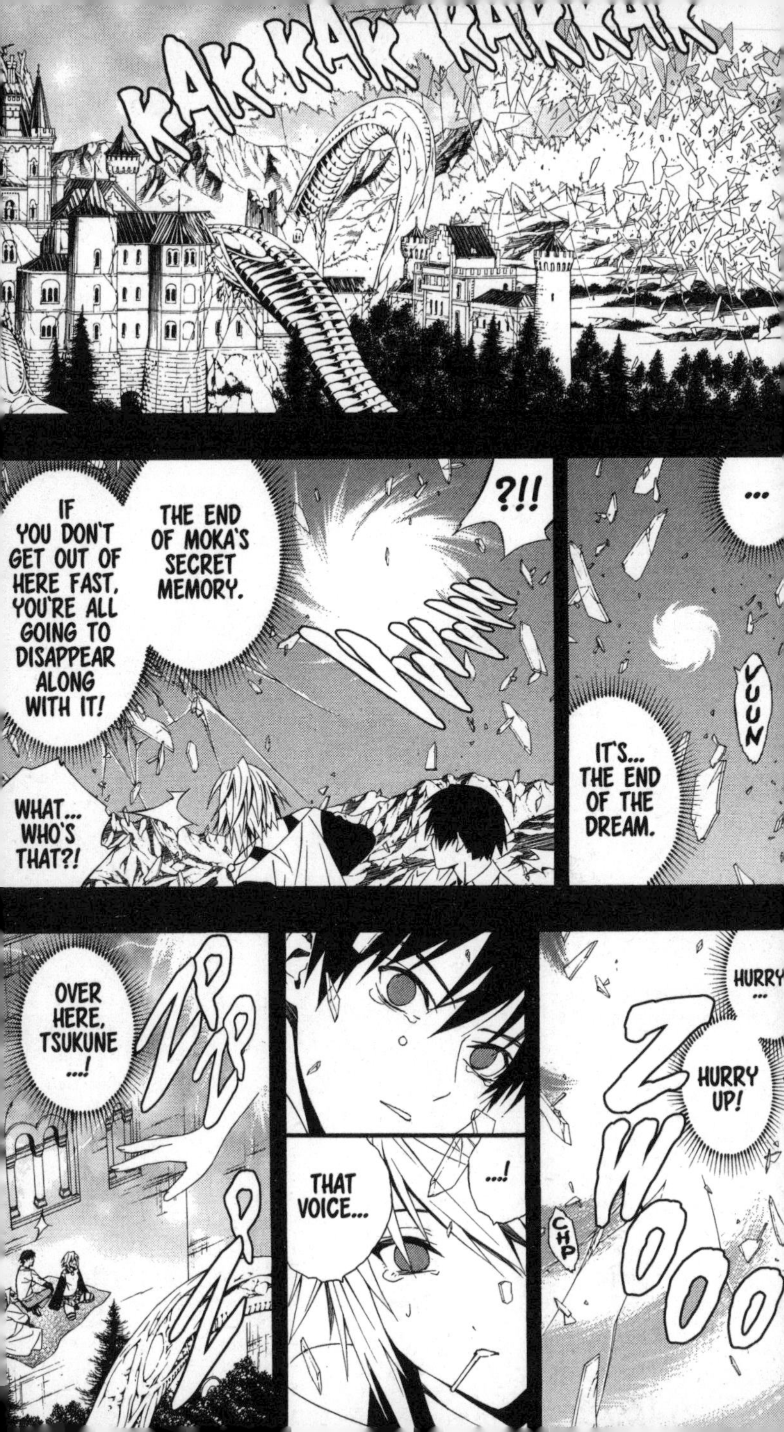
KAK KAK KAKKAK
...
VUUN
IT'S... THE END OF THE DREAM.
?!!
THE END OF MOKA'S SECRET MEMORY.
IF YOU DON'T GET OUT OF HERE FAST, YOU'RE ALL GOING TO DISAPPEAR ALONG WITH IT!
WHAT... WHO'S THAT?!
HURRY...
ZWOOOO
HURRY UP!
CHP
...!
THAT VOICE...
OVER HERE, TSUKUNE...!

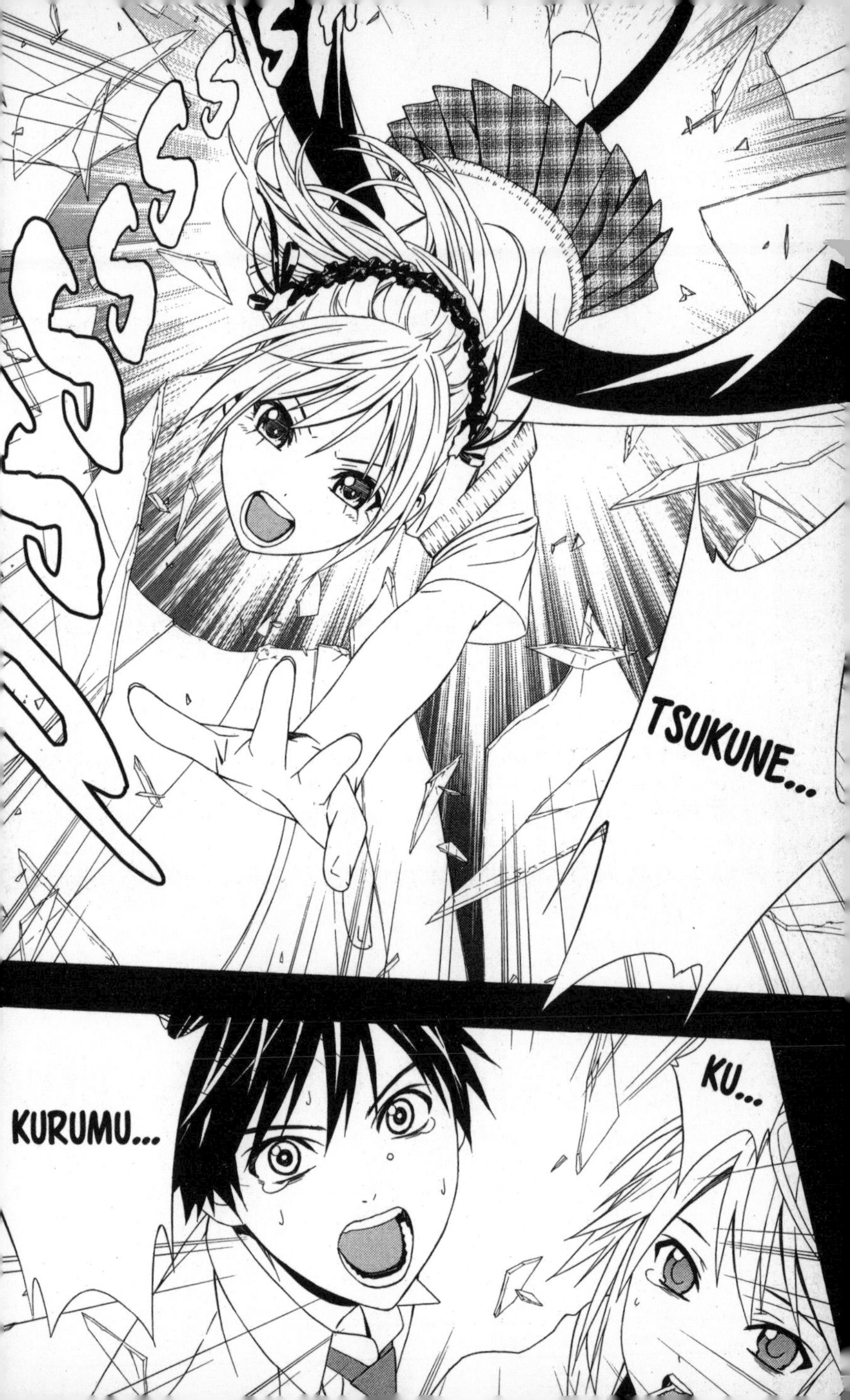
TSUKUNE...
KU...
KURUMU...

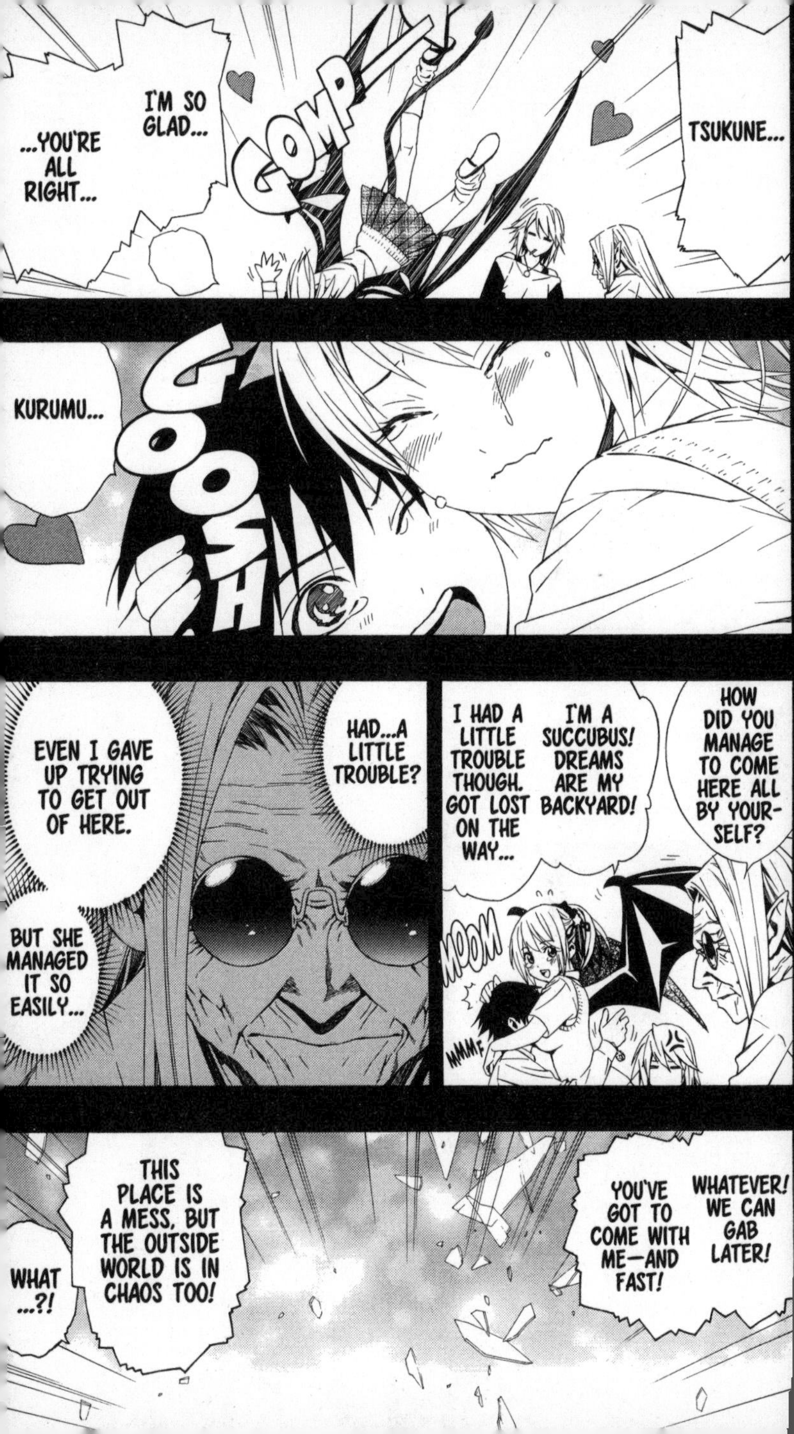
TSUKUNE...
GOMP
I'M SO GLAD...
...YOU'RE ALL RIGHT...
GOOSH
KURUMU...
HOW DID YOU MANAGE TO COME HERE ALL BY YOURSELF?
I'M A SUCCUBUS! DREAMS ARE MY BACKYARD!
I HAD A LITTLE TROUBLE THOUGH. GOT LOST ON THE WAY...
MOOM
MMMF
HAD...A LITTLE TROUBLE?
EVEN I GAVE UP TRYING TO GET OUT OF HERE.
BUT SHE MANAGED IT SO EASILY...
WHATEVER! WE CAN GAB LATER!
YOU'VE GOT TO COME WITH ME—AND FAST!
THIS PLACE IS A MESS, BUT THE OUTSIDE WORLD IS IN CHAOS TOO!
WHAT ...?!

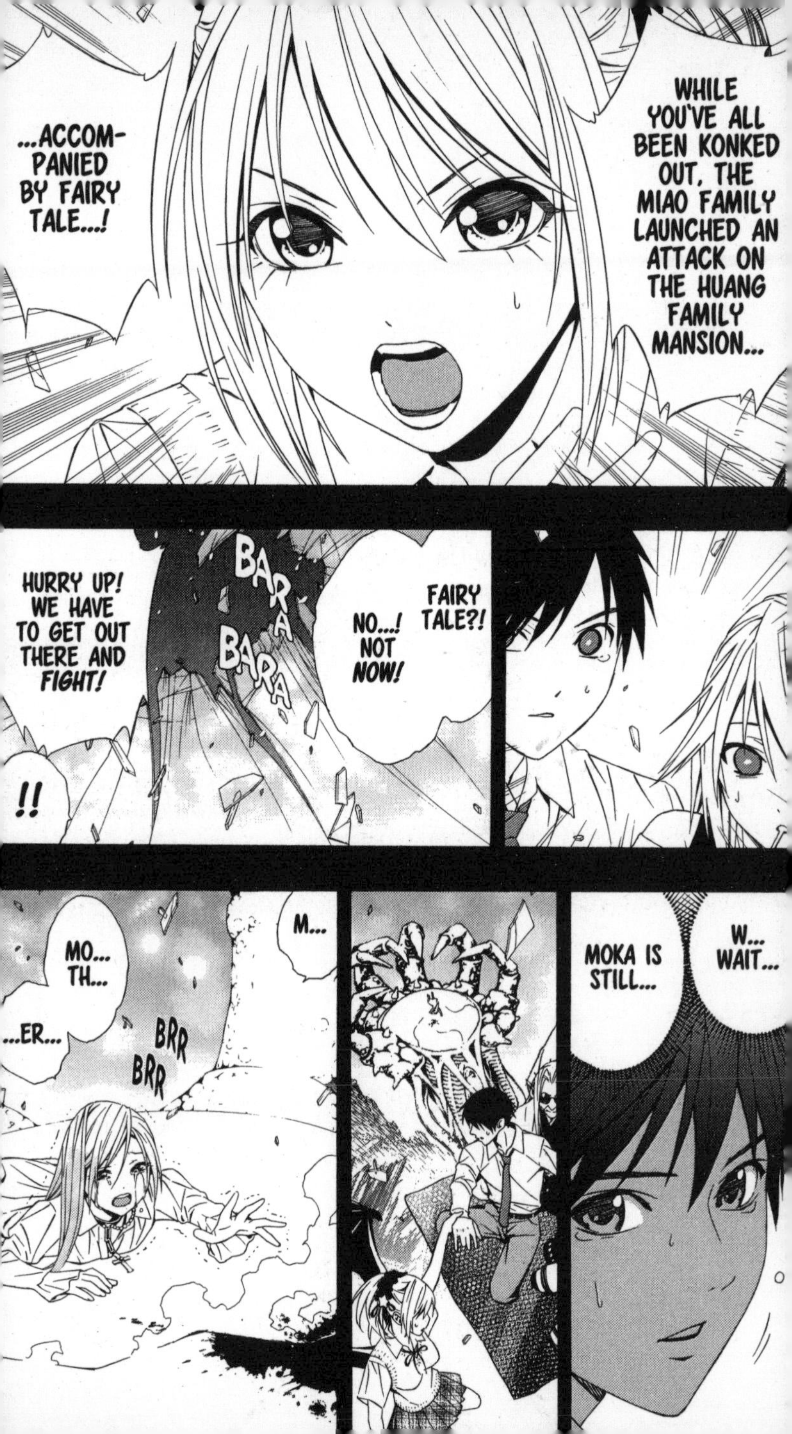
WHILE YOU'VE ALL BEEN KONKED OUT, THE MIAO FAMILY LAUNCHED AN ATTACK ON THE HUANG FAMILY MANSION...
...ACCOM-PANIED BY FAIRY TALE...!
FAIRY TALE?!
NO...! NOT NOW!
BARA BARA
HURRY UP! WE HAVE TO GET OUT THERE AND FIGHT!
!!
W... WAIT...
MOKA IS STILL...
M...
MO... TH...
...ER...
BRR BRR

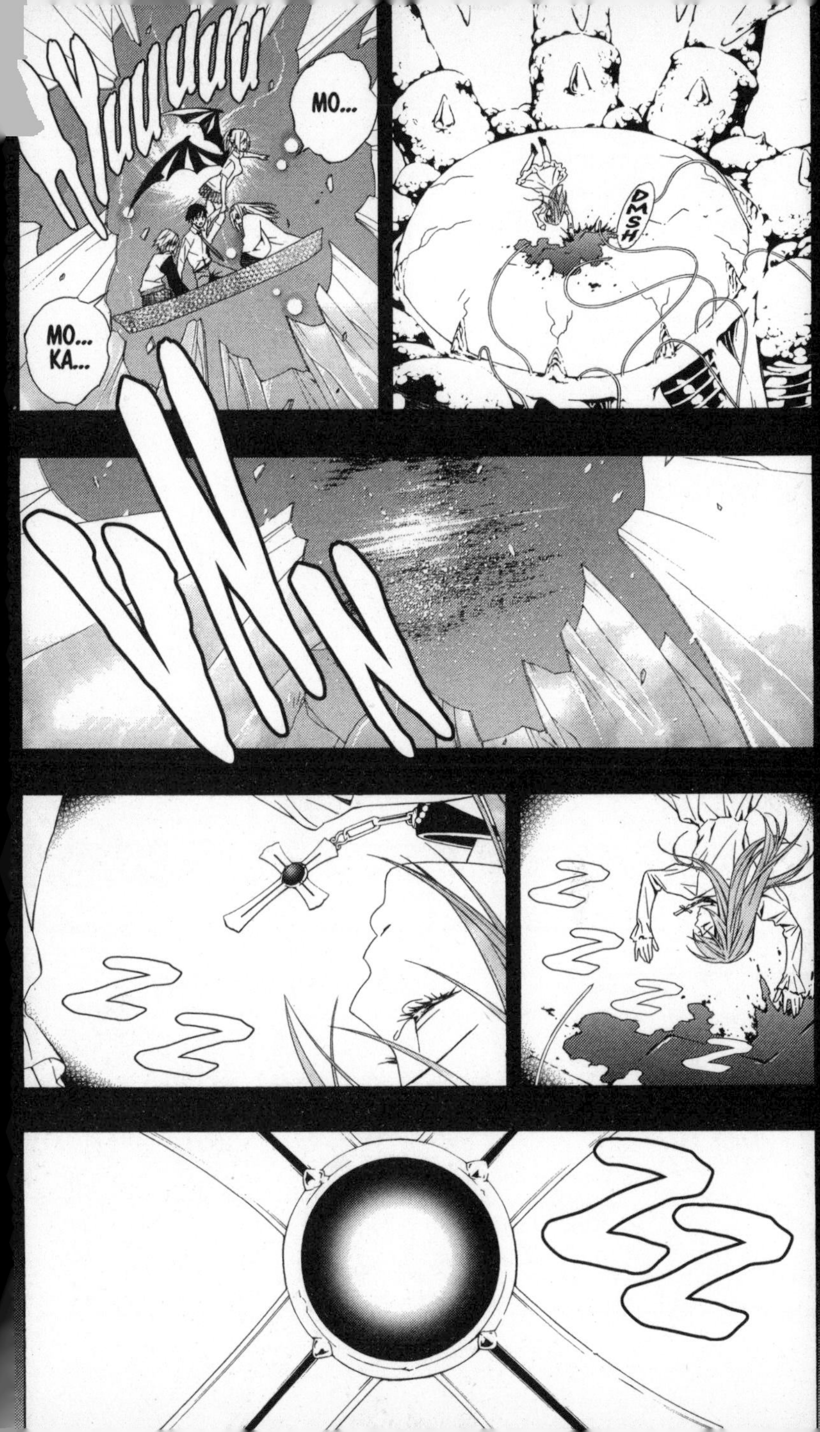
DMSH
MO...
MO...
KA...

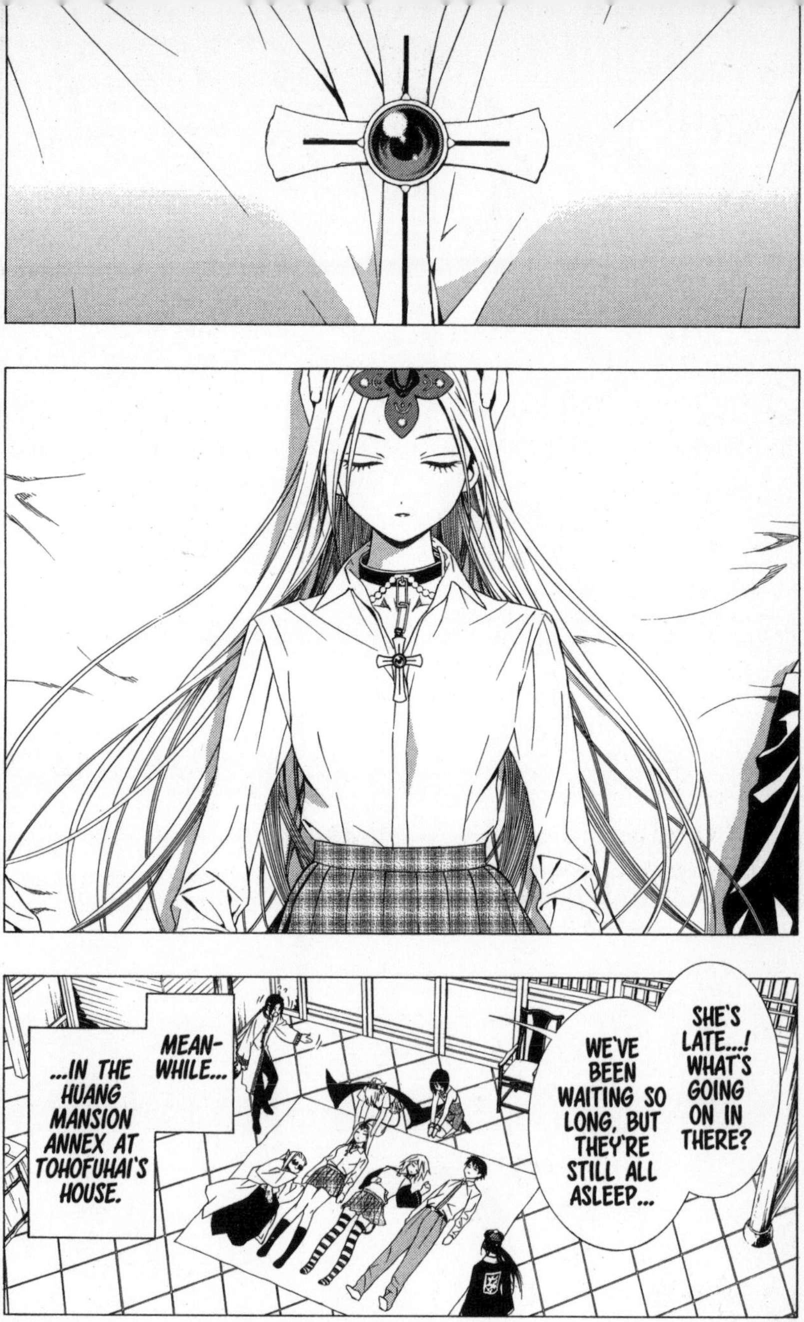
SHE'S LATE...! WHAT'S GOING ON IN THERE?
WE'VE BEEN WAITING SO LONG, BUT THEY'RE STILL ALL ASLEEP...
MEAN-WHILE...
...IN THE HUANG MANSION ANNEX AT TOHOFUHAI'S HOUSE.

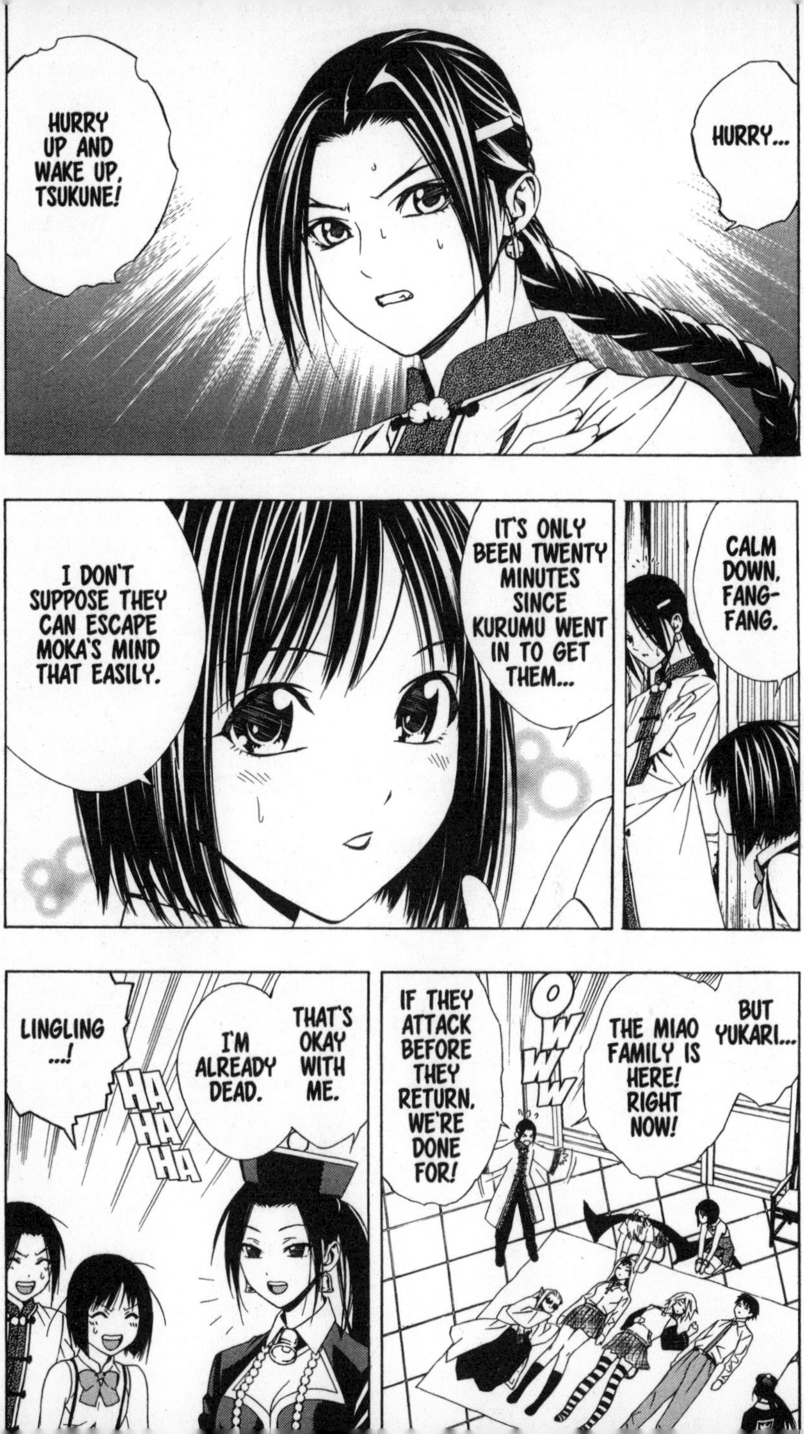
HURRY...
HURRY UP AND WAKE UP, TSUKUNE!
CALM DOWN, FANG-FANG.
IT'S ONLY BEEN TWENTY MINUTES SINCE KURUMU WENT IN TO GET THEM...
I DON'T SUPPOSE THEY CAN ESCAPE MOKA'S MIND THAT EASILY.
BUT YUKARI...
THE MIAO FAMILY IS HERE! RIGHT NOW!
OWWWW
IF THEY ATTACK BEFORE THEY RETURN, WE'RE DONE FOR!
THAT'S OKAY WITH ME.
I'M ALREADY DEAD.
HAHAHAHA
LINGLING...!

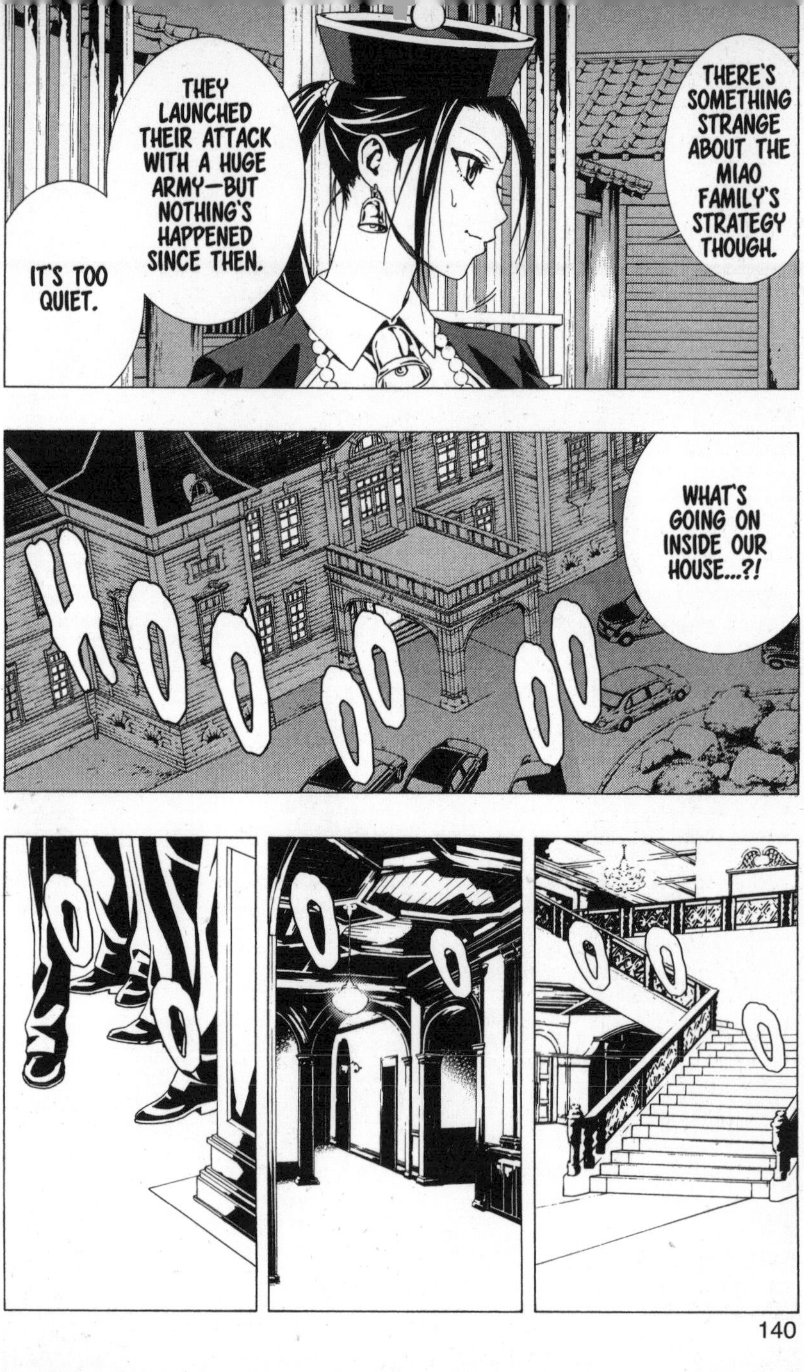
THERE'S SOMETHING STRANGE ABOUT THE MIAO FAMILY'S STRATEGY THOUGH.
THEY LAUNCHED THEIR ATTACK WITH A HUGE ARMY—BUT NOTHING'S HAPPENED SINCE THEN.
IT'S TOO QUIET.
WHAT'S GOING ON INSIDE OUR HOUSE...?!
HOOOOOO

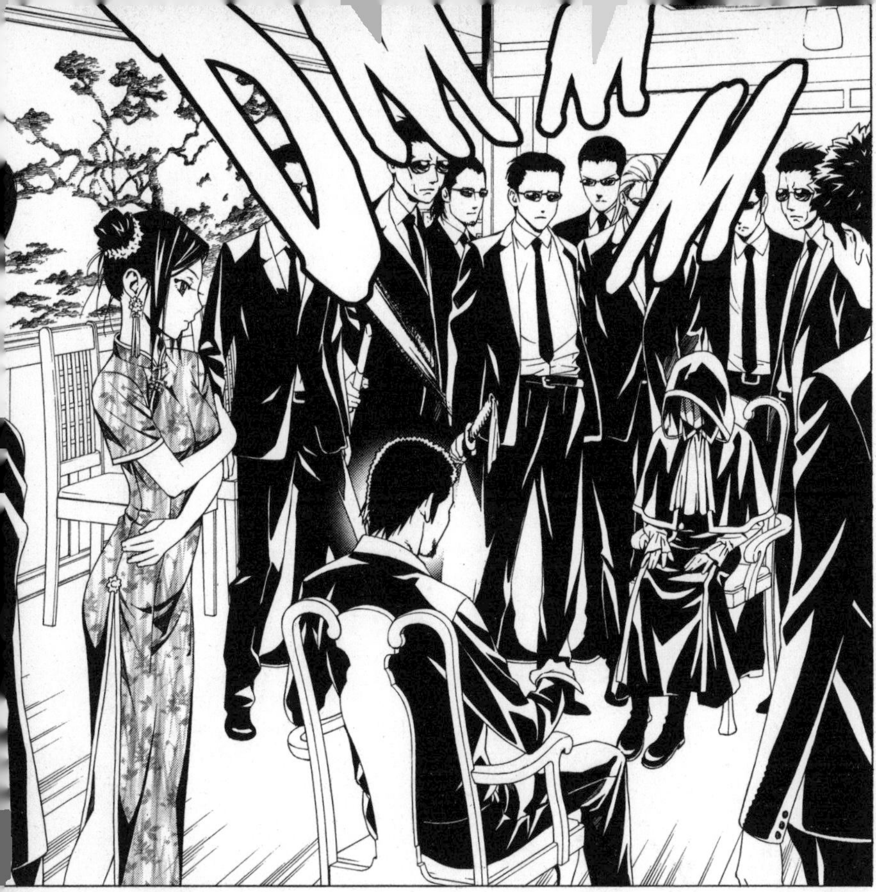
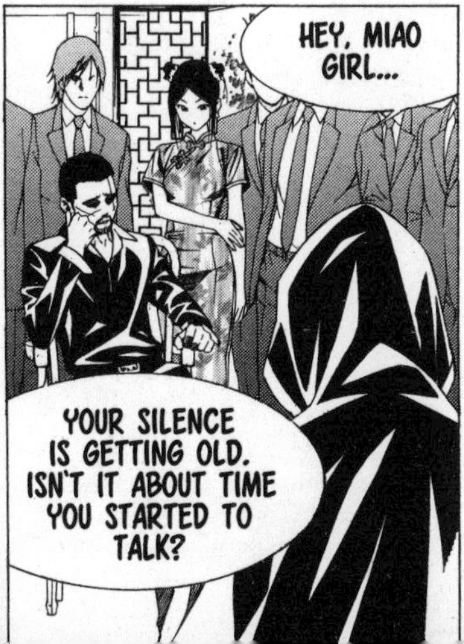
HEY, MIAO GIRL...
YOUR SILENCE IS GETTING OLD. ISN'T IT ABOUT TIME YOU STARTED TO TALK?
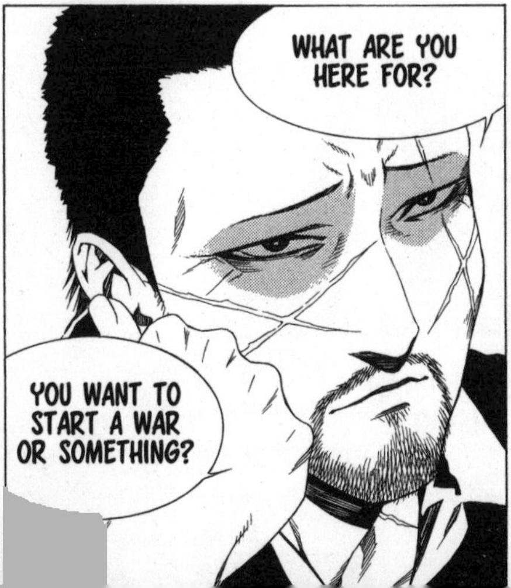
WHAT ARE YOU HERE FOR?
YOU WANT TO START A WAR OR SOMETHING?

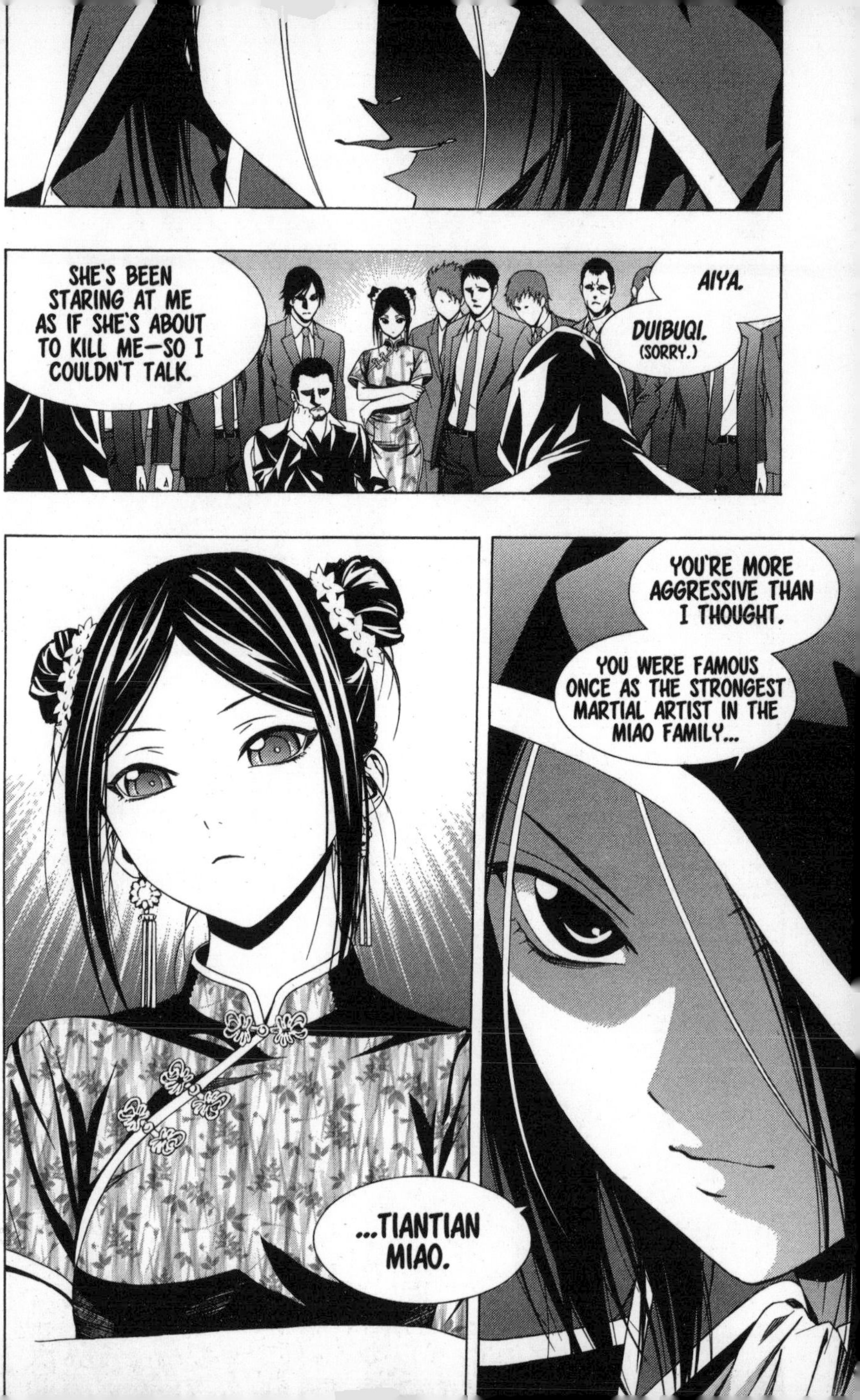
AIYA.
DUIBUQI. (SORRY.)
SHE'S BEEN STARING AT ME AS IF SHE'S ABOUT TO KILL ME—SO I COULDN'T TALK.
YOU'RE MORE AGGRESSIVE THAN I THOUGHT.
YOU WERE FAMOUS ONCE AS THE STRONGEST MARTIAL ARTIST IN THE MIAO FAMILY...
...TIANTIAN MIAO.

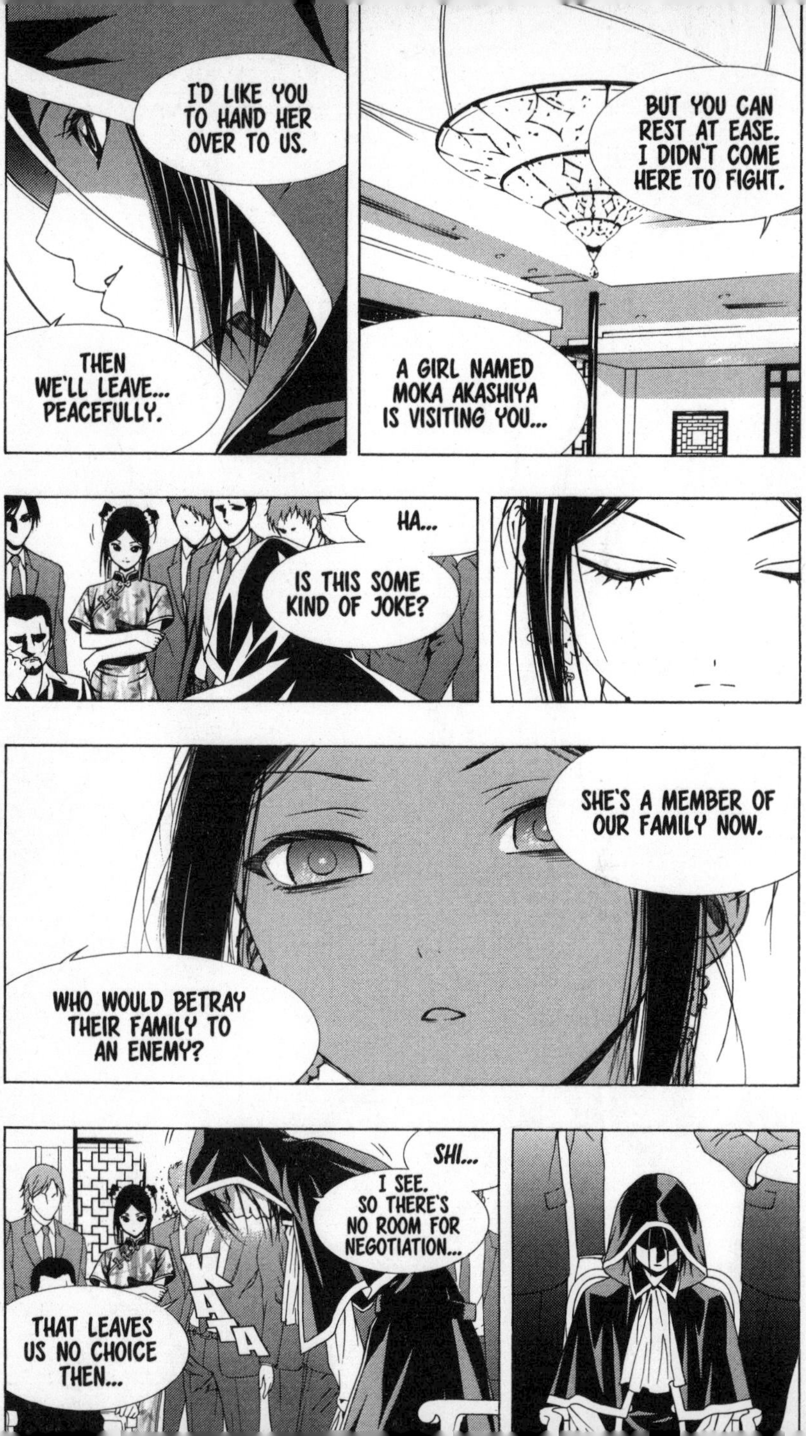
BUT YOU CAN REST AT EASE. I DIDN'T COME HERE TO FIGHT.
A GIRL NAMED MOKA AKASHIYA IS VISITING YOU...
I'D LIKE YOU TO HAND HER OVER TO US.
THEN WE'LL LEAVE... PEACEFULLY.
HA...
IS THIS SOME KIND OF JOKE?
SHE'S A MEMBER OF OUR FAMILY NOW.
WHO WOULD BETRAY THEIR FAMILY TO AN ENEMY?
SHI...
I SEE. SO THERE'S NO ROOM FOR NEGOTIATION...
KATA
THAT LEAVES US NO CHOICE THEN...

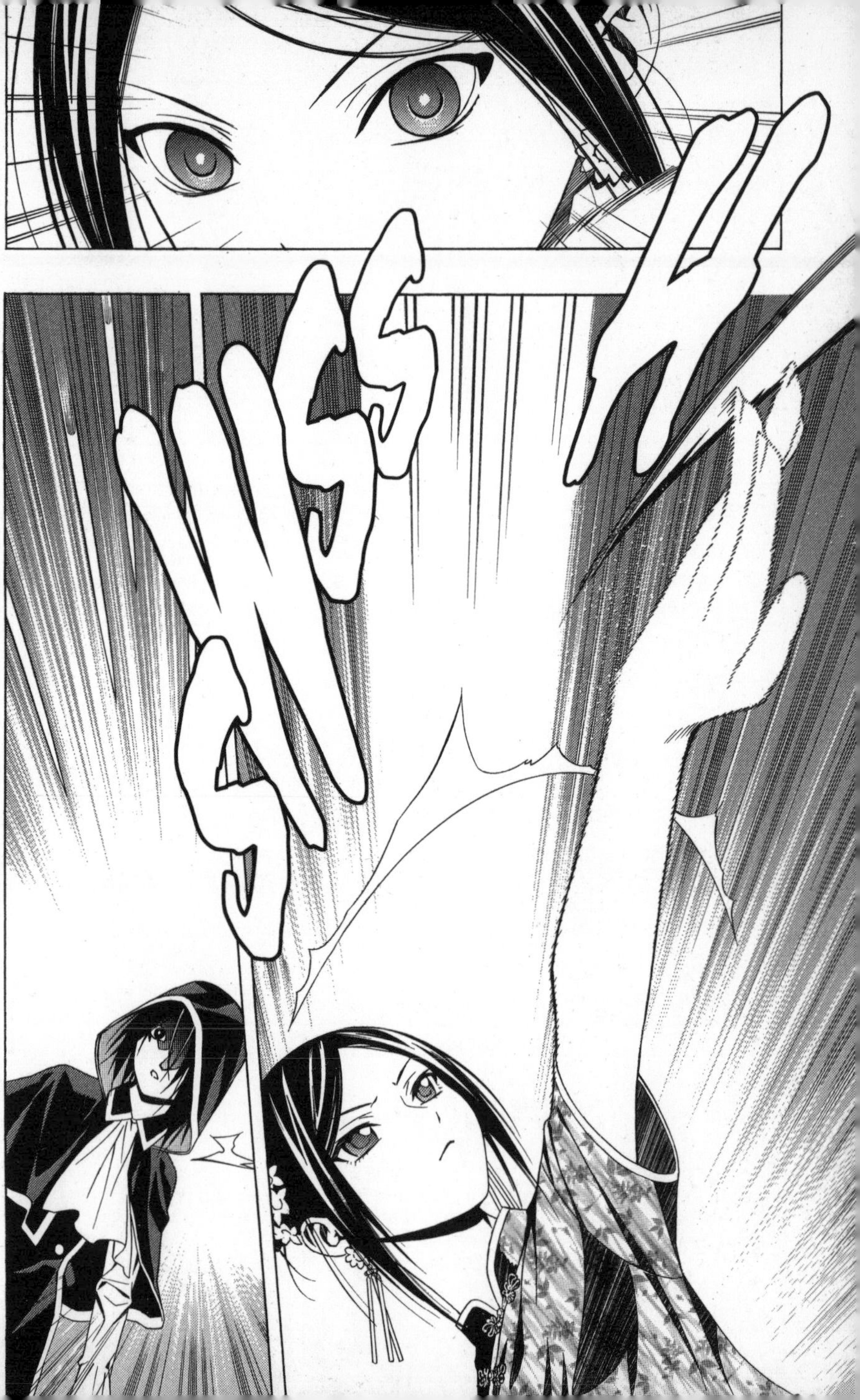
SWISSH

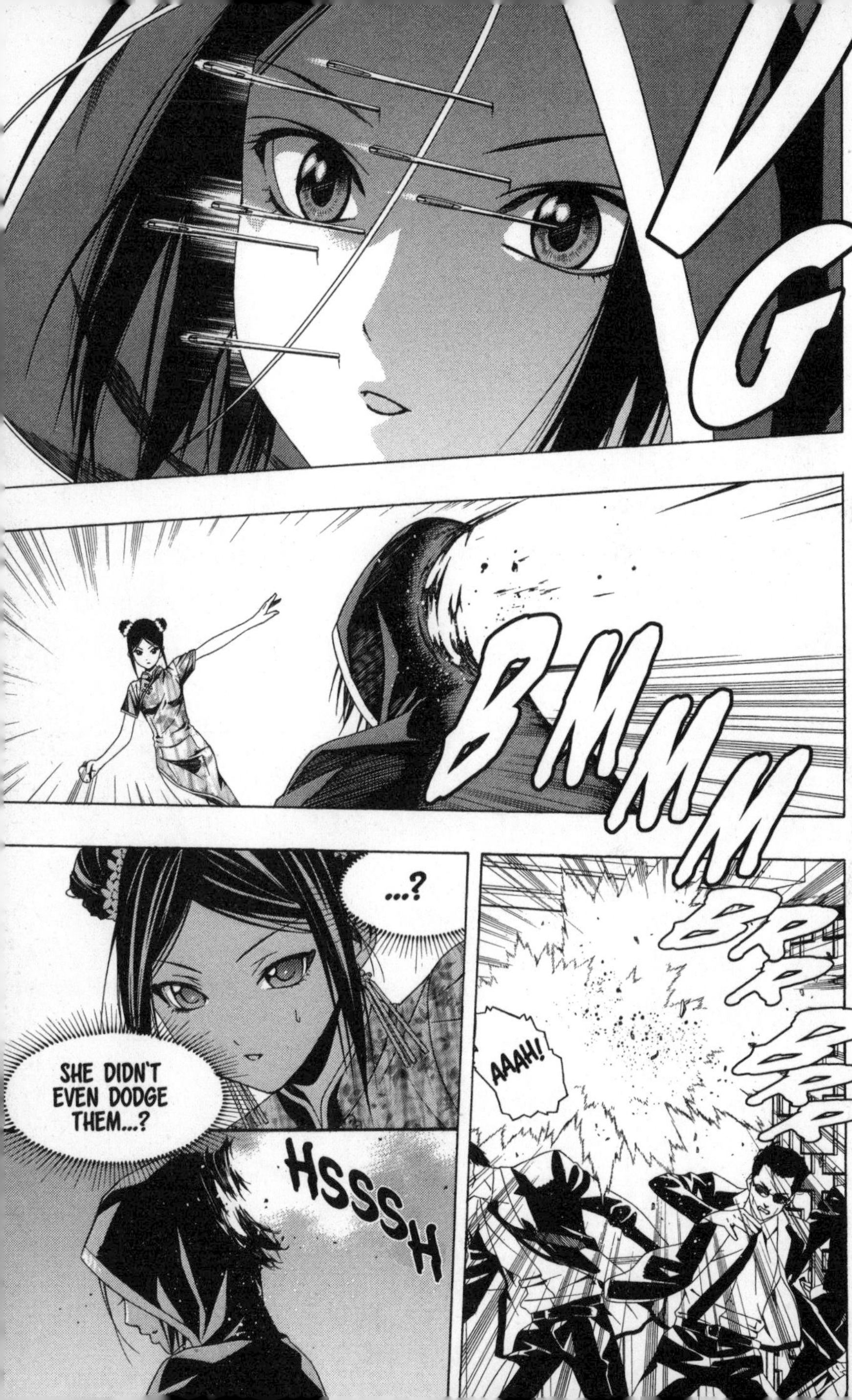
VG
BMMMM
BRRRRRR
AAAH!
...?
SHE DIDN'T EVEN DODGE THEM...?
HSSSH

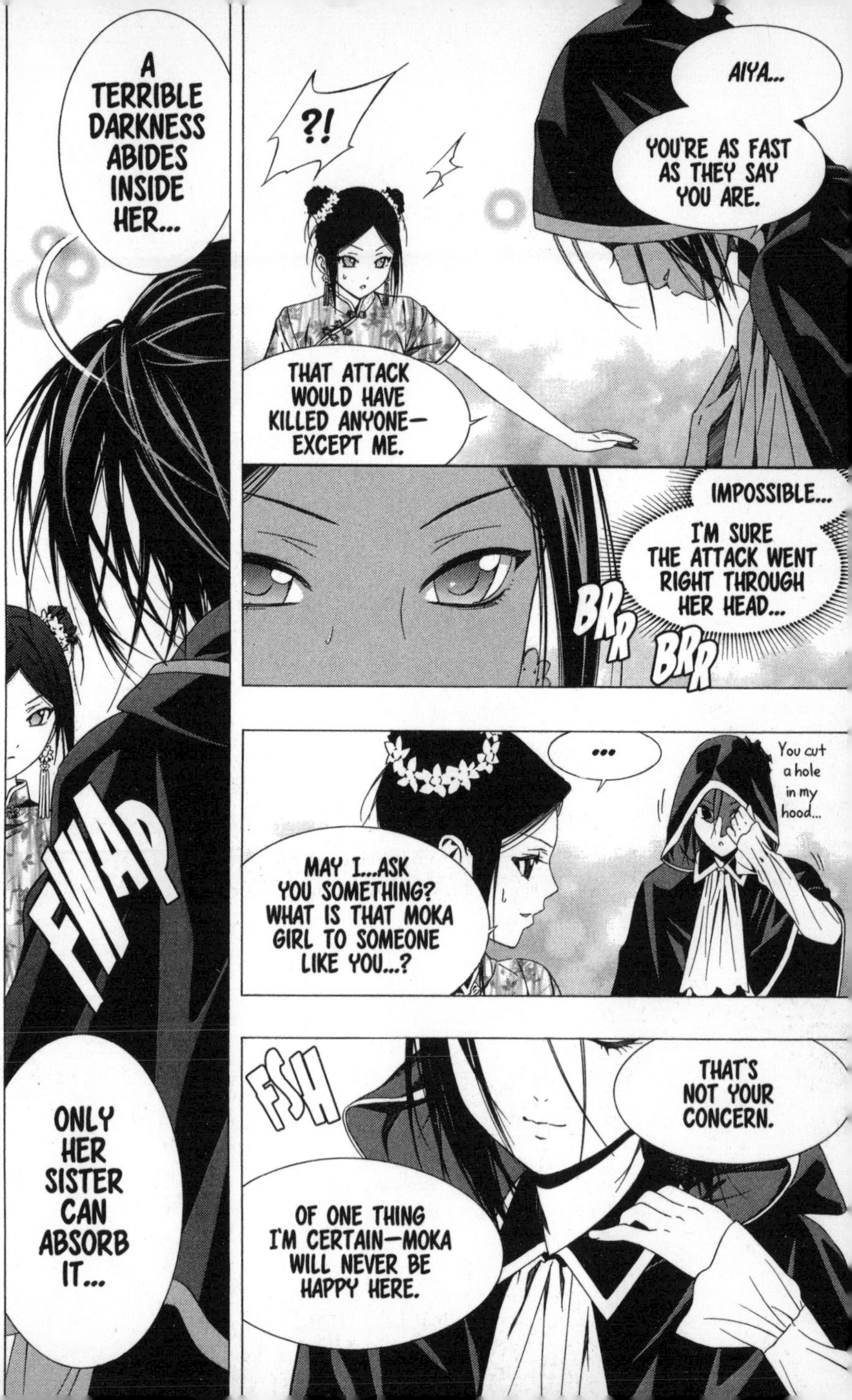
AIYA...
YOU'RE AS FAST AS THEY SAY YOU ARE.
?!
THAT ATTACK WOULD HAVE KILLED ANYONE—EXCEPT ME.
IMPOSSIBLE...
I'M SURE THE ATTACK WENT RIGHT THROUGH HER HEAD...
BRR
BRR
You cut a hole in my hood...
...
MAY I...ASK YOU SOMETHING? WHAT IS THAT MOKA GIRL TO SOMEONE LIKE YOU...?
THAT'S NOT YOUR CONCERN.
FSH
OF ONE THING I'M CERTAIN—MOKA WILL NEVER BE HAPPY HERE.
A TERRIBLE DARKNESS ABIDES INSIDE HER...
FWAP
ONLY HER SISTER CAN ABSORB IT...

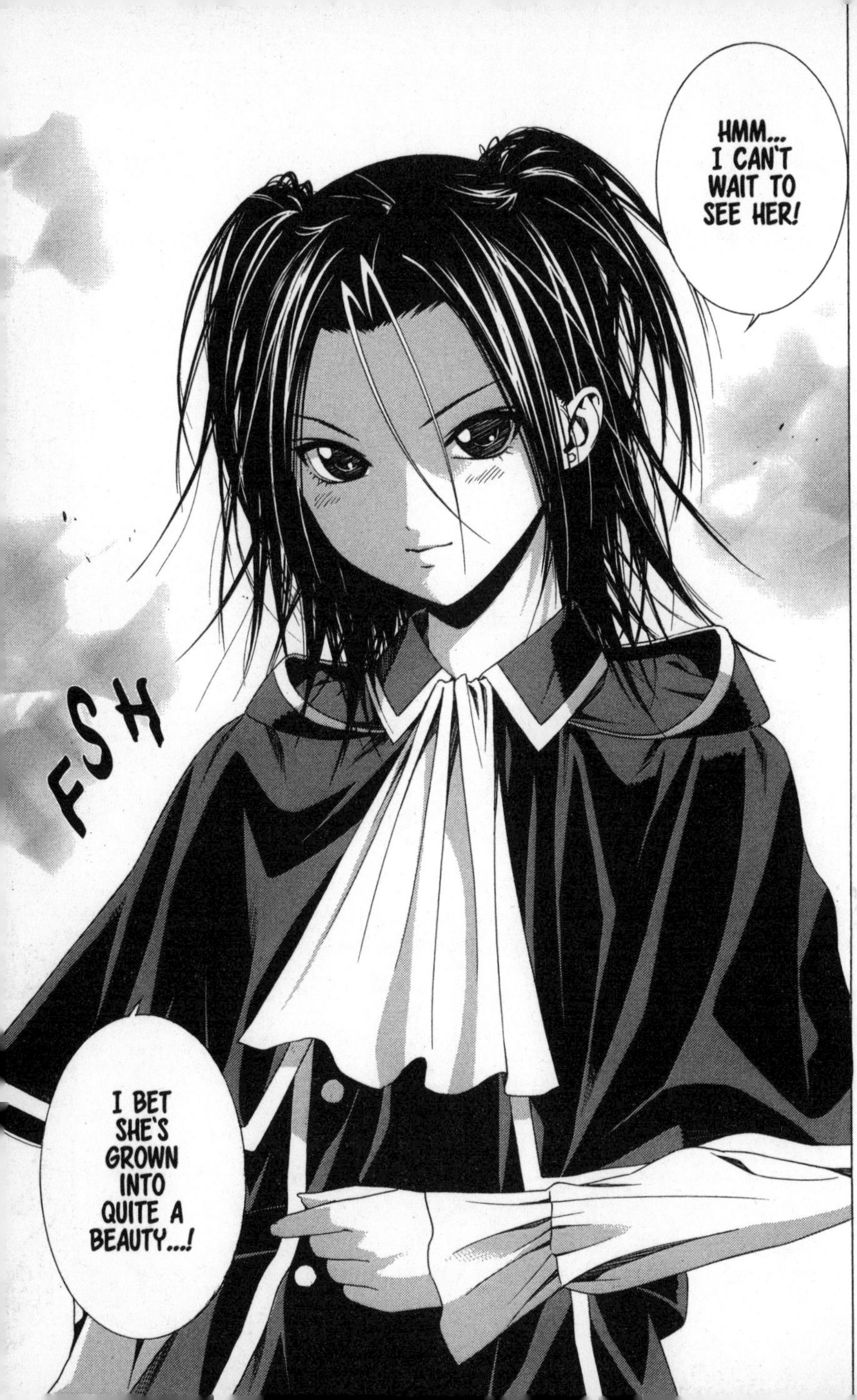
HMM... I CAN'T WAIT TO SEE HER!
FSH
I BET SHE'S GROWN INTO QUITE A BEAUTY...!

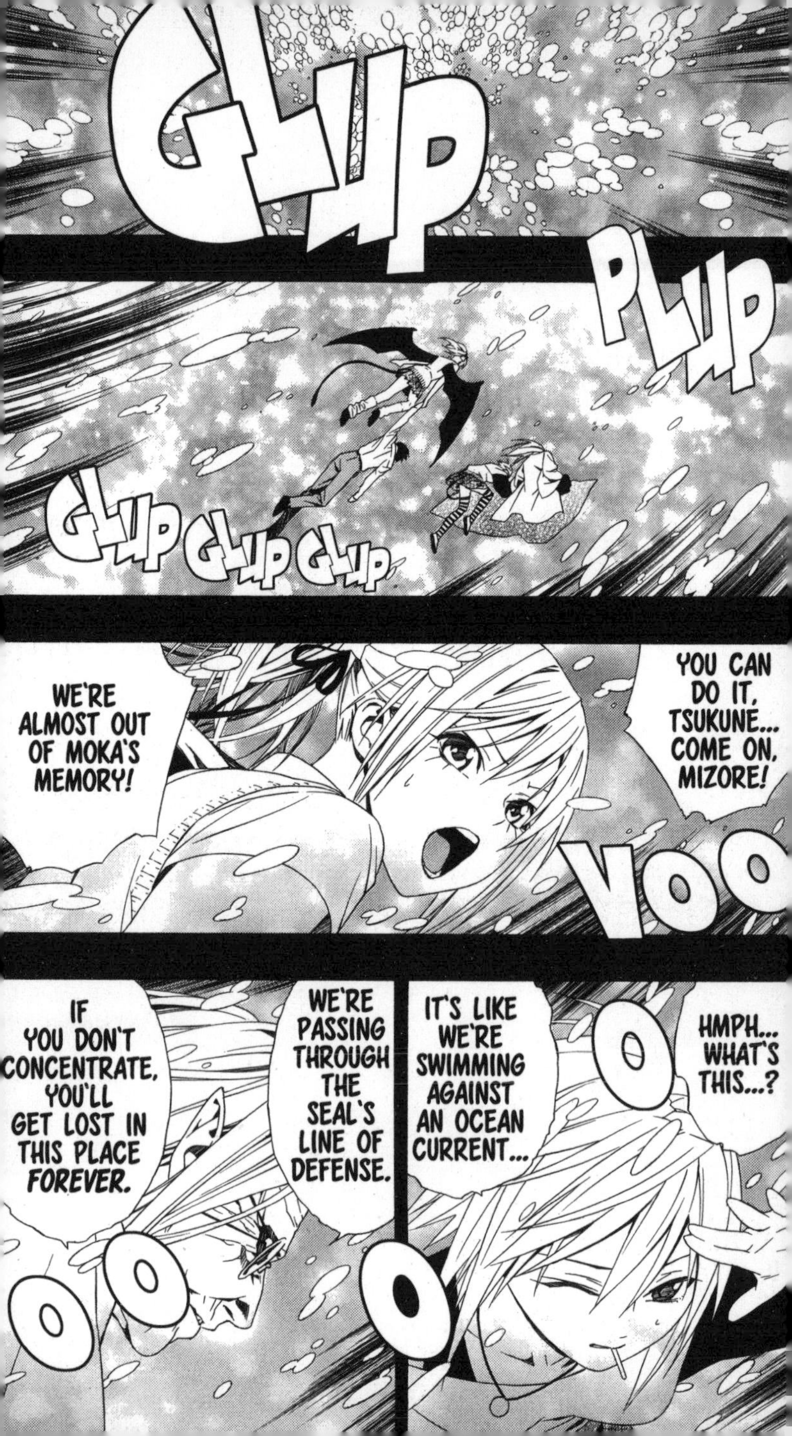
GLUP
PLUP
GLUP GLUP GLUP
YOU CAN DO IT, TSUKUNE... COME ON, MIZORE!
WE'RE ALMOST OUT OF MOKA'S MEMORY!
VOO
HMPH... WHAT'S THIS...?
IT'S LIKE WE'RE SWIMMING AGAINST AN OCEAN CURRENT...
OO
WE'RE PASSING THROUGH THE SEAL'S LINE OF DEFENSE.
IF YOU DON'T CONCENTRATE, YOU'LL GET LOST IN THIS PLACE FOREVER.
OOO

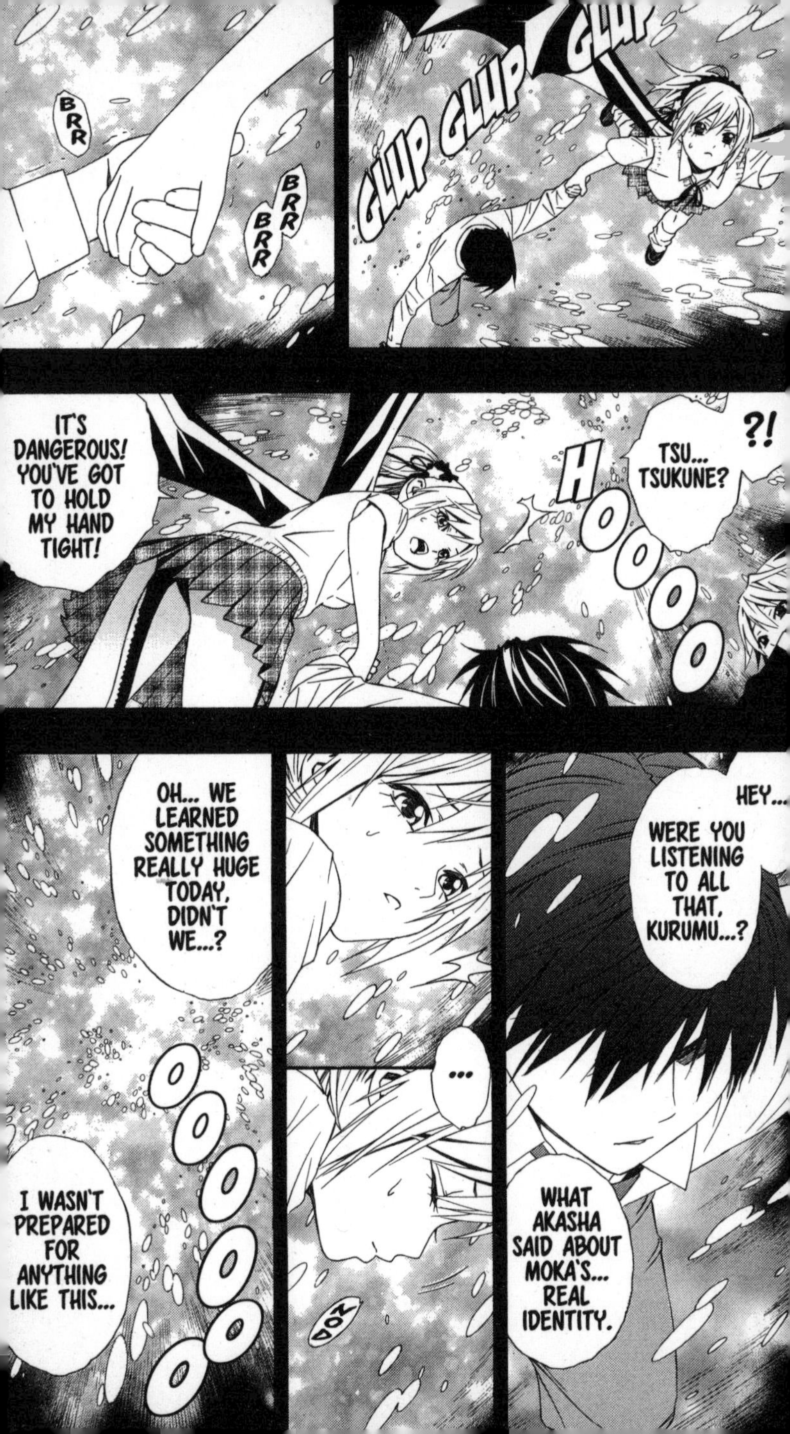
GLUP GLUP GLUP GLUP
BRR
BRR BRR
?!
TSU... TSUKUNE?
HOOOOO
IT'S DANGEROUS! YOU'VE GOT TO HOLD MY HAND TIGHT!
HEY...
WERE YOU LISTENING TO ALL THAT, KURUMU...?
WHAT AKASHA SAID ABOUT MOKA'S... REAL IDENTITY.
...
NOD
OH... WE LEARNED SOMETHING REALLY HUGE TODAY, DIDN'T WE...?
OOOOOOO
I WASN'T PREPARED FOR ANYTHING LIKE THIS...

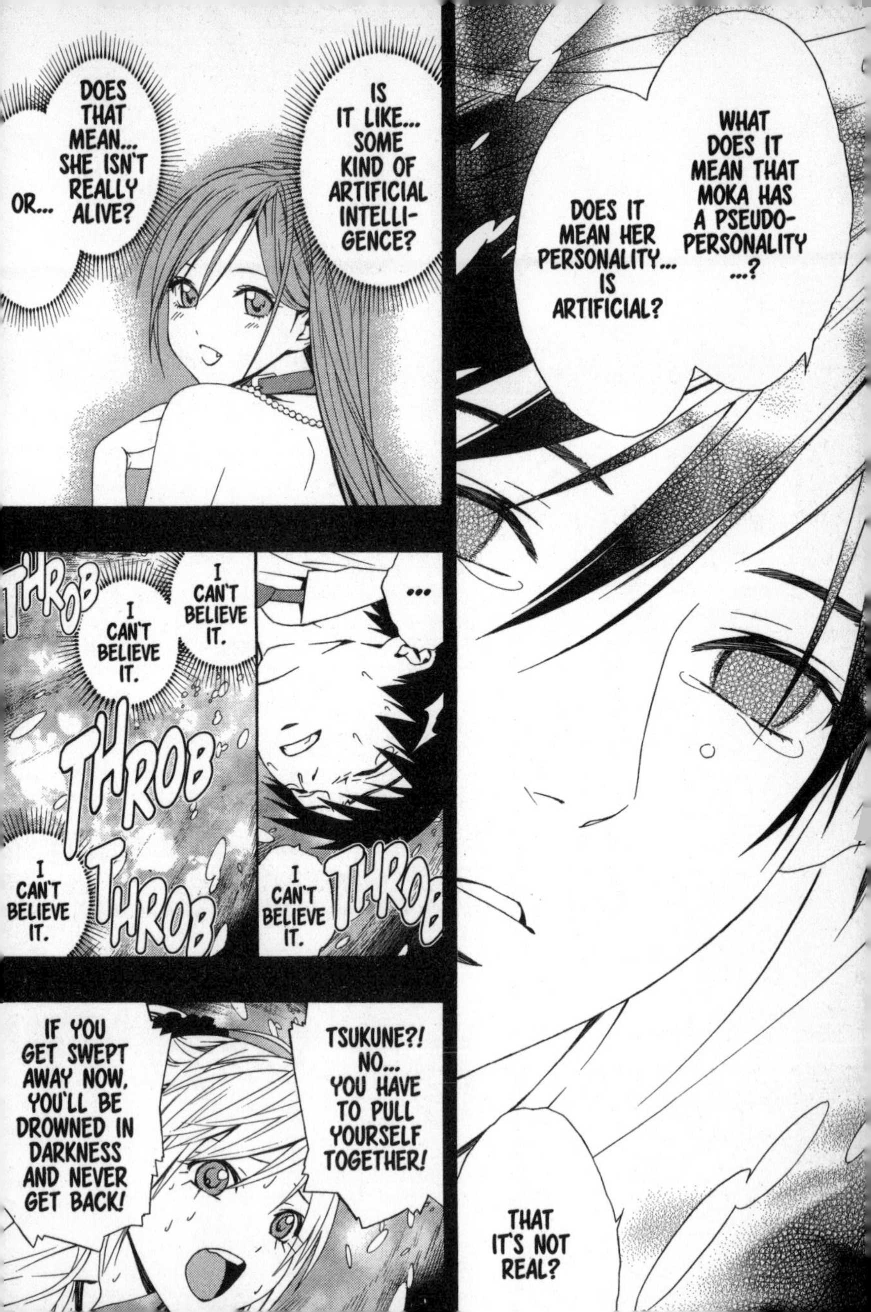
WHAT DOES IT MEAN THAT MOKA HAS A PSEUDO-PERSONALITY ...?
DOES IT MEAN HER PERSONALITY... IS ARTIFICIAL?
THAT IT'S NOT REAL?
IS IT LIKE... SOME KIND OF ARTIFICIAL INTELLIGENCE?
DOES THAT MEAN... SHE ISN'T REALLY ALIVE?
OR...
...
I CAN'T BELIEVE IT.
THROB
I CAN'T BELIEVE IT.
I CAN'T BELIEVE IT.
THROB
THROB
THROB
I CAN'T BELIEVE IT.
TSUKUNE?! NO... YOU HAVE TO PULL YOURSELF TOGETHER!
IF YOU GET SWEPT AWAY NOW, YOU'LL BE DROWNED IN DARKNESS AND NEVER GET BACK!

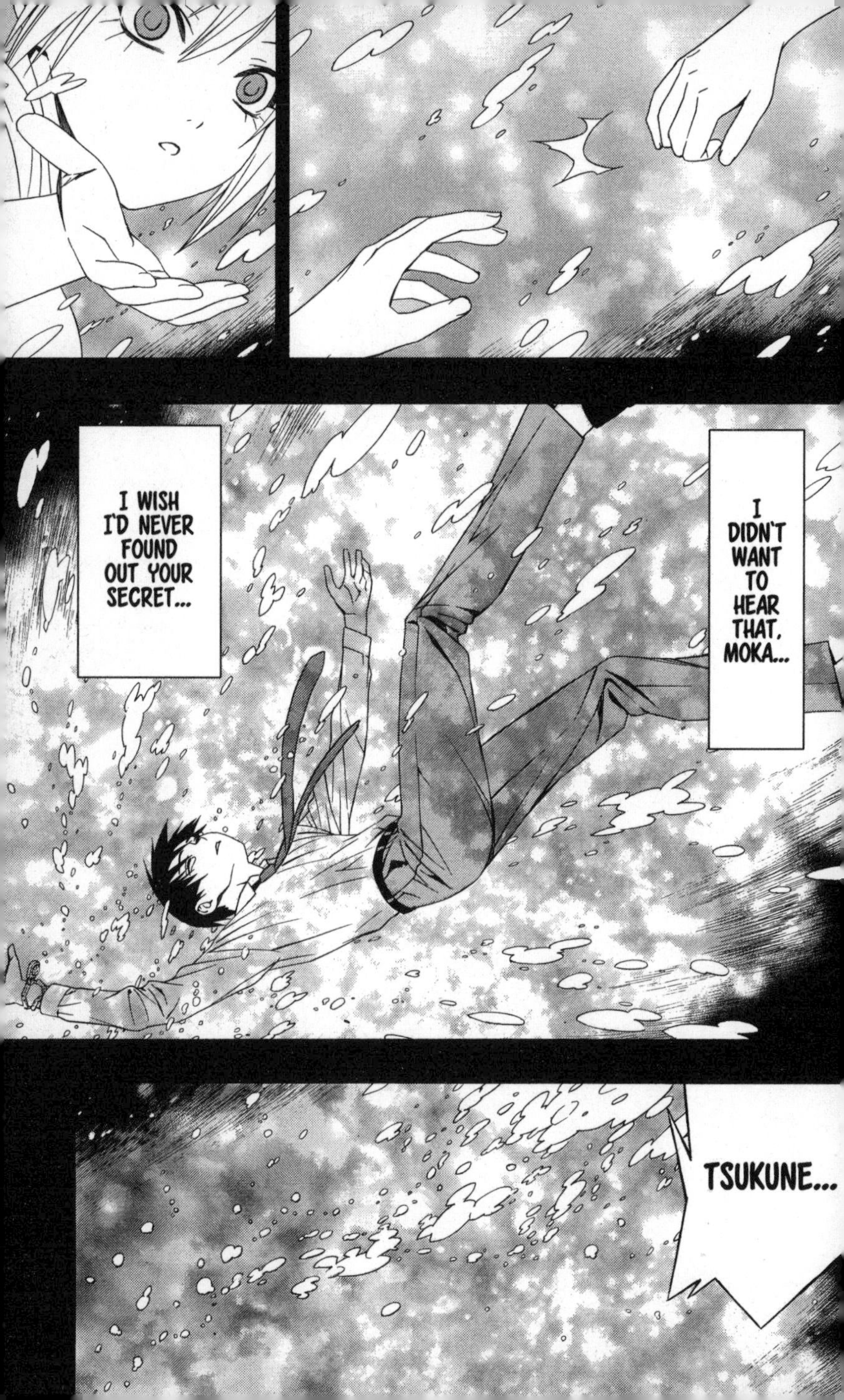
I DIDN'T WANT TO HEAR THAT, MOKA...
I WISH I'D NEVER FOUND OUT YOUR SECRET...
TSUKUNE...

# 35: Confession

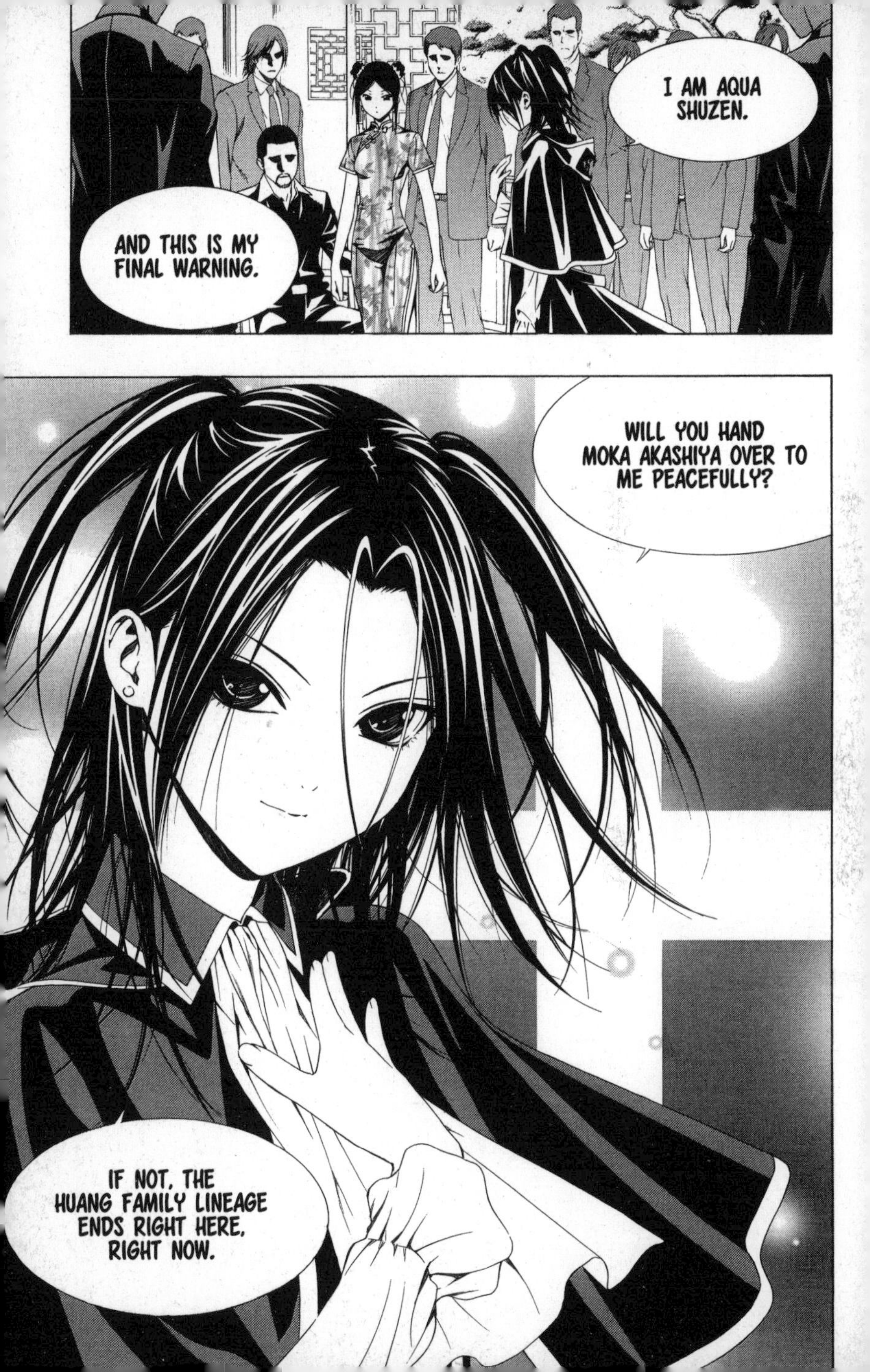
I AM AQUA SHUZEN.
AND THIS IS MY FINAL WARNING.
WILL YOU HAND MOKA AKASHIYA OVER TO ME PEACEFULLY?
IF NOT, THE HUANG FAMILY LINEAGE ENDS RIGHT HERE, RIGHT NOW.

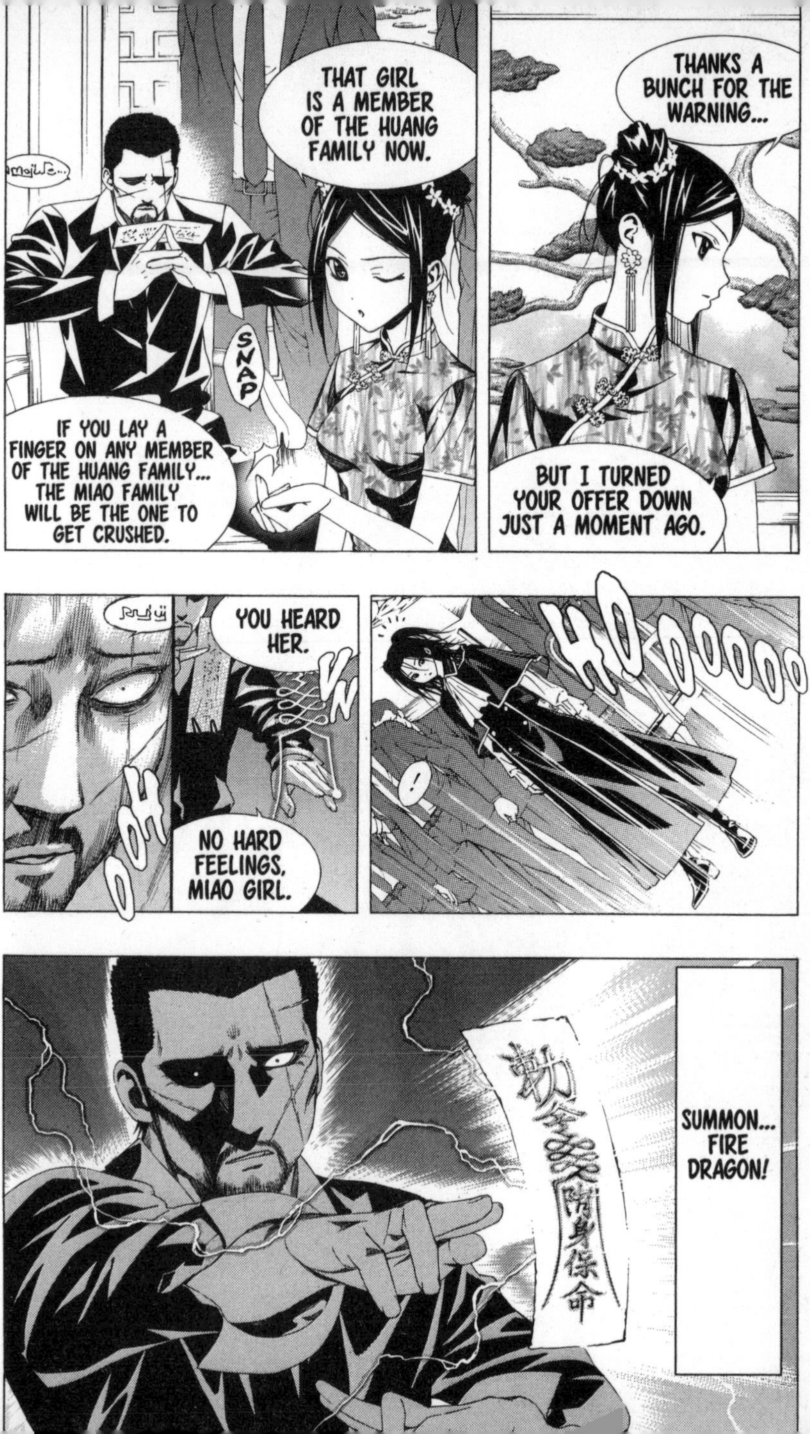
THAT GIRL IS A MEMBER OF THE HUANG FAMILY NOW.
SNAP
IF YOU LAY A FINGER ON ANY MEMBER OF THE HUANG FAMILY... THE MIAO FAMILY WILL BE THE ONE TO GET CRUSHED.
THANKS A BUNCH FOR THE WARNING...
BUT I TURNED YOUR OFFER DOWN JUST A MOMENT AGO.
YOU HEARD HER.
NO HARD FEELINGS, MIAO GIRL.
!
HOOOOOO
SUMMON... FIRE DRAGON!

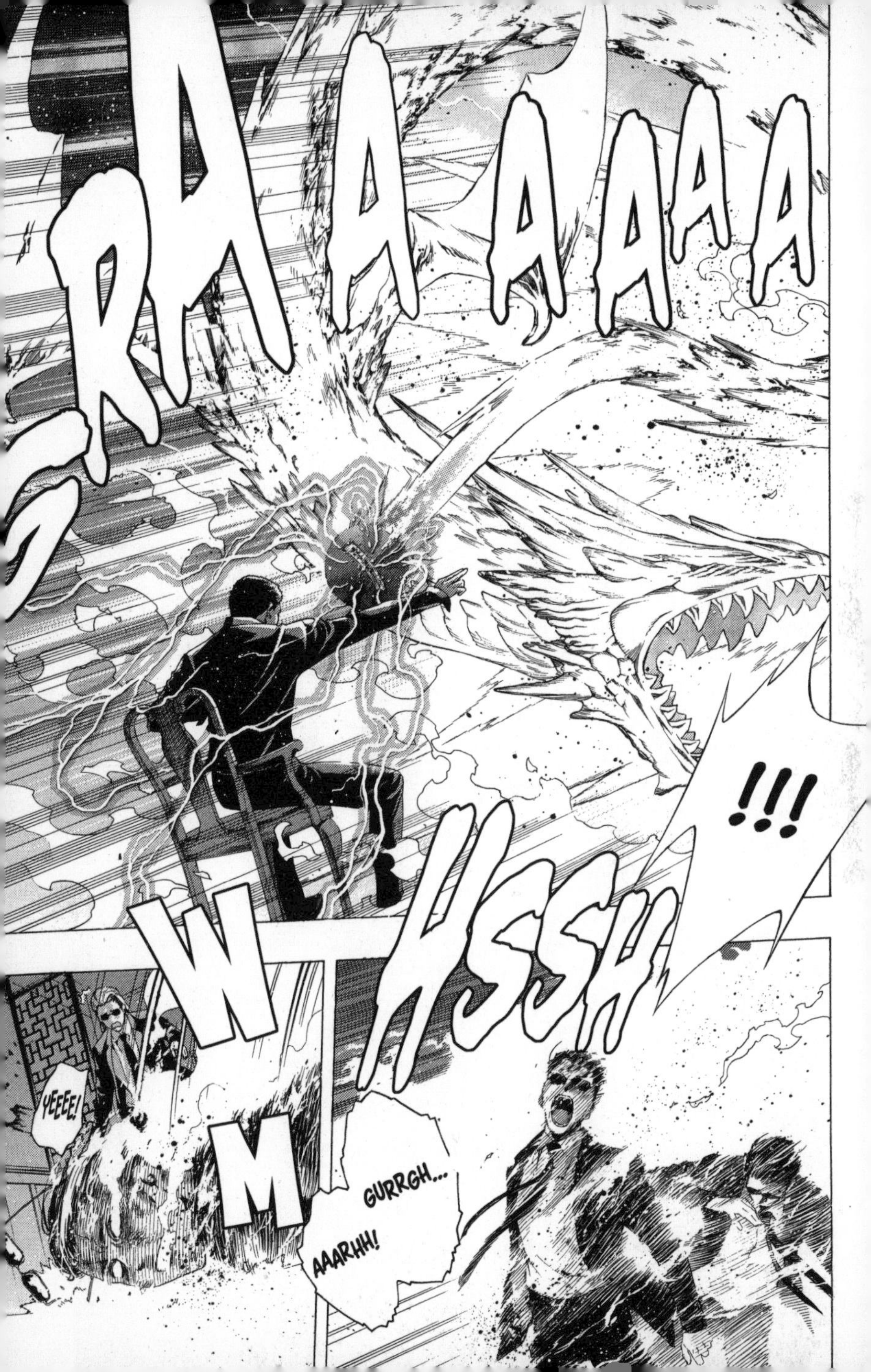
GRAAAAAA
!!!
WHSSH
WM
GURRGH...
AAARHH!
YEEEE!

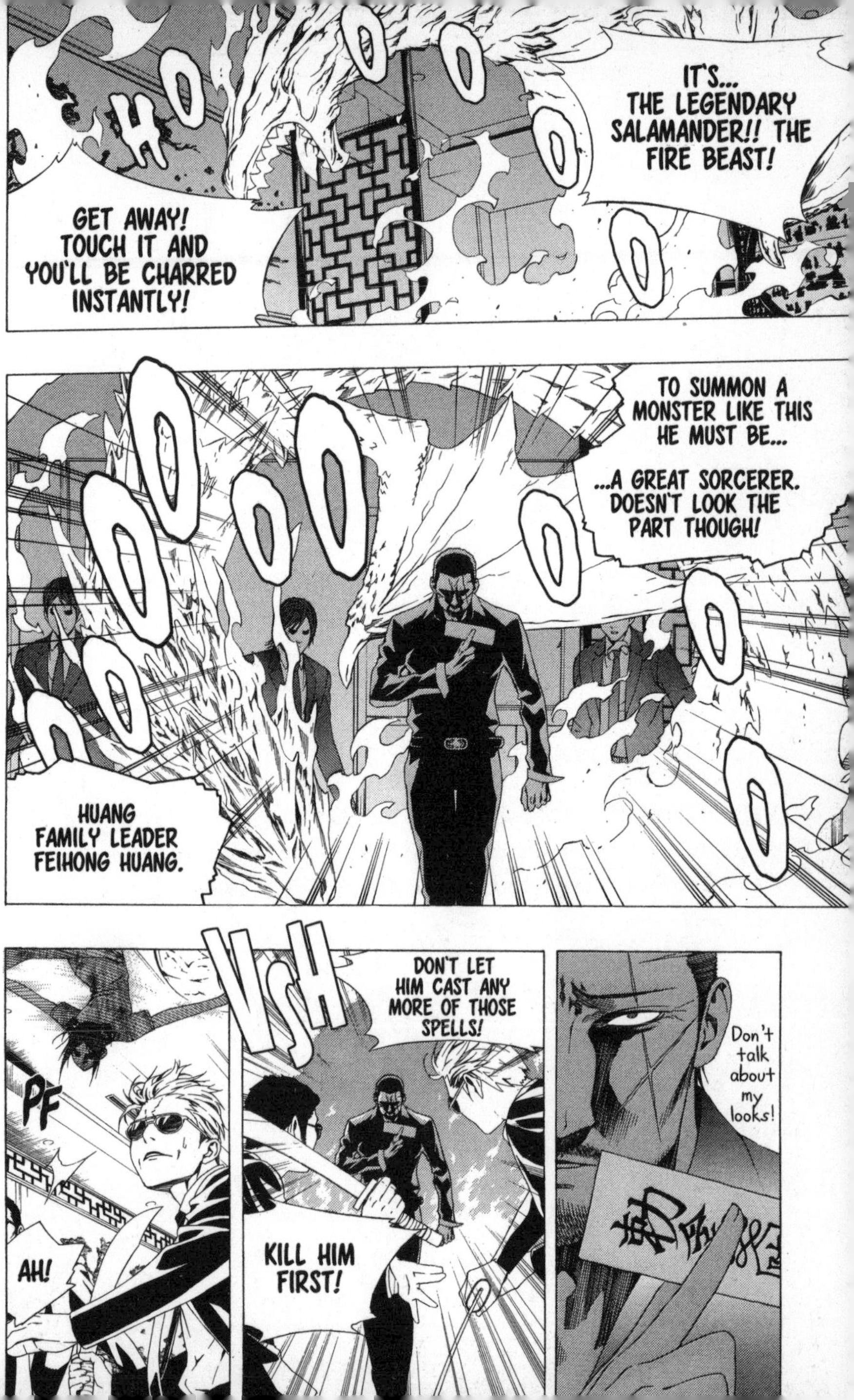
IT'S... THE LEGENDARY SALAMANDER!! THE FIRE BEAST!
HOOOOOOOO
GET AWAY! TOUCH IT AND YOU'LL BE CHARRED INSTANTLY!
TO SUMMON A MONSTER LIKE THIS HE MUST BE...
...A GREAT SORCERER. DOESN'T LOOK THE PART THOUGH!
OOOOOOOOOO
HUANG FAMILY LEADER FEIHONG HUANG.
Don't talk about my looks!
VSH
DON'T LET HIM CAST ANY MORE OF THOSE SPELLS!
KILL HIM FIRST!
PF
AH!

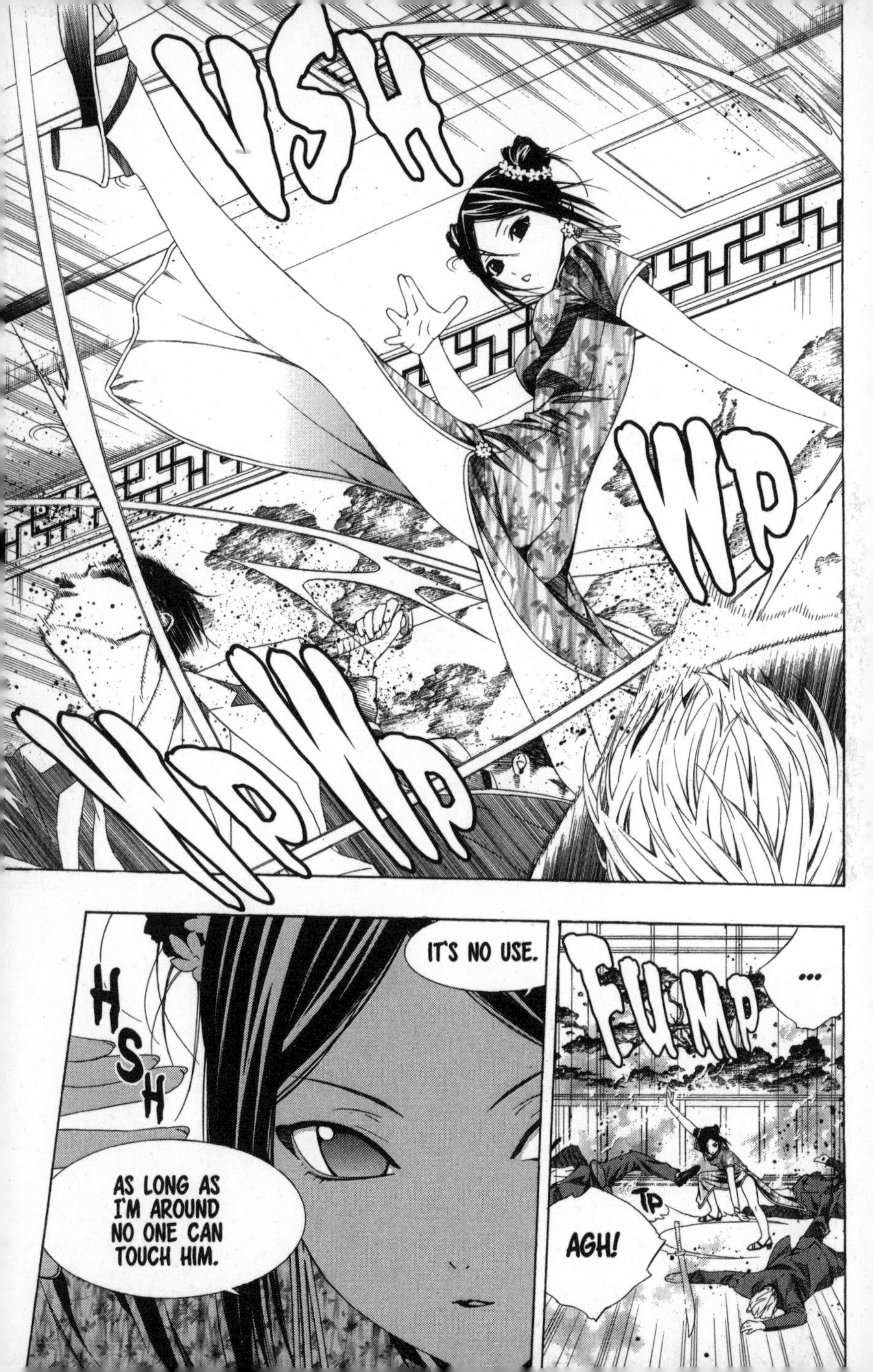
WIP
VSH
WAMP
...
FUMP
TP
AGH!
IT'S NO USE.
HSH
AS LONG AS I'M AROUND NO ONE CAN TOUCH HIM.

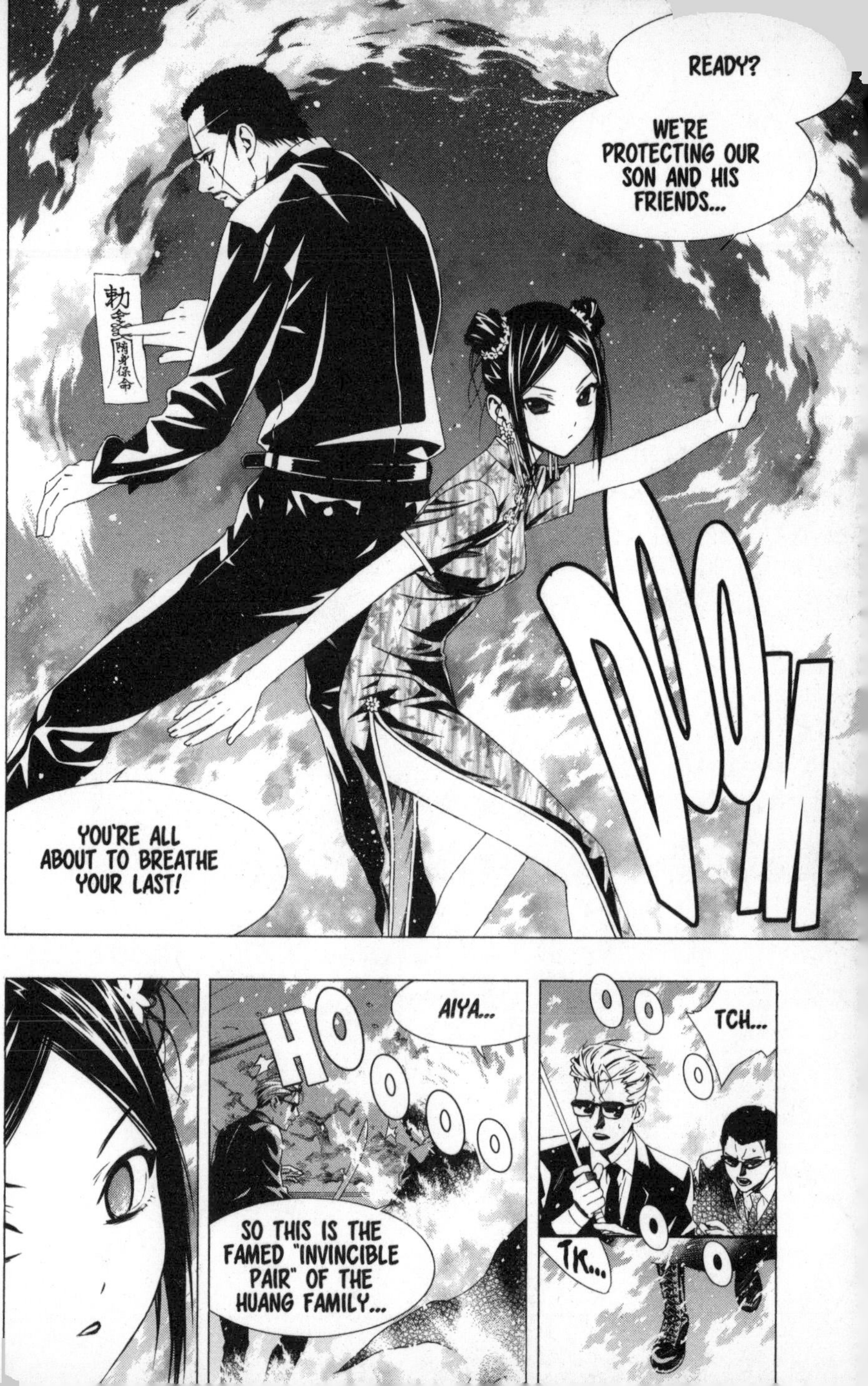
READY?
WE'RE PROTECTING OUR SON AND HIS FRIENDS...
隨身保命
DOOM
YOU'RE ALL ABOUT TO BREATHE YOUR LAST!
TCH...
OOOOOO
TK...
AIYA...
HOOOOOO
SO THIS IS THE FAMED "INVINCIBLE PAIR" OF THE HUANG FAMILY...

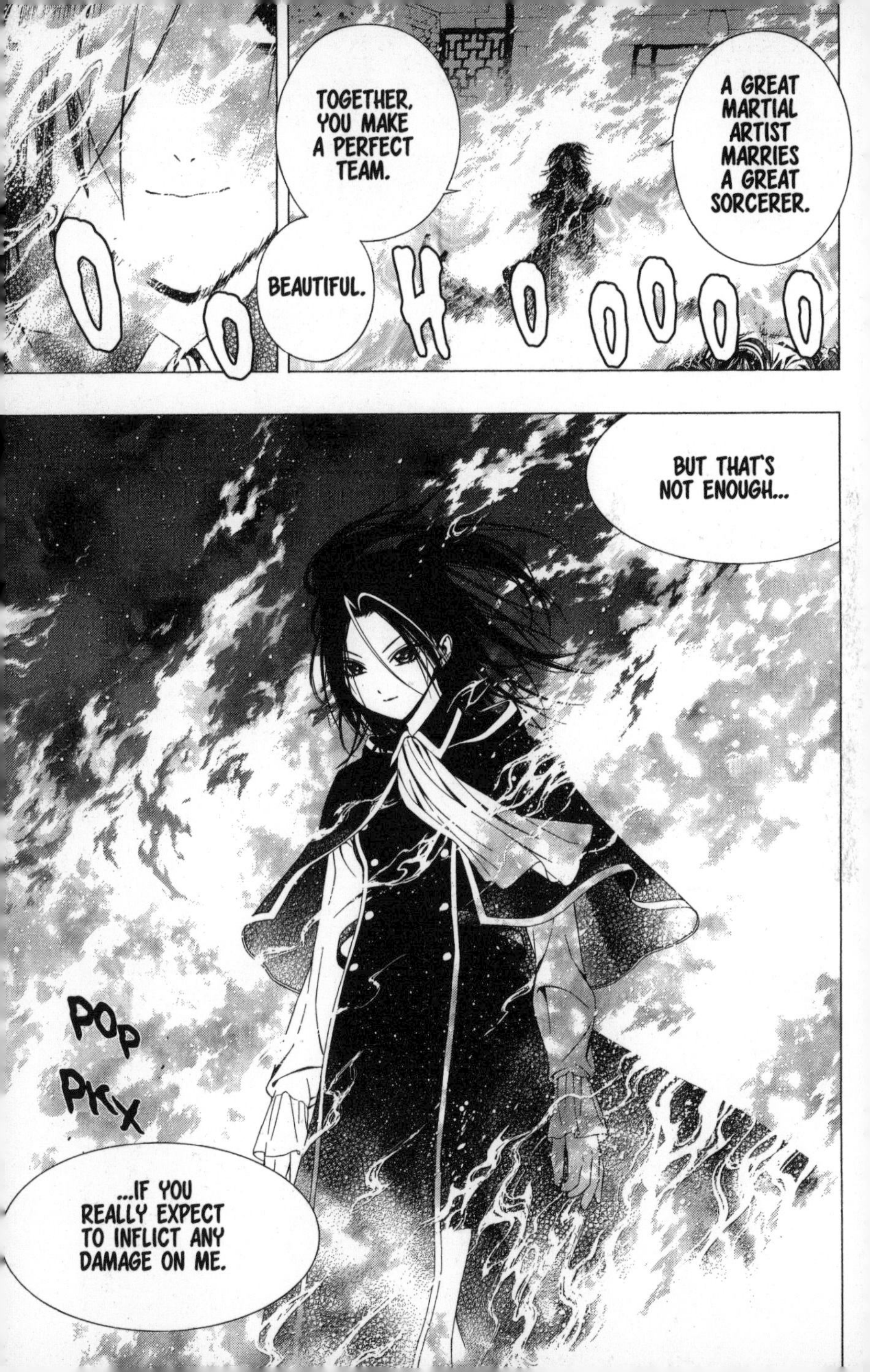
A GREAT MARTIAL ARTIST MARRIES A GREAT SORCERER.
TOGETHER, YOU MAKE A PERFECT TEAM.
BEAUTIFUL.
OOHOOOOO
BUT THAT'S NOT ENOUGH...
POP
PKX
...IF YOU REALLY EXPECT TO INFLICT ANY DAMAGE ON ME.

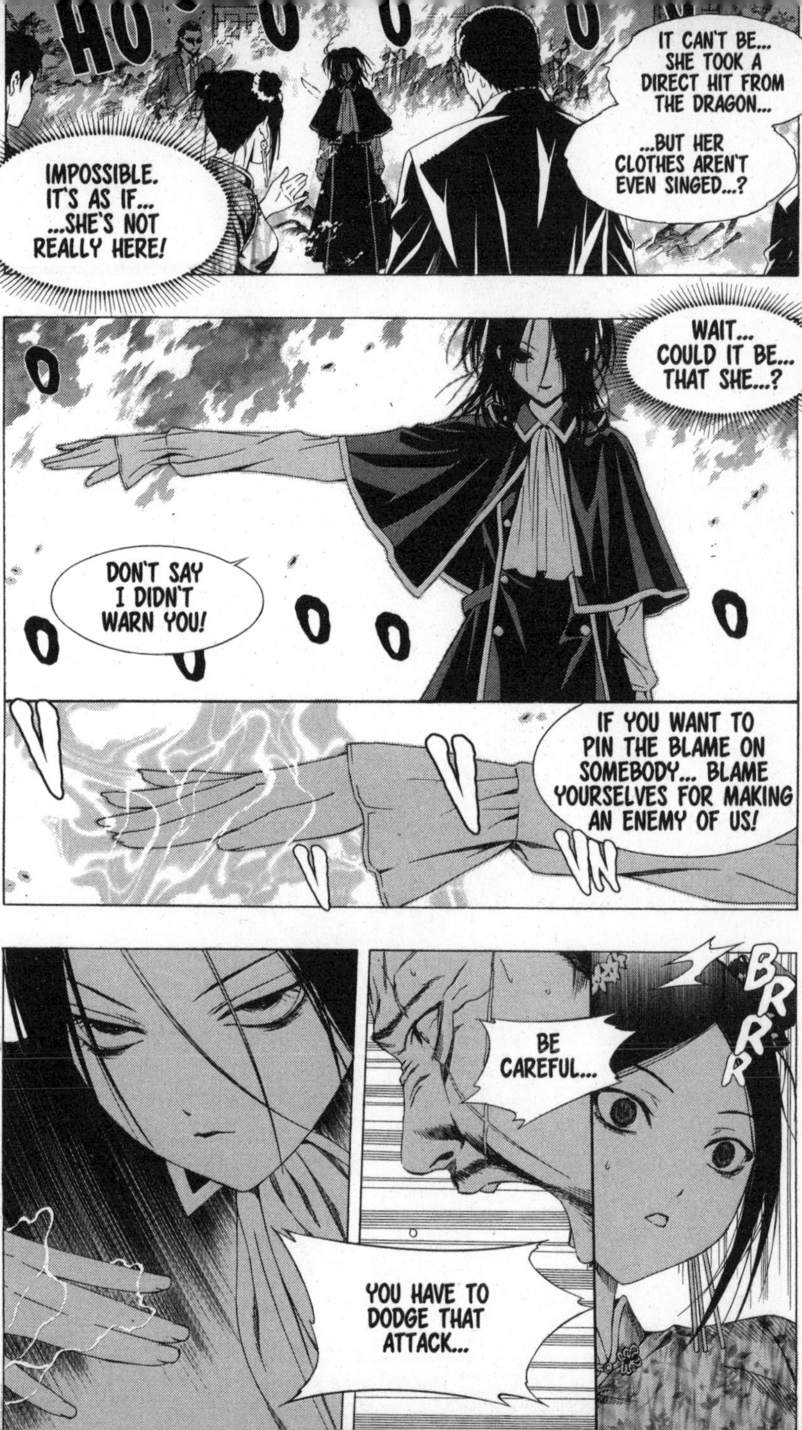
HOOOO
IT CAN'T BE... SHE TOOK A DIRECT HIT FROM THE DRAGON...
...BUT HER CLOTHES AREN'T EVEN SINGED...?
IMPOSSIBLE. IT'S AS IF... ...SHE'S NOT REALLY HERE!
WAIT... COULD IT BE... THAT SHE...?
DON'T SAY I DIDN'T WARN YOU!
IF YOU WANT TO PIN THE BLAME ON SOMEBODY... BLAME YOURSELVES FOR MAKING AN ENEMY OF US!
BRRRR
BE CAREFUL...
YOU HAVE TO DODGE THAT ATTACK...

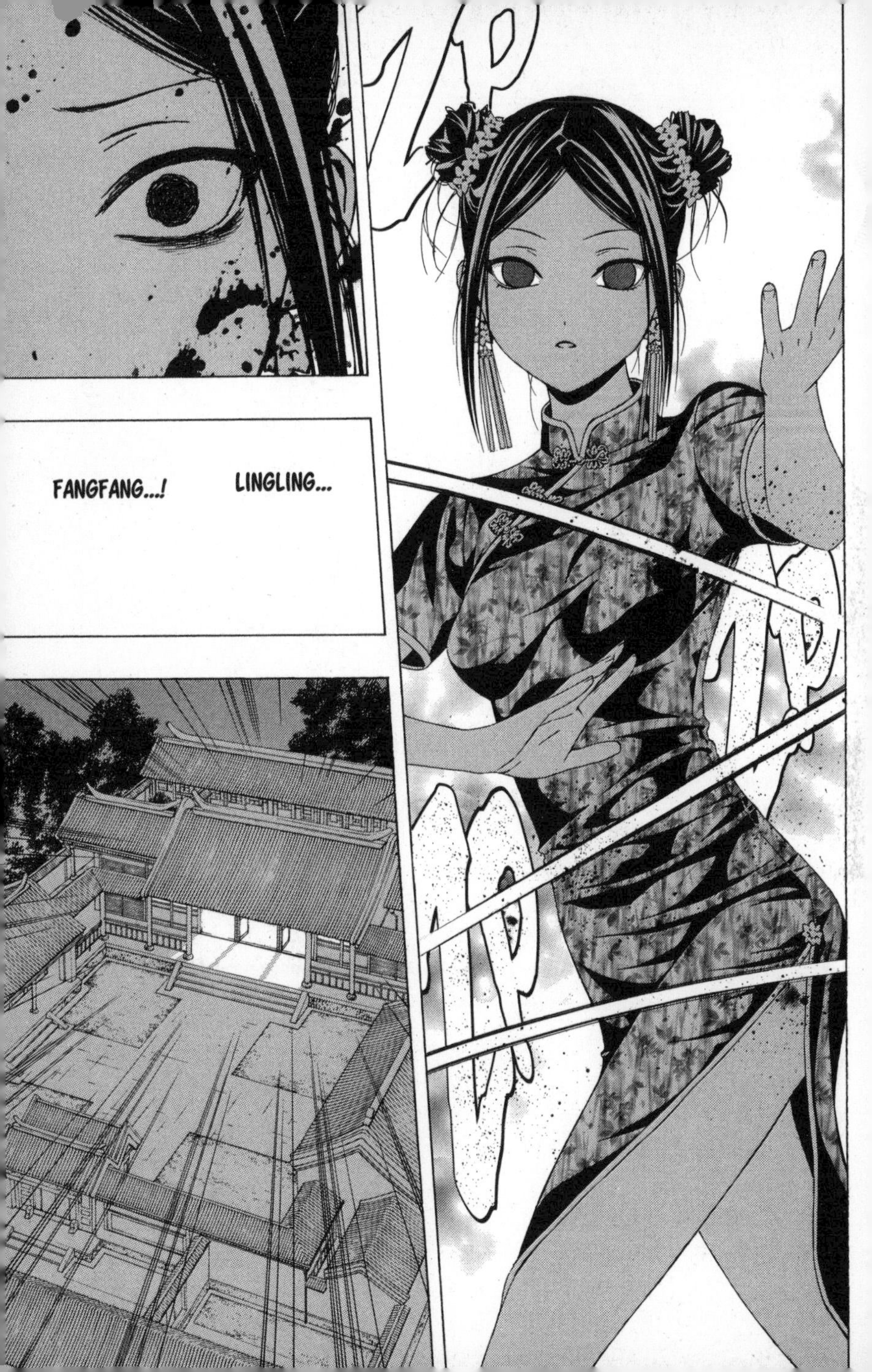
LINGLING...
FANGFANG...!

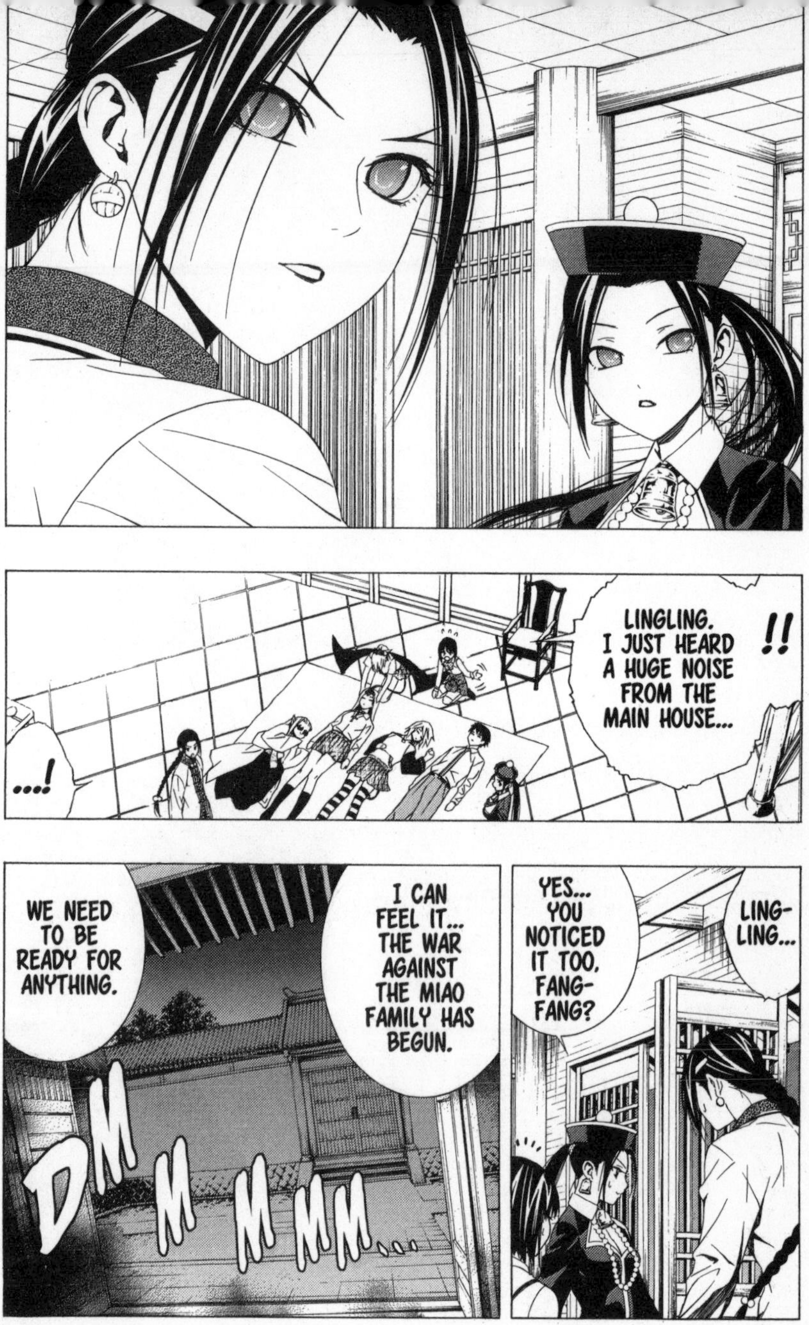
LINGLING. I JUST HEARD A HUGE NOISE FROM THE MAIN HOUSE...
!!
...!
LING-LING...
YES... YOU NOTICED IT TOO, FANG-FANG?
I CAN FEEL IT... THE WAR AGAINST THE MIAO FAMILY HAS BEGUN.
WE NEED TO BE READY FOR ANYTHING.
DMMMMM...

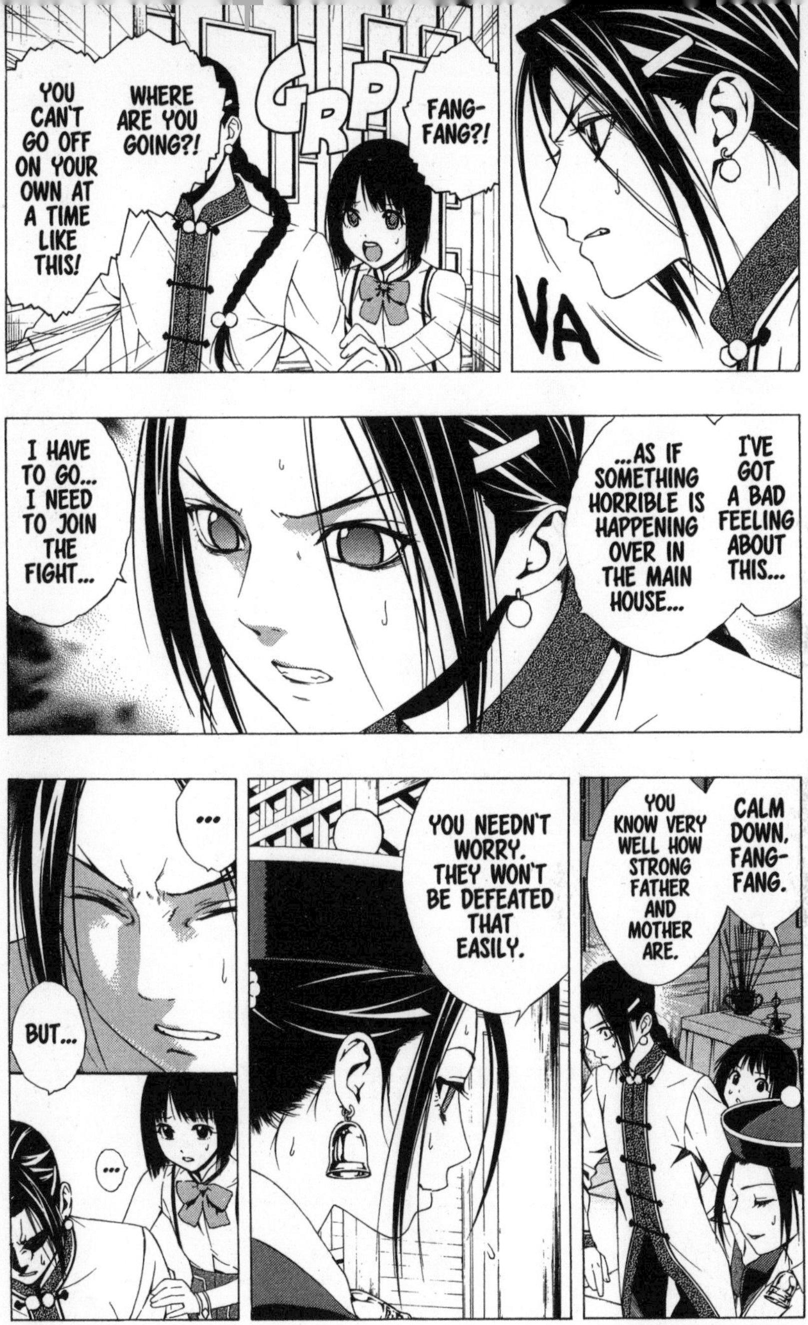
VA
FANG-FANG?!
GRP
WHERE ARE YOU GOING?!
YOU CAN'T GO OFF ON YOUR OWN AT A TIME LIKE THIS!
I'VE GOT A BAD FEELING ABOUT THIS...
...AS IF SOMETHING HORRIBLE IS HAPPENING OVER IN THE MAIN HOUSE...
I HAVE TO GO... I NEED TO JOIN THE FIGHT...
CALM DOWN, FANG-FANG.
YOU KNOW VERY WELL HOW STRONG FATHER AND MOTHER ARE.
YOU NEEDN'T WORRY. THEY WON'T BE DEFEATED THAT EASILY.
...
BUT...
...

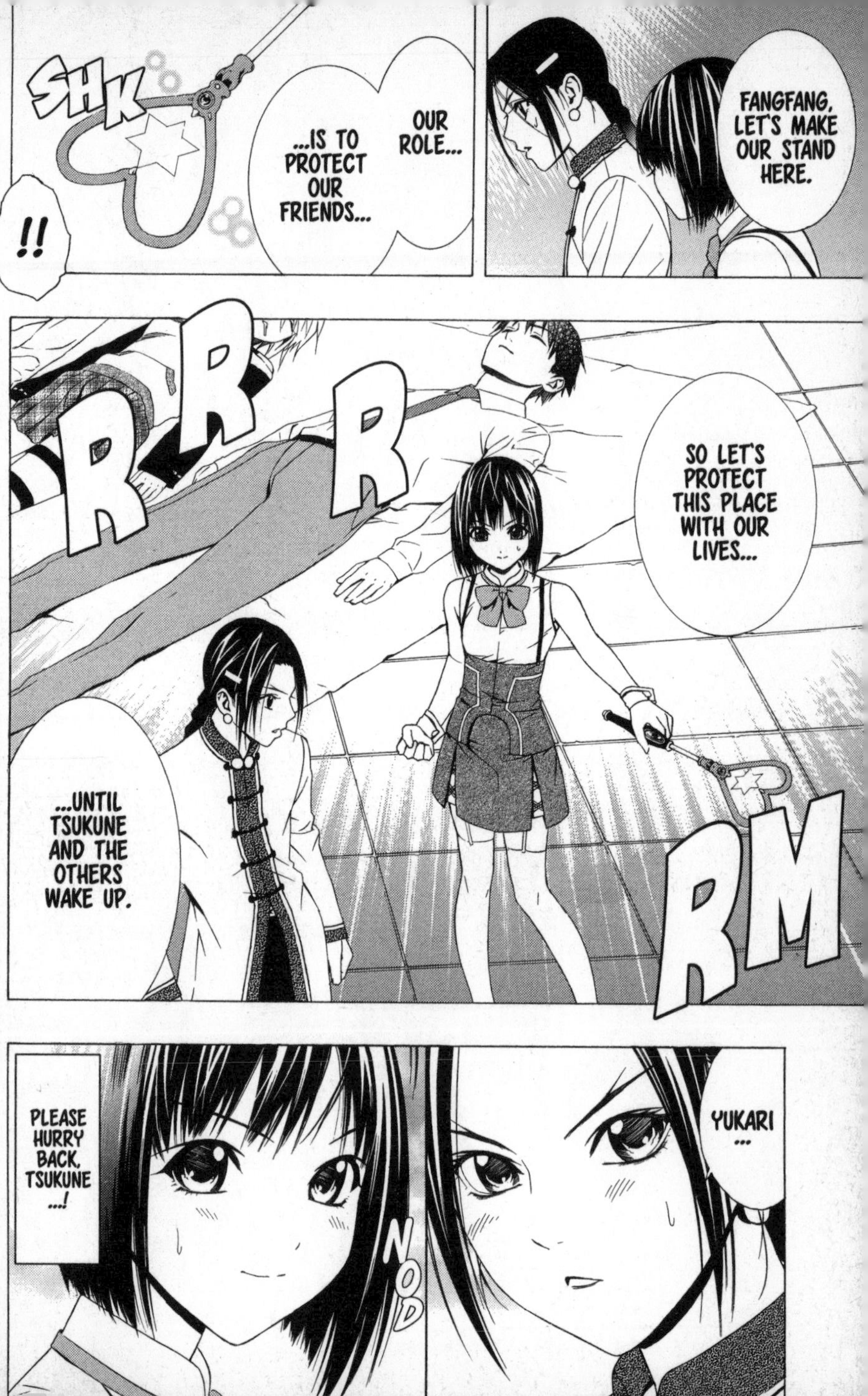
FANGFANG, LET'S MAKE OUR STAND HERE.
OUR ROLE...
...IS TO PROTECT OUR FRIENDS...
SHK
!!
SO LET'S PROTECT THIS PLACE WITH OUR LIVES...
RRR
...UNTIL TSUKUNE AND THE OTHERS WAKE UP.
RM
YUKARI ...
NOD
PLEASE HURRY BACK, TSUKUNE ...!

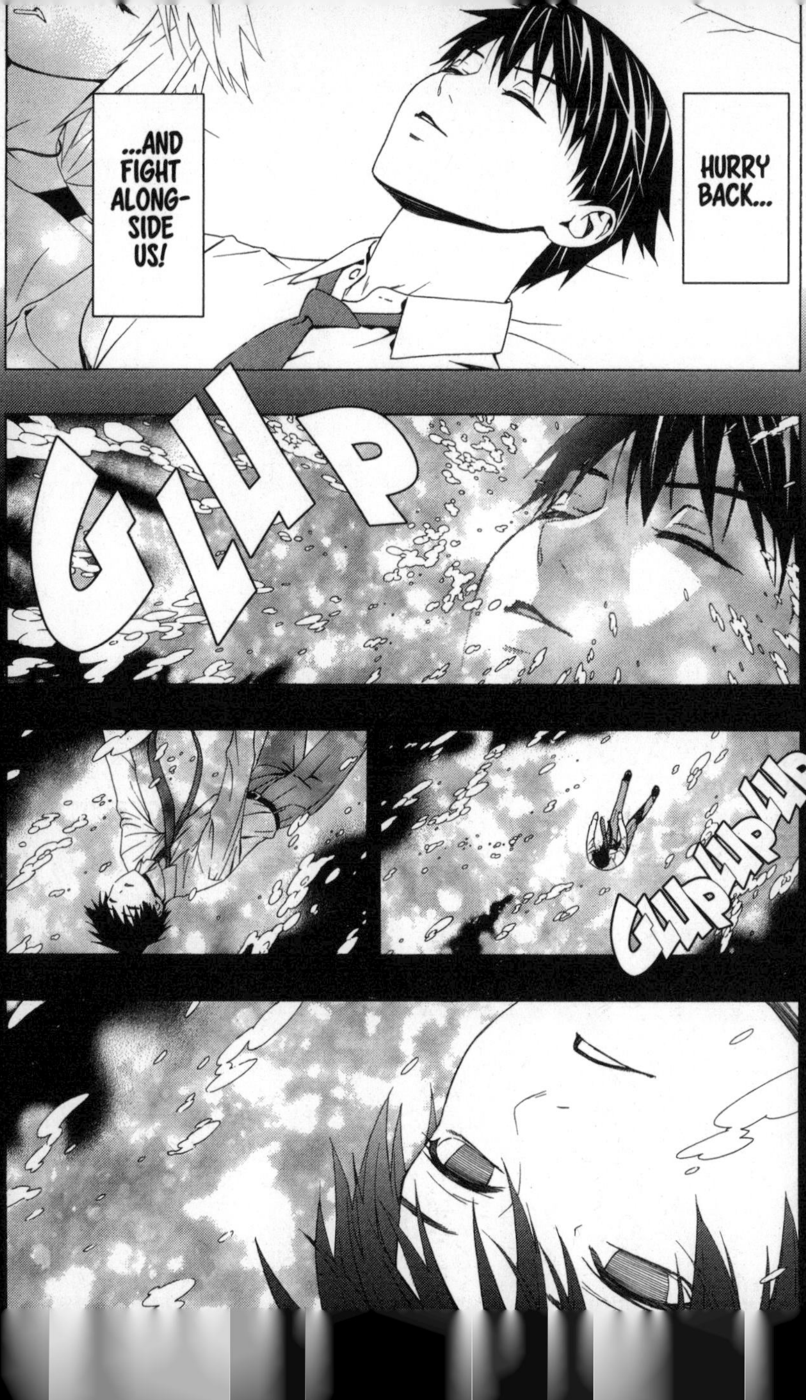
HURRY BACK...
...AND FIGHT ALONG-SIDE US!
GLUP
GLUPGLUPGLUP

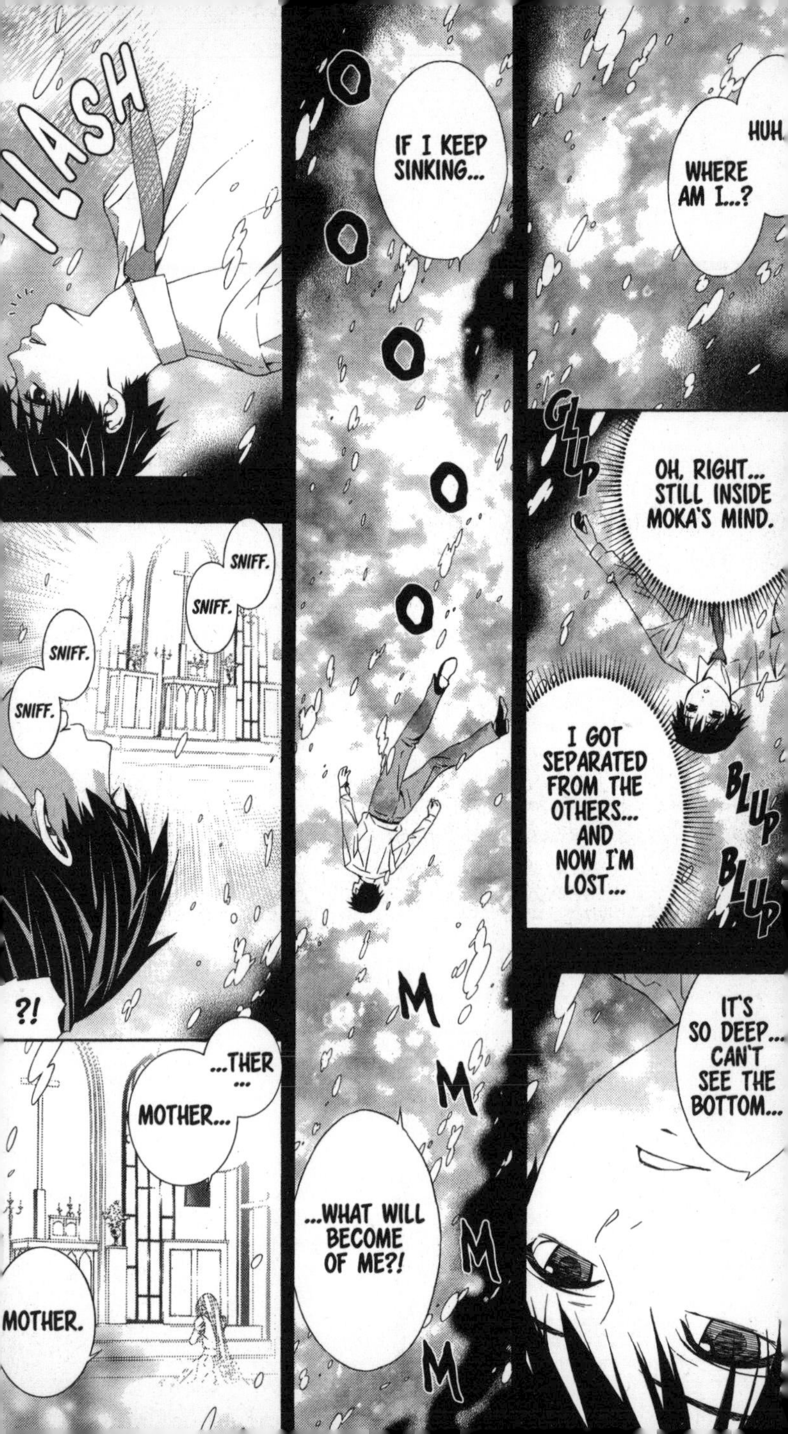
HUH...
WHERE AM I...?
GLUP
OH, RIGHT... STILL INSIDE MOKA'S MIND.
I GOT SEPARATED FROM THE OTHERS... AND NOW I'M LOST...
BLUP BLUP
IT'S SO DEEP... CAN'T SEE THE BOTTOM...
IF I KEEP SINKING...
MMMM
...WHAT WILL BECOME OF ME?!
FLASH
SNIFF.
SNIFF.
SNIFF.
SNIFF.
?!
...THER...
MOTHER...
MOTHER.

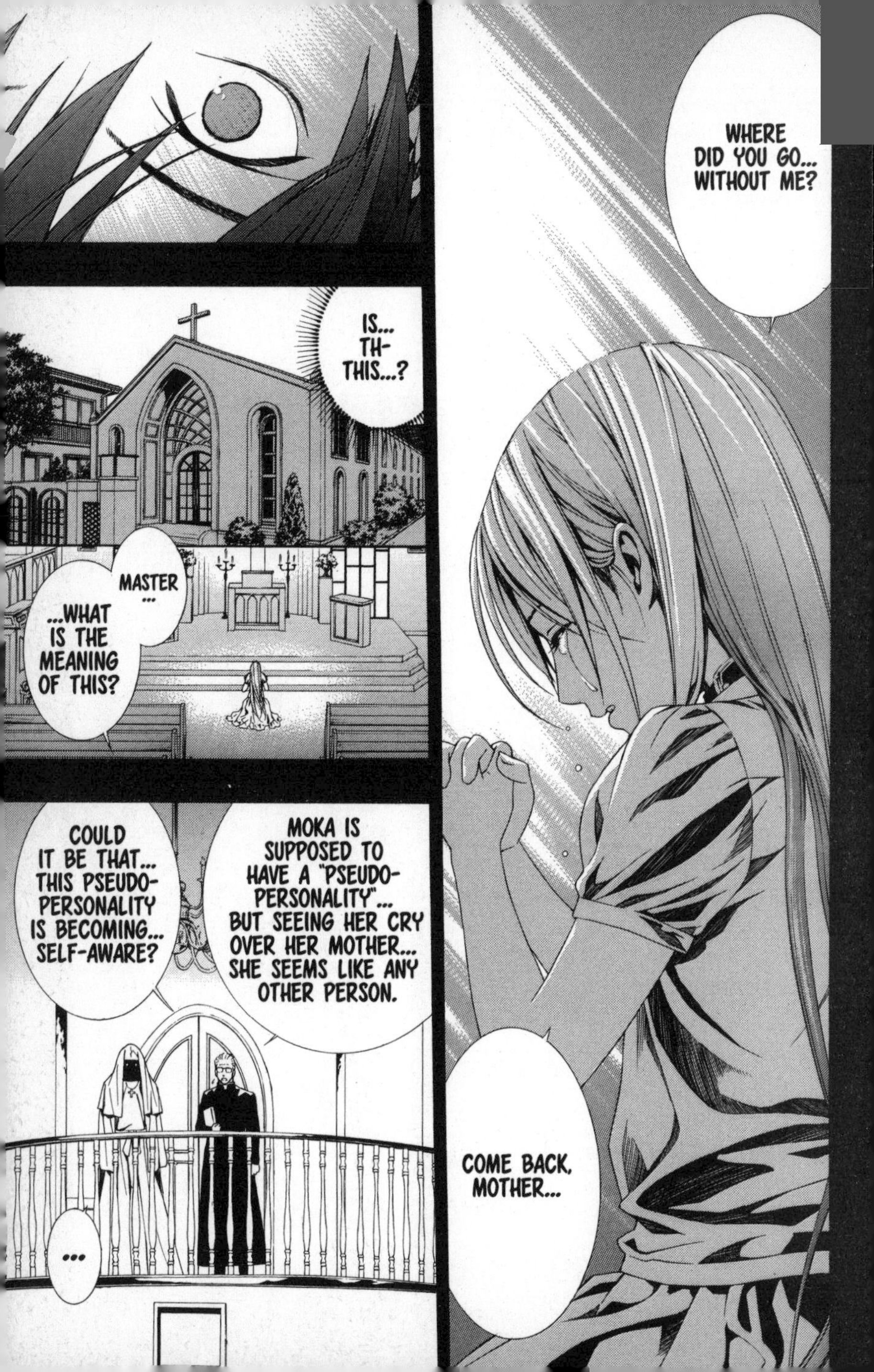
WHERE DID YOU GO... WITHOUT ME?
COME BACK, MOTHER...
IS... TH- THIS...?
MASTER...
...WHAT IS THE MEANING OF THIS?
MOKA IS SUPPOSED TO HAVE A "PSEUDO-PERSONALITY"... BUT SEEING HER CRY OVER HER MOTHER... SHE SEEMS LIKE ANY OTHER PERSON.
COULD IT BE THAT... THIS PSEUDO-PERSONALITY IS BECOMING... SELF-AWARE?
...

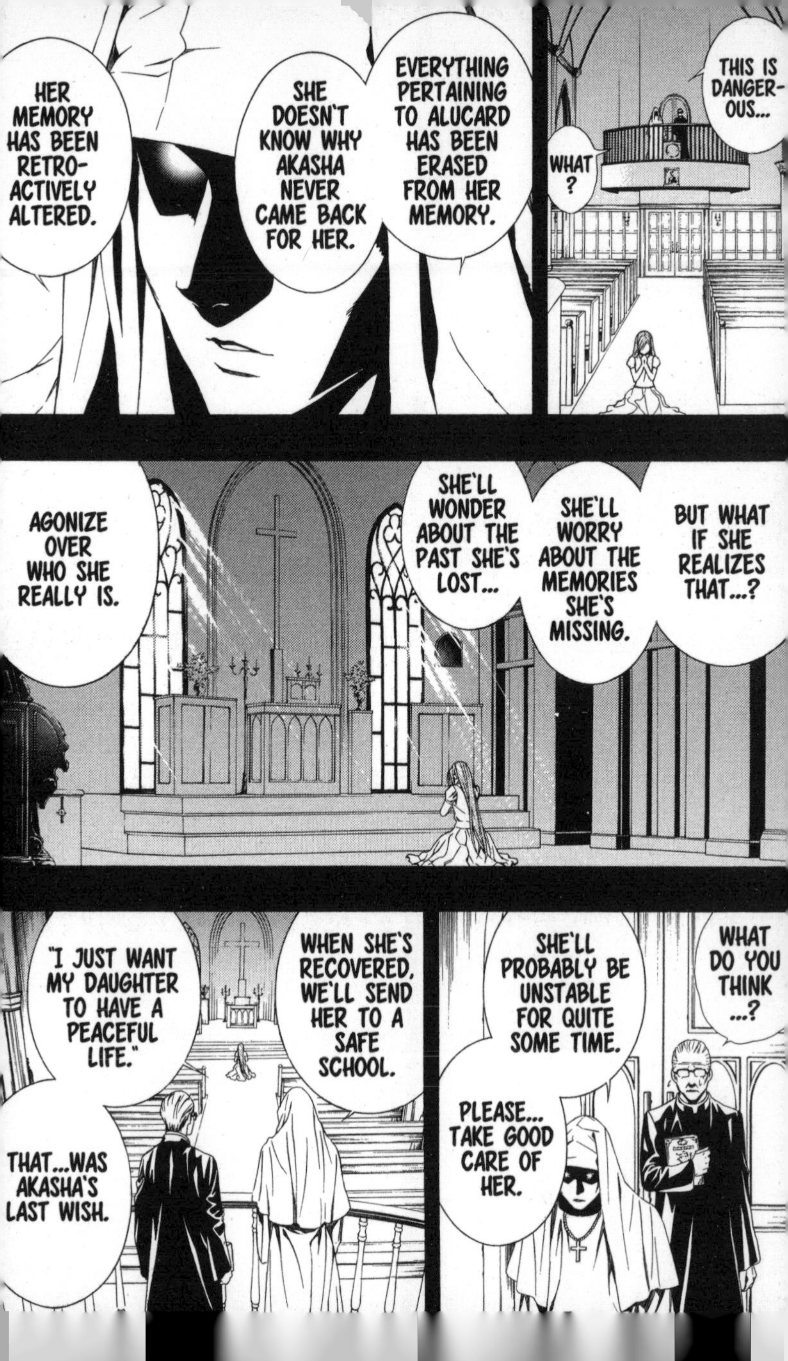
THIS IS DANGEROUS...
WHAT?
EVERYTHING PERTAINING TO ALUCARD HAS BEEN ERASED FROM HER MEMORY.
SHE DOESN'T KNOW WHY AKASHA NEVER CAME BACK FOR HER.
HER MEMORY HAS BEEN RETROACTIVELY ALTERED.
BUT WHAT IF SHE REALIZES THAT...?
SHE'LL WORRY ABOUT THE MEMORIES SHE'S MISSING.
SHE'LL WONDER ABOUT THE PAST SHE'S LOST...
AGONIZE OVER WHO SHE REALLY IS.
WHAT DO YOU THINK...?
SHE'LL PROBABLY BE UNSTABLE FOR QUITE SOME TIME.
PLEASE... TAKE GOOD CARE OF HER.
WHEN SHE'S RECOVERED, WE'LL SEND HER TO A SAFE SCHOOL.
"I JUST WANT MY DAUGHTER TO HAVE A PEACEFUL LIFE."
THAT...WAS AKASHA'S LAST WISH.

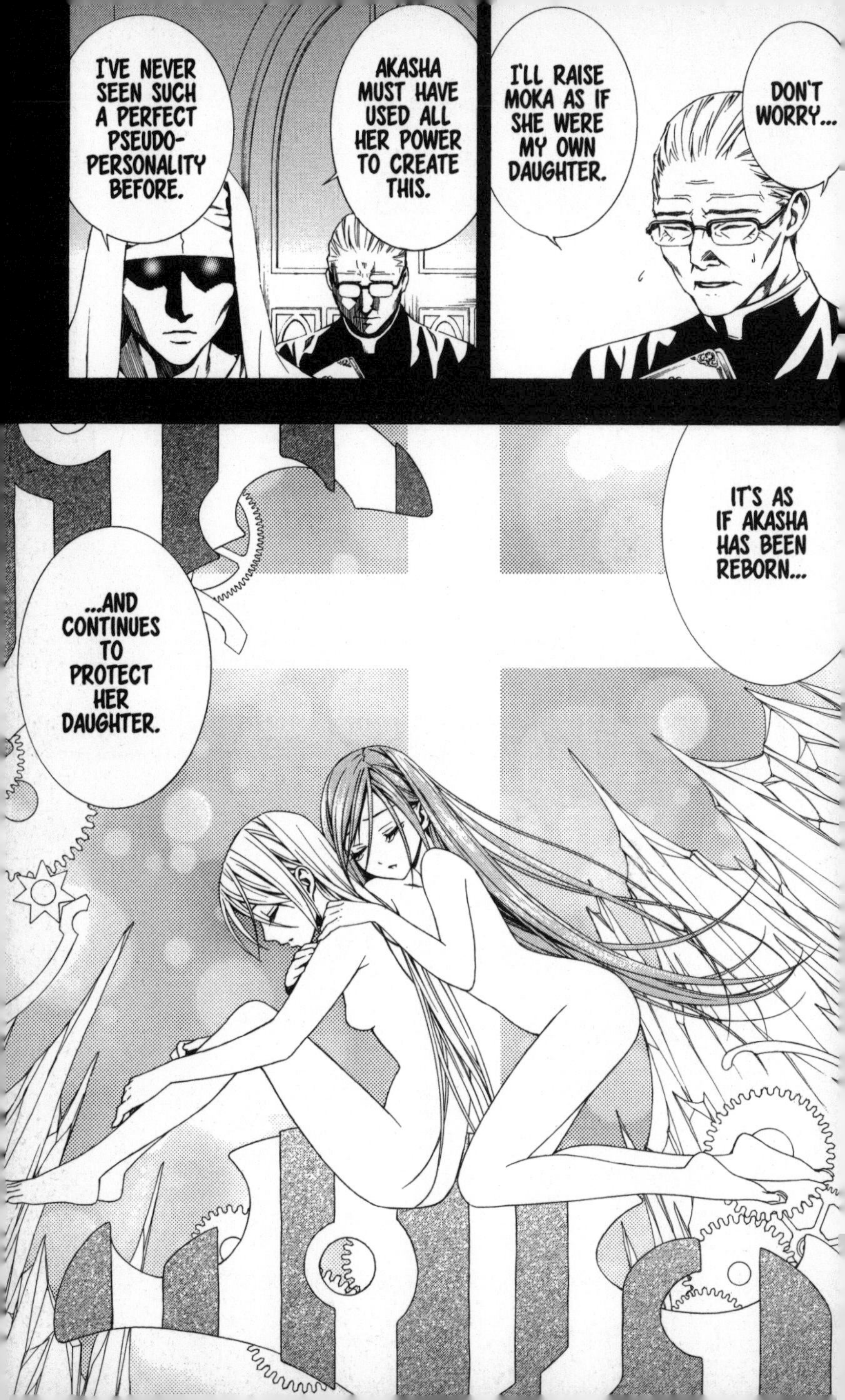
DON'T WORRY...
I'LL RAISE MOKA AS IF SHE WERE MY OWN DAUGHTER.
AKASHA MUST HAVE USED ALL HER POWER TO CREATE THIS.
I'VE NEVER SEEN SUCH A PERFECT PSEUDO-PERSONALITY BEFORE.
IT'S AS IF AKASHA HAS BEEN REBORN...
...AND CONTINUES TO PROTECT HER DAUGHTER.

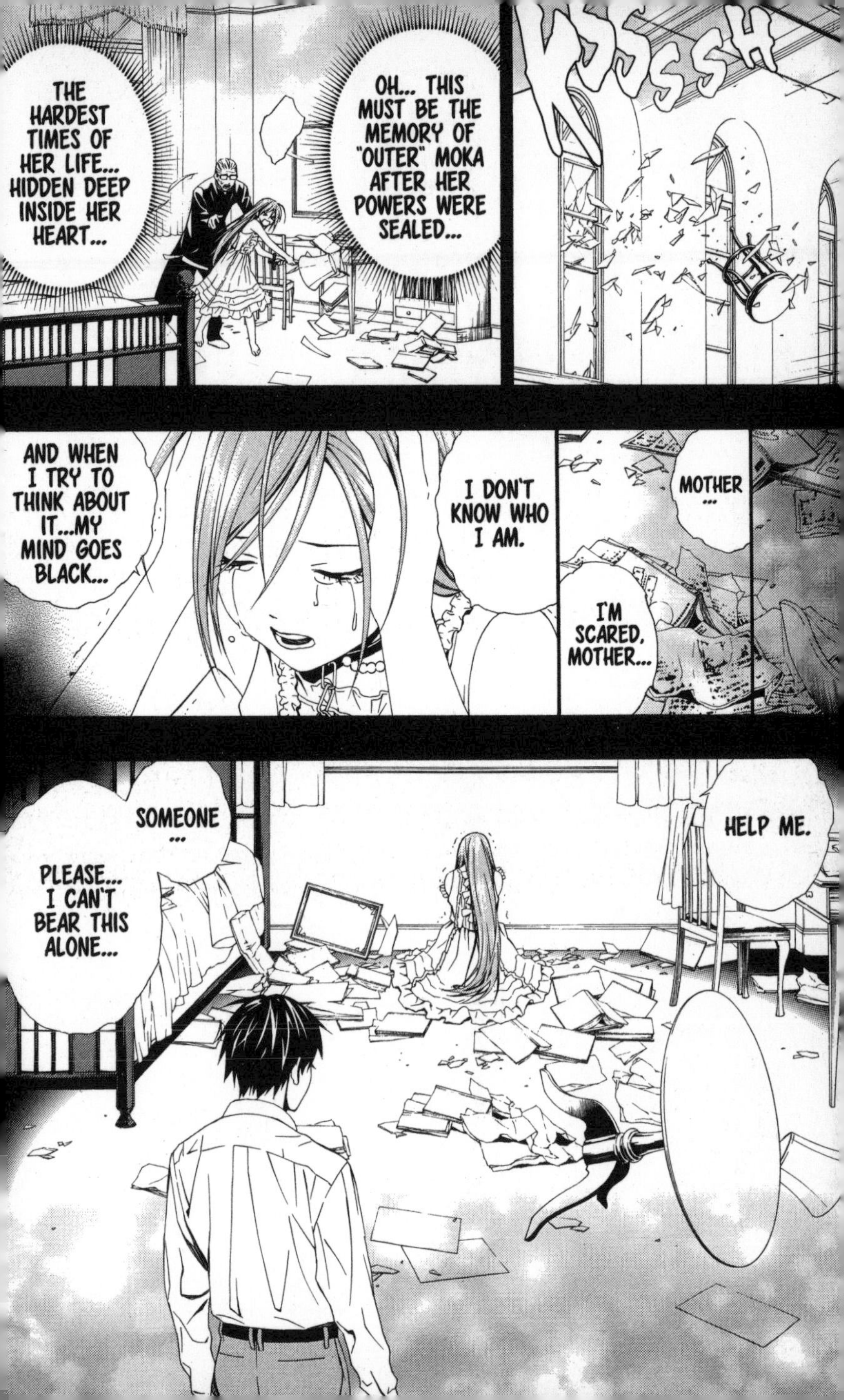
KSSSSH
OH... THIS MUST BE THE MEMORY OF "OUTER" MOKA AFTER HER POWERS WERE SEALED...
THE HARDEST TIMES OF HER LIFE... HIDDEN DEEP INSIDE HER HEART...
MOTHER ...
I'M SCARED, MOTHER...
I DON'T KNOW WHO I AM.
AND WHEN I TRY TO THINK ABOUT IT...MY MIND GOES BLACK...
HELP ME.
SOMEONE ...
PLEASE... I CAN'T BEAR THIS ALONE...

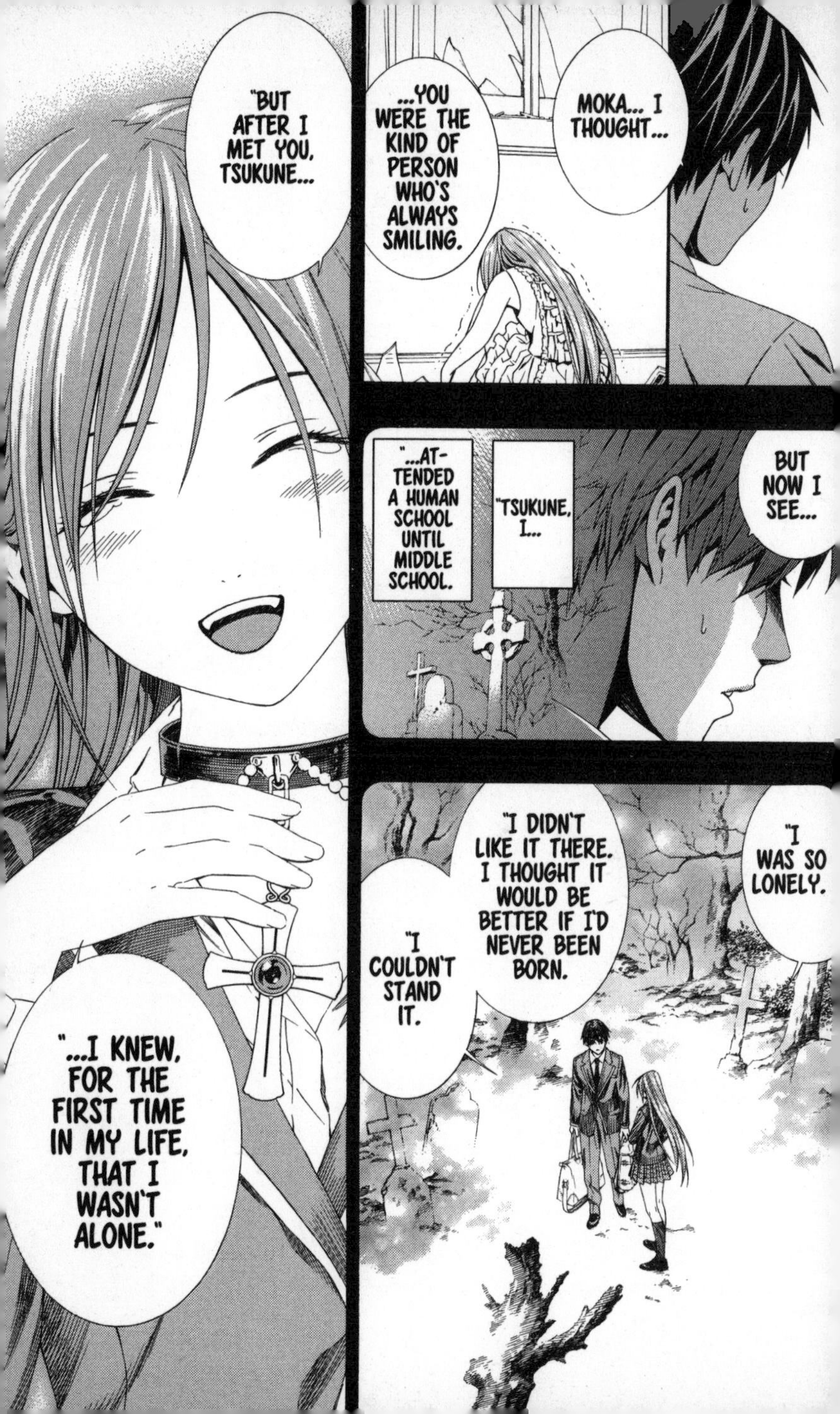
MOKA... I THOUGHT...
...YOU WERE THE KIND OF PERSON WHO'S ALWAYS SMILING.
BUT NOW I SEE...
"TSUKUNE, I...
"...AT-TENDED A HUMAN SCHOOL UNTIL MIDDLE SCHOOL.
"I WAS SO LONELY.
"I DIDN'T LIKE IT THERE. I THOUGHT IT WOULD BE BETTER IF I'D NEVER BEEN BORN.
"I COULDN'T STAND IT.
"BUT AFTER I MET YOU, TSUKUNE...
"...I KNEW, FOR THE FIRST TIME IN MY LIFE, THAT I WASN'T ALONE."

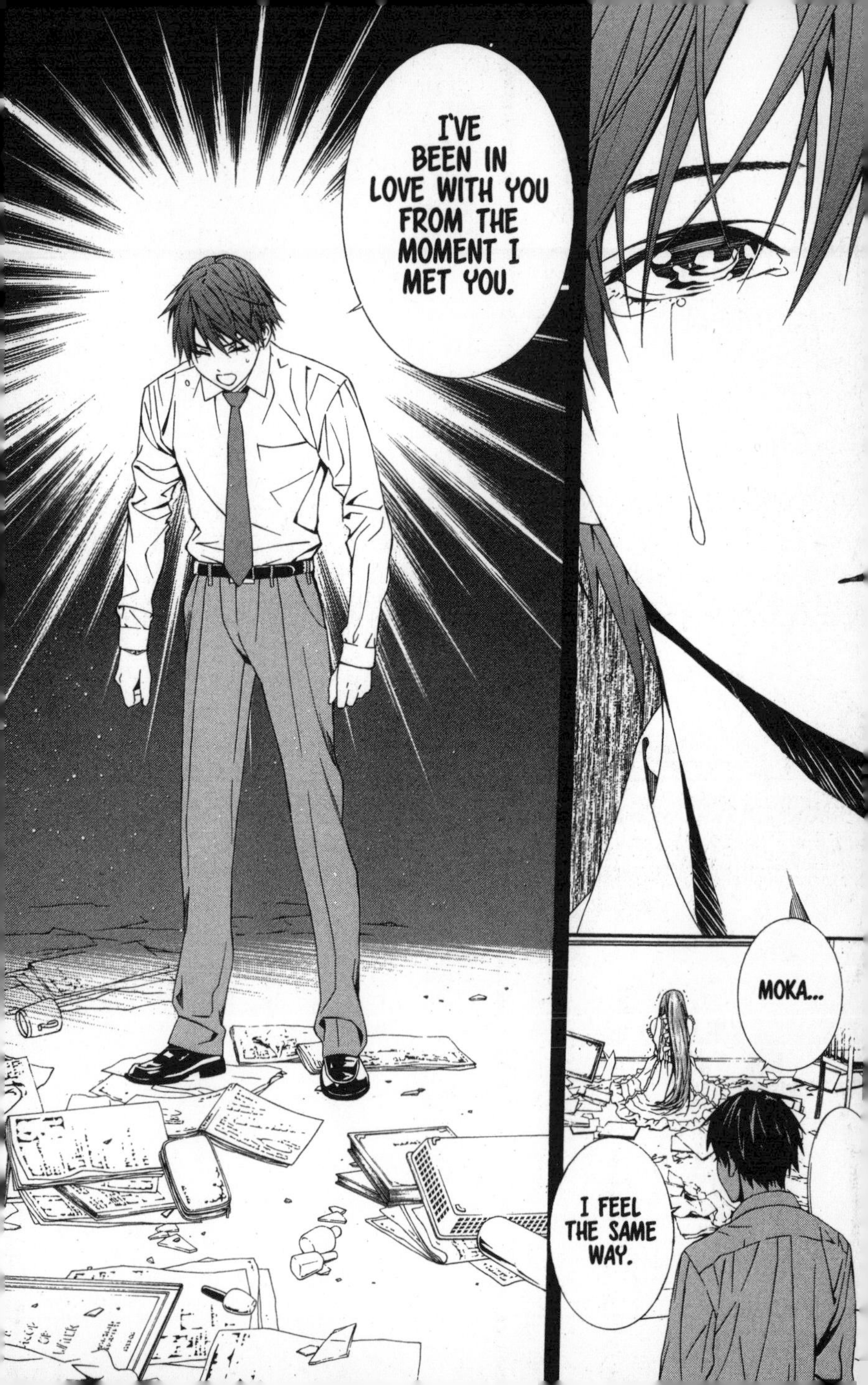
MOKA...
I FEEL THE SAME WAY.
I'VE BEEN IN LOVE WITH YOU FROM THE MOMENT I MET YOU.

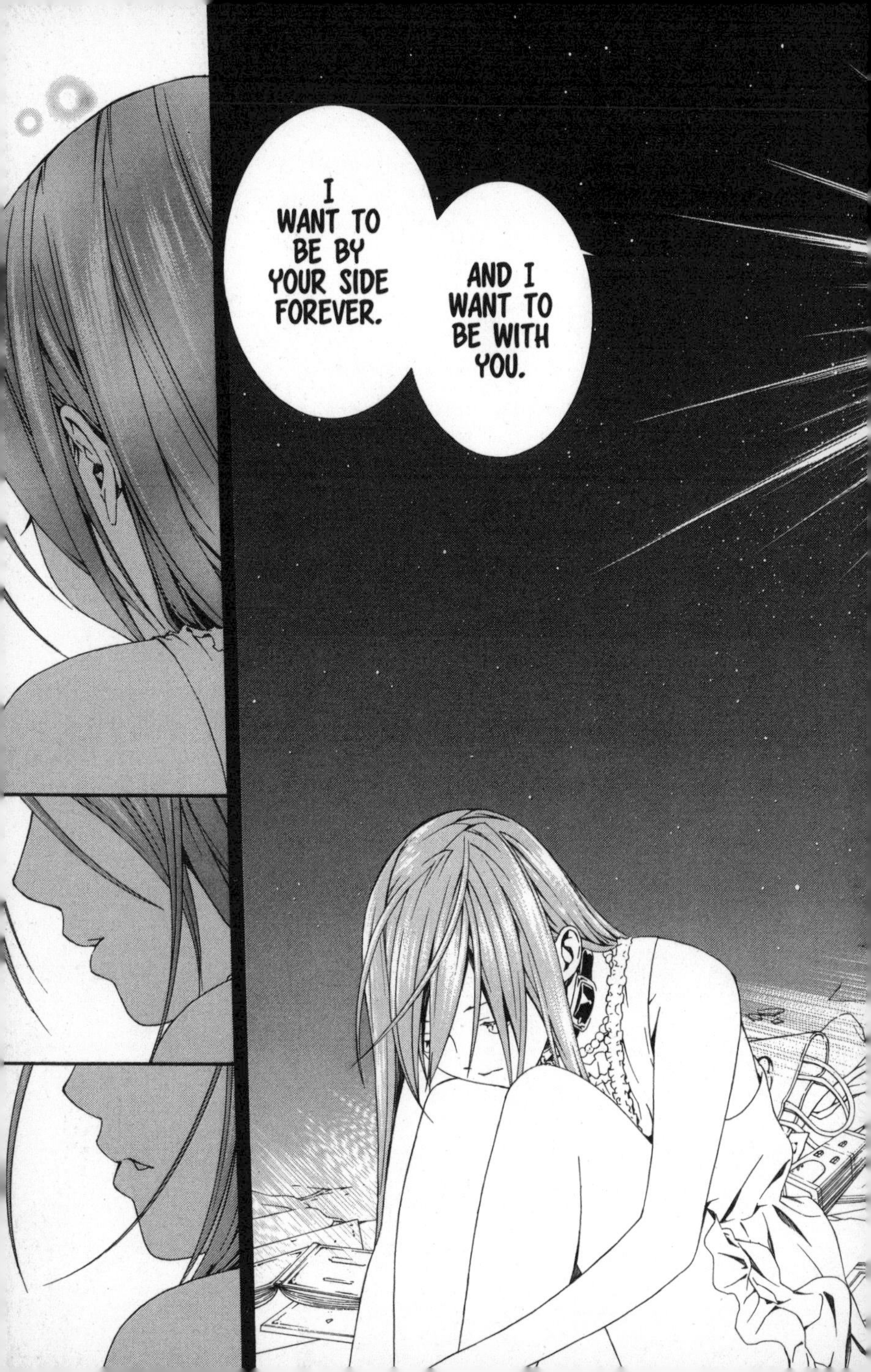
I WANT TO BE BY YOUR SIDE FOREVER.
AND I WANT TO BE WITH YOU.

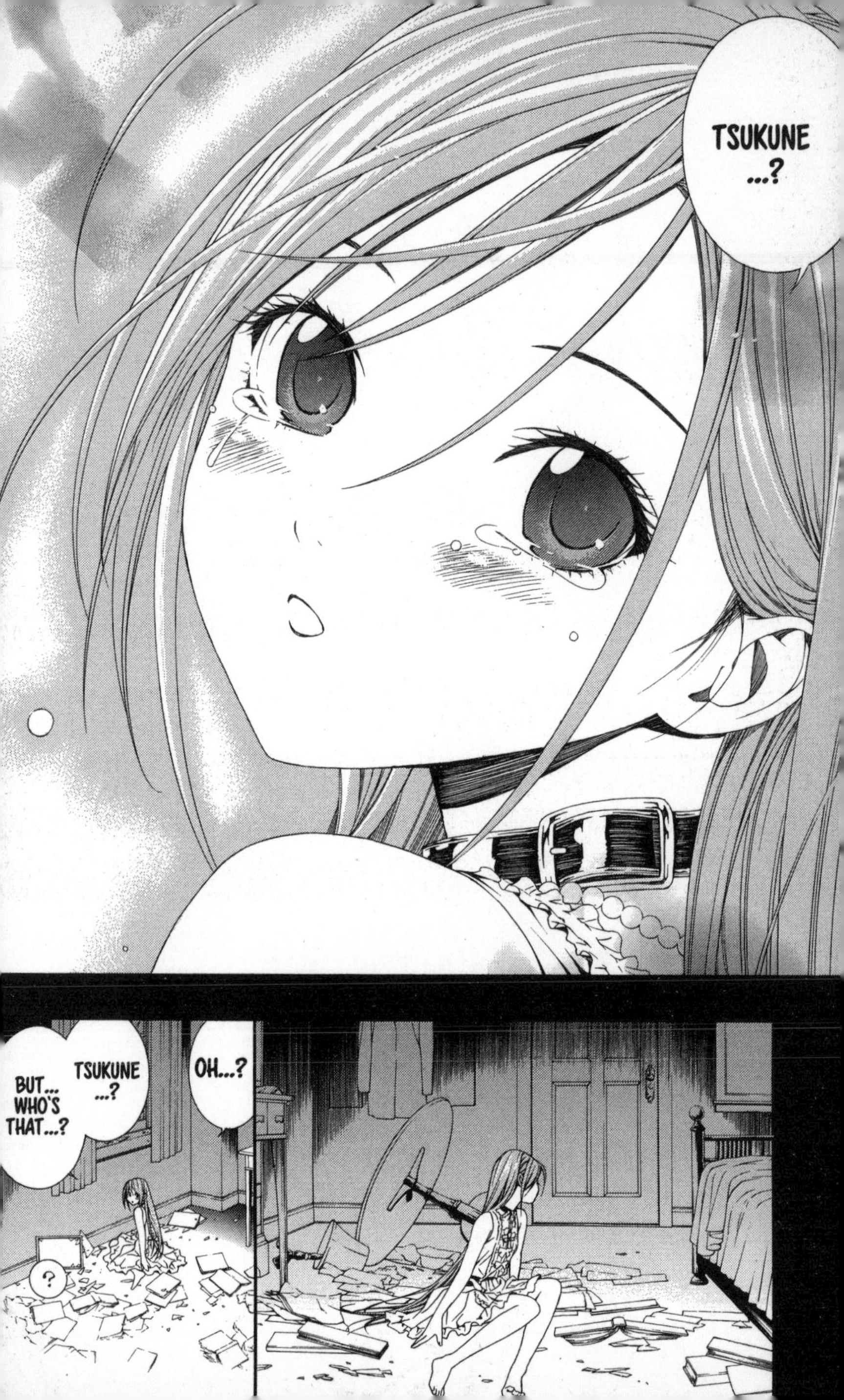
TSUKUNE ...?
OH...?
TSUKUNE ...?
BUT... WHO'S THAT...?
?

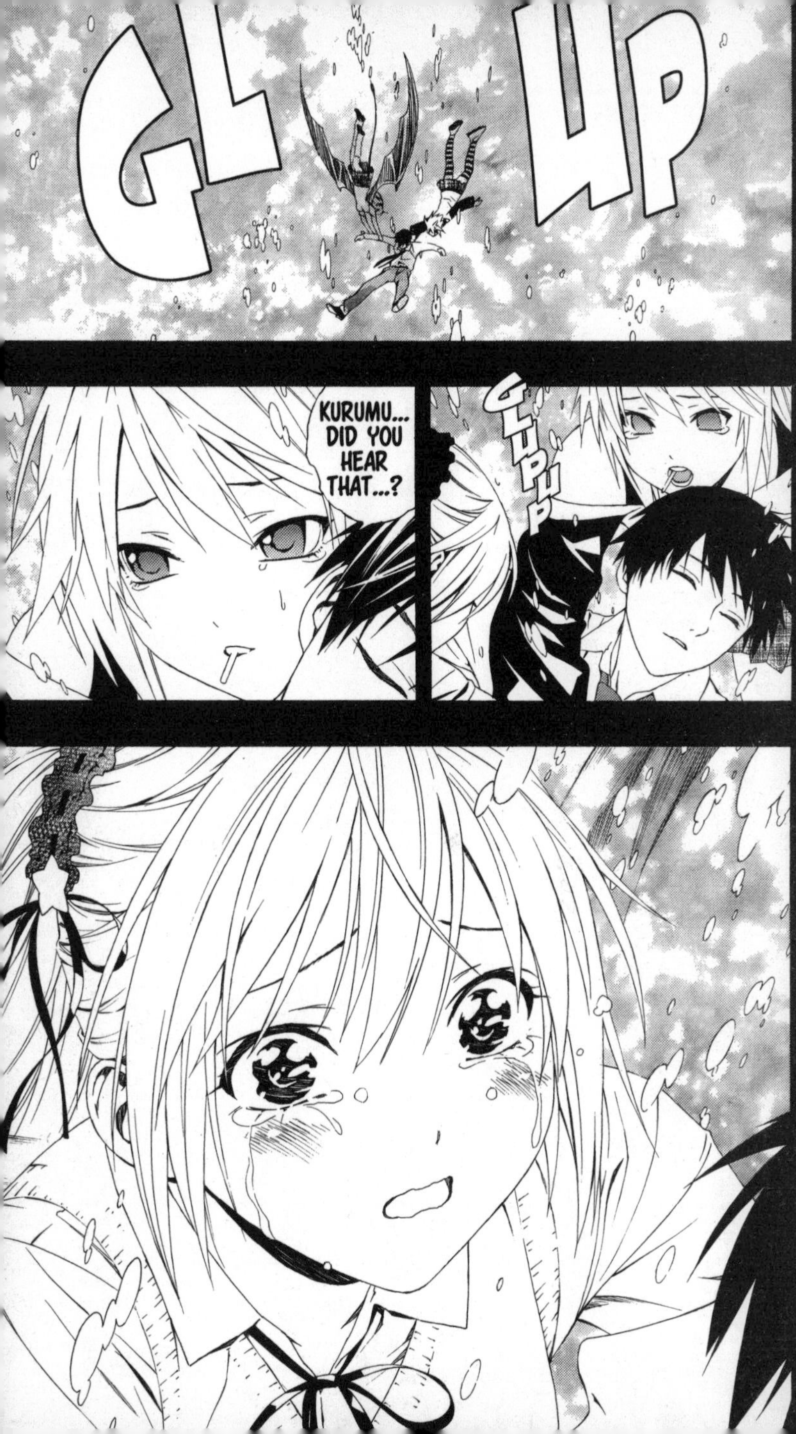
GL UP
GLUPUP
KURUMU... DID YOU HEAR THAT...?

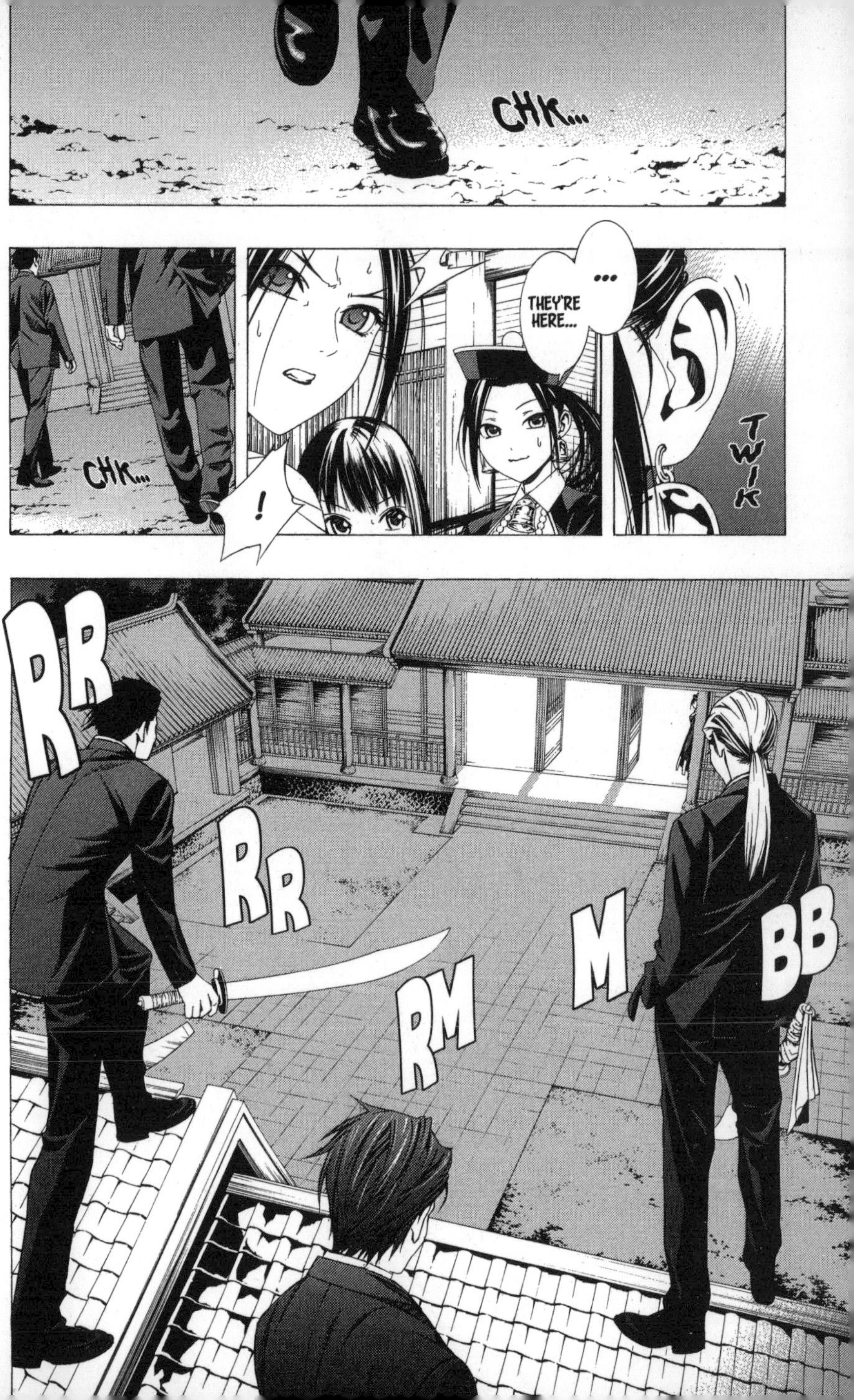
CHK...
TWIK
...
THEY'RE HERE...
!
CHK...
RR
RR
RM
M
BB

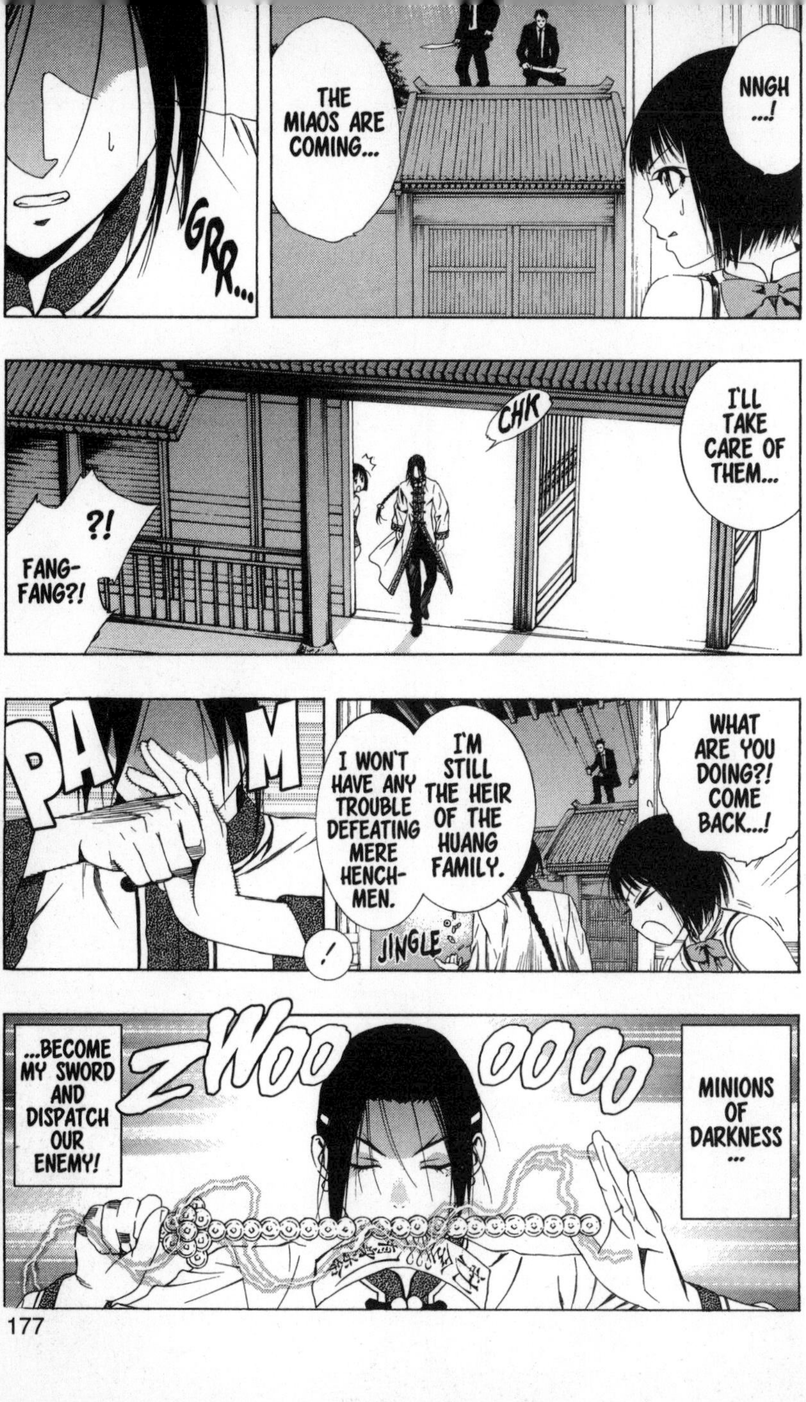
NNGH ...!
THE MIAOS ARE COMING...
GRR...
I'LL TAKE CARE OF THEM...
CHK
?!
FANG-FANG?!
WHAT ARE YOU DOING?! COME BACK...!
I'M STILL THE HEIR OF THE HUANG FAMILY.
I WON'T HAVE ANY TROUBLE DEFEATING MERE HENCH-MEN.
JINGLE
!
PAM
MINIONS OF DARKNESS ...
ZWOOOOOOO
...BECOME MY SWORD AND DISPATCH OUR ENEMY!

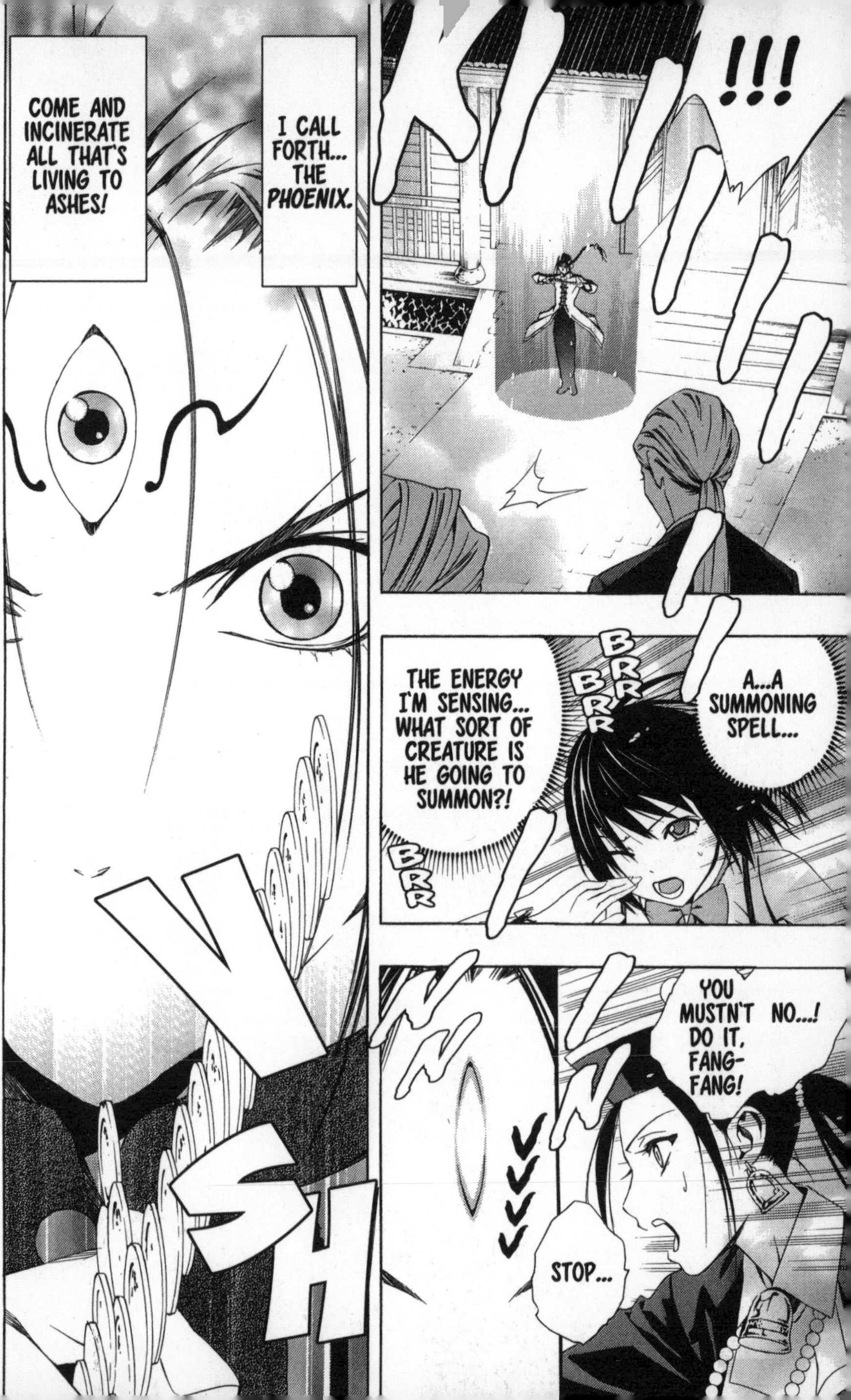
!!!
BRR
BRR
BRR
A...A SUMMONING SPELL...
THE ENERGY I'M SENSING... WHAT SORT OF CREATURE IS HE GOING TO SUMMON?!
BRR
NO...!
YOU MUSTN'T DO IT, FANG-FANG!
STOP...
I CALL FORTH... THE PHOENIX.
COME AND INCINERATE ALL THAT'S LIVING TO ASHES!
VSH

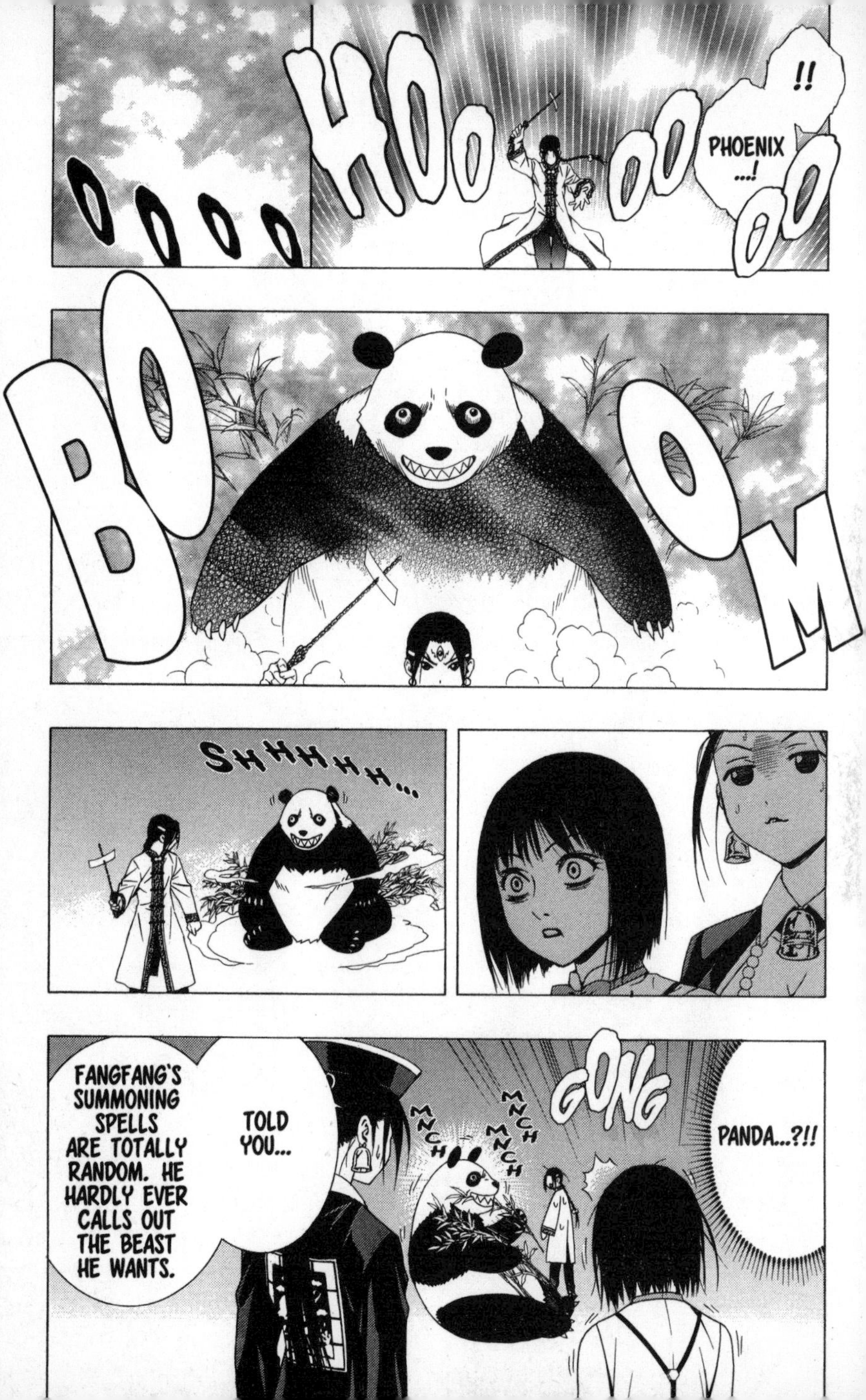
PHOENIX ...!
OOOO HOOOOOOOO!!
BOOOOM
SHHHHHH...
PANDA...?!!
GONG
MNCH MNCH
MNCH
TOLD YOU...
FANGFANG'S SUMMONING SPELLS ARE TOTALLY RANDOM. HE HARDLY EVER CALLS OUT THE BEAST HE WANTS.

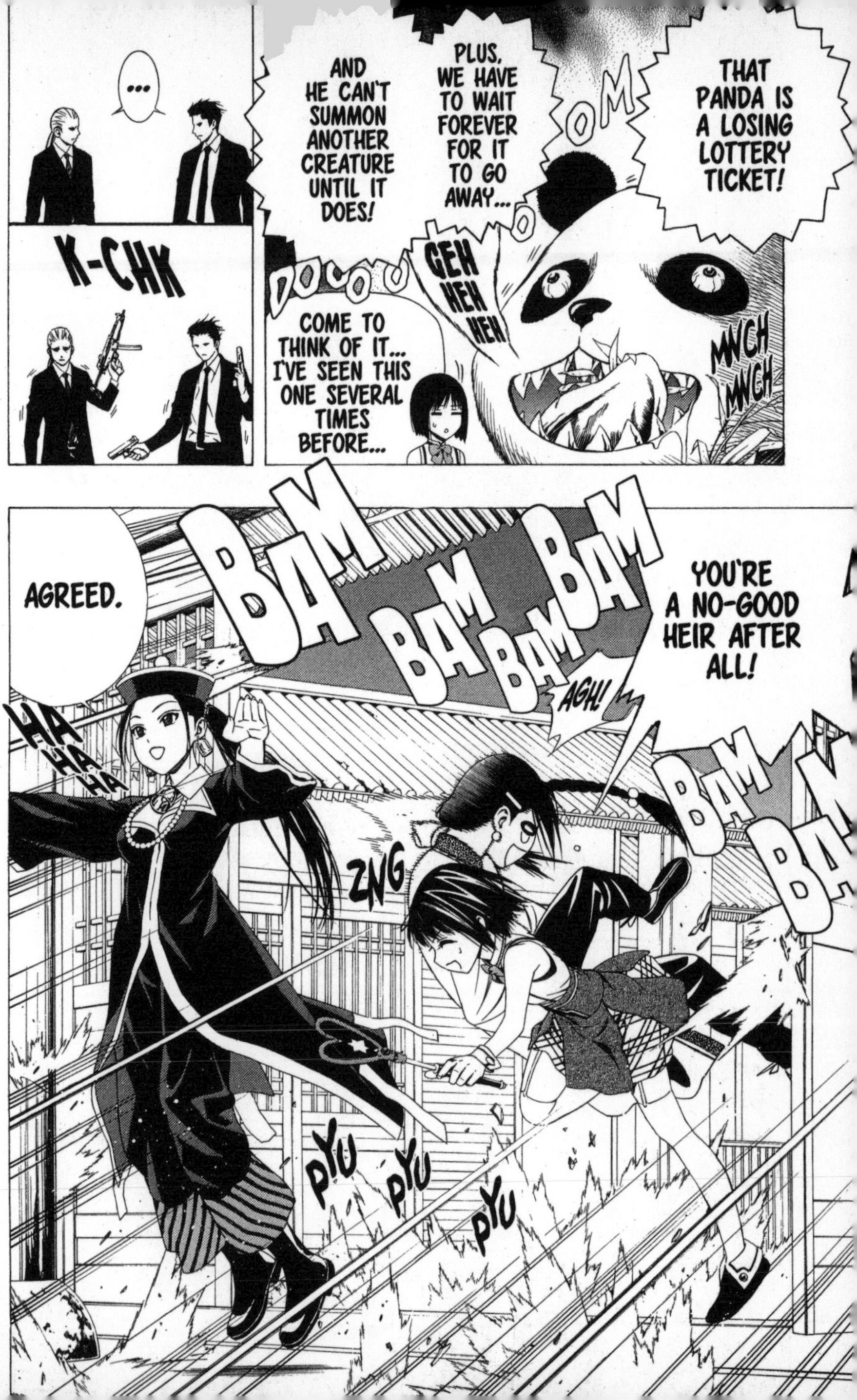
THAT PANDA IS A LOSING LOTTERY TICKET!
PLUS, WE HAVE TO WAIT FOREVER FOR IT TO GO AWAY...
AND HE CAN'T SUMMON ANOTHER CREATURE UNTIL IT DOES!
GEH HEH HEH
MNCH MNCH
COME TO THINK OF IT... I'VE SEEN THIS ONE SEVERAL TIMES BEFORE...
...
K-CHK
YOU'RE A NO-GOOD HEIR AFTER ALL!
BAM BAM
AGH!
BAM BAM BAM BAM
AGREED.
HA HA HA
ZNG
PYU PYU PYU

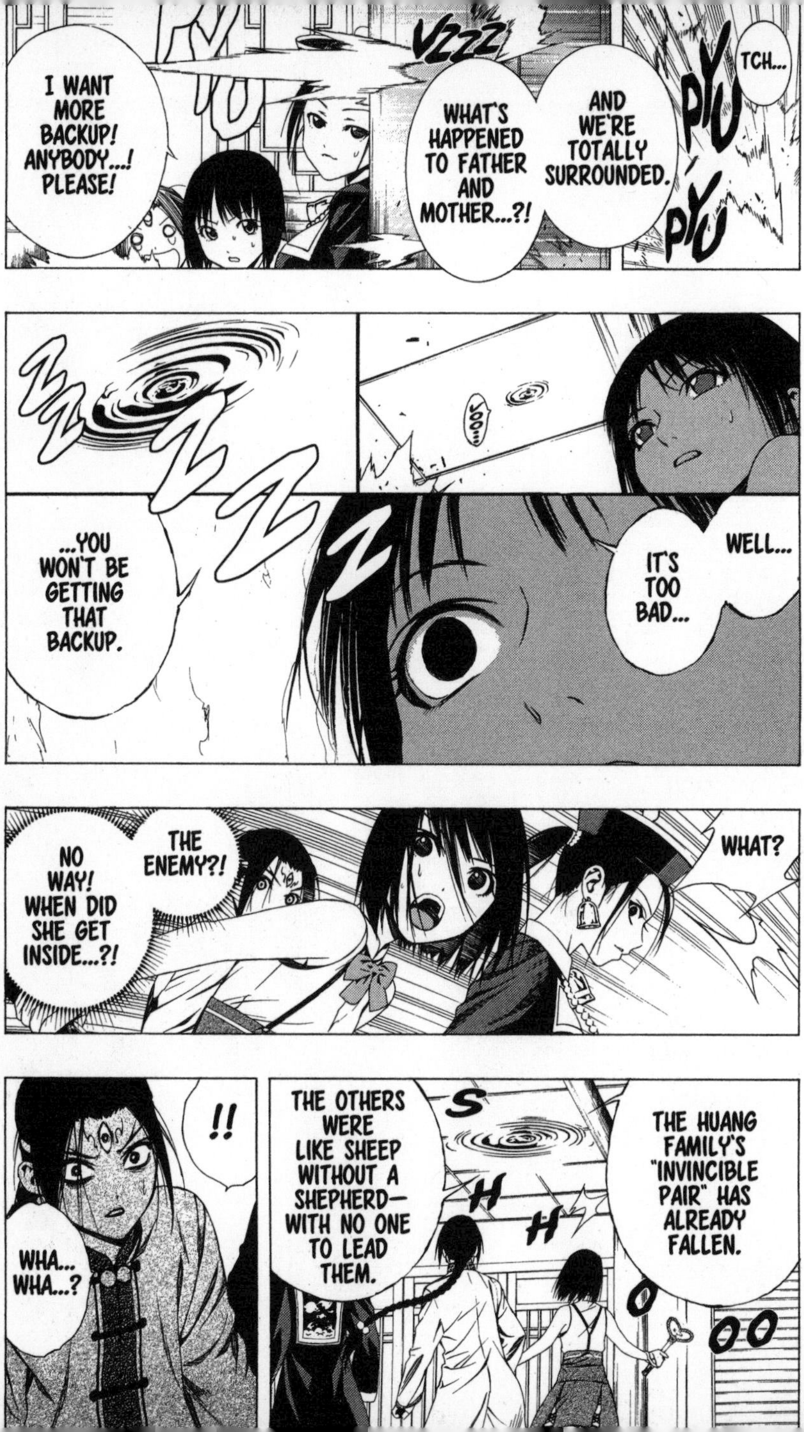
TCH...
PYU
PYU
AND WE'RE TOTALLY SURROUNDED.
WHAT'S HAPPENED TO FATHER AND MOTHER...?!
VZZZ
I WANT MORE BACKUP! ANYBODY...! PLEASE!
JOO...
WELL...
IT'S TOO BAD...
...YOU WON'T BE GETTING THAT BACKUP.
WHAT?
THE ENEMY?!
NO WAY! WHEN DID SHE GET INSIDE...?!
THE HUANG FAMILY'S "INVINCIBLE PAIR" HAS ALREADY FALLEN.
SHH
THE OTHERS WERE LIKE SHEEP WITHOUT A SHEPHERD—WITH NO ONE TO LEAD THEM.
!!
WHA... WHA...?

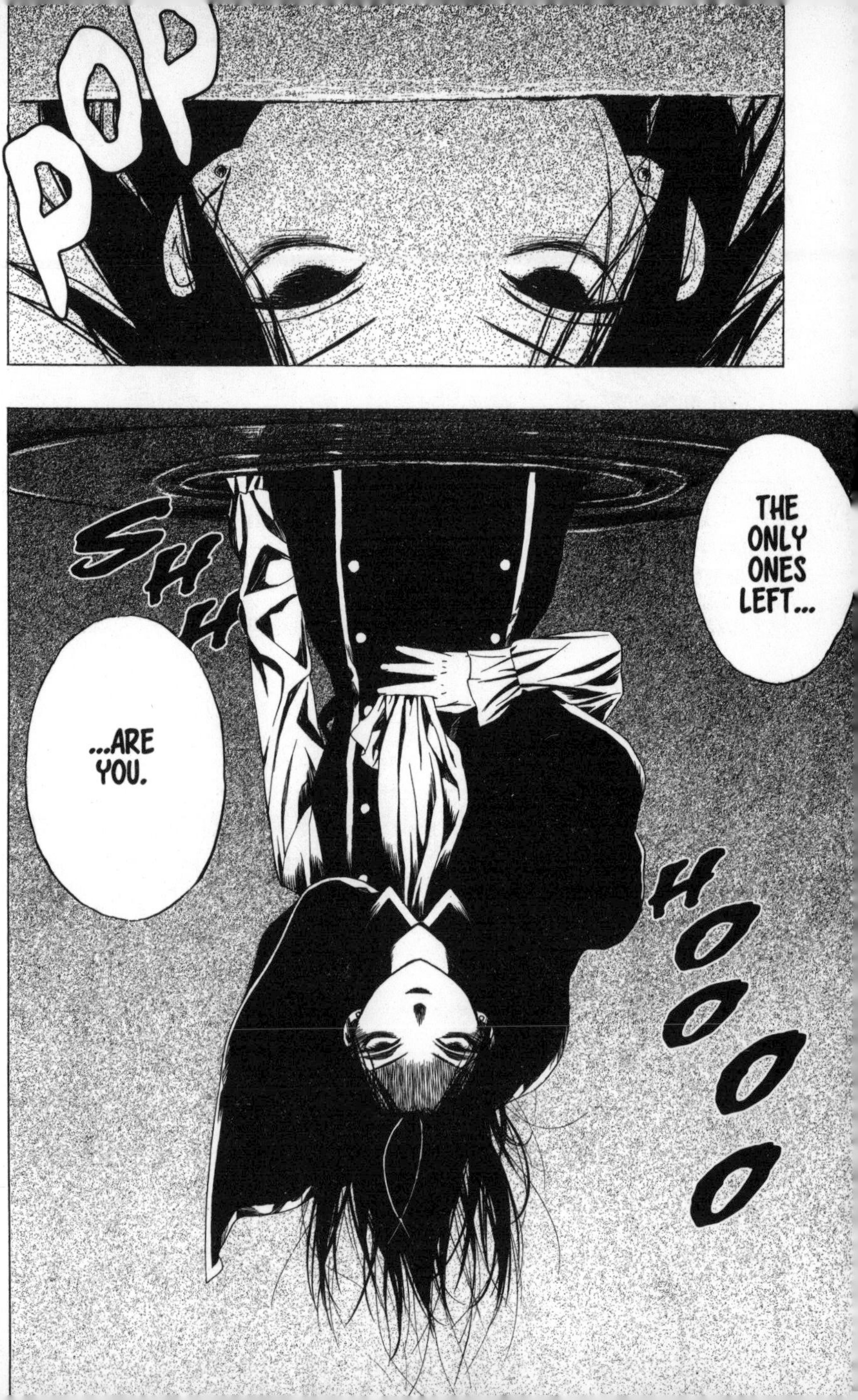
POP
THE ONLY ONES LEFT...
SHH
...ARE YOU.
HOOOO

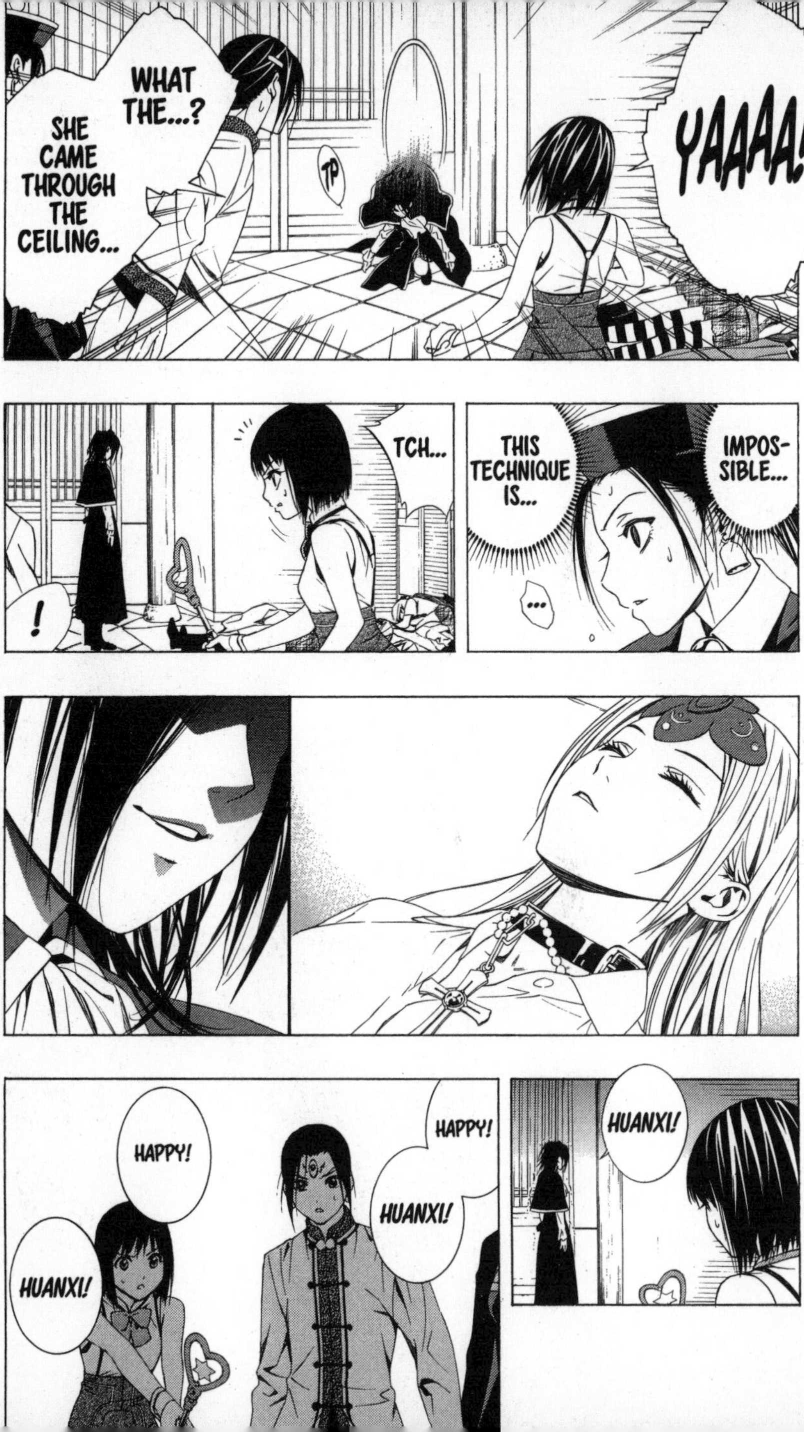
YAAAA!
TP
WHAT THE...?
SHE CAME THROUGH THE CEILING...
IMPOS-SIBLE...
THIS TECHNIQUE IS...
...
TCH...
!
HUANXI!
HAPPY!
HUANXI!
HAPPY!
HUANXI!

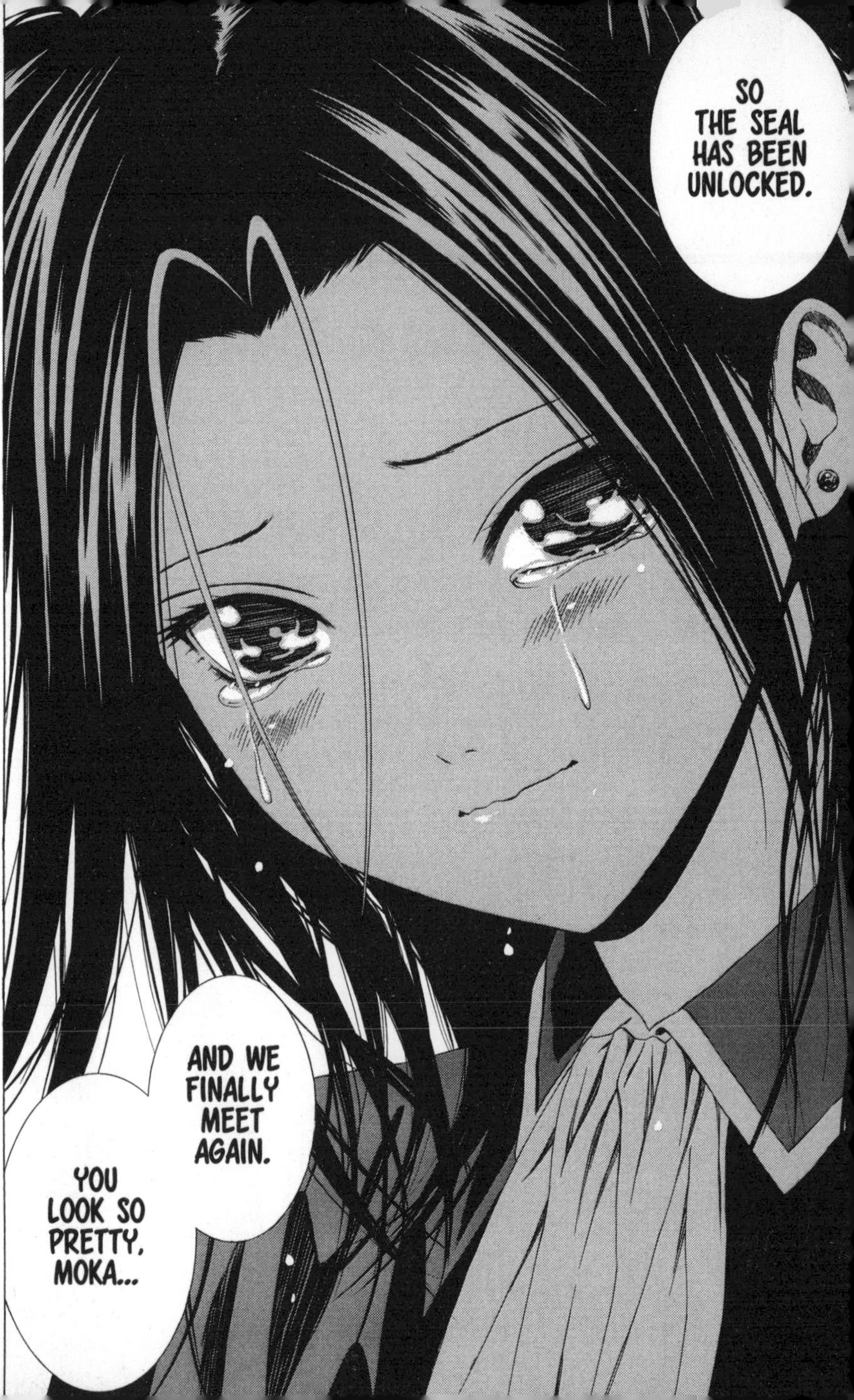
SO THE SEAL HAS BEEN UNLOCKED.
AND WE FINALLY MEET AGAIN.
YOU LOOK SO PRETTY, MOKA...

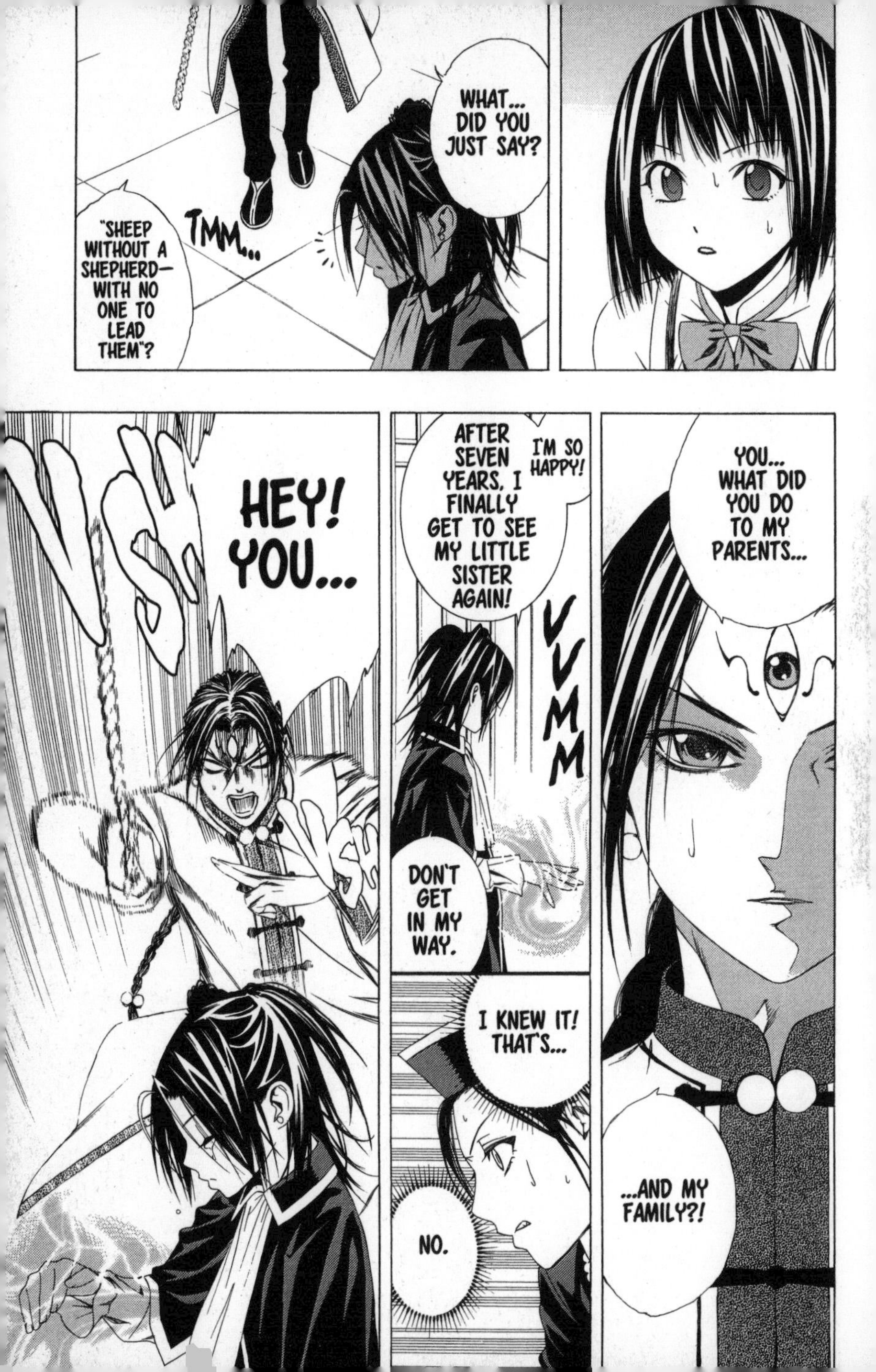
WHAT... DID YOU JUST SAY?
TMM...
"SHEEP WITHOUT A SHEPHERD— WITH NO ONE TO LEAD THEM"?
YOU... WHAT DID YOU DO TO MY PARENTS...
...AND MY FAMILY?!
I'M SO HAPPY!
AFTER SEVEN YEARS, I FINALLY GET TO SEE MY LITTLE SISTER AGAIN!
VUMM
DON'T GET IN MY WAY.
I KNEW IT! THAT'S...
NO.
HEY! YOU...
VSH

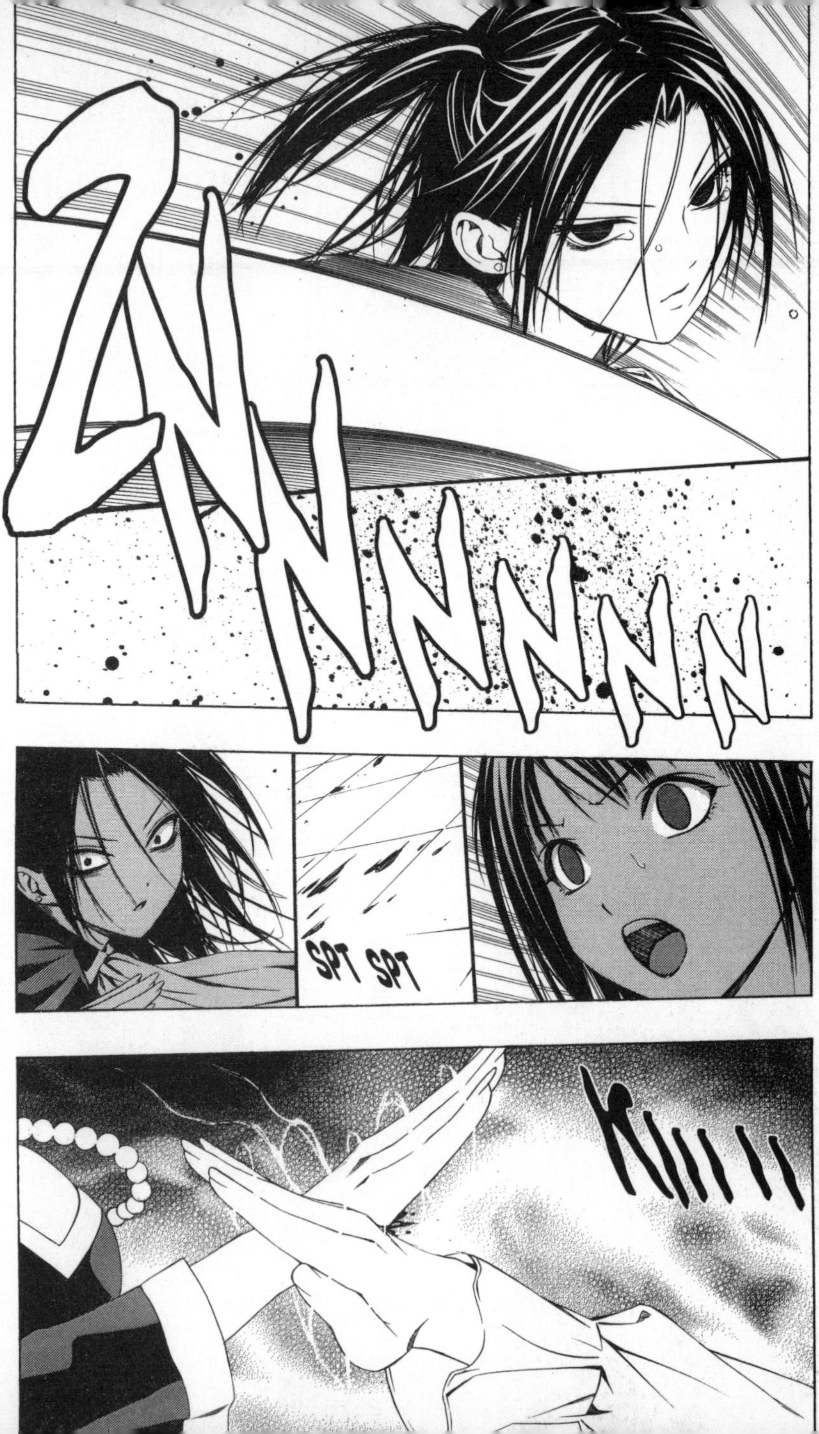
ZNNNNNNN
SPT SPT
KIIIII

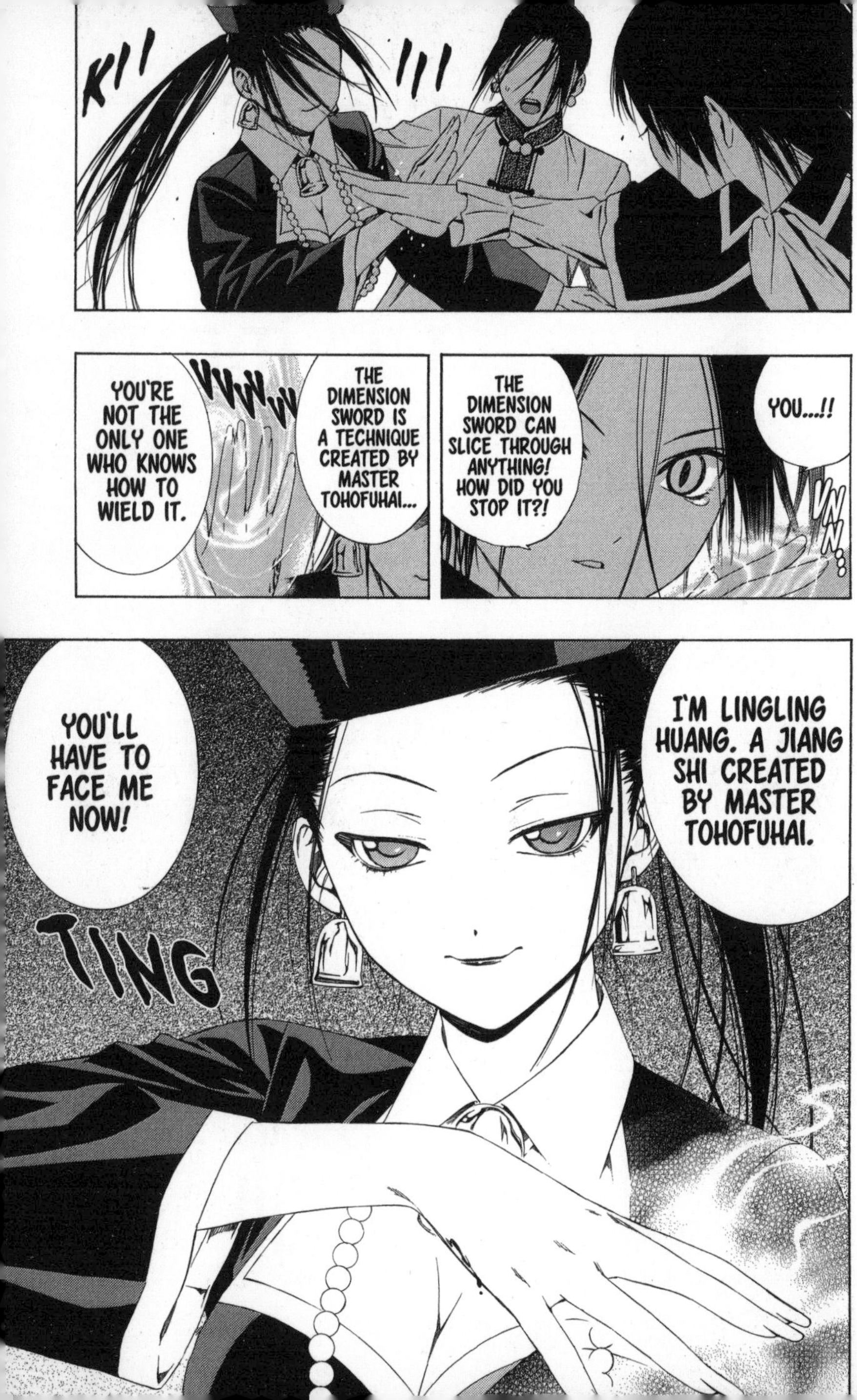
KI!! !!!
YOU...!!
VNN..
THE DIMENSION SWORD CAN SLICE THROUGH ANYTHING! HOW DID YOU STOP IT?!
THE DIMENSION SWORD IS A TECHNIQUE CREATED BY MASTER TOHOFUHAI...
VVVVV
YOU'RE NOT THE ONLY ONE WHO KNOWS HOW TO WIELD IT.
I'M LINGLING HUANG. A JIANG SHI CREATED BY MASTER TOHOFUHAI.
YOU'LL HAVE TO FACE ME NOW!
TING

# ROSARIO + VAMPIRE

## Season II

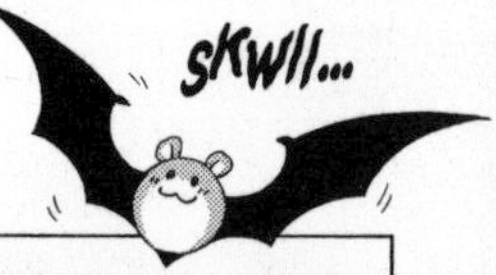
SKWII...

**This End-of-Volume Theater takes place after Aqua joins the Shuzen Family.**

## Meaningless End-of-Volume Theater VIII

### • Home Alone •

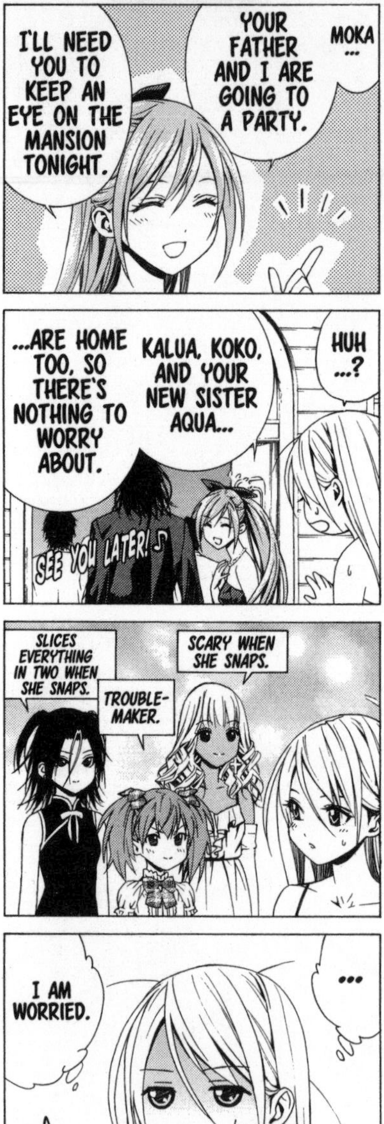
MOKA...
YOUR FATHER AND I ARE GOING TO A PARTY.
I'LL NEED YOU TO KEEP AN EYE ON THE MANSION TONIGHT.
HUH...?
KALUA, KOKO, AND YOUR NEW SISTER AQUA...
...ARE HOME TOO, SO THERE'S NOTHING TO WORRY ABOUT.
SEE YOU LATER! ♪
SCARY WHEN SHE SNAPS.
TROUBLE-MAKER.
SLICES EVERYTHING IN TWO WHEN SHE SNAPS.
...
I AM WORRIED.
A little...

**•Childish?•**

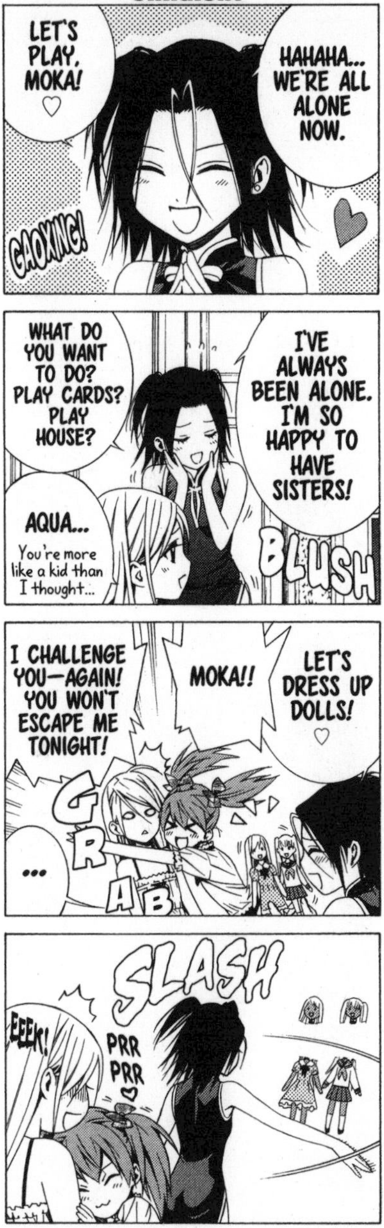
HAHAHA... WE'RE ALL ALONE NOW.
LET'S PLAY, MOKA! ♡
GAOXING!
I'VE ALWAYS BEEN ALONE. I'M SO HAPPY TO HAVE SISTERS!
WHAT DO YOU WANT TO DO? PLAY CARDS? PLAY HOUSE?
BLUSH
AQUA... You're more like a kid than I thought...
LET'S DRESS UP DOLLS! ♡
MOKA!!
I CHALLENGE YOU—AGAIN! YOU WON'T ESCAPE ME TONIGHT!
GRAB
...
SLASH
PRR PRR ♡
EEEK!

**•Childish!•**

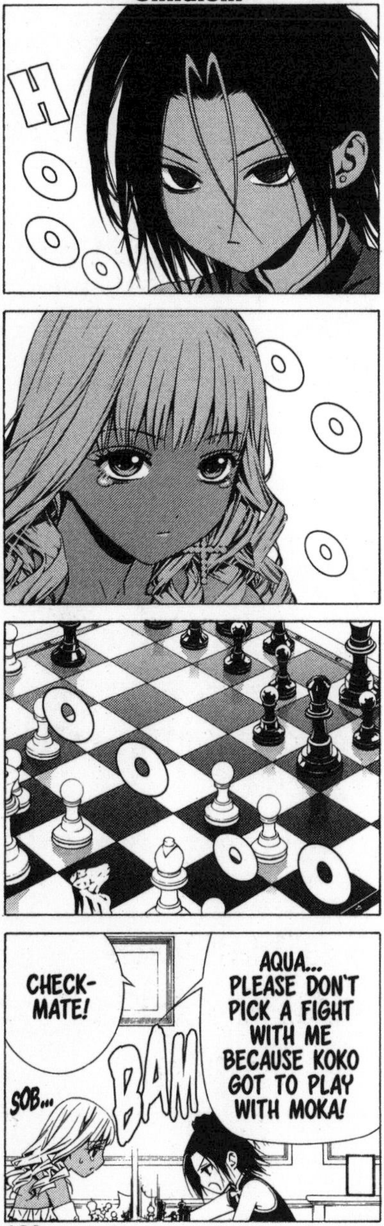
HOOOO
OOOO
OOOOOO
AQUA... PLEASE DON'T PICK A FIGHT WITH ME BECAUSE KOKO GOT TO PLAY WITH MOKA!
CHECK-MATE!
BAM
SOB...

## •Let's Cool Off•

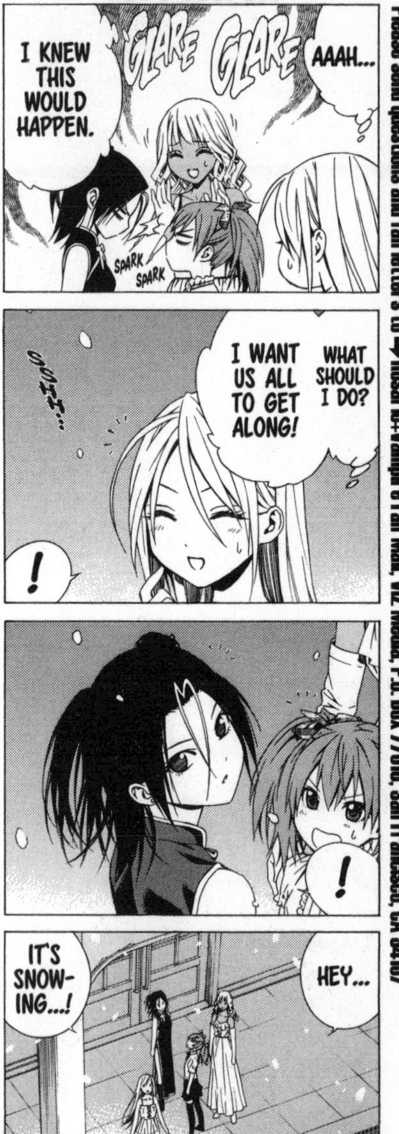

AAAH...
GLARE GLARE
I KNEW THIS WOULD HAPPEN.
SPARK SPARK
WHAT SHOULD I DO?
I WANT US ALL TO GET ALONG!
SSHH...
!
!
HEY...
IT'S SNOW-ING...!


## •Four Sisters, One Blanket•

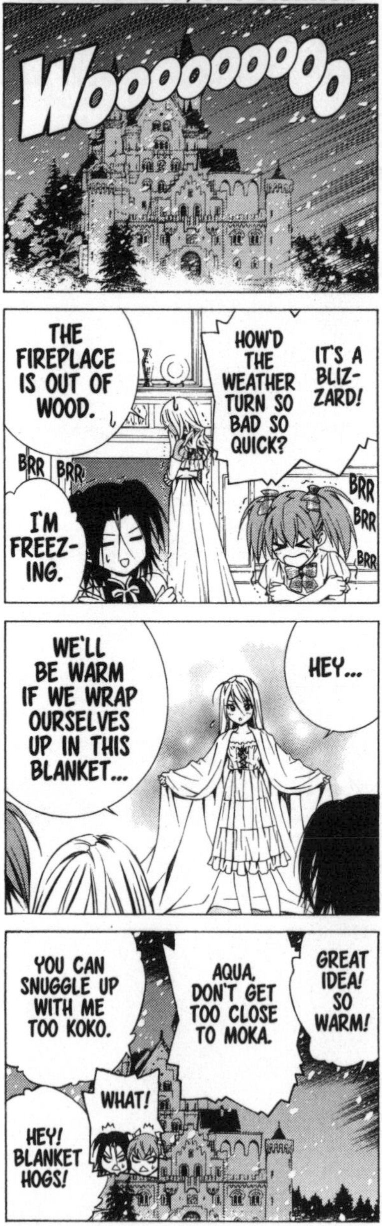

WOOOOOOOOO
IT'S A BLIZ-ZARD!
HOW'D THE WEATHER TURN SO BAD SO QUICK?
THE FIREPLACE IS OUT OF WOOD.
BRR BRR BRR
BRR BRR
I'M FREEZ-ING.
HEY...
WE'LL BE WARM IF WE WRAP OURSELVES UP IN THIS BLANKET...
GREAT IDEA! SO WARM!
AQUA, DON'T GET TOO CLOSE TO MOKA.
YOU CAN SNUGGLE UP WITH ME TOO KOKO.
WHAT!
HEY! BLANKET HOGS!


Please send questions and fan letters to ➡ Rosario+Vampire Fan Mail, VIZ Media, P.O. Box 77010, San Francisco, CA 94107

## • Sweet Dreams...for Now •

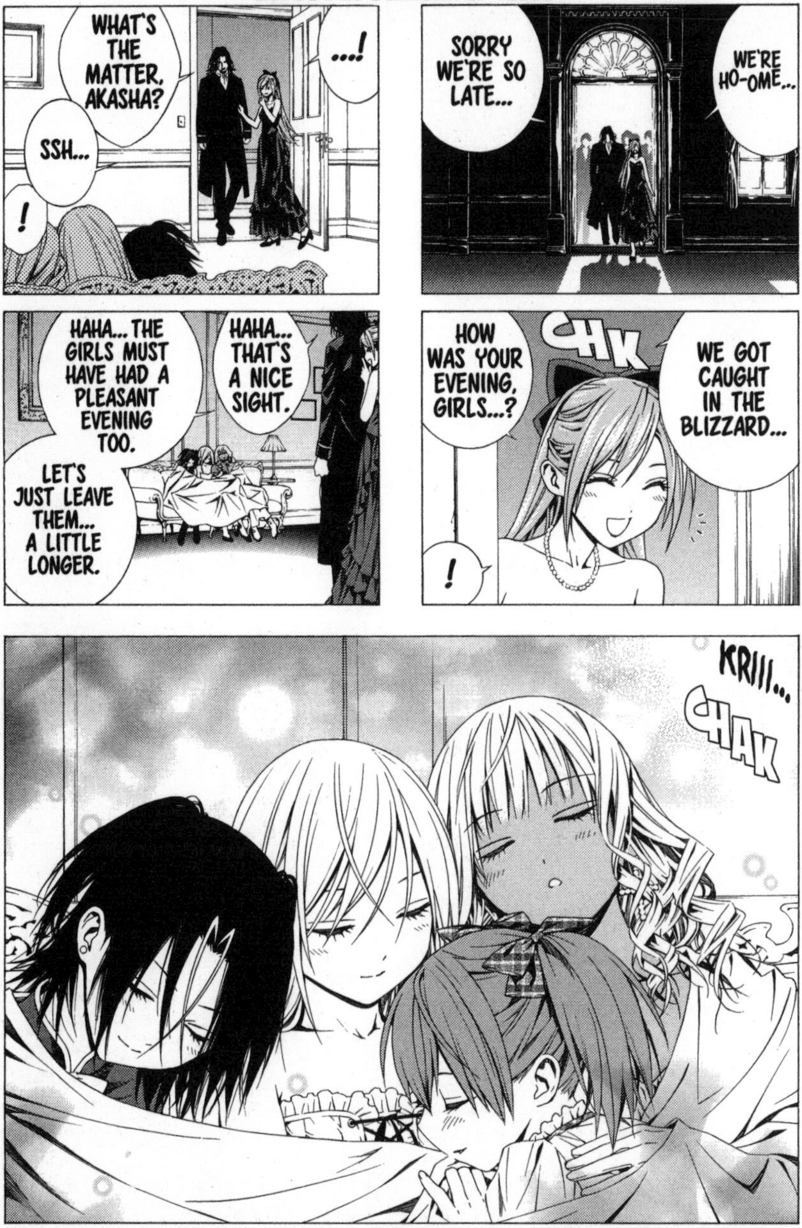
WE'RE HO-OME...
SORRY WE'RE SO LATE...
...!
WHAT'S THE MATTER, AKASHA?
SSH...
!
WE GOT CAUGHT IN THE BLIZZARD...
CHK
HOW WAS YOUR EVENING, GIRLS...?
!
HAHA... THAT'S A NICE SIGHT.
HAHA... THE GIRLS MUST HAVE HAD A PLEASANT EVENING TOO.
LET'S JUST LEAVE THEM... A LITTLE LONGER.
KRIII...
CHAK

**Staff: Akihisa Ikeda, Makoto Saito, Nobuyuki Hayashi, Rika Shirota, Tomoharu Shimomura**

**Editor: Takanori Asada, Junichi Tamada** **Comic: Kenju Noro**

# NEXT VOLUME...
# PROTECTED BY LOVE FROM THE DEPTHS OF THE HEART...

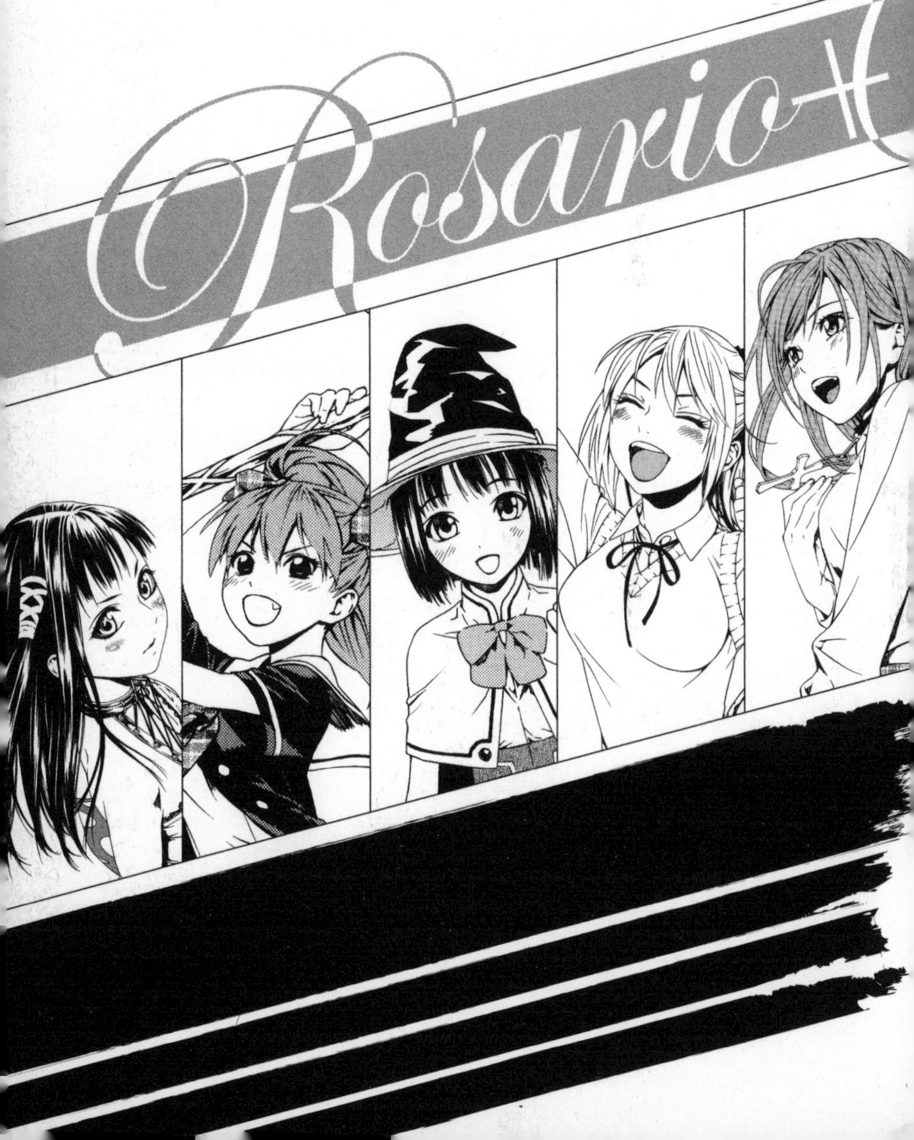
Rosario+

**AKIHISA IKEDA**

The *Rosario+Vampire* graphic novels have been published every four months up to now... But this volume broke that cycle. My apologies to everyone who has been waiting for this volume to come out!

The story arc continues from the last volume—you'll learn more about the Shuzen family's history. The drawings for this volume took so much time that the release date got pushed back. But the pages are filled with action and special effects which you'll really like...! (I hope.) It will make me very happy if you enjoy this volume!

What...? Is there any romantic comedy in this volume, you ask?
Um... Romantic comedy...?
Uh... Anyway, I hope you enjoy it!

Akihisa Ikeda was born in 1976 in Miyazaki. He debuted as a mangaka with the four-volume magical warrior fantasy series *Kiruto* in 2002, which was serialized in *Monthly Shonen Jump*. *Rosario+Vampire* debuted in *Monthly Shonen Jump* in March of 2004 and is continuing in the magazine *Jump Square (Jump SQ)* as *Rosario+Vampire: Season II*. In Japan, *Rosario+Vampire* is also available as a drama CD. In 2008, the story was released as an anime. Season II is also available as an anime now. And in Japan, there is a Nintendo DS game based on the series.

Ikeda has been a huge fan of vampires and monsters since he was a little kid. He says one of the perks of being a manga artist is being able to go for walks during the day when everybody else is stuck in the office.

# ROSARIO+VAMPIRE: Season II
# 8
### SHONEN JUMP ADVANCED Manga Edition

## STORY & ART BY **AKIHISA IKEDA**

Translation/Kaori Inoue
English Adaptation/Gerard Jones
Touch-up Art & Lettering/Stephen Dutro
Cover & Interior Design/Ronnie Casson
Editor/Annette Roman

ROSARIO + VAMPIRE SEASON II © 2007 by Akihisa Ikeda
All rights reserved. First published in Japan in 2007 by SHUEISHA Inc.,
Tokyo. English translation rights arranged by SHUEISHA Inc.

The rights of the author(s) of the work(s) in this publication to be so
identified have been asserted in accordance with the Copyright, Designs
and Patents Act 1988. A CIP catalogue record for this book is available
from the British Library.

Printed in the U.S.A.

Published by VIZ Media, LLC
P.O. Box 77010
San Francisco, CA 94107

10 9 8 7 6 5 4 3 2 1
First printing, April 2012

www.viz.com

www.shonenjump.com

## CRYPT SHEET FOR
# ROSARIO+VAMPIRE: SEASON II, VOL. 9
# *FAIRY TALE*

**TEST 9**

**COMPARED TO FAIRY TALE HQ, WHAT IS THE GOAL OF FAIRY TALE'S BRANCH OFFICE?**

a. the same

b. the opposite

c. better parking spots

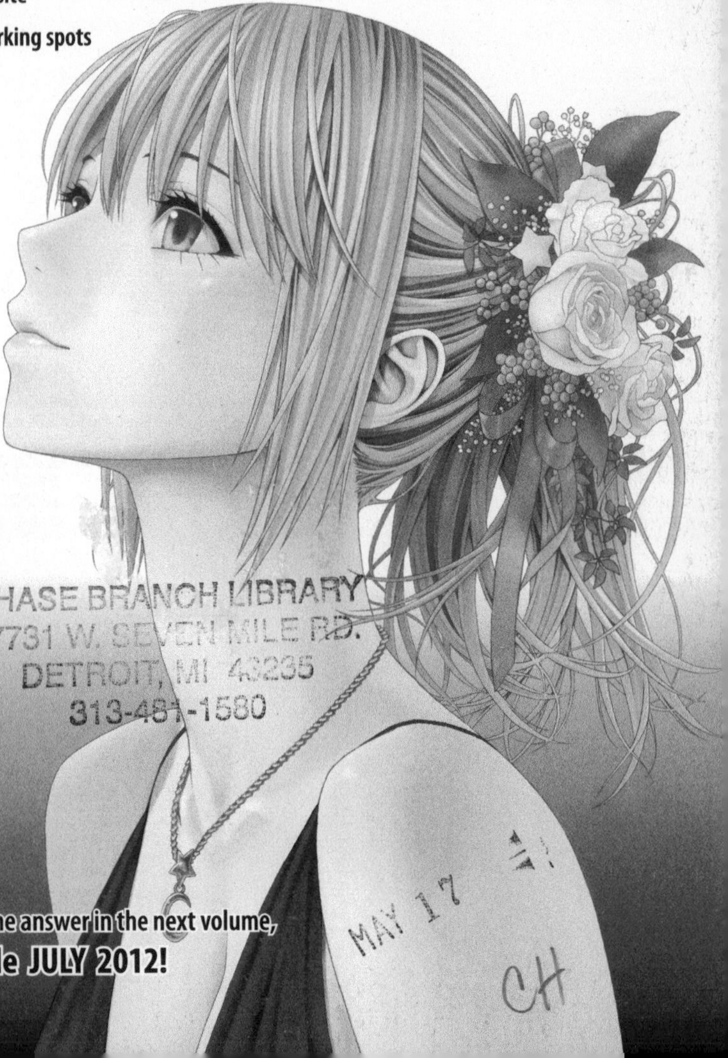



**Find out the answer in the next volume, available JULY 2012!**